DIFFERENT DRUMMERS
Banking and Politics in Canada
Robert MacIntosh

Macmillan Canada
Toronto, Ontario, Canada

Canadian Cataloguing in Publication Data

MacIntosh, Robert, 1923-
    Different drummers : banking and politics in Canada

Includes bibliographical references and index.
ISBN 0-7715-9146-2

1. Banks and banking – Canada – State supervision.
I. Title.

HG1778.C2M25 1991   332.1'0971   C91-094522-5

Illustration credits:

Title page: Grahame Arnould
Frontispiece: Donald Reilly, *Harvard Business Review*
Page 60: Toronto *Globe*, May 23, 1924
Pages 187 and 257: Philip Mallette, *Financial Post*

Jacket design by Kirk Stephens, Southside Studios

Macmillan Canada
A Division of Canada Publishing Corporation
Toronto, Ontario, Canada

1 2 3 4 5   GP   95 94 93 92 91

Printed in Canada

Printed on paper containing over 50% recycled paper including 5% post-consumer fibre.

CONTENTS

For Lynn

ACKNOWLEDGEMENTS

This book could not have been written without the help of: Peggy Reuber, who created the archives of the Canadian Bankers' Association out of unorganized files in cardboard boxes; Philippa Campsie, Macmillan's editor-in-chief, whose wise advice belied her years; Brian Davidson, librarian at the CBA whose total recall and great patience were instrumental in finding sources; Jan Hall, who did all the word processing with speed and good cheer; and Perrin Lewis, who put the manuscript through his fine screen for accuracy. Thanks are due to many others who helped with archives, library resources and the reading of manuscript material. Among these are Jane Nokes and Charlie Dougall at the Bank of Nova Scotia archives; Gord Rabchuk at the Royal Bank archives; Yolaine Toussaint, Bank of Montreal archives; the library staff at the Metro Toronto Reference Library and the CIBC library; and Shawn Cooper. A long list of individuals was imposed upon: John Altenau, Barb Amsden, John Angus, Grahame Arnould, Mike Bradley, Hugh Brown, Lynn Buckle, Bradley Crawford, Joanne De Laurentiis, George Girouard, Shelly Jourard, Henry Knowles, Nancy Leamen, W.A.C. Macdonald, Justine MacIntosh, Bud McMorran, Jim Mizen, Peggy Morgan, Brian O'Brien, Bill Randle, Michael Thompson, Rob Turnbull, Mark Weseluck, and Nancy Whynot. All the errors are entirely the fault of my research staff—myself.

"I see a level playing field for your company, but unfortunately, it's some years after your retirement." Reprinted from *Harvard Business Review* by permission of D. Reilly

CHAPTER 1

INTRODUCTION

E ver since the days of the Medicis, banks and bankers have not
been popular with the general public nor with their governments
except perhaps in Switzerland. The Swiss regard their banks as a
national asset, but some Canadians treat theirs as a national fire
hydrant. Sir Edmund Walker, president of the Canadian Bank of
Commerce early in the century, said, "As democracy does not love
banks, progress is very limited." Sixty years later, Pierre Trudeau said,
"People beef all the time, and it doesn't impress me . . . you know, the
worst bitchers are bankers."

There are few economic issues in the life of a country that do not
involve the banks in one way or another. And if they involve the
banks, they also touch on politics.

This book takes a short tour around the playing field of banking and
politics, showing how the various teams march to the beat of different
drums. The rules of the game have always been essentially the same,
though increasingly complex in response to social change. As we
shall see, the sound of the drums becomes louder and more insistent
over Canadian financial history, but the conflicting themes are even
harder to sort out. And the marching feet tend to tear up the turf.

When I joined the Bank of Nova Scotia in 1953, my mother said,
"Robert, why are you throwing away your education?" She could
hardly bring herself to mention it to the neighbours. I might as well
have gone to the Kingston Penitentiary. In those days, people with
university degrees did not go into banking. As it turned out, I never
had a boring day in twenty-seven years at the bank followed by ten
years at the Canadian Bankers' Association. There was an endless
variety of problems to solve, and an almost unlimited opportunity to
learn about the complex relationships between financial affairs, people, and politics.

The average reader probably thinks that banking is an extremely dull subject, and looked at from the point of view of routine transactions across the counter, it probably is. Behind the routine business of paying bills and drawing cash, however, there is an intricate structure which is intended to maintain confidence in the soundness of a country's money system. People are almost as fussy about the sanctity of their financial affairs as they are about the sanctity of their marital affairs (these days, maybe more so). Few things cause people to get more upset than feeling that some or all of their life savings are at risk, or even that they have been charged too much for a small transaction. Later on, in my version of the battle over bank service charges in the 1980s, that point is examined. The service charge issue generated more political heat for the banks than perhaps any other issue in recent years, although it could not compare in importance with more fundamental questions.

But it was important in terms of image — that is, it was a question of trust and confidence, which is the basis of the financial system. Eventually the government and the banks reached common ground on the service charge issue; it has largely ceased to be a bone of contention in the last year or two, even though the legislation implementing the ground rules has not yet been passed at the time of writing. This demonstrates as clearly as anything could that the strict letter of the law is not necessarily a governing consideration in the relations between the banks and their customers and the government.

The first few chapters of this book try to explain how the Canadian banking system got to be the way it is. As Canadians look at the woeful state of affairs in the banking system south of the border, it is relevant right now to understand how we diverged from the United States in banking matters. Self-denigration is such a common Canadian trait that some may find it hard to believe in the merits of our banks compared to those elsewhere. Having spent a lifetime observing our performance compared to that of others, however, I support the assertion that there is no better system in the world.

The general theme of this book is that the banking system is a mirror of social and political change. The reason that we developed national branch banking was not so much a question of intelligent planning and foresight as it was a response to the combined forces of economics and politics, some of them related to banking and some not. The political forces which led the American and Canadian systems to diverge so greatly 150 years ago have continued until quite recent times. But now we are being treated to the spectacle of the

American banking system moving rapidly in the direction of the Canadian model, in response to tremendous regional economic forces and modern technology.

One undercurrent in the theme of social and political change is the peculiarly Canadian notion that banks are a public utility; that everyone should be able to plug into the service at little cost, and that the overriding corporate goal of banks should be to accommodate social and political objectives rather than to make a profit. Thus we find a continuing demand for branches to be available in tiny hamlets, for banks to make credit freely available for risky small business proposals in areas of high unemployment, for banks to provide free basic services to lower income groups, and so on and so on. For some reason, journalists sometimes share the perception that banking services are a public utility. To these people I would suggest that free banking should go on the agenda right after the provision of free daily newspapers. Most people are pretty good at defining social goals to be accomplished with other people's money. My own view is that social goals are set by government, through the consensus of duly elected representatives who decide the standards of society, and not by self-appointed authorities.

There are all sorts of fascinating players out there on the field, even if sometimes it's hard to tell what teams they represent, and which way they are running. The amusing similarities between the banking buccaneers early in this century and the trust company buccaneers of the 1980s are certainly worthy of a visit. And of course the role of western dissent against the eastern banking and political establishment could hardly be overlooked. This pops up three times, first in the founding of the Bank of Canada, then in the astonishing years of Aberhart, and finally in the rise and fall of the two banks in Alberta.

The banking system has changed out of all recognition since Stephen Leacock recorded his quaking fear about going into a bank in Orillia, Ontario. There are still plenty of critics whose perception of a bank branch is coloured by the Leacock story: the dark oak fittings, the brass teller's cage, the fusty bureaucratic teller in the cage, and the terrifying manager back in the corner. When readers get over the shock of finding out that Stephen Leacock worked for the Canadian Bankers' Association in the 1930s, they may be prepared to continue the tour by looking at the tremendous changes in the 1950s and the 1960s.

What happened was almost revolutionary, because the laws were changed to bring the banks into contact with millions of ordinary middle-class Canadians, something which had not been possible before. The flowering of the relationship between millions of households and the banks led to a fundamental change in the politics of banking. The number of stakeholders in the banking system has increased dramatically. At one time the stakeholders were the federal government, the central bank, the chartered banks, industry and agriculture, and the affluent middle class. Now there are the provincial and municipal governments and special interest groups representing a wide diversity of economic forces: consumers, residential mortgage debtors, importers and exporters, computer software companies, rival segments of the financial system, crown corporations, environmentalists, issuers of plastic cards, human rights advocates, and many others I have left out. Most of these groups are users of banking services, although some are suppliers or competitors.

And always, always, there are politicians. They represent local interests, regional and occupational interests, and ideological points of view. It is not for nothing that the Canadian Bankers' Association had—at one point in the 1980s—129 committees. While this may sound like an astonishing feat in empire-building, every single committee came into being because the banks needed to have it. In the current environment of restraint and downsizing, the number of committees has decreased somewhat, but the issues with which they deal have not gone away. Not surprisingly, there is now a committee devoted to environmental concerns, for example.

Professor William Coleman has recently written a thoughtful article, "The Banking Policy Community," which examines the "changing patterns of power and influence." He notes the increasing capacity of government to supervise financial firms and the growth of "bureaucratic pluralism," as the federal government shares power with the provinces. He adds that the "breakdown of market compartmentalization in the financial sector" has also "led to a significant growth in the number of actors in the banking policy community." Quite so.

Forty years ago, significant changes in the Bank Act were made after the intervention of relatively few players. Nowadays, the process of reform of financial legislation is practically an ongoing game. After the Bank Act Revision of 1980, the "banking policy community" plunged immediately into the struggle over the Bank Act revision of 1990, which has not yet quite run its course. The decennial revision will continue (after an initial review in five years), and this will involve not just the banks, but also the trust and loan companies, credit unions, and insurance companies. Meanwhile, the Canadian system is being influenced by the rapidly changing American scene, and also by the European Community. Although there is widespread fatigue among the players, it is unlikely that they will get much rest before the next round.

Coleman's article did not include a discussion of the profound influence of the media on public policy. In my experience, the media have had a deep and lasting influence on the making of public policy in the financial services field. Like most people who have been extensively involved in these questions, I could produce a litany of complaints: the inadequate education of certain journalists in business and economics; the leftist bias of many reporters and editors; the deliberate manipulation of the news columns to advocate positions; the frequent absence of fair-mindedness and balance; and even, from time to time, unethical behaviour in observing the agreed-upon terms of an interview.

An example of the uneven treatment accorded to an event is best summarized by a news story: on August 8, 1977, 150 gallons of ink spilled into Toronto harbour from a storage tank at the main printing plant at the *Toronto Star*. The next day, this environmental disaster was reported in the *Globe and Mail* in a story five columns wide and ten inches high, including a picture. The same story was covered in the *Toronto Star* in the second section in one column five inches high; in other words, 10 percent of the size of the *Globe and Mail* story.

During a decade of turbulent events in the financial system, I had unnumbered jousts with the media. On one occasion I was even sued for $300,000 personally (and the CBA for a matching amount) for having described a journalist's writing as "sleazy." The action was eventually dropped by the plaintiff, whom I later encountered in a parliamentary committee.

That run-in was a bit extreme, but there were many occasions when there were sharp elbows and kicks to the shin on the playing field. Most other bankers tend to be reticent—even secretive—and the media always seemed to me to be ambivalent about someone who is relatively outspoken on financial issues; they love to have fresh copy, but are often prickly about candid opinions which they do not share. With my unfortunate tendency to call a spade a bloody shovel, I sometimes thought I was miscast as a Canadian, and perhaps should have been born south of the border.

On reflection I have to acknowledge that there are quite a few excellent financial writers, especially in the field of investigative business journalism. Their work—and the passage of time—have helped me to put the story of the past decade into some perspective. I have borrowed extensively (with acknowledgements in the endnotes) from the huge stack of contemporary writings as well as from a roomful of archival material. In case this makes what follows sound like a memoir, the reader will soon see otherwise; it is a mixture of history, journalism, argumentation which is usually (but not always) in defence of my industry, and personal reflections. There is still plenty of room for other voices, because the range of issues cannot possibly be covered entirely in a book this size and, just possibly, someone else might have a different point of view!

CHAPTER 2

THE ROOTS OF CANADIAN BANKING

THE POLITICS OF THE FIRST BANK CHARTERS

From its earliest years, banking has been inseparable from politics. The founders of banks were usually prominent members of the merchant establishment in the larger communities, which in the early nineteenth century were Montreal, Quebec City, Halifax, Saint John, and Kingston. They were normally well represented in the legislative assembly or, better still, in the legislative council, which was the appointed executive before the days of full responsible government. Modern notions of conflict of interest hardly existed, and it was not until the early twentieth century that there began to emerge a more clearly defined line between business and government.

Nevertheless, it was not that easy for these early bankers to get the exclusive charters with the permissive terms that they wanted. The Bank of Montreal, which is generally considered Canada's first bank, was an association of business partners for its first five years beginning in 1817. It was not until 1822 that the founders succeeded in getting their charter approved by the Imperial Government in London as well as by the Government of Lower Canada.

The first Canadian bank charter granted was that of the Bank of New Brunswick in 1820. Not surprisingly, the merchant founders in Saint John were much influenced by the experience of the earliest banks in Massachusetts, and as a result, some rather populist notions appeared in this first charter: no one could vote more than ten shares of the stock, and the directors were personally liable for any shortfall of assets to liabilities.

In Halifax, a private banking corporation called the Halifax Banking Company was founded in 1825. Its efforts to get a Royal charter failed, mainly because of its demand for a ten-year monopoly. Despite its political support in the twelve-member executive council of the province, its efforts to block the more populist Bank of Nova Scotia from getting a charter in 1832 failed. The political man-oeuvrings of the earliest bankers to keep out other banks never succeeded for very long.

In Lower Canada, the Quebec Bank and another called the Bank of Canada were established not long after the Bank of Montreal, but the Bank of Montreal took advantage of its head start and became by far the most important bank in the nineteenth century.

In Upper Canada, the politicking for bank charters could almost be described as bizarre. Requests for a bank charter came first from Kingston, which was then about twice as large as York (which had a population of 868 in 1817), and was closer to export markets. When the Bank of Montreal opened agencies in Kingston and York in 1818, the Kingston merchant community reacted by promoting a Bank of Upper Canada. The charter was passed through the legislative assem-bly and the executive council at York, and sent by the Lieutenant Governor to the authorities in London for final approval. There it got lost in a bureaucratic jungle, and by the time approval came two years later, the expiry date of the charter had already passed.

The political establishment at York, the famous Family Compact, then skated the Kingston crowd into the boards, getting a charter for a different Bank of Upper Canada, this one based in York. In order to appease the Kingston merchant community, a compromise was reached between the legislative assembly and the executive council, providing for a Bank of Kingston as well. This bank never got off the ground, and an unchartered Bank of Upper Canada at Kingston, called the "Pretended Bank" of Upper Canada, also failed.

Altogether, eighty bank charters were issued by the provincial legislatures up to 1867, and of these, thirty-five survived to Confedera-tion. Two banks, the Bank of Montreal and the Bank of Nova Scotia, have continued to operate under their own names to the present day. Each of the other four of today's big six banks had predecessor banks which can be traced back to these early days. The Halifax Banking Company became part of the Canadian Imperial Bank of Commerce of today; the Quebec Bank founded in 1818 became part of the Royal Bank of Canada; La Banque Nationale founded in 1859 became part of the present National; and the Bank of Toronto, founded in 1855, is now the Toronto-Dominion Bank.

In the British North America Act of 1867, banking was placed under federal jurisdiction. All of the bank charters issued by the five easternmost provincial legislatures were continued under the new federal legislation. British Columbia received a bank charter directly from the Imperial Government in London and this bank's charter was also continued under the new Dominion legislation in 1871, when British Columbia joined Confederation.

SETTING THE GROUND RULES

The charter of the Bank of Montreal established some of the most basic characteristics of the Canadian banking system which last to this day. It was copied pretty well directly from that of the First Bank of the United States founded in 1791, some sections being word for word. Most of its features were then repeated in the charters issued in Upper and Lower Canada before Confederation. The Bank of New Brunswick Charter of 1820, however, contained some features which also influenced subsequent banking charters, especially the "double liability" clause which will be discussed further on.

It was not only American ideas, but American capital which influenced the first Canadian bank charters. One of the biggest problems in getting new banks started was the lack of capital. Even the Montreal community did not have sufficient local resources to found the Bank of Montreal. A substantial number of the first shares were held by wealthy families in Boston, New York, and Philadelphia. But if the founders of the Bank of Montreal wanted the Americans' money, they didn't want their votes. The articles of incorporation of the Bank of Montreal restricted voting powers to residents of Montreal and British subjects, and no one could vote more than twenty shares of the stock. In the case of the Bank of New Brunswick (and the Eastern Townships Bank as well), the maximum voting power was ten shares.

The U.S. constitution did not provide explicit federal authority over banking. Despite this, Alexander Hamilton, the Secretary of the Treasury, pushed the charter of the First Bank of the United States through Congress in 1791. Its charter had many features drawn from the Bank of England's charter of 1694. Its twenty-year mandate was not renewed by Congress in 1811 partly because the bank's stockholders included many British with whom the U.S. was on the brink of war. A second, federally chartered Bank of the United States was founded in 1816 but killed by Andrew Jackson in 1836. The political circumstances which led to its demise are entertainingly recorded in Bray Hammond's Pulitzer-Prize-winning *Banks and Politics in Amer-*

ica. In brief, there was a coalition of forces: western agrarian dislike of the eastern seaboard banking establishment, competing financial interests in New York and Philadelphia, and advocates of easy credit and states rights (which often go together).

The United States subsequently abandoned the idea of individual bank charters in favour of "free banking." Instead of the state legislature considering each application for a charter, anyone could get one providing he put up the small capital requirements. But as Hammond wrote, "A good banker was apt to prefer a special charter . . . [to] a new-fangled one handed out at a window."

There were significant political forces in Upper Canada who wanted to follow the United States into "free banking." In fact the legislature of the Province of Canada created a Free Banking Act in 1850. As Hammond puts it, "The Lords of the Treasury in Whitehall were not struck with admiration . . . and the less because it followed American precedent." A few banks were licensed under this legislation, but the Canadian preference was for a special individual charter for each bank. A century and a half later, economic forces are driving the American system towards the Canadian model.

Perhaps the most important characteristic of the Bank of Montreal charter was that it said nothing about branching. When its provincial charter became a federal one in 1867, the foundation was laid for nationwide branch banking in Canada.

After Confederation, the third Minister of Finance, Sir John Rose, tried once more to introduce the American notion of small unit banks to collect the savings of the people in the hinterland. But his vision was based on his experience as a director of the Bank of Montreal. He believed that there should be only a very few large banks in the big cities which could conduct the commercial and government business, gathering their deposits from rural banks. But political resistance to this American approach was too great even for the Minister of Finance, and the idea did not survive.

Another feature of the Bank of Montreal charter was that it was valid for only ten years. This decennial review process has continued down to our times, and would have required a regular revision in 1990, had it not been for the legislative slippage.

Nowadays, the insurance and trust company lobbyists talk as if the decennial revision of banking legislation were a great benefit conferred on the banks by a beneficent government. On the contrary, the review process was created because the legislature of Lower Canada wanted to keep its hand on the collar of the Bank of Montreal, so that it could have a second look at its offspring and at the proposals of other candidates for bank charters.

In fact, the first renewal in 1831 was a dicey affair. The renewal bill was referred to a committee of the legislative assembly, where the Speaker, Louis-Joseph Papineau, attacked the bank. He accused it of exercising a monopoly over the government's foreign exchange business and cast doubt on the quality of its paper money in circulation (at that time, French Canadians tended to distrust paper money). Papineau's attack on the bank was part of a wider political objective, intended to push the British government towards responsible government in Lower Canada. The reformers in the assembly also supported the incorporation of a French-Canadian bank, the Banque du Peuple, which was founded in 1835 and which eventually got a charter in 1844.

Most of the fifteen-odd revisions of banking legislation that occurred after 1817 were designed to expand the scope of government regulation, not to broaden the banks' powers. (The first federal Bank Act of 1871 was six pages long; the 1980 version was 245 pages, not including 262 pages of regulations.) It was only in the revisions of 1954 and 1967 that enlarged powers were conferred on the banks, and some of these were resisted by the bankers. The periodic revisions to the Bank Act became an occasion on which policy makers could review the relevance of the legislation to the needs of the economy, but the original intention was to provide for further control, not for competitive advantage against other financial institutions.

Several other characteristics of the Bank of Montreal's charter deserve comment, because they are relevant to contemporary concerns. There was a prohibition against a bank being involved in any other trade or business—a principle dating back to the Bank of England. The bank was also prohibited from taking real property as security.

The principle of separating banking from commercial or industrial ownership and control has always been fundamental to the Canadian system. The idea behind the separation of powers is very simple: there is an inherent conflict of interest between the bank as lender and the customer who borrows funds to employ in his or her business. If the bank controls the borrower, or the borrower controls the bank, there is a very real possibility that the public's deposits will be used to further the private interests of the controlling borrower rather than the overall interests of the bank and its shareholders and depositors. This separation of function prevails pretty well everywhere that the principles of English common law apply, and also in Japan. In Europe, however, banks are allowed to own a portion of other industries (although the reverse does not apply, because in general no shareholder is allowed to get control of a bank).

The prohibition against taking real property as security had a significant effect in Canadian economic history. It prevented land speculation based on short-term bank loans; as a result the Canadian banking system has avoided some of the excessive instability which is associated with fluctuations in the value of real property. We do not have to look far to find a vivid example of the opposite case: since 1974, the United States savings and loan industry has been permitted to engage in financing land speculation. On top of this, the principle of protecting banking from self-dealing owners was violated. The result is that the U.S. government is now faced with a bail-out of the savings and loan industry which may run to $500 billion.

But there was also a drawback to the prohibition against taking real property as security. In the first place, the banks were prevented from making residential mortgage loans until 1954. This meant that the banks could not deal with millions of householders on the most important transaction of their lives, which was the financing of a house.

The prohibition against lending on real estate also extended to farm property and buildings, and to the real property of small businessmen. One of the most durable pieces of mythology in our economic history is that the banks closed in on the farmers on the prairies during the tough times of the 1930s. In fact the banks had always been prevented by law from financing the purchase of farm lands, and could only take security over real property to bolster an existing working capital loan.

The clauses which restricted voting rights to twenty in the case of the Bank of Montreal and ten in the case of the Bank of New Brunswick is a telling commentary on the nineteenth-century opposition to closely held ownership. It is also a commentary on foreign ownership of banks, then and now. In fact, there is no developed country in the world which allows foreigners to own and control its banking system.

One important feature of nineteenth-century Canadian banking was the provision for "double liability" of shareholders for the bank notes (paper money) issued by the bank. This provision was not contained in the Bank of Montreal's charter, but appeared for the first time in the charter of the Bank of Nova Scotia in 1832. The Bank of

Nova Scotia was, in fact, the first "joint stock bank," unlike the earlier banks, which were private. What this means is that the bank's stock consisted of common shares which could be bought and sold by anyone, rather than closely held private shares.

Until late in the nineteenth century, deposits were usually less important than bank notes in the liabilities of a bank. In the simplest terms, any commercial bank has a share capital, which is the amount originally paid in by the shareholders. The bank then makes loans, not limited to its capital, but based on its power to give the borrower a credit on its books, either in the form of a deposit or in the form of notes issued by the bank. A bank can "lever" its capital, depending on the legal limits placed on the ratio of capital to assets in the law. In effect, the bank can create credit within the limits imposed by the authorities.

Nowadays that limit is strictly controlled by the Bank of Canada, which is the government-owned bank responsible for official monetary policy, and the banks no longer issue their own paper money. But in the earliest days, when chequable deposits did not exist, the issuing of notes was fundamental to providing credit to borrowers, and of course also provided the general means of payment for the public.

In order to prevent a bank from issuing too many of its own bank notes, the Nova Scotia legislation, in the event of bank failure, required the shareholders, with money still owing to noteholders and depositors, to pay over as much money as they had already invested in the shares of the bank. This meant that the board of directors would think twice before issuing too many notes or making too many risky loans.

As we shall see shortly, the double liability became an important element in the politics of bank mergers for almost a century, up to 1923. To make doubly sure that a bank did not issue too many notes, there were provisions in all bank charters which limited the liabilities of a bank to two or three times its shareholders' capital. After Confederation, this very basic constraint disappeared from Canadian banking, thereby making possible some of the excesses of the 1970s and 1980s. It was not until very recent times that "capital ratios" were restored.

BANKERS AS POLITICIANS

It is hardly surprising that there was a close connection between banking and politics throughout the nineteenth century. The mercantile community was looking for a reliable mechanism to finance the export of raw materials to Great Britain. It could take two years to receive payment for lumber and potash shipped to England, whereas goods imported from New York had to be paid for in cash. The merchants also needed domestic financial institutions that were independent of the whims of the bureaucracy in Whitehall, which was at least two months away in terms of getting decisions made. And everyone needed a standardized currency to replace the confusing mixture of British sterling, American dollars, Spanish doubloons, and a wide range of paper currency, some of it fraudulent, which constituted the means of payment in those days.

The requirements of the business community for banking facilities were matched by the financial needs of governments. The fiscal requirements of the provincial governments included a practical mechanism for gathering taxes (principally customs revenues), for placing their deposits in safekeeping, and for arranging loans to tide them over during periods of low revenue. The opening up of the country placed heavy demands on the infrastructure of transport and communications, so the governments were also borrowers for their own longer-term requirements as well.

The competitive struggle for early bank charters was often a matter of political influence. By the middle of the century, banking became even more an arena for partisan politics. There was a new class of financial entrepreneurs, men who had acquired experience as bank owners and directors, and who were frequently involved in active political careers. For example, the first three Ministers of Finance in the new Dominion government were all closely associated with banks. Alexander Tilloch Galt, the first Minister of Finance, had been an original applicant for a charter for the Eastern Townships Bank (later absorbed into the Bank of Commerce). In 1867 he was a large shareholder of the failing Commercial Bank in Ontario while Minister of Finance, and later, after leaving office, he became a director of the Bank of Montreal.

Sir John Rose, who succeeded Galt as Minister of Finance in 1867, had been a director of the Bank of Montreal from 1859 until taking office. (Apart from his undoubted qualifications for the job, in his youth he had gone along on a sort of vaudeville tour of the United States with Sir John A. Macdonald, who played "a rude instrument" while Rose capered around dressed as a dancing bear.) As Minister of Finance, Sir John chaired the parliamentary committee which was trying to steer the first Bank Act through Parliament from 1867 to

1869. His own vision of banking legislation was that corporate banking should be confined to the big players like the Bank of Montreal and the Bank of British North America, and that Canada should copy the American system of rural unit banking. Despite his dual position as minister and chairman of the committee, he failed to push his version of the Bank Act through Parliament and quit politics in disgust.

The third Minister of Finance, Sir Francis Hincks, succeeded Rose in 1869. He had been a founder of the Farmers' Bank in 1835, but its Tory connections caused him to move very soon to the Bank of the People as manager. This reform-minded bank, which was associated with William Lyon Mackenzie and was a counterpart to the francophone reformist Banque du Peuple in Quebec, only lasted from 1835 until 1838, when it was absorbed by the Bank of Montreal. Much later on, after a career abroad, Hincks was recruited by Sir John A. Macdonald (who had a coalition cabinet) to be Minister of Finance. After leaving office in 1873 he became president of the City Bank, which merged with the Royal Canadian Bank into the Consolidated Bank, which in turn failed in 1879. (Hincks was later indicted for fraud in connection with this failure, but he was seventy-two years old at the time, and it was not entirely clear to the courts whether his actions were due to dishonesty or senility.)

The translation of bank directors and bank solicitors into Ministers of Finance or other ministerial positions neither began nor ended around Confederation. However, certain standards of propriety gradually evolved; it would be inconceivable today for the Minister of Finance to be a significant bank shareholder, much less chair the House of Commons Committee on Finance, Trade and Economic Affairs. However, in the Senate perceptions of conflict of interest have been slower to change. When Sir John Rose was chairing the House committee, the chairman of the Senate Committee on Banking was Sir William McMaster, who also happened to be the founding president of the Bank of Commerce. In our own day, Senator Salter Hayden, a director of the Bank of Nova Scotia, held the chair of the banking committee in the Senate until 1983, when he was in his eighties.

In 1891-92, Sir John Abbott was Prime Minister while holding a seat in the Senate and retaining his directorship on the board of the Bank of Montreal. However, later prime ministers attained high political office only after severing their bank connections. This has happened quite often. Robert Borden, Prime Minister from 1911 to

1920, had been a director of the Bank of Nova Scotia for many years and later was president of Barclays Bank (Canada). R.B. Bennett was a director of the Royal Bank from 1924 to 1947, except for his years as Conservative leader and Prime Minister, 1927-38. For that matter, Brian Mulroney was briefly a director of the Canadian Imperial Bank of Commerce, prior to becoming Prime Minister, although this has never been seen by bankers as a plus for the banking industry.

THE PAPER MONEY DISPUTE

Although ideas about conflict of interest have changed since the nineteenth century, the fact is that politicians with banking connections did not always succeed in getting their own way on banking policy. There were almost always competing interests in Parliament and in the government of the day that were strong enough to offset an insider position.

As already noted, the chartered banks had originally had the power to issue their own notes in certain denominations, a power which lasted from 1817 until the creation of the Bank of Canada in 1935. The note-issuing power was fundamental to profitability in the days before deposits in banks became significant. When a bank issued notes, it in effect created liabilities (which are the equivalent of non-interest-bearing deposits). The charters of the banks placed constraints on issuing notes, usually one or two times paid-up capital. There was also a requirement to hold some portion of the note issue as a cash reserve in the form of gold and silver coins ("specie") or provincial (later Dominion) notes.

The first great confrontation between the banks and government after Confederation was over the note-issuing power. The first three Ministers of Finance under Sir John A. Macdonald — Galt, Rose, and Hincks — all wanted to remove the note-issuing power from the banks and transfer it to the new Dominion of Canada. The principal reason for this was that the government was strapped for cash. It could not roll over a maturing short-term obligation in the London money market, and needed a new source of funds. In this endeavour they were supported by the Bank of Montreal, which represented one-quarter of the whole banking system, and which wanted to become a central bank as well as a commercial bank, like the Bank of England.

The Bank of Montreal also had a commercial interest in the government's proposals, inasmuch as it would be paid a commission for issuing Dominion notes and would be freed from its unofficial obligation to keep some of its more speculative fellow banks in line by demanding payment in gold for their excessive note issues. It would also realize on its holdings of government bonds. As well, the bank wanted to regain its position as the exclusive fiscal agent for the Dominion of Canada, and to represent it in the London money market. These aspirations were given a great boost when the Province of Canada's principal banker, the Bank of Upper Canada, failed in 1866.

Of all the failures in Canadian banking history, it would seem that that of the Bank of Upper Canada was the least justified and the most irresponsible. It did about 15 percent of the banking business in Upper Canada, and 8 percent in the Canadas as a whole. Not only that, it was for a time principal banker to the Province of Canada, and had from its very beginnings been identified with the Family Compact in York.

The basic reason it failed was bad management. Having started business soon after the Bank of Montreal, and being dependent on the rapidly growing economy of Upper Canada, its early success was gradually eroded by excessive lending to the new railways, especially the Grand Trunk. Its note issue became excessive in relation to its capital, and its general lending policies became overly speculative. For years it survived by arranging railway bond financings in London, with the help of the brokers there (rather like the Campeau junk-bond financings in New York in the late 1980s).

When the bank failed a few months before Confederation, the new Dominion of Canada took a heavy loss, because most of its deposits handed down from the Province of Canada were at the Bank of Upper Canada. Rather than pursue the shareholders for the double liability, Sir John A. Macdonald buried the whole issue as quickly as possible, probably because most of the shareholders were Tory party supporters. To prevent questions being asked about the failure, the government saw to it that all the books and records of the bank were sold to a waste paper dealer for $20 a ton, thus providing the earliest known instance of waste recycling in Canada.

After the failure of the Bank of Upper Canada, the Commercial Bank (headquartered in Kingston) also went down, and soon after that the Gore Bank in Hamilton. One could almost say that there was systemic failure, because these three banks were the largest in Upper Canada, and the business community had interrelationships with all of them. The Commercial Bank was the Montreal agent for the Gore Bank, so when the former closed, the latter ended up with unpaid liabilities. The loss of confidence which followed the failure of the Bank of Upper Canada is almost a laboratory case of the consequences for the whole financial system of a significant banking failure.

With the demise of the Bank of Upper Canada and the subsequent failure of the Commercial Bank, the principal competitors in Ontario of the Bank of Montreal were wiped out and the bank fell heir to the federal government's business. Although considered ruthless, the Bank of Montreal was in fact well managed. It kept its note issue and its total liabilities within prudent limits in relation to its capital, and it avoided excessive railway financing. The following table shows the approximate share of the total market (measured in terms of the total assets of twenty-four reporting banks rounded off to the nearest 1 percent).

The "Big Six" in 1867
Share of Market of 24* Reporting Banks
(Approximate Percent of Total Assets)

Bank of Montreal	25
Bank of Nova Scotia	2
Bank of Commerce	1
Bank of Toronto	4
Banque Nationale	2
Royal Bank**	3
	37

Major Competitors that Disappeared 1868-1890

Commercial Bank	12
Gore Bank	3
City Bank	2
Royal Canadian	3
	20

* 14 more banks did not report.
** Quebec Bank, a component of Royal after 1917, had 3%; the Merchant Bank of Halifax had not yet been founded.

Out of the speculative wreckage in Upper Canada emerged the Bank of Commerce and the Toronto Bank, both of which found opportunities caused by the bank failures.

Whether the Bank of Montreal used its dominant position to lessen competition in its own interest, or to prevent the survival of weak institutions in the public interest, is a matter of opinion. Certainly its president in the years 1869-73, Edwin King, was much feared and disliked by his rivals. Adam Shortt, the distinguished historian of early Canadian banking, wrote in his article "The History of Canadian Currency":

> A circumstantial story [about King], given in the leading New York papers, told of how the Bank of Montreal, after acquiring command of a large percentage of the available gold on the New York market, ostentatiously sent a considerable proportion of it down to a steamer leaving for London, much to the dismay of the market and the sudden elevation of the rate for gold. The gold, however, was afterwards returned to the vaults of the bank under cover of darkness, and was disposed of at a considerable premium on the following day. Certain it is that numerous, though often bitter tributes were paid to the power of the Bank of Montreal by the New York papers, which attributed several of the periodic crises on the New York gold market to the operations of the Bank of Montreal. As usual, such transactions were righteously denounced by those whose speculative ventures had gone astray.

The turbulent events in banking around the time of Confederation provided the background for the struggle over the note issue, which was in part a struggle about financing the government's deficit. But there were other questions of public policy at stake. Notes issued by the Upper Canadian banks were redeemed only at a discount in Montreal; and the Bank of Montreal undertook to redeem its notes only at head office; thus the paper money issued by the banks was usually worth its face value only in the city of issue and not elsewhere. Obviously government-issued paper money would trade at its full face value everywhere, which would remove the cost, inconvenience, and risk of shipping paper money back to its home base for redemption in gold or silver coin or Dominion notes.

The problem of redeeming bank notes at their par value was only one element in the rivalry between Toronto and Montreal, a rivalry which went back to the very beginning of the system in 1817. Montreal was much the older and more developed city, and also the centre of the export trade in grain, potash, and timber. Upper Canada was dependent on Montreal for its pipeline to Great Britain. But even with the strong support of the Bank of Montreal, three successive Ministers of Finance did not have the political clout to overcome the united opposition of the twenty-odd other banks which opposed an exclusive Dominion note issue.

Among the leading lobbyists for the banking community was Senator William McMaster, who had quit the board of the Bank of Montreal because of his dissatisfaction with its treatment of Upper Canada. He founded the Bank of Commerce, which eventually exceeded the Bank of Montreal in size. McMaster had plenty of allies, not only in Toronto and Montreal, but also in the Maritimes, in his battle with the Minister of Finance.

The outcome of the struggle was a compromise imposed by the Prime Minister and the rest of his cabinet on the Minister of Finance: the banks would retain the right to issue notes in denominations of $4 or more (changed to $5 in 1881), while the government issued smaller denominations.

THE POLITICS OF BANK FAILURES

Despite the serious bank failures around the time of Confederation, and the worldwide financial panic in 1879 which took down more banks, by 1890 there were still thirty-eight banks reporting to the government. This was about the same number as there had been in 1867, but there had been considerable turnover since then. There were some further banking failures, but none as spectacular as the ones in the period 1866-69.

When banks got into trouble, it was not unusual for the government to encourage the strongest banks to intervene and try to bail them out. Governments always prefer a bail-out, especially if other people's money can be used for it. As we have seen so many times in recent years, depositors who suffer losses or who might suffer losses make unhappy voters.

In any event, it was not unusual for a consortium of banks to meet together to pick up the pieces of a failure. The branch system of the Consolidated Bank, for example, was dismembered and parcelled out to a number of banks when it failed in 1879. If a bank was completely insolvent, that is, if the creditors could not all be paid in full, the other banks backed away. But if a bank was not insolvent but only illiquid, that is, if there were enough genuine assets to realize so that everyone could be paid out eventually, they would intervene. The doors of the failing bank would be kept open until the deposits had been entirely withdrawn and the notes retired; this ensured against a general loss of confidence in the system.

Although losses to holders of the paper money of failed banks were comparatively slight in the two decades following the first Bank Act of 1871, politicians were afraid of future bank failures. In the first Bank Act Revision of 1881, bank note liabilities were made a "first call" on the assets of a failed bank, meaning that noteholders would be paid before anyone else.

When the second bank revision was coming up in 1890, the government decided to create an insurance fund for the notes of all the banks. Every bank had to pay a small percentage of its note circulation into a central fund, which was called the Bank Circulation Redemption Fund. In effect, this put all bank notes of the different issuing banks on an equal footing, because they would be paid out in full from the fund in the event of a failure of one of the weaker members. The Bank of Montreal opposed the creation of this fund, on the not unreasonable grounds that it would put all other bank notes on an equal footing with its own, which were of undoubted quality. But the balance of political forces was in favour of protecting the lowest common denominator.

It was the Bank Act Revision of 1890 which led the banks to get together for joint discussions with the Minister of Finance. Though divided over the issue of the Bank Circulation Redemption Fund, the banks decided that the time had come to create an industry association. In December 1891, the Canadian Bankers' Association (CBA) was founded as a voluntary association of banks. The principal purpose of the association, then as now, was to provide a forum in which the banks could consider legislation affecting banking. In 1900, the CBA was incorporated by an act of Parliament, making it one of the few trade or industry associations which has a statutory existence. The act has not been changed since 1900, although the creation of the Canadian Payments Association Act of 1980 removed its responsibility for operating the clearing system.

CHAPTER 3

WHY THERE ARE ONLY SIX BIG BANKS

CONCENTRATION AND COMPETITION

The consolidation of the banking establishment which took place between 1879 and 1925 provides a fascinating panorama of the economic forces at work across the country. The consolidation was the result of ineluctable economic forces. Canada was a thinly populated country when the first banks came into existence, and remained thinly populated as the banks marched across the continent in step with economic development. In many regions, the local economy depended on a narrow base of primary industries, not a good foundation for establishing new financial institutions. Any bank, even a well-run bank, can only reflect the real economy in which it dwells. The growth of its deposits depends on the income and savings of its customers, and the viability of its loan portfolio depends on the capacity of borrowers to employ funds profitably and pay them back.

The following table shows that in 1890 the Bank of Montreal was still by far the dominant bank, with 19 percent of the system's total assets. The Bank of Commerce was emerging as a major challenger, with 9 percent of total assets. The Royal Bank was still very small, and the other three of the present "big six" were not yet in their period of major growth. At that point, there were only three other banks with a significant share of the market, of which the Merchants' Bank of Canada in Montreal was the most important with 9 percent. (The Merchants' Bank of Halifax decided to change its name to the Royal Bank in 1901, in order not to be confused with its powerful Montreal competitor. One could speculate that the change in name was a factor in the Royal's subsequent take-off into growth.)

The "Big Six" in 1890
Share of Market of 38 Reporting Banks
(Approximate Percent of Total Assets)

Bank of Montreal	19
Bank of Commerce	9
Bank of Toronto	5
Bank of Nova Scotia	4
Royal Bank (Merchants' Bank of Halifax)	3
Banque Nationale	2
	42

While a thin population living on a narrow industrial base is the broad general reason for the nature of our banking structure, the specific circumstances which led to the consolidation of the system into six big banks were remarkably different. At one extreme were small banks that were thinly capitalized and sometimes owned by a small group of self-dealing speculators; and at the other extreme was the Bank of Upper Canada, founded under the best possible establishment auspices, with a relatively broad geographic and industrial base, but mismanaged into failure.

In some cases, the immediate cause of mergers and contractions was mismanagement and incompetence, and occasionally even outright fraud. Small banks could not easily survive rumours or published reports that a senior officer had absconded with most of the cash. The larger banks were more resilient. The Bank of Nova Scotia's first general manager, J.T. Forman, fled to England after embezzling for thirty-eight years, but the bank survived. Canadian banking history is full of the noise of galloping hooves as bankers headed south, as did J.S. Bousquet of the Banque du Peuple in Quebec, for example, and the "cashier" of the Bank of Prince Edward Island, Joseph Brecken. Others died under a cloud of doubt, like Sir Francis Hincks, the former Minister of Finance; or Sam Zimmerman, who owned his own bank in Niagara Falls. One banker, the general manager of the Ontario Bank in Toronto, was sent to the Kingston Penitentiary.

Banking by its very nature provides opportunities for theft or mismanagement, because it deals with money and depends on human judgement. The examples which we deal with here illustrate another theme in the period 1890 to 1925, which was the need for better regulation. Banking has become a highly regulated industry. The general reason for this is that it takes only a single individual, sometimes a dishonest one, but more often a person lacking in balanced judgement, to take down an institution, and thereby damage a much wider community.

Let us take a guided tour of Canadian regional banking in the period 1890 to 1925. Our first port of call is St. John's, Newfoundland, where the two existing banks, the Commercial and Union, both failed in 1894.

BLACK MONDAY IN NEWFOUNDLAND

A century ago, the Newfoundland economy was even more dependent on the fishing industry than it is today. The population of 190,000 was served by two commercial banks, the Union and the Commercial, and by the Newfoundland Savings Bank, a government-owned institution. The two commercial banks were owned and controlled by the fish merchants of St. John's, who in turn supplied credit to the fishermen. Until the fishing catch was sold, the fishermen were entirely dependent on credit extended to them by the merchants for their supplies and bait, indeed for everything. This "truck system," as it was called, lasted well into the twentieth century along the Atlantic seaboard. The merchants in turn depended on the banks, which recovered their advances when the fishing catch was sold in Britain.

In the early 1890s, bank credit became greatly overextended because the merchants operated on bank overdrafts and passed the costs on to the poor fishermen who had no alternative but to pay. There was no one to regulate the financial situation, because the merchants themselves controlled the banks, and the politicians (including successive Prime Ministers) were themselves shareholders in the banks. The government was itself overextended in railway finance and hardly able to keep afloat. A disastrous fire in the City of St. John's in 1892 and a poor fishing catch the following year compounded the banks' problems.

"Black Monday" on December 10, 1894, was an infamous day in Newfoundland history. On that day, the Commercial bank closed its doors, and the Union Bank immediately followed. The shock wave of failure nearly took down the Newfoundland Savings Bank, because there was a run on deposits. The government itself was overextended and quite unable to help its offspring. "The country found itself without a currency; business was brought to a standstill with many firms never to reopen," wrote Francis Rowe in 1971.

The government was anything but anxious to investigate the circumstances of the bank failures, because the Prime Minister, Sir William Whiteaway, and other cabinet ministers were themselves shareholders. Most of them, and many of the merchants, quickly retired to a more comfortable life in the United Kingdom. In desperation, the government invited three Canadian banks, the Bank of Nova Scotia, the Bank of Montreal, and the Merchants' Bank of Halifax to open for business in Newfoundland. The Bank of Nova Scotia opened an office on December 21, eleven days after Black Monday, and the Bank of Montreal opened in January 1895.

In 1990, the Bank of Nova Scotia had sixty-two branches in Newfoundland, and the Bank of Montreal twenty-seven branches. All other banks put together had forty-six branches. This preponderant share held by two banks can be directly traced to the events of 1894. One could hardly imagine a more clear-cut case of a calamitous economic event leading towards a national branch banking system.

THE LIVERPOOL BOODLERS

In *The Scotiabank Story*, Joseph Schull and Douglas Gibson describe the demise of a small bank in Liverpool, Nova Scotia, in 1879. Here again we find a small bank serving an economy based solely on fishing and forest products.

For a time in the nineteenth century, Nova Scotia enjoyed a booming triangular trade: wooden sailing ships built on the Atlantic seaboard carried lumber and salt cod to the Caribbean, where the cargo was off-loaded and replaced with sugar and molasses bound for Britain. The ships then returned with manufactured goods to Halifax and the seacoast ports. But then the sailing ships were replaced by steamships, and as we have seen, the fishing industry was always vulnerable to economic conditions.

In 1867, the Bank of Nova Scotia had $1.3 million in assets, which about equalled the assets of all the other banks in Nova Scotia put together. These included the Halifax Banking Company, which had not yet obtained a charter, and a few smaller banks in Halifax, Yarmouth, Windsor, and Pictou.

In December 1875, the president of the Bank of Liverpool

provided his shareholders with the sort of assurance which sometimes
precedes an imminent disaster.

> Your Directors beg to remind you that the chief industries of
> this county still remain in a depressed condition. Although
> the excessive losses suffered by the bank have absorbed a very
> large proportion of your capital, your directors are of the
> opinion that with what remains, you can continue to offer
> banking facilities sufficient for legitimate local requirements.

"It was soon evident," Gibson writes, "that the Bank of Liverpool's
Directors were desperately attempting to stave off liquidation in view
of their double liability. The bank's statements were suspect, large
loans were renewed again and again ... Politics had entered the
picture because prominent Liverpool citizens, many of whom owned
shares in the Bank of Liverpool, were proclaiming the need to
maintain the bank as the backbone of the community."

The Bank of Liverpool had many overdue loans including debts to
the federal government and to the Bank of Nova Scotia. Thomas
Fyshe, the general manager of the Bank of Nova Scotia, pursued the
directors of the Bank of Liverpool for their double liability on the
paper money issued by the bank. After twelve years of litigation, the
"Liverpool Boodlers," as Fyshe described them, were forced to pay
up. "Among the shareholders were Senators, Members of Parliament,
and important ecclesiastics, who made every effort to avoid honour-
ing their double liability obligation."

By 1890, the Bank of Nova Scotia constituted almost half of the
total banking system in Nova Scotia, and the participation of three
Halifax banks in the construction of national institutions had not yet
begun. (These were the Bank of Nova Scotia, the Merchants' Bank of
Halifax which became the Royal, and the Halifax Banking Company
which became a unit in the Bank of Commerce.)

In 1905, the Bank of Yarmouth failed, "as a consequence of loans
to one firm out of all proportion to its own means," according to R.M.
Breckenridge, in his book, *Banking in Canada*. The Commercial
Bank of Windsor was acquired by the Union Bank of Halifax in 1892,
which in turn was absorbed by the Royal in 1910. The very small
Exchange Bank of Yarmouth became part of the Bank of Montreal in
1903; the People's Bank of Halifax with its twenty-six branches was
bought for shares and cash by the Bank of Montreal in 1907. The
other local banks in Nova Scotia lasted only a short time. Market
forces were driving the system towards national consolidation.

DOMINOES ON THE ISLAND

Independent banks on Prince Edward Island lasted for exactly fifty years, from the founding of the first bank in 1856 to the merging of the last bank in 1906. The Bank of Prince Edward Island was established rather late (in 1856), considering that there were already a number of banks in Nova Scotia and New Brunswick, whose currency circulated on P.E.I.

Victor Ross, the historian of the Bank of Commerce, notes that "the Island had long been disturbed by a system of absentee landlordism ... In a single day, in 1767, almost the whole island had been divided by lot among 67 proprietors, chiefly army and navy officers, government officials, and landed gentry, all residing in England." Thus Prince Edward Island was an economy of tenant farmers until Confederation. There was a wooden shipbuilding industry, which suffered the same fate as that in Nova Scotia with the decline of wooden sailing ships and the rise of steamships made of iron and steel.

Prince Edward Island rejected Confederation in 1867, but had second thoughts when railway speculation got the province overextended in debt instruments that could not be peddled on the London market. The government financed a narrow-gauge railway by putting up $25,000 of debentures per mile, but neglected to stipulate the mileage. The contractor took a meandering route across the beautiful countryside, and the province found itself with an unmanageable debt. The banks were left holding unmarketable bonds beyond their capacity to carry. The local establishment, whose members owned the banks, had no choice but to capitulate to Confederation in 1873. As part of the deal, the federal government assumed responsibility for the railway debt.

In 1881, Joseph Brecken, the cashier (general manager) of the Bank of Prince Edward Island absconded. The resulting losses exceeded twice the bank's capital. This produced the domino effect which we have already seen in Newfoundland. The Union Bank of Prince Edward Island took refuge by merging with the Bank of Nova Scotia in 1883; the Merchants' Bank of Prince Edward Island, which had been founded under very strong political auspices just before Confederation, struggled on until 1906, when it merged with the Canadian Bank of Commerce.

Clearly, the economic base of Prince Edward Island, with its declining shipbuilding industry and railway speculation supported by the politicians of the day, could not support an independent banking system. More than a century later, the two largest of the big six banks represented in Prince Edward Island are the Bank of Nova Scotia with nine branches and the Canadian Imperial Bank of Commerce with eight, reflecting events a century ago.

THE BEANCOUNTERS SELL OUT

Although the Bank of New Brunswick was the first bank in Canada to get a charter, it was a very conservative institution. In 1908, it still had assets of only $7 million compared to $45 million for the Bank of Nova Scotia. It had been very reluctant to open branches in New Brunswick, which may explain why fifteen other banks also received charters in New Brunswick in the nineteenth century. Some of these were in relatively small communities such as St. Andrews or St. Stephen. The only serious local competition which the Bank of New Brunswick had was the People's Bank of New Brunswick, which was absorbed by the Bank of Montreal in 1907.

According to Douglas Gibson, "The Directors (of the Bank of New Brunswick) voted on discounts by using black and white beans." Whether or not the expression "beancounters," which is usually applied to chartered accountants, originated in Saint John is uncertain. In any event the conservative style of the bank eventually made it a target for the Bank of Nova Scotia, which had already shifted its base of operations from Halifax to Toronto in 1900. The Bank of New Brunswick had failed to develop a management succession, but its directors resisted a takeover for several years. At one point, Sir William Stavert, who had been its general manager, tried to engineer a merger with the Bank of Montreal, but this project fell through.

In the first decade of the twentieth century, the Montreal, Royal, Nova Scotia, and Commerce all opened branches in the province, and the Bank of New Brunswick was feeling the heat. In its annual report to the shareholders in October 1912, the president wrote, "During the past few years banks with large capital and branches extending to the Pacific have invaded our territory, intensifying the keen competition in banking." He went on to say that the bank needed more capital to expand and compete, and that the bank should really be opening branches in Ontario and the West. But there was no one to provide the leadership, and in 1913 the Bank of New Brunswick finally capitulated to the Bank of Nova Scotia and sold out with a share exchange. So ended almost a century of regional banking in New Brunswick.

THE FRANCOPHONE FACTOR

One of the big six banks of today is the Banque Nationale. When I became president of the Canadian Bankers' Association in 1980, I made a point of replacing all references to "The Big Five" by references to "The Big Six" in order to recognize the fact that the National Bank had to be considered comparable to the large anglophone banks, even though it is the smallest of the six. Perhaps even more important, the National Bank now holds about one third of the banking system's assets in Quebec, and one cannot talk about Canada's financial policies without taking account of the Quebec factor.

We have already seen that the Bank of Montreal dominated the whole banking scene throughout the nineteenth century. It was an urban and anglophone bank, founded by the unilingual and British-oriented business community of Montreal. The corporate style of the Bank of Montreal was to concentrate on the commercial sector, and even as late as 1900, there were only three branches in the province of Quebec, two in Montreal, and one in Quebec City. French Canada, on the other hand, was very largely an agricultural community, lacking both the capital and the business traditions of the anglophone business sector in Montreal and Quebec City.

The first francophone bank was the Banque du Peuple, formed in 1835 and chartered in 1844. It is possible that the Bank of Montreal used its connections on the legislative council to stall the granting of a charter to the Banque du Peuple, although relations were cordial enough on the surface. (Both the president of the Bank of Montreal, Peter McGill, and its vice-president, Joseph Masson, were on the legislative council during the years 1835 to 1844.)

The Banque du Peuple might have survived and continued to the present day, except that it fell victim to excessive expansion after 1885. Branches were opened rapidly, the note issue was almost doubled in ten years, and the bank took on more deposits than its capital could support. The general manager, J.S. Bousquet, made large loans not authorized by the directors, and word got around that the bank was in shaky condition. This led to a run on deposits, and in 1895 the bank went into liquidation.

Under its peculiar charter, the Banque du Peuple directors had unlimited liability, and they spent the next few years trying to avoid their financial responsibility. In the end, Parliament passed a special bill to limit the liability of the directors, with the result that small depositors recovered only about seventy-five cents on the dollar. Although this failure occurred before the creation of the office of Inspector General of Banks, Ronald Rudin, in his recent history of francophone banks, *Banking en français*, notes that the Department of Finance was aware of other bad debts totalling nearly $500,000 on the bank's books.

The loss of its largest and most respected bank was a serious setback to the francophone financial community. This left three larger banks: the Banque Nationale (founded in 1859), La Banque Jacques Cartier (founded in 1862), and the Banque d'Hochelaga (founded in 1873). In 1900, the Jacques Cartier became the Provincial Bank. In 1924, three became two, when the Banque Nationale was forced into a merger with the Banque d'Hochelaga.

This came about primarily through the Banque Nationale's excessive lending to an agricultural machinery company, Machine Agricole, at Montmagny, down river from Quebec City. The Banque Nationale had already been weakened by the sharp business recession of 1921, during which there was a decline in its deposits from about $50 million to about $33 million. Machine Agricole, which had prospered on government contracts for road machinery during the First World War, was considered to be in dubious financial condition. The situation was not improved when the manager of the rival Provincial Bank started spreading rumours about the Banque Nationale. These so frightened the depositors that the bank entered into a shotgun marriage with the Banque d'Hochelaga in 1924, after the efforts by both Conservative and Liberal governments to prop it up had failed. The merged bank took the name Banque Canadienne Nationale in 1925.

Meanwhile, nearly a dozen other Quebec banks were formed in the nineteenth century, but all had fallen by the wayside by 1908. Ronald Rudin writes, "All of Canada's small town banks suffered from the restricted nature of their operations, which made them particularly vulnerable to bad management, recessions, and the designs of larger banks, but this was particularly the case for the smallest of the French banks, whose operations were further circumscribed by language."

It is not hard to understand the origins of the caisses populaires in Quebec, when we look at the statistics of branch penetration in the province. According to Rudin, in 1871 only one in three towns with a population of 5,000 to 10,000 people had a bank branch; in 1881 this had changed to one in two. In 1891 the City of Lévis, across the river from Quebec City, with a population of 7,000, had no bank. The first "caisse pop" was formed in this town in 1901, and the headquarters of the movement is still located there.

The final episode in the concentration of the francophone banking industry occurred in 1979, when the Nationale and the Provincial banks merged to form the Banque Nationale of today. This provided the French-Canadian business community with a bank strong enough to compete with its anglophone rivals. In fact, the policy of the Banque Nationale has been one of widening the scope of its operations from its largely Quebec base to the rest of Canada and to the international banking community.

BRITISH COLUMBIA JOINS THE MAINSTREAM

Before the Canadian Pacific Railway was completed in 1885, the colonies of Vancouver Island and British Columbia were not effectively connected to eastern Canada. The most efficient route from England was by ship to Panama, overland to the Pacific, and then up the coast to Victoria.

The first bank on the west coast was a branch of the Bank of British North America, which was already well established in eastern Canada. This bank had a royal charter rather than a Canadian provincial charter, and was brought under the Canadian Bank Act some time after Confederation.

In 1862, a group of financial entrepreneurs in London obtained a royal charter for the Bank of British Columbia. At that time, the principal economic activity on the coast was gold mining, which had attracted a rush beginning in 1858. Those who were successful in panning for gold had no place to put their treasure except to bury it in the woods.

Before the coming of the railway, business activity in Victoria and in the lower Fraser Valley was very slow and the Bank of British Columbia made most of its money at its branches in San Francisco, Seattle, and Portland, Oregon. When Vancouver was selected in 1886 as the terminus of the Canadian Pacific Railway, the sleepy times were over for the Bank of British Columbia. Its Victoria manager wrote to head office in London:

Rumours are frequent as to the intention of Eastern Canadian banks to establish at Coal Harbour [Vancouver], but at present they are doubtless premature and very probably emanate from land speculators interested in property on the spot.

Nevertheless, to protect its turf the Bank of British Columbia opened about ten branches on the mainland in 1891.

But in 1897, the Merchants' Bank of Halifax opened three branches in British Columbia and by 1899 it had ten branches. The Canadian Bank of Commerce opened in both Vancouver and the Yukon in 1899, and by 1901 it had ten branches in British Columbia. The Commerce, which was already the correspondent bank for the Bank of British Columbia in eastern Canada, represented a major competitive threat to the Bank of British Columbia not only in the province but in San Francisco. The shares of the Bank of British Columbia fell by more than 50 percent as it struggled to compete with the eastern banks. Meanwhile the Bank of British Columbia had come under the Canadian federal banking legislation in 1893, and when its charter came up for review the second time, in 1901, the directors decided to sell out to save their investment.

THE BANKS FOLLOW THE RAILWAY

When the first Bank Act was passed in 1871, the province of Manitoba was one year old. The population of the Red River settlement was approximately 1,500 white settlers and 10,000 Métis and Indians. It would be another thirty-four years before the Provinces of Saskatchewan and Alberta were formed out of the Northwest Territories.

Banking followed the path of settlement, the governing factor being the advance of the Canadian Pacific Railway. Even so, several of the larger eastern Canadian banks had opened branches in the Red River Settlement before the railway was completed in 1885. In the vanguard was the Merchants' Bank, which opened in 1873. The population of Winnipeg rocketed to 15,000 by 1885, and there was heavy speculation in land. In The Last Spike, Pierre Berton wrote, "In Winnipeg, on Main Street, the price rose as high as $2,000 a front foot for choice locations." The real estate bubble burst in only six months, and Berton notes that it was almost a century before the price of real estate at Portage and Main got back to the price in 1882, but in depreciated dollars.

The head of rail reached Regina and beyond in 1882, and arrived in Calgary in 1883. The Bank of Montreal opened in Calgary in 1886, when there were 1,200 people in the area. But most of the banks were more cautious in assessing business prospects along the rail right of way, having been badly burned in the Winnipeg collapse in 1882. The Commerce opened a branch in Medicine Hat in 1902 and in Regina in 1903, while the Nova Scotia opened branches in both Edmonton and Calgary in 1903 and in Saskatoon in 1906.

There was little chance of forming a successful, locally owned western bank in the late nineteenth century. The huge inflow of population after the completion of the northern Ontario section of the line in 1885 spread out thinly over the Prairies looking for good land, and there was no such thing as a local concentration of capital and commercial knowledge to form a bank. The eastern banks, on the other hand, had experienced staff who could be transferred to the growing western communities and provided with capital and guidance from their home base.

Despite the enormous difficulties in founding an indigenous bank, there were quite a few attempts. Seven charters were granted for banks in Manitoba which were never used, and two more in Saskatchewan. Two banks got off the ground in Winnipeg, one being the Commercial Bank of Manitoba in 1885, and the second being the Northern Bank in 1904. The first of these failed after eight years, while the second merged with the Crown Bank of Toronto in 1908, and the resulting Northern Crown Bank was absorbed by the Royal Bank in 1918.

In Saskatchewan, the Weyburn Security Bank operated from 1910 until 1931, when it was merged into the Imperial. There were never any homegrown banks in Alberta before the creation of the two ill-fated banks of the 1980s.

THE EMERGENCE OF NATIONWIDE BANKS

Around the turn of the century, four of the present big six banks embarked on ambitious programs to extend their branch networks from coast to coast. This was accomplished in part by a rapid growth in new branches, as a wave of immigration and prosperity swept across the West in the first two decades of the twentieth century.

The Bank of Commerce was, until 1892, an all-Ontario bank, except for its Chicago and New York offices. With forty-nine branches in Ontario, its first domestic branch outside the province was a small one in Montreal opened in 1892. At that point a decision was made to embark on a huge plan of expansion across the country. Between 1898 and 1918, the Commerce opened 174 branches in the three Prairie provinces and a further thirty-nine in British Columbia. In addition, the Commerce acquired the Bank of British Columbia with its ten branches in 1901, the Halifax Banking Company with seventeen branches in 1903, and the Eastern Townships Bank in 1912 with no fewer than ninety-four branches and sub-branches. Thus in only two decades, the Commerce changed itself from being an Ontario bank into a national institution with branches from coast to coast.

But the national expansion was also influenced by a key change in the Bank Act of 1900, which permitted banks to merge by mutual agreement without the need of a specific act of Parliament. Provided two-thirds of the shareholders agreed, banks could merge with the approval of the Treasury Board and the Governor in Council. There was a growing awareness that there were too many small floundering banks which were not in fact contributing to the growth of the economy. Bank failures were disrupting the payments system, throwing the business and farming community into turmoil, and causing losses for shareholders and to some extent for depositors and noteholders.

The evidence is overwhelming that local and regional institutions were not well adapted to the conditions of the Canadian economy. Even relatively sound banks, like the Halifax Banking Company, the Quebec Bank, the Merchants' Bank of Canada, or the Eastern Townships Bank, found themselves lacking the capital and experienced personnel to compete with the Montreal and Commerce and others. The Eastern Townships Bank was a good case in point. Based in Sherbrooke, Quebec, it served the thirteen almost entirely anglophone counties southeast of Montreal which are known as the Eastern Townships, and in 1912 had ninety-four units. The directors reached the conclusion that if the bank were to compete successfully for commercial customers, it would have to be widely represented across Canada. In 1911, they made a trip through western Canada, and came to the conclusion that their bank did not have the capital and personnel resources to take the great leap forward. Immediately after returning from the western trip in 1912, they accepted a share-exchange proposal from the Bank of Commerce on a one-for-one basis. (The Commerce subsequently eliminated some marginal units, but not the branch in Rock Island, with its grandiose Ionic granite columns. That branch held my first savings account.)

The response of the Bank of Montreal to the expansion of the Commerce and the Royal Bank was late in coming, but when it came it was massive. In 1918, the Bank of Montreal took over the Bank of British North America; in 1922 it acquired the Merchants' Bank of Canada, and in 1925 it added Molson's Bank to its acquisitions. These three acquisitions more than tripled the branch system of the Bank of Montreal from about 200 to more than 600.

It has already been noted that the two Halifax-based banks, the Bank of Nova Scotia and the Merchants' Bank of Halifax, moved to the national stage after the turn of the century. The Bank of Nova Scotia shifted its head office from Halifax to Toronto in 1900; it acquired the Metropolitan Bank in 1902 and the Bank of Ottawa in 1919. The Merchants' Bank of Halifax changed its name to the Royal Bank in 1901, and moved its head office to Montreal in 1907. Under Sir Herbert Holt and Edson L. Pease, the Royal embarked on a remarkable period of growth which took its branch system from eighty-six Canadian units in 1907 to 801 units in 1925. About half of this huge increase represented acquisitions: the Union Bank of Halifax in 1910, the Traders' Bank in 1910, the Quebec Bank in 1914, the Northern Crown in 1918, and the Union Bank of Canada in 1925. In little more than two decades, the Royal had placed itself on the same footing as the Commerce and Montreal. The huge expansion of these two banks over thousands of miles of territory, in villages and towns, is testimony to the great administrative talents that had emerged in the top hierarchies of banking. In the Royal it was Edson Pease, and in the Commerce Sir Edmund Walker.

Alone among the big six banks of today, the Toronto-Dominion Bank never expanded by way of merger, except in 1954 for its two elements, the Toronto and the Dominion banks. The combined bank then had about 450 branches, of which about 375 were in Ontario. Since the merger, the number of Canadian branches has more than doubled, and many of these are in Quebec and western Canada.

Thus we find that in the early decades of this century, the present structure of the banking system took shape, with a few large institutions expanding from coast to coast. While the merger movement was a significant factor in the emergence of a few large institutions, internal growth was at least as important in the development of the branch banking system. While all this was going on, the system was plagued by periodic episodes of fraud and failure which embarrassed the industry. Although the regulatory system had been gradually strengthened through four Bank Act revisions prior to 1913, there were still some glaring weaknesses. These, and the response to them, will be explored in the next chapter.

CHAPTER 4

THE SHORT UNHAPPY LIFE OF THE SOVEREIGN BANK

CRUSTY HENRY MCLEOD

While there were plenty of bank failures between Confederation and the turn of the century, the losses to the general public were quite small. In some cases the shareholders were wiped out, but losses to depositors were generally avoided by last-minute mergers or successful liquidations. Losses to noteholders were small, and the Bank Circulation Redemption Fund of 1890 established a government-sponsored fund which all the banks had to support. There had been three threats of systemic failure, that is, a domino collapse of the whole system: the first in Upper Canada, brought on by the disastrous failure of the Bank of Upper Canada; and later the collapse of the Prince Edward Island and Newfoundland banks.

In the first quarter of the twentieth century there were several shocking bank failures. They were marked by a pattern of fraud and self-dealing which we have seen repeated in the trust companies in the 1980s. It took almost twenty years for the reluctant bankers and politicians to introduce financial reforms to protect the public. This chapter is a short history of one case—the Sovereign.

Although the Bank Act had been strengthened by three revisions up to 1903, there were few provisions to control internal fraud. Standards of accountability which might have been more or less tolerable in the middle of the nineteenth century were no longer sufficient in the early twentieth.

The undoubted leader in the drive to raise standards and eliminate embezzlers from the system was Henry C. McLeod, the general manager of the Bank of Nova Scotia. McLeod was a crusty, courageous, and unbending man, who started his career in Prince Edward Island. His first objective was to establish the practice of having outside auditors examine a bank's financial statements. Douglas Gibson has described how he brought over some chartered accountants from Scotland who understood banking, advising his board: "If we take the initiative in having chartered accountants verify our next annual statement I think we will still further entitle ourselves to the full confidence of depositors and of the public generally." In 1907 the Bank of Nova Scotia produced the first outside shareholders' audit of a Canadian bank.

McLeod's second objective was to lobby for an office of bank inspection under the Department of Finance. He started campaigning for such a position as early as 1901, but met with stony resistance from almost the whole banking community and indifference from J.M. Courtney, the deputy minister of finance. But a series of disasters gradually altered public perceptions.

In July of 1907, the Knickerbocker Trust Company failed in New York City. There was a panic and a run on the banks, and for a few months the American financial system was in grave danger. Call loan rates on the New York money market went from 6 percent in July 1907 to 20 percent towards the end of the year, and six months later were back to 5 percent.

The severity of the crisis led to the creation of a National Monetary Commission by Congress. This American version of a Royal Commission led to the creation of the Federal Reserve System in 1913. In 1909-10 a sub-committee chaired by Edward Vreeland of New York journeyed to Toronto to take evidence from the general managers of the large banks. Henry McLeod, always one to call a spade a spade, had a public disagreement on the witness stand with his fellow general manager, Duncan Coulson of the Bank of Toronto:

> Chairman Vreeland: Is it your opinion that confidence is created by supporting and standing by each other, and by liquidating banks and paying off the depositors?
>
> Coulson: That all helps, and we have a large paid up capital and paid up reserve, and upon that the government returns are issued from month to month and the people can use them.
>
> McLeod: They are not worth the paper they are written on.
>
> Coulson: I say 99 out of every 100 are fairly correct. I will not admit any such laxity in the government as to say they are not worth the paper they are written on at all.

McLeod: I do not regard them as worth the paper they are written on because there's no supervision. In the case of the failed banks they have made them with every degree of falsification and there's no check or supervision.

McLeod and Coulson and ten other general managers of large banks had just been through the process of liquidating the remains of the Sovereign Bank of Canada. The failure of the Sovereign in 1908 had been preceded by the failure of the Ontario Bank in 1906, and both of them provided vivid examples of the point that McLeod was trying to make. There was no outside audit of the banks, and no check by the government on the validity of financial statements issued by the banks. The general public was left with the false impression that publication of monthly and annual statements submitted to the Department of Finance provided some assurance of their accuracy and honesty. The short unhappy life of the Sovereign Bank of Canada was evidence to the contrary.

THE SAD STORY OF THE SOVEREIGN

The Sovereign Bank was founded in 1901 by Herbert (later Sir Herbert) Holt, who became president of the Royal Bank of Canada and a famous figure in Canadian business history. The first general manager was Duncan M. Stewart, a Montreal stockbroker who had previously worked for the Royal Bank and before that the Bank of Commerce. Of the Sovereign's original six directors, two were senators and one was a New Yorker named H.R. Wilson, who appears to have represented financier J. Pierpont Morgan.

(The appearance of J.P. Morgan on the Canadian banking scene is not well-known or documented, although it has been identified by Thomas Naylor in *The History of Canadian Business*. An unpublished thesis by Nancy Whynot has traced a connection between Stewart and J.P. Morgan "with whom he had been associated in parish work at St. George's Church," when Stewart was an employee of the Commerce in New York.)

In 1902 Duncan Stewart launched the Sovereign Bank on a reckless expansion. Between 1902 and 1907, Stewart opened sixty-eight branches and sub-branches, including ones in such high-growth areas as Beebe Plain, Quebec, and Harrietsville, Ontario. Stewart continued to live in Montreal, although the head office of the bank was in Toronto. During this huge expansion, Stewart nevertheless managed to spend three months in the summer of 1904 travelling around Europe making international contacts for the bank. He also made an uncollectable loan of $126,000 to his brother, F.H. Stewart, who was involved in the promotion of the Alaska Central Railway. According to John E. Ballaine, who was the founder and promoter of the Alaska Central, he secured the backing of the Sovereign Bank of Canada in 1905 "to the extent of $3,500,000 with a contingent promise of more, up to $18 millions." Ballaine founded the town of Seward, Alaska, which was to be the seaboard terminus for his railway, which ran seventy-two miles to nowhere. F.H. Stewart was his agent in Seward.

Herbert Holt wisely resigned the presidency of the bank (for unstated reasons) in 1904, leaving a board of directors made up mostly of senators and members of Parliament. In 1906, the bank doubled its capital from $2 million to $4 million; the striking thing about this new share issue was that more than 15,000 shares of the 20,000 issued were taken up by J.P. Morgan and the Dresdner Bank.

Stewart undercut the lending rates of the other banks and he instituted the practice of paying a quarterly dividend to shareholders, which forced the other banks to do likewise, much to their annoyance. Pressure tactics were Stewart's stock in trade. The Sovereign Bank put ads in the Toronto streetcars which read, "Government supervision — a guarantee of safety." (This sort of misleading claim is still being made by some non-bank deposit institutions today.)

Several banks wrote to J.M. Courtney, the deputy minister of finance, complaining about the misleading advertising of the Sovereign. W.D. Ross of the Metropolitan Bank wrote: "The advertising practice of the Sovereign Bank is usually misleading and deceptive but hitherto they have not made their government a party to the deception." After a good deal of pressure, Stewart agreed to withdraw the misleading ads.

When Stewart was making plans for the second issue of stock, he evidently felt that matters would be advanced if the deputy minister of finance were offered some stock in advance at a favourable price. In June 1905 he wrote to Courtney:

I do not know whether your official position debars you from holding stock in a bank, but if not, and you would care to obtain a few shares in the Sovereign Bank, please let me know at your earliest convenience, as I might be able to procure some for you at a satisfactory figure.

There is no record that Courtney bothered to answer this letter.

The Dresdner Bank had hardly completed its acquisition of additional Sovereign Bank stock when it became alarmed about rumours of the bank's condition. In the fall of 1906, J. Shuster, the executive head of the Dresdner Bank, decided to visit Toronto and see for himself. He called on the general manager of the Bank of Commerce, Byron (later Sir Edmund) Walker. Walker was then the leading figure in the Toronto banking community, and he evidently advised the Dresdner and J.P. Morgan to get rid of Stewart. At the fifth annual meeting in June 1907, Stewart was granted a "leave of absence," and in his place, a senior officer of the Bank of Commerce, F.G. Jemmett, was brought in. The second president of the Sovereign, Randolph Macdonald, resigned and was replaced by Aemilius Jarvis.

Jarvis was a prominent stockbroker and member of the distinguished family which had lent its name to Jarvis Street, Toronto. He was the grandson of Sam Jarvis, who had killed eighteen-year-old John Rideout in a notorious duel in Toronto in 1817. Jarvis had already been a shareholder of the bank behind the scenes, and may indeed have also been known to J.P. Morgan. (According to the biographer of the Jarvis family, Aemilius Jarvis was also instrumental in the building of the King Edward Hotel, and in 1904 Morgan had stayed there. Whether he came to Toronto as a stockholder in the Sovereign Bank is unclear.)

It soon became obvious to Jemmett that the Sovereign Bank was hopelessly insolvent. The "rest fund" (a bank's retained earnings) had to be wiped out and the capital reduced from $4 million to $3 million. In January 1908, a group of twelve "assisting banks" was formed to bail out the Sovereign. Their motive was to prevent a run on the banks in general, especially given the recent failure of the Ontario Bank. The objective was to keep the doors of the Sovereign Bank open in order to meet all deposit liabilities and thereby prevent a panic.

It was six years before the Sovereign Bank went into liquidation. The Bank Act provided a mechanism for the winding up of a bank, but in 1908 the banks did not want to liquidate the Sovereign. There was a consensus that the assets could be gradually liquidated, the deposits paid out, and the note issue redeemed. And then there was always the double liability, that is, the call on the shareholders to put up as much again to meet the uncovered liabilities of the bank.

The assisting banks made large loans and guaranteed the liabilities of the Sovereign; the branches and sub-branches were sold out to the different banks; and the Bank of Montreal bought out a good part of the realizable assets. Still, when Sir William Stavert (the banks' agent) took a close look at things, he concluded that Duncan Stewart and also the Montreal branch manager of the Sovereign, W.Graham Browne, had been secretly trading in the Sovereign Bank's stock. He identified $478,000 (more than 10 percent of the bank's stock) in promissory notes signed by Stewart and by several directors of the bank, which had been granted to support the bank's stock on the market. The monthly returns to the Minister of Finance, signed by Stewart and Browne, were clearly false in the opinion of the crown attorney, Colonel F.W. Hibbard.

Then began a lengthy process of backing and filling. No one wanted to take responsibility for going after Stewart. There was an extensive correspondence between the banks and the departments of Finance and Justice. By that time, there were new faces in Ottawa. In September 1908, the deputy minister of finance, T.C. Boville, wrote to the deputy minister of justice, E.L. Newcombe, "I now beg to state that it is not the desire of the Minister (W.S. Fielding) that any prosecution should be entered upon without an adequate basis of reasonable ground for belief that such prosecution can be fully sustained in the courts." This, despite Hibbard's advice to the minister that the false returns were a clear contravention of the Bank Act, and that the courts would sustain an action by the Crown.

At this point, Zebulon A. Lash, who was counsel to the Sovereign Bank—and also to the Canadian Bankers' Association—jumped into the fray. His intervention is a vivid illustration of the difference between business sense and legal quibbles. Although the bank had been for all practical purposes dismembered, Lash wrote to Jemmett in October, 1908 as follows: "I wish to correct the erroneous impression of the assistant deputy minister of finance (Henry T. Ross) that the Sovereign Bank is being wound up. Nothing which has taken place so far as the Sovereign Bank is concerned justifies this assumption . . . The Sovereign Bank has never suspended payment of any of its liabilities as they became due." In a narrow legal sense Lash was right; although the body had gone to the crematorium, the legal soul of the bank still existed under the Bank Act, because the "assisting banks" were putting up the cash to meet its liabilities. Lash urged the government and the bankers to drop the charges against Stewart, asserting that Stavert wished to withdraw his charges.

A VISIT TO ALASKA FOR HEALTH REASONS

But in September 1908 a warrant was issued for the arrest of Stewart. The charge was laid by the Department of Finance, but according to a

newspaper report, "Major Stewart was granted leave of absence by the
Militia Department and said farewell to his Sunday school class in
Montreal several weeks ago." Duncan Stewart had wisely taken off for
Alaska, where his brother F.H. was still promoting the Alaska Central
Railway.

In February 1909, the Department of Finance finally agreed to lay
criminal charges against the Montreal branch manager, W. Graham
Browne, for signing false returns to the Minister. But the magistrate
ruled in a preliminary hearing that there was no case against Browne,
because he hadn't known what he was signing. Once again, but not for
the last time in Canadian financial history, the courts, against all the
evidence, took a permissive view of financial fraud.

The case against Stewart having been thoroughly botched, and that
against Browne lost, the twelve assisting banks turned their attention
to minimizing their losses. But the twelve banks soon became eleven.
Henry McLeod of the Bank of Nova Scotia felt that the other banks
were kidding themselves in thinking that they would realize fully on
the assets of the Sovereign Bank.

In his testimony to the U.S. sub-committee of the National Monetary Commission in 1910 the following passage occurred:

Mr. Vreeland: You are familiar with the circumstances of its
[the Sovereign's] failure?

McLeod: Yes.

Vreeland: Would you object to stating?

McLeod: Bad management—corrupt management.

Vreeland: Corrupt management?

McLeod: Yes; false returns. That is true of the Ontario bank
as well.

McLeod bought his way out of the twelve-bank syndicate by putting
up fifty cents cash on the dollar for his share of the liability.

The other banks were fully aware that the liquidation of the
Sovereign would have a bearing on the upcoming revision of the Bank
Act, which was supposed to occur in 1910 but in fact was not com-
pleted until 1913. The question at issue was the position of the CBA
on the proposals of Henry McLeod to have outside auditors, or even,
God forbid, government inspectors, audit bank financial statements.
The banks were divided on whether to let Stewart off the hook or
pursue him to Alaska, but they insisted that further government

intervention was unnecessary. Daniel Wilkie, the general manager of the Imperial Bank who was now also president of the Canadian Bankers' Association, wrote to George Burn, vice-president of the CBA and general manager of the Bank of Ottawa: "It would be farcical for Parliament to be making stricter rules for the inspection and administration of banks at a time that the Association would be endeavouring to secure relief for a fugitive from justice."

At this point the major shareholders, J.P. Morgan and Dresdner Bank, apparently concluded that matters should not be allowed to drag on, because there was the overhanging threat of double liability for all the shareholders and the embarrassment to their reputations. Apart from the two big institutional holders, there were very few other large shareholders except Duncan Stewart himself and Aemilius Jarvis, who had bought half of Stewart's stock when he took over as president. A new company called the International Assets Company was created with $3,750,000 cash put up by the Sovereign Bank shareholders. This, in effect, covered the double liability of the larger shareholders, and no effort was made to pursue the dozens of small shareholders in the towns and villages of Ontario and Quebec.

In the meantime, Duncan Stewart had stayed out of Canada for fear of prosecution. On May 4, 1913, writing on the letterhead of the Racquet and Tennis Club in New York City to Bicknell, the lawyer for G.T. Clarkson, the liquidator of the Sovereign, Stewart said:

> There are just two points I would like to emphasize. *First* that I left Canada because I had collapsed, physically, for the *second* time since leaving the bank, and went to Alaska because my brother there urged my family to send me on account of the exceptional salubrity of the climate. I had absolutely no idea that a warrant was issued, and never heard of such action until several months after I had been in Alaska. Only the very dangerous condition of my health, and the urgent pleading of my family prevented my return *then*.
>
> *Second* I could not, and *would* not, ask for the sympathy or assistance of anyone now if I were really guilty of the charges laid against me. I simply wish to avoid the publicity and expense of a trial and there are *many* reasons why it would be in the *public interest* as well as my own to avoid it. I am not going back to Canada to reside, or maintain an office, but I want to be free to visit my family and friends there . . . I want to thank you on behalf of my wife, my mother and my

daughter as well as for myself, for your sympathy and aid which I assure you are not misdirected or misplaced.

Yours very sincerely,

D.M. Stewart

Stewart continued to pull what strings he could to get the charges against him dropped. In 1918, he managed to get Henry Darling, the treasurer of the U.S. General Electric Co., to write to Boville, the deputy minister of finance, asking him to reopen the case.

There is a very tart letter in the archives of the Department of Finance, dated April 3, 1918:

Dear Mr. Darling:

I have your letter of 26th-ultimo respecting our friend Mr. Duncan Stewart.

The Sovereign Bank, after a considerable splurge in the banking world, finally "came a cropper" owing to bad investments and reckless management. I do not know anything of a judgement of $125,000 against him but certainly would not be surprised if it were so. Criminal action was taken against him by the Department of Finance for making false returns. Stewart fled from Canada and so far has never returned. A warrant was issued for his arrest and is still outstanding. This in brief seems to be the situation as far as this Department is concerned.

Yours very truly,

T.C. Boville

Meanwhile, the third and last president of the Sovereign Bank, Aemilius Jarvis, was having his own troubles with the courts. During the time that Jarvis was involved with the Sovereign, he was also a stockbroker and bond dealer and a customer of the Bank of Nova Scotia. His relations with Henry McLeod were anything but cordial. In 1907 Jarvis arranged a call loan with the Bank of Nova Scotia, for which the collateral was some Penman Company bonds. Jarvis said the bonds were sold to one of his customers and would be taken out shortly when his customer took delivery. In fact the bonds were neither sold nor removed as promised; they were still there when the New York market crashed in 1907, and of course depreciated in value so that the bank's collateral was inadequate to pay off the loan. McLeod was not pleased.

But Jarvis was a shareholder of the bank and a powerful member of the Toronto establishment. He was infuriated when McLeod published a pamphlet titled *Bank Inspection: The Necessity for External Examination.* McLeod circulated his pamphlet not only to the shareholders of the Bank of Nova Scotia but to all bank shareholders he could trace.

Aemilius Jarvis went over McLeod's head and wrote to John Y. Payzant, the president of the Bank of Nova Scotia who lived in Halifax: "I fail to see why our General Manager should constitute himself the financial policeman for the Dominion." He asked that his correspondence be placed before the board of directors. McLeod defended himself to his president:

> So far as Mr. Jarvis's arguments against bank inspection go,
> they are the arguments of B.E. Walker [president of the Bank
> of Commerce] and I look upon the whole scheme as an
> attempt to intimidate the directors in order to produce friction
> between the Board and the management.

In November 1909, Jarvis again wrote to Payzant:

> A rumour is abroad here that the Bank of Nova Scotia
> through its general manager, is going to take an independent
> position to that of the Bankers' Association in dealing with
> the government with regard to the renewal of the Bank Act, at
> the coming session of Parliament.
>
> As a shareholder of the Bank of Nova Scotia, and having
> put a good many of my clients into the investment, I view
> with some degree of apprehension such a course . . . I should
> very much like to be in a position to contradict this rumour,
> and be able to say that the bank is going to act in conjunction
> with the others.

But Payzant defended his general manager. Five days later he replied from Halifax:

> I am in receipt of your letter of the 26th-ultimo. I presume
> that the "rumour" you speak of has reference to the matter of
> providing for some independent inspection of Canadian
> banks, a provision which this bank has as you know for some
> years been advocating.
>
> I regret that the bankers of Canada as a body have not thus
> far seen their way clear to give us their support, but I trust

that this will ultimately be done. As to any action the bank may possibly see fit to take in Parliament, I do not share any apprehensions you express.

Unfortunately, McLeod did not have many banking colleagues on his side. Even the great Thomas Fyshe, who had preceded McLeod as general manager of the Bank of Nova Scotia, but who was now with the Merchants' Bank, wrote: "So far as I know our friend McLeod is the only prominent banker who favours government inspection, and I never heard him make out anything of a case for it."

While this was going on, the correspondence between McLeod and Jarvis became increasingly hostile. On December 30, 1909, McLeod wrote to Jarvis: "I do not take seriously your recent attack on me for I am peculiarly indifferent to anything of the sort, so long as I am conscious of right." Jarvis replied that he had been good enough to give the bank his business "purely out of friendship to yourself and in sympathy to your local manager, whose difficulties in having to deal with an autocrat I thoroughly realized."

Two weeks later, McLeod accused Jarvis of having recommended some bonds to the bank on which the bank had taken a loss. Four days later, the prickly McLeod resigned as general manager of the bank, having antagonized most of the banking community, including some of his directors. Although he lost the battle, McLeod won the war. In the Bank Act Revision of 1913, provision was made for outside shareholders' auditors. But McLeod's case for a government inspector did not succeed, and there was still some grief ahead for the banking industry before his point was won.

As for Aemilius Jarvis, he wound up in the county jail at Langstaff. But this had nothing directly to do with his time at the Sovereign Bank. In 1920, Jarvis worked out a deal with Peter Smith, provincial treasurer in the Ontario Farmer-Labour Government, to buy back three issues of Government of Ontario bonds which had been placed on the London money market. These bonds had fallen in value on the market, and sterling was very cheap. Jarvis proposed to the government that he go to London and buy back the bonds, delivering them at a fixed price to the province for redemption. It turned out that Jarvis and Smith took a large cut on the way through. But this did not come out for several years and only after a change of government in Ontario. In fact, it surfaced when the Home Bank failed in 1923 and investigators were going through the papers. They found evidence of kickbacks to Peter Smith from the Jarvis brokerage firm, not only in connection with some Home Bank transactions in Ontario bonds, but going back to the bond transactions in 1920.

After a celebrated trial, Peter Smith went to penitentiary and Jarvis to jail, and both were heavily fined. But Jarvis always maintained that he had been made the scapegoat. The Jarvis family and many prominent citizens lobbied to reopen the case for years afterwards. In 1931, the Toronto *Mail and Empire* published an editorial arguing for a reopening of the case: "Those who are familiar with his record as a clean sportsman and with his patriotic efforts on behalf of the nation and the Empire do not believe that he could have been guilty of the charge upon which he was convicted."

In 1933, *Maclean's* magazine published a three-part article by E.C. Drury, who had been premier of the Ontario Farmer-Labour government at the time of the bond purchase from London. These articles were titled "Have we a Canadian Dreyfus?" Drury argued strenuously that the bond purchase in 1920 had not been a conspiracy which enriched Jarvis, because there had been a firm price deal which the government had entered into with full knowledge of the cabinet. By then Jarvis was seventy-three and he had fought the issue for ten years. It appears that a reopening of the Jarvis case never occurred.

THE STRUGGLE FOR THE SHAREHOLDERS' AUDIT

The scandalous failure of the Sovereign Bank, and of the Ontario Bank before it, increased public awareness of the need for closer audit and inspection of the banks. According to Benjamin Beckhart (whose book *The Banking System of Canada* was the standard work on Canadian banking for many years after its publication in the United States in 1929), the failure of the Farmers' Bank in 1910 "crystallized public sentiment in favour of some form of supervision." Thomas Naylor noted that a Royal Commission report on the failure concluded: "The subsequent management of the affair was characterized by gross extravagance, incompetence, dishonesty and fraud." The Farmers' case may have been the last straw, but the preceding failures had already dismayed the public.

Within the Canadian Bankers' Association a lengthy and vigorous debate developed, which involved the general managers of about fifteen banks. The minutes of the Canadian Bankers' Association's executive council record that "at the annual meeting of the Association in 1909 the draft of an Act suggested by Henry McLeod of the Bank of Nova Scotia—relating to examination of banks by independent officials—was introduced and briefly discussed. Mr. McLeod's proposal was not accepted but led to a general discussion upon the necessity of some closer supervision of chartered banks."

Among the bankers, the most influential was Sir Edmund Walker, the president of the Bank of Commerce. Walker had started his career as a brokerage clerk in Hamilton, and had risen quickly to become general manager of the Commerce in 1886. In 1907 he was made president and chief executive officer, and in 1910 he was knighted and became chairman of the Board of Governors of the University of Toronto, a position which he held until 1923.

At a meeting of the CBA Executive Council in 1910, Sir Edmund, now an honorary president of the CBA (he had been president in 1904), stated that "it was evident that the members of the Association did not at present desire any closer examination of their respective institutions than that now given to same by (internal) bank inspection."

As the banks tried to find a common position before having to face the House of Commons for the Bank Act Revision, a more important event intervened which delayed the Bank Act until 1913. This was Laurier's reciprocity bill of 1911, which suddenly aroused powerful opposition from the Conservatives and from much of anglophone Canada, which was still strongly British and anti-republican in character. Many Liberals deserted Laurier, and even Sir Edmund Walker intervened in the political debate, opposing reciprocity with the United States.

The Conservatives won the election of 1911. Robert Borden became Prime Minister in place of Laurier, and the new Minister of Finance was Sir Thomas White, replacing Fielding. But the change in government and in the complexion of the House did not really alter the growing concern about inadequate banking supervision.

By the time the newly elected Conservative government got around to dealing with the Bank Act in 1913, the new minister, Sir Thomas White, was at last prepared to move on the bank audit issue. "The audit which is provided in this Bill is the audit which Mr. H.C. McLeod, former General Manager of the Bank of Nova Scotia, had in mind." White said that he was eliminating the discretionary character of the audit as proposed by his predecessor Fielding, and making it compulsory. In its final form, the act stipulated that the directors could appoint one or more auditors, and that the list of eligible auditors would be drawn up by the Canadian Bankers' Association and placed before the Minister of Finance for approval.

To implement this legislation, the banks advertised for auditors, and there was an unseemly scramble to get on the list. In August 1913, representatives from twenty-five banks met and agreed on a list of sixty-four eligible candidates. Most of these were professional chartered accountants like G.T. Clarkson; but there was no requirement that an auditor had to be an accountant, chartered or otherwise. One of the exceptions who was not an accountant was Sidney H. Jones, the auditor of Trinity College, whom we shall encounter shortly as the auditor of the Home Bank.

The wrangling over bank auditors was soon set aside, however, because on August 1, 1914, Germany declared war on Russia. Sir Thomas White summoned Sir Edmund Walker to Ottawa to discuss suspension of the gold standard. On Sunday morning August 2, Sir Edmund got up very early at his summer place at deGrassi Point on Lake Simcoe, in order to make the long drive to Toronto to catch the afternoon train for Ottawa. At a meeting with the minister on Monday morning, it was agreed that the redemption of bank notes in gold would be suspended, and that the banks would stay open in order to avoid any financial panic. Shortly afterwards, Parliament passed the Finance Act of 1914, which ended the direct linkage between the supply of money and the nation's gold reserves.

Preoccupation with wartime finance meant that little or no attention could be given to bank regulation for several years. But it became apparent several years after the war that the problems had not all been resolved. In 1922, the Merchants' Bank of Montreal, which was considered to be one of the oldest and soundest of banks, had to be rescued by the Bank of Montreal. In the spring of 1923, the Bank Act was once again before the Standing Committee on Banking and Commerce to be considered in the decennial revision. Led by Sir Edmund Walker and Sir John Aird, both from the Bank of Commerce, there was a move to strengthen the clause relating to shareholders' audits. It became mandatory for a bank to have two auditors, each appointed for three years; moreover the eligible list had to be drawn up from professional members of the provincial accounting institutes.

But the concept of government inspection was rejected in the Bank Act Revisions of both 1913 and 1923. In 1913, Sir Thomas White reported back to the House of Commons "that the evidence before the Banking and Commerce Committee had indicated that government inspection would be practically impossible in the case of the Canadian banking system."

Ten years later, things had not changed much. The Liberal Minister of Finance (once again Fielding), introducing the 1923 revision to the House of Commons, said: "Every Minister of Finance who has preceded me reached the conclusion that it was not wise to adopt a system of government inspection. I have myself taken that view and I adhere to that view at present." Speaking for the banks, Sir John Aird said: "The government inspection of banks would throw a responsibility upon the government and naturally people would say in the event of trouble, well, the government inspector or auditor signed this statement as correct, and we naturally look to the government to protect us."

As it turned out, the theme of moral responsibility on the part of the government was put to the test within months after the passage of the 1923 revision.

CHAPTER 5

THE HOME BANK SAGA

CASA LOMA'S PLACE IN BANKING HISTORY

Casa Loma is one of the best-known landmarks in the city of Toronto, but its place in Canadian banking history is scarcely known at all. Its creator and owner, Sir Henry Pellatt, was the grandfather of real estate land "flips" using other people's money. In relative terms, Sir Henry Pellatt's misuse of bank depositors' funds, which led to the failure of the Home Bank in 1923, was on a scale as large as the trust company scandals of the 1980s.

The Home Bank had been founded in 1854 as the Toronto Savings Bank, an institution whose purpose was to provide banking services for the Irish Catholic working class in Toronto. When the Savings Bank Act was repealed in 1878, the Toronto Savings Bank became the Home Savings and Loan Company Ltd. By 1903, when the Home Savings and Loan Company was converted into the Home Bank, the company had 6,000 depositors. The capital was $1,750,000 and there was $2 million on deposit. It is more than a little ironic, in the light of the current savings and loan industry disaster in the United States, that the Home Bank's role had been the same as that of savings and loans institutions in the United States, which was to provide a place of safekeeping for the small depositor, and also a source of home mortgage financing.

A person can have fifty years' experience, or he can have one year's experience fifty times over. Such was the case with Brigadier General the Honourable James Mason, senator and for fifty years an officer and finally president of the Home Bank and its predecessor institutions. Mason was of Irish descent and a Roman Catholic, but nevertheless an establishment figure at a time when Toronto was a mainly Protestant community. He was an active officer opposing the Fenian raids, and served as a captain in the Royal Grenadiers during the Riel rebellion.

James Mason had a son, James Cooper Mason, who joined the Queen's Own Rifles of Canada in 1891, where he met Henry Pellatt, a pompous and showy officer who delighted in dressing up in huge cockaded hats and extravagant uniforms. Pellatt's closest proximity to military action had been a riot in Belleville in 1877. But the younger Mason fought in the South African campaign, and was wounded at Paardeberg in 1900. He was also a member of the Argonaut eights rowing champions of 1901. Pellatt was himself a considerable athlete, so Mason and Pellatt had much in common.

Henry Pellatt came from a banking background. His father, Henry Sr., had started out with the Bank of Upper Canada but had lost his job when the bank failed in 1866. Henry Sr. then went to the Bank of British North America, but later left banking and founded a brokerage firm with E.B. Osler. Osler wisely left the partnership in 1882 and thereby kept the distinguished Osler name free from the subsequent disasters. The brokerage firm was subsequently called Pellatt and Pellatt. Young Henry assumed sole control in 1892. He soon struck it very rich through the vehicle of land speculation companies in western Canada, using the Home Savings and Loan as his source of funds. In 1901 he became the commanding officer of the Queen's Own Rifles, and in 1902 he made a celebrated trip to England for the coronation of Edward VII. Pellatt personally paid to equip the regimental band and ship it to England. Sir Wilfrid Laurier knighted him in 1905 for his distinguished services.

Sir Henry made a huge splash in Toronto society. He was a member of the board of the Manufacturers Life Insurance Company and the director who was assigned responsibility over the company's investments. This provided a splendid client for Pellatt and Pellatt, since attitudes toward conflict of interest were rudimentary at best. According to one biographer, he and some partners cornered the market in Dominion Coal stock using the life insurance company's funds. In 1906 there was a Royal Commission inquiry into the operations of the insurance industry, which turned up the fact that the Manufacturers Life had funded the Pellatt-controlled Lake and Ocean Navigation Company, which in turn bought several steamers (one of which was called the *HMS Pellatt*). But Sir Henry managed to avoid appearing at the inquiry altogether, by taking the Queen's Own Rifles to New York City for a parade.

Sir Henry was not above stock promotion even in wartime. In 1915 he told the *Wall Street Journal* that he had a contract for producing artillery shells at the Steel and Radiation Company of which he was president. He said the contract was for about $2 million and he forecast a profit of over $1 million. The Toronto *Globe* commented: "Love of liberty, determination to preserve the Empire and a profit of 50% on the turnover make an irresistible combination." Prime Minister Robert Borden was so incensed that he got the "Shell Committee" (the government's purchasing arm) to require Pellatt to appear before it and issue a denial of the New York statement.

Around 1910 Sir Henry Pellatt turned his attention to real estate speculation in Toronto. He reckoned that the St. Clair Avenue-Bathurst Street-Vaughan Road area northwest of Toronto was ripe for real estate development, reflecting the booming economic conditions of the time. In 1910 he launched the four-year job of building Casa Loma, both to provide himself with adequate accommodation and to draw attention to the northwest extension of the city. In 1912 he bought a large farm area just north of the Casa Loma site for $321,000, of which $200,000 was by way of mortgage. A month later he incorporated a company called Home City Estates, and shortly thereafter he sold the farm to this company for $1,205,000. The price was $205,000 in cash, a promissory note to Sir Henry for another $200,000, the assumption of the $200,000 mortgage by the buyer, and $600,000 in stock to Sir Henry. In two months he had managed to make a cash profit of $84,000 and a total profit of $889,000, all accomplished on loans from the Home Bank which were not repaid.

But Sir Henry soon ran into new problems. The direction of real estate development was to the northeast through Rosedale to Moore Park, rather than the northwest. Then the war came along, and Sir Henry found himself with a large number of unsaleable building lots. In the meantime, Casa Loma had been under construction since 1910, and by the time it was finished in 1914 it had eaten up enormous amounts of money. No one knows the cost, but it was estimated to have been as much as $3.5 million. Henry Pellatt's loans at the Home Bank accumulated, with interest being added to principal as time went on. In 1921, with rumours circulating that Pellatt was overextended, the Chartered Trust Company was appointed by the Home Bank to investigate Pellatt's land companies. The trust company soon found that the property values had been greatly inflated for purposes of bank borrowings.

But clouds had begun to gather over the Home Bank at least as early as 1915. In that year, three western directors, led by Thomas

Crerar of Winnipeg, became concerned that they were not receiving full disclosure from the management of the Home Bank and their fellow directors in the east. After visiting Toronto and receiving no satisfaction, they wrote to the Minister of Finance, Sir Thomas White, requesting an investigation. White consulted his old and trusted friend, Zebulon A. Lash, whom we have already encountered in the Sovereign Bank affair, and who was now counsel to the Home Bank as well as a director and vice-president at the Bank of Commerce. Lash was aware that there were several very large loans on the books of the Home Bank. Later he wrote to the western directors: "The amount locked up indefinitely in four large accounts is probably three times the paid up capital and more than half the total deposits" of the bank. Pellatt and Pellatt, the brokerage firm, owed $1.7 million through various land companies. Another loan was to the Prudential Trust Company, which used the funds to finance the New Orleans Southern and Grande Isle Railway Company. Part of the funds for this dubious investment seem to have come from deposits placed by the government of Ontario with the Home Bank.

The scale of fraudulent self-dealing by the directors was massive. The Masons, father and son, owed nearly $100,000 when the bank was liquidated in 1923. H.J. Daly, the president from 1919 to 1923, was involved in loans not only to the A.C. Frost Company of Chicago, but also to the Arnprior Cabinet Company and the False Creek Timber Company in British Columbia, in all of which he was an officer and shareholder. C.A. Barnard, another director, had a loan from the Home Bank with which to carry 2,622 shares of the bank's stock, held for himself and Pellatt in trust. And so on and so on. All this was not to come out for seven years, first in the curator's report, then in the reports of the liquidator, and finally in a Royal Commission report in June 1924.

But in 1916, Zebulon Lash advised the Minister of Finance that things could be straightened out quietly at the Home Bank by removing James Mason Sr., then seventy-three years old. Sir Thomas White debated with himself whether to call in the CBA to investigate the situation, but decided to write Mason and request an explanation for the large loans. He directed Mason to appoint his internal auditor, Sidney H. Jones, to answer the concerns of the western directors. When there was no initial response to his letter from the Home Bank, Sir Thomas White wrote again, requesting a report from the auditor. This time, Jones only gave him some information about one borrower. James Mason Sr. was replaced as president, and his son moved up to be general manager.

Much later, the 1924 Royal Commission report of Chief Justice Harrison A. McKeown noted that "the government could have closed the bank (in 1916) and forced liquidation at a time when, in my opinion, no loss would have fallen upon the depositors." But White chose to do nothing. In June 1925 he told the Banking and Commerce Committee of the House that he could not have allowed the bank to fail in wartime because it might have destabilized the banking system. The Finance Department later dismissed this assertion.

In August 1918, a former assistant to the president of the Home Bank, W.A. MacHaffie, sent a registered letter to the Minister of Finance, recommending an inquiry, given his internal knowledge of the bank's affairs. Again White referred the inquiry to the bank, where the eastern directors cast doubts on MacHaffie's motivation, saying that he was looking for a better severance contract.

Whether White's inaction in dealing with the complaints against the Home Bank was politically motivated is hard to say. Thomas Crerar, one of the western directors who had first blown the whistle on the Home Bank, was also president of the United Grain Growers Company, and a leading figure in the Prairie farm community. In fact, Robert Borden invited him to join the wartime Unionist government, where he became a cabinet colleague of Sir Thomas White. Crerar may have decided not to press his case, because the Grain Growers was itself a borrowing customer of the Home Bank, and used some of the funds to speculate in the grain futures market. But Crerar was the leader of the growing agricultural dissent movement in western Canada, and the failure of the government to take his concerns seriously must have confirmed western grievances against the eastern financial establishment.

After the war, matters continued to drift along, with government procrastination leading to a further deterioration in the Home Bank's affairs. The financial affairs of its most prominent customer, Sir Henry Pellatt, were a major factor. The city of Toronto decided to increase the assessment on Casa Loma from $50,000 to $250,000. Sir Henry's household bills went unpaid. The accruing interest on his network of land company loans was added to principal, but even as late as June 1920, the Dominion Bank responded to an American bank inquiry: "We consider him a man of means."

As far as the Canadian Bankers' Association was concerned, the

Home Bank was meeting its obligations. The annual audit showed that the note circulation of the Home Bank was no greater than its capital, although what the banks did not know was that the capital was wildly overstated. But a true picture of Pellatt's affairs must have been emerging. In February 1921, H.D. Burns, an officer and later president of the Bank of Nova Scotia, wrote to another American banker: "He is always hard up, has no credit, and we wonder at times how he manages to get enough income together to pay interest and taxes."

In 1919, Borden resigned as Prime Minister and invited Sir Thomas White to succeed him. However, White turned down the invitation, and returned to Toronto to become a vice-president of the Bank of Commerce. Arthur Meighen became Prime Minister in the Conservative government for about a year before being defeated in the election of 1921 by the Liberals, led by William Lyon Mackenzie King. It is perhaps not a coincidence that the collapse of the Home Bank did not occur until after the Conservatives had left office; it was Mackenzie King, with the support of the National Progressives led by Thomas Crerar, who had to ride out the political storm when the Home Bank closed its doors on August 17, 1923.

What finally triggered the collapse of the house of cards was the death of Colonel James Cooper Mason, the general manager of the Home Bank, on August 9, 1923. The directors of the Home Bank then ordered a special examination of the bank's affairs, and found that $7 million in loans, or about half the portfolio, was "locked up" in unsaleable assets.

On August 17, the bank suspended business, and the Canadian Bankers' Association appointed a curator, A.B. Barker, that same day. Barker finished his work quickly and submitted his report on September 28 to Sir Frederick Williams-Taylor, president of the Canadian Bankers' Association and president of the Bank of Montreal. Barker found that, out of $18 million in assets, about $6 million were realizable at full value. Most of the loans consisted of the debris of borrowings by the directors and companies controlled by the directors. As for the deposits, there were nearly 47,000 depositors with less than $500 each, and 53,000 deposit accounts altogether.

What made the Home Bank failure such a celebrated political case was that a handful of self-dealing speculators in Toronto had used other people's money, which had been collected in small deposits across the country. There was the shocking revelation that the strengthening of the Bank Act in 1913 and again in 1923, just before the failure of the Home, had failed to protect the public against fraud and speculation by directors and management of a bank. And there was a good deal of justifiable western anger at manipulation from the east.

Since the curator realized that there was no hope of recovery, the Home Bank was immediately put into the hands of the liquidator, the ubiquitous G.T. Clarkson, in October 1923. He summarized the liabilities of the Home Bank as follows:

Note circulation	$1.7 million
Preferred claims (Government of Canada and Government of Ontario deposits)	1.5 million
Deposits of domestic and foreign banks	1.0 million
Public deposits	15.5 million
Total deposit liabilities	19.7 million

There were seventy-one branches and sub-branches, many of them in small western communities as well as in Ontario. There was a branch in Fernie, British Columbia, where the municipality had $116,000 on deposit, probably a quid pro quo for opening the branch. The City of Toronto had $280,000 on deposit and the Toronto Separate School Board $48,000.

From the good assets available, Clarkson was able to retire the whole note circulation of $1,700,000 and in December he borrowed $3,750,000 from eleven banks in order to pay the depositors twenty-five cents on the dollar. In submitting his report, Clarkson said: "Never at any time in its career was an experienced and trained banker at the head of the bank and in control of its affairs. It can be said that the late James Mason and the late Colonel Mason utterly failed to pay regard to or impose elementary safeguards in protection of the business of the bank."

The highly partisan Toronto *Telegram*, in an editorial on December 12, 1923, said: "If the Bankers' Association had gone up against the MANHOOD represented by Sir Thomas White's mastery of the Finance Department, instead of going up against the mush represented by Honourable W.S. Fielding's mismanagement of that department, the Canadian Bankers' Association would have taken over the Home Bank or have liquidated that institution, and no depositor would have lost a dollar." In fact White had been presented with the problem as early as 1916, but had managed to do nothing until he left office in 1919.

Meanwhile the depositors were forming committees in Vancouver,

Winnipeg, and Toronto, and they created a national executive committee. In early 1924 they sent a petition to the Governor General,
Lord Byng, with a supporting statement of claims which held the
government responsible for their losses. Their petition was set out in a
series of statements:

> First Statement: The unstable condition of the bank was
> known to the Dominion Finance Department for many years.
>
> Second Statement: No adequate action was taken to safeguard
> depositors.
>
> Third Statement: The charter was renewed just preceding the
> date of the bank's suspension.

All of these statements were true. The depositors' petition wound
up with the comment that public confidence in the banks had been
shaken. To this the Department of Finance replied:

> The depositors in that institution had approximately 1% of the
> total deposits in all the banks in Canada, and while the failure
> of that institution is regrettable, the fact mentioned indicates
> that there is no loss of confidence by the public in the banks
> as a whole.

With the outright rejection of their claims by the government, the
depositors turned up the heat on their members of Parliament and on
the Canadian Bankers' Association. The chairman of the Vancouver
Home Bank Depositors' Committee wrote to Sir John Aird, who had
succeeded Williams-Taylor as president of the CBA: "We know that
the subsequent disclosures of crookedness and bad management
caused a feeling of distress and suspicion of Canadian banking institutions amongst the people generally. We are venturing to ask that you
support our claim with the government."

The CBA received scores of letters to the general effect that, had
the banks not opposed the creation of an outside inspection office, the
Home Bank failure would never have occurred. The truth is that the
Department of Finance had been provided with adequate information on which to act, but the minister had swept the problem under
the rug. Sir Thomas White even asserted later that he had had
dealings with Sir Henry Pellatt when he himself was general manager
of the National Trust, and had never had a problem. The Toronto
Mail and Empire of January 7, 1924, quoted Sir Thomas as saying:
"No facts were at any time brought to my attention while I was

Minister justifying action on my part which would have brought about suspension." White's failure to act does not seem to have impaired his relations with the Canadian Bankers' Association. In July 1924 he was paid a fee of $5,000 by the CBA for having acted as counsel during the Bank Act revision in the preceding year.

BAILING OUT DEPOSITORS

Lawsuits began to fly in all directions. The liquidator went after the shareholders for their double liability, and this caused a great shock when relatively small shareholders discovered that they were being forced to pay up an amount equal to their holdings. There was even a letter in the press from Bishop Fallon of London, Ontario, in which he opposed the double liability of his parishioners.

There were suits for "misfeasance," suits by depositors who had placed funds with the bank at the last moment, and suits for cheques in transit. In December 1923, civil and criminal charges were laid against the president, the vice-president, five directors, the general manager, the chief accountant, and the auditor of the Home Bank.

Despite the 25 percent payment to depositors, there is no doubt that real hardship was experienced by hundreds and perhaps thousands of depositors. One of the many letters to the CBA was from a Dr. A. MacDonald of Khedive, Saskatchewan:

The failure of Home Bank has crippled both towns [Khedive and Amulet], as men in business as well as a great many farmers lost heavily. A number of farmers were hailed out in 1923 - had only received their hail insurance and deposited same in Home Bank, where they lost it all. There were a number of sad cases. One case was a poor old man and his wife who had saved up $1,200 all his life from repairing shoes. He had his son deposit it in the Home Bank. The bank's failure left him without a cent. He is now 68 years of age and unable to do much.

Another letter from William Mellor of Toronto enclosed a clipping from the *Mail and Empire* of November 26, 1923, which stated: "Despondent because of long illness and the loss of his life savings in the Home Bank, Charles L. Fitzpatrick, 30 years old, farmer of Maidstone, ended his life this afternoon into the river from the Walkerville ferry boat."

A DARK AND DANGEROUS CORNER

MR. CANUCK—PUT A GOVERNMENT OFFICER ON THAT CORNER, SIR. THE PEOPLE DEMAND IT!

Mackenzie King, having chaired the Privy Council meeting which had met representatives from the National Depositors' Committee and had rejected their demands, took the classic step of a government seeking delay: in February 1924, he appointed a one-person Royal Commission, naming Chief Justice Harrison A. McKeown as the Commissioner. McKeown took evidence in April and May and submitted his report on June 10, 1924. He concluded that perhaps something might have been done, but that Sir Thomas White could not be blamed because he had thought about it a good deal. He added that Sir Thomas had told him that the appointment of an outside auditor would have precipitated a crisis.

The minority Liberal government was feeling the heat from the thousands of angry depositors in the Home Bank, and of course from the media. Mackenzie King did not wait to receive the report of the Royal Commission, but referred the Bank Act, which had just been amended after its decennial review in 1923, to the Standing Committee on Banking and Commerce. The committee was asked to consider what should be done to prevent another failure like the Home Bank, and to receive the report of the Royal Commission.

The committee reported back to the House in June 1925. Its major recommendation was to create the Office of Inspector General. The report was adopted by the House and became law a month later. The nature and duties of the Office of Inspector General, as set out by the committee, remained essentially unchanged until 1987 when a broader office covering all federal financial institutions was created. It was recognized that the Inspector General could not inspect the whole branch system of a bank but would primarily examine the books at head office and rely on the shareholders' auditors of the banks to be kept fully informed.

The committee also proposed that the Office of Inspector General be financed out of general revenues (called the Consolidated Revenue Fund), but recommended that the chartered banks be required to reimburse the government for the cost of running the office. Over the years, politicians have sometimes asserted that this clause gives the banks control over the size and scope of the Inspector General's office, but this is in fact not the case. Policy, the composition of personnel, and the budget are wholly within the control of the government.

The hasty amendment of the Bank Act to create the Office of Inspector General did not end the political uproar over the losses to Home Bank depositors. During the hearings of the Standing Committee on Banking and Commerce in the spring of 1925, the secretary of the Canadian Bankers' Association, H.T. Ross, convinced the committee that the banks could not be held responsible for something they had known nothing about. (Ross, a distinguished Maritime lawyer, had been assistant deputy minister of finance before joining the CBA in 1916.) He pointed out that the CBA had no power to verify the annual reports of a member bank. In the case of the Home Bank, the false returns were the responsibility of the directors and management. Tommy Church, MP (later the mayor of Toronto), suggested that if the courts did not act to "do something" about the directors of the Home Bank, then Canada should look at a system of electing judges, rather than "handing [appointments] out like Christmas presents."

The Standing Committee on Banking and Commerce, accepting a report of a special sub-committee, told the House that the government had a "moral claim in equity" to the Home Bank depositors. This conclusion was based on the finding of the Royal Commission that the government had been aware of the problem in 1916.

In June 1925, the House of Commons approved by a vote of 100 to 20 the Home Bank Creditors' Relief Act, which authorized a payment of $5,450,000 to the Home Bank depositors. At this point the Liberal government of Mackenzie King was hanging on to power by a slender thread; with 101 seats in the House of Commons, the Liberals were outnumbered by the Conservatives with 116 seats, and dependent on the support of the Progressive Party with 24 seats. And it was the Progressives, the agrarian reformers, who were still unhappy about the Home Bank.

Mackenzie King whittled down the size of the payment from $5.4 million to $3.4 million. This amounted to a "compassionate payment" of thirty-five cents on the dollar to depositors with less than $500 each on deposit. The act also barred any payments to directors of the Home Bank, to other banks, and to governments and corporations.

Towards the end of May 1925, the secretary of the CBA, H.T. Ross, corresponded directly with Mackenzie King on the subject of moral responsibility for the Home Bank. Ross claimed that the phrase "moral claim in equity" used by the parliamentary committee had been dismissed in British common law. Mackenzie King's secretary, F.A. McGregor, replied to Ross that the Prime Minister was too busy to respond personally, but wished Ross to know that "he has had exactly the same feelings and understanding as yourself."

At this point, depositors had recovered sixty cents on the dollar, but there was still about $6 million owing. By 1927 Clarkson, the liquidator, was still digging away at the remaining assets, and still hoping to realize 5 percent or 10 percent more.

Of course it was not only the depositors who were unhappy about their losses. The shareholders were pursued relentlessly for their double liability payment. As late as May 1931, Prime Minister R.B. Bennett told the House that the liquidator had collected $1.1 million from 1,686 shareholders.

Tommy Church's apprehensions about the courts were unfortunately well founded. Charges had been brought against H.J. Daly, the president, R.P. Gough, the vice-president, and five directors, C.A.

Barnard, Q.C.; P.A. Mitchell; Lieutenant Colonel C.F. Smith; J.F.M. Stewart; and Casey Wood, K.C., as well as against the general manager, James Cooper Mason, the chief accountant, S.H. Jones, and the auditor. The trial ground on through 1924, but was more than a little impaired by the fact that Mason had died a week before the bank closed in August 1923, and then Daly died two weeks before the report of the Royal Commission in June 1924.

On December 5, 1924, the surviving defendants were found guilty by the trial judge, Emerson Coatsworth Jr. There was promptly an appeal to the Appellate Division Court of Ontario. The decision of the trial judge was overturned by the appeal court justice, Frank E. Hodgins. He ruled that the directors could not be found guilty, because they were entitled to rely on the reports presented to them by the general manager, who was dead.

The Attorney General, W.F. Nickle, K.C., was stunned by the decision. Nickle decided against appealing to a higher court, and also dropped all charges against M.J. Haney, who had been president from 1916 to 1919. Everyone could blame Mason and Daly, who were both in their graves. In commenting on the case, the Attorney General said: "The less a director knows about the bank's business and the more careful he is to stay away from directors' meetings, the less chance there is of his being found liable. Where ignorance is bliss 'tis folly to be wise."

As the *Western Record* of July 14, 1925, said: "Thus ends the Home Bank fiasco. Reduced to a logical conclusion, the Ontario Court of appeals judgement means that a director can not be held responsible for the deceptions and fraud committed by the General Manager and the 1923 Bank Act is not adequate to meet the situation ... The release of the Home Bank directors is nothing short of letting down the safeguards that were so laboriously constructed to meet the palpable weakness of the 1913 act."

But the seeds had been planted for the idea of a central bank, and it could be said that the Home Bank disaster was a significant milepost leading to the creation of the Bank of Canada in 1935.

The last asset of the Home Bank which was realized was the sale of the West Coast Collieries on Vancouver Island for $7,500 in 1960. In 1961 A.E. Calvert died; Calvert had been an assistant manager of the Home Bank at the time of its failure, and had worked for forty years with the liquidator to wind up the affairs of the bank. In 1965, his widow auctioned off the books and papers of the bank, which had been stored in a barn near Pickering, Ontario, for many years.

The fallout of the Home Bank episode was a further consolidation of the banking system, because of public apprehension about the soundness of some banks like the Merchants' Bank in Montreal and the Bank of Hamilton. By 1925, the big six banks of today accounted for almost all the system's assets, although three big mergers were still many years ahead.

Big Six Share of Market, 1925
(Approximate Percent of Total Assets)

Royal Bank	26.5
Bank of Montreal	26.2
Commerce (and Imperial)	21.4
Bank of Nova Scotia	8.4
Toronto (and Dominion)	8.0
Provincial (and National)	6.1

CHAPTER 6

THE FOUNDING OF THE BANK OF CANADA

The bank failures described in the preceding chapters led to the reform of bank audit and inspection, but were a relatively minor part of the banking system as a whole. By the late 1920s, the ten surviving banks were solidly run, with very large branch networks which served the needs of the community. There was a high level of confidence in the safety of bank deposits. The exchange rate was stable, apart from a bad blip in 1921. There was growing dissatisfaction in the western farming communities, but the rest of the general public had few complaints with things as they were.

Various observers have asked why Canada was so late in acquiring a central bank. The U.S. Federal Reserve System was founded in 1913, after the National Monetary Commission had analyzed the financial panic of 1907. The Bank of England had long since emerged as the dominant central bank in the world, exercising its influence not only in Great Britain and the sterling area, but throughout the international financial system. Even Canada's fellow dominions had developed central banking institutions before the Bank of Canada was founded. The Reserve Bank of South Africa opened in 1921. The Commonwealth Bank of Australia, founded in 1911, assumed central banking powers in 1924. The Reserve Bank of New Zealand was created in 1933.

The chartered banks were fundamentally opposed to having a central bank, for reasons which will be discussed shortly. The only banker who seems to have been advocating a central bank was Edson Pease, who was vice-president and managing director of the Royal Bank in 1918, and also president of the Canadian Bankers' Association in that year. According to Douglas Fullerton, the biographer of

Graham Towers (first governor of the Bank of Canada), Pease stated at the Royal Bank's annual meeting in 1918 that he was in favour of a central bank, and suggested that "the government should appoint a committee of experts to investigate the matter." Fullerton adds that "Pease had a rough ride from the other bankers, and received no government support."

In 1923, the House of Commons Committee on Banking and Commerce wanted its terms of reference broadened, in order to study the need for "one type of properly administered central or reserve bank." Significant support for the proposal came only from the Progressive Party, which represented western agrarian discontent. But the Progressive Party faded away in the 1920s, reflecting the booming conditions in the wheat economy, which lasted until late in the decade.

From a public policy point of view, there were several reasons for the lack of interest before about 1932 in a central bank. First of all, there was better monetary and financial stability in Canada than in the United States. The Canadian banking system had weathered the financial panic of 1907 in New York. Wartime finances had been handled with smooth cooperation between the Department of Finance and the chartered banks. The postwar recession in 1921, which again found the American banking system in trouble, passed with relative comfort in Canada.

At the institutional level, the Canadian Bankers' Association provided a vehicle through which the government of Canada could provide informal policy guidance to the banking system, a process which is now called "moral suasion." On a practical level the CBA was useful: there was the mechanism for monitoring the note issue — the Bank Circulation Redemption Fund. And the banks had for many years operated the clearing system without the need of government intervention.

Canada's monetary stability may have been due more to good luck than to good management, but in fact there was a rudimentary mechanism of monetary control called the Finance Act. This Act enabled the banks to borrow from the government, under certain conditions, to meet unusual demands for currency, especially during the crop-moving season. It was only in the late 1920s, when the system for controlling the volume of money began to get out of hand, that professional economists began to sound the alarm for a central bank.

THE NATURE OF MONEY

To understand the reason for the economists' concern, it is necessary to take a step backward and review briefly the nature of a monetary system. The principal functions of money are to provide a means of exchange, a method of keeping accounts, and a store of value. All sorts of commodities have been used by mankind to perform the money function. But in the last few centuries, most civilizations fixed on gold and silver. These had the advantage of being very limited in supply, durable, readily turned into identical coins, and therefore easily recognizable and transportable.

It is only within the last two or three centuries that people realized that gold and silver could be left in a safe vault, and negotiable receipts or vouchers issued for them. When vouchers or paper money were issued against gold in the vault, the amount of paper money could not exceed, dollar for dollar, the gold reserves in the vault.

From there it was a fairly short step to conclude that it was not necessary to have such an extravagant system as a 100 percent reserve of gold in safekeeping. Since it was highly unlikely that all those holding paper currency would descend on the bank to withdraw their gold reserves all at once, it was feasible to have a percentage reserve of gold, such as 25 percent. And from there it was not such a big step to say that all the gold would be held by the central authority, but the amount of paper in circulation would be strictly limited in relation to the central gold reserve. At that point it did not seem necessary to have the gold at all, as long as there was a legal mechanism for limiting the amount of paper money in circulation.

When banks came into existence, they provided deposit facilities, but the paper currency in circulation was completely interchangeable with deposits. Cheques are not themselves deposits, but are messages to transfer value from the payer to the payee on the ledger books of the bank. Since deposits and paper currency are interchangeable, then the underlying legal system which limits the combined total amount in circulation must, of course, apply to both paper currency and deposits.

Before 1935 the sovereign authority of the Government of Canada over money and banking was exercised through several statutes: the Bank Act, the Finance Act, the Bills of Exchange Act, and the Interest Act. The Bank Act defined the powers and restrictions on banks, including the requirement to hold cash reserves, which set a potential limit on their capacity to expand. The Finance Act enabled the banks to borrow from the government, and was in effect a rudimentary central bank mechanism. The Bills of Exchange Act defined "legal tender" and therefore provided a legal framework for commercial transactions. The Interest Act defined the meaning of interest on borrowed money. Taken together, these four pieces of legislation established the framework of the monetary system. But the first two— the Bank Act and the Finance Act—did not spell out in detail the nature of the government's control over the banking system, nor did they provide for an institution devoted exclusively to exercising monetary authority.

A fundamental feature of the gold standard was that it provided a mechanism for the settlement of international accounts. This is the feature that made it so attractive in theory, and for a while in practice, over the last two centuries. If a country imports more than it exports, then it must settle the difference in some means of payment acceptable to the creditor country. Since Britain was on the gold standard, and sterling was tied to gold, then other currencies could also be safely tied to gold; therefore there was a fixed exchange rate mechanism between the currencies of the trading nations. According to the theory, if a country's trade and capital flows were out of balance, gold would flow in or out of the country, thereby automatically forcing monetary discipline on the government.

The Canadian dollar was defined in terms of gold in 1853, when the Province of Canada fixed the content of the dollar at 23.22 grains of pure gold, identical to the gold content of the U.S. dollar. This was equivalent to $20.87 per ounce of gold. The British pound was 113 grains of gold, so that by definition the pound sterling was worth $4.867. Thus the relationship between the Canadian dollar, the U.S. dollar, and the British pound was fixed by a set of arbitrary government definitions.

After Confederation there was a struggle between the Bank of Montreal and the government on the one hand, and the rest of the banking system on the other, over the power to issue notes. A compromise allowed the banks to continue issuing notes in denominations of $4 and $5 (and multiples of $5) while the government issued Dominion notes in denominations of $1 and $2 as well as the coinage.

Although there was no defined cash reserve requirement for the chartered banks, they were expected to keep one-third of their reserves in the form of Dominion notes. The total amount of Dominion notes that could be issued by the Department of Finance had to be covered by a 100 percent reserve of gold, except for a small underlying amount with no gold backing.

This system worked quite well from 1853 until 1914. If the banks needed more currency to satisfy public demand for a circulating medium, or to settle accounts between themselves, they could sell more stock, use the money to buy gold, deposit the gold at the Department of Finance and draw out Dominion notes; or, better still, they could issue their own bank notes, keeping a reserve of one-third in Dominion notes.

When war broke out in August 1914, the government was immediately forced to suspend the gold standard. As the MacMillan Royal Commission later reported in 1933 on this period: "Many runs upon the banks took place throughout the country, withdrawals of gold in Montreal and Toronto were particularly heavy and in general an atmosphere of incipient financial panic prevailed." The Finance Act of 1914 (and the related Dominion Notes Act) allowed the banks to obtain more Dominion notes by depositing government bonds with the Department of Finance. The Treasury Board (which consisted of the Minister of Finance and five cabinet ministers, with the deputy minister of finance as Secretary) fixed the rate of interest on such borrowings. The rate stayed at 5 percent from 1914 to 1924. George Watts (a retired Bank of Canada officer) has described the arrangement as "a highly permissive, open-ended form of central banking."

GETTING BACK TO GOLD

After the war, the Finance Act of 1914 was extended, first in 1919 and then in 1923. Robert Bryce, the deputy minister of finance in the years 1963-1970, has described this pre-Bank of Canada era in *Maturing In Hard Times*, which is a history of the Department of Finance up to 1940. The Finance Act of 1923 allowed the chartered banks to borrow from the Department of Finance at rates of interest below the yield on the assets which they could acquire with the borrowed money. In effect, this provided a built-in incentive for a bank to borrow from the government and therefore to inflate the money supply. Such borrowing could have been discouraged by the Treasury Board, but as Bryce explains, the Department of Finance was run essentially by lawyers who weren't too familiar with monetary theory; the first professional economist to work for the minister was Clifford Clark, who was appointed in 1932. In fact, R.B. Viets, the internal solicitor to the department, wrote a clause into the 1923 Finance Act which required the government to return to the gold standard in 1926. Bryce writes:

> The President of the Bank of Montreal wrote to Finance Minister [J.A.] Robb that it would be financial suicide to return to the gold standard unless gold reserves were substantially increased. The Royal Bank, however, which was more involved than the others in international banking, favoured an immediate return to gold . . . The Bankers' Association could give no agreed advice with the Royal opposed to the general view of the other banks.

The Minister of Finance then turned to Gilbert Jackson, a Toronto economist whose air of authority exceeded his monetary grasp. Jackson advised the minister to go ahead with the return to gold, and the government unwisely took his advice.

This set the stage for a financial expansion in the late 1920s which got out of control. The banks borrowed heavily under the Finance Act, with borrowings increasing from $12 million in January 1927 to $112 million in December 1929. Most of the financial expansion was used to make call loans in the New York money market. (Call loans are wholesale loans to investment brokers and bond dealers for carrying their inventories of securities, both government and corporate.) After the crash of the stock market in New York in 1929, the banks reduced their call loans and paid off their borrowings from the Department of Finance.

The calamitous downward spiral of the world economy which followed led to vast changes in the world's financial system and in international trading arrangements. As Bryce notes, the Canadian Gross National Product declined about 43 percent between 1929 and 1933, of which 30 percent was a real decline and 13 percent a fall in prices. On the Prairies, the decline was much worse than this. For the banking system, one of the most important consequences of the fallout from the crash was the creation of the Bank of Canada.

The absence of a central monetary authority, and indeed of anyone qualified to advise the Minister of Finance on money and banking matters, was strikingly illustrated in October 1931. Britain had gone off the gold standard, but Prime Minister R.B. Bennett insisted that Canada remain on gold. Stephen Leacock, the famous humorist, who was also head of the Department of Political Economy at McGill University, decided to put Bennett's assertion to the test. If Bennett was right, anyone could obtain gold in exchange for paper currency.

Leacock's biographer, David Legate, described how Leacock took $10,000 worth of $1 and $2 bills to the Receiver General's office in Montreal and demanded gold in payment for this legal tender. But the government office had got wind of his coming, and paid him in very small coins, which he then found impossible to ship to New York. Eventually Leacock had to redeem his coins for paper money again, after the government took off a percentage for "wear and abrasion." Legate wrote, "However, if Leacock lost the battle, he won the war. He had proved that Canada was not on the gold standard."

THE BANKERS LOSE THE BATTLE: THE MACMILLAN COMMISSION

The absurdity of a situation in which the government did not know whether it was on the gold standard or not was not lost on the Faculty of Economics at Queen's University. Clifford Curtis, one of its able group of economists, published an article in the U.S. *Journal of Political Economy* entitled "The Canadian Monetary Situation" in June 1932, which was privately circulated to the interested players. Curtis drew attention to the fact that Prime Minister Bennett had announced in the House of Commons on February 29, 1932, that a central banking institution might be considered in the 1933 revision of the Bank Act. Curtis concluded, "Canada will have no monetary stability until such an institution—in fact if not in name—is developed." Douglas Fullerton says that Curtis was "instrumental in swinging Mackenzie King in the Liberal opposition around to supporting a central bank."

At the same time, after a two-year hiatus during which there had been no deputy minister of finance (the department having been damaged by internal embezzlement), Bennett appointed W. Clifford Clark. The department entered a period of outstanding leadership which lasted through Bryce and Reisman for more than thirty years.

Meanwhile, the chartered banks were less than enthusiastic about notions of a central bank. Beaudry Leman, who was general manager of the Banque Canadienne Nationale and the first francophone president of the Canadian Bankers' Association, said in 1931, "Throughout this financial and economic upheaval, young Canada has not suffered a single bank failure. Nothing much can be wrong with a system that produces such results."

His successor as president of the CBA was J.A. McLeod, general manager of the Bank of Nova Scotia and a distant relation of Henry C.

McLeod. In his presidential address of 1932, McLeod reflected the feelings of his colleagues: "Without wishing to be flippant, I may fairly say that it suddenly became fashionable, after the war, for governments to create central banks . . . now it is easy to pass legislation creating a central bank; but whether a central bank, when once created, can control credit, can stabilize business and lessen the strain of economic depression—that is another question."

There was one banker who disagreed with the industry consensus—Graham Towers. He had started with the Royal in 1920 at the age of twenty-three having been persuaded by Edson Pease to give up law school at McGill. In the next year he wrote an internal guide to financing foreign trade for the bank. Nine years later he was chief inspector, which is a key staff job in the head office of a bank, and one which requires practical operating knowledge. Thus Towers was more than the resident intellect of the Royal Bank. In 1933 he became assistant general manager of the bank at the age of thirty-six. This was a meteoric rise in an industry where experience in a great variety of posts, both geographically and functionally, was considered fundamental.

Douglas Fullerton notes that Graham Towers was well-known to Clifford Clark. He may also have been known to R.B. Bennett, although this is less clear, as Bennett was a director of the Royal Bank of Canada from 1924 to 1928.

Whether Bennett discussed the possibility of a central bank with Edson Pease and other senior officers of the Royal (including Towers) is a matter of conjecture. Fullerton tells us that Bennett, on his rather frequent trips to Great Britain, met Montague Norman, the Governor of the Bank of England, and also Sir Edward Peacock, a Canadian-born financier who maintained close connections with Toronto. Fullerton writes, "Bennett had no doubt observed the important part the Bank of England played in that country's financial affairs."

It was Clifford Curtis of Queen's who suggested a Royal Commission, and in March 1933 Bennett acted on the idea. Bennett must have already made up his mind as to the conclusion he wanted, based on his selection of five Royal Commissioners. He chose as chairman Lord MacMillan, who had just completed serving as chairman of a Commission on Finance and Industry in Great Britain. MacMillan suggested another Englishman, Sir Charles Addis, who had been a director of the Bank of England. He also brought along (as an adviser) Raymond Kershaw, an officer of the Bank of England who had advised other Commonwealth countries on setting up their central banks. According to Fullerton, Kershaw wrote the key section of the report which recommended the establishment of a central bank.

A third member of the commission was J.E. Brownlee, premier of Alberta, and in effect the voice of the western demand for a public institution to control the credit system. There were two bankers on the commission, Beaudry Leman and Sir Thomas White. Leman was the general manager of the Banque Canadienne Nationale and White was a vice-president of the Bank of Commerce. The assistant secretary of the commission was A.F. Wynne Plumptre, who became assistant deputy minister of finance in the 1960s.

The Royal Commission was appointed on July 31, 1933, held hearings from August 8 until September 11, and submitted a report to the government on September 28. In fifty-nine days, the MacMillan Commission did its job, including public hearings from coast to coast and extensive hearings at the beginning and end in Ottawa. In the West, the commission heard all four premiers (in Alberta the acting premier, because the premier was on the commission), and numerous representatives of farm organizations and municipalities.

AN EARFUL FROM THE WEST

In the summer of 1933, when the MacMillan Commission visited the western provincial capitals, the economic situation was disastrous. The average farm price of wheat was thirty-four cents a bushel for the crop year just ended, which was the lowest price in the whole dismal period from 1929 to 1939. (To put this price in perspective, the price of "number one northern" at Fort William [now Thunder Bay] averaged $1.07 per bushel from 1910 to 1916, and rose to a war-inflated level of $2.31 in the period 1917 to 1920. From a peak price of $2.73 in 1920 the price fell to $1.07 in 1924. For several subsequent years the price was quite good, but then came the disastrous decline in the 1930s.)

Not only was the price of wheat extremely volatile, but so were yields per acre. Coinciding with the crash of the stock market in October 1929, the average yield per seeded acre fell by 50 percent, from twenty-four to twelve bushels per acre. But this was not the bottom; in the crop year 1937/38, the average yield fell to six bushels per acre. Multiplying the volume of production times the price obtained, the value of the wheat crop fell by two-thirds from 1929 to 1933.

Against this background, it is small wonder that the banks came in for a barrage of criticism in the West. There was the long-standing grievance, still nursed to this day, that the banks had an eastern bias against the West. This deeply held point of view was expressed in testimony to the Royal Commission by John Bracken, then premier of Manitoba, and later national leader of the Conservative Party:

> The Canadian banks of the future must be built upon a broader philosophy; they must recognize that they have a social obligation to the public as well as an obligation to their shareholders . . . they ought to recognize, however well intentioned eastern officials may be, the possibility of unconscious bias in decisions which are left to officials living in Montréal and Toronto.

The general manager of the Royal Bank, Morris Wilson, gave the same response to this criticism as would be given today. All but a tiny fraction of decisions on loan applications are made on the spot, either at the branch level or by the regional headquarters of the bank: "The records show that out of thousands of borrowing accounts in the three Prairie Provinces, 99.64 percent were dealt with before being referred to head office."

W.T. Easterbrook, an economic historian and student of farm credit in Canada, has written, "It was clear that the chartered banks, with their emphasis on liquidity and on commercial loans, were far from being as closely in tune with the needs of the farmer as to those of the merchants, implement companies, and others with whom the farmer had business dealings." While this is perfectly true, the banks at the time were not authorized to provide intermediate or long-term credit. The taking of mortgage security was ruled out, except as a supplement to an existing non-performing loan. There was indeed a significant gap in the institutional structure for farm credit.

Another criticism was that interest rates were too high and often exceeded the legal ceiling rate of 7 percent. We have not so far dealt with interest rate considerations, because they had not been a significant factor in the politics of banking. In fact there had always been a 7 percent ceiling on interest rates in the Bank Act, from 1871 onwards, and even before that, but the structure of interest rates in Canada was normally well below 7 percent. It must be remembered that at that time the banks were not empowered to make residential mortgage loans or consumer credit loans. Bank lending was overwhelmingly a question of commercial loans repayable on demand.

As for deposits, the product line of the banks was extremely simple:

there were demand deposits, which paid no interest, and savings deposits, which paid a standard rate of interest explicitly negotiated by the banks between themselves, and with the concurrence of the government. The following testimony to the MacMillan Commission by Jackson Dodds, the general manager of the Bank of Montreal, gives some flavour of the times: "For very many years the rate paid on time deposits or savings bank deposits has been fixed at 3 percent per annum, and the standard rate for first class commercial loans has been 6 percent per annum." Dodds went on to say that, after making salary cuts, the banks still could not meet their overhead costs under depression conditions.

> For this reason . . . the banks, after discussion and with the approval of the Dominion government, reluctantly were compelled to break the old tradition, and on the first of May, 1933, reduced the interest on savings deposits to 2½ percent per annum . . . In the case of the farmers' loans . . . the banks reduced the rate of interest charged by double, and in many cases more than double, the reduction in the deposit rate. The maximum rate for farm loans is reduced to 7 percent per annum, country-wide.

It may be wondered how the maximum rate could be reduced to 7 percent, when there was a ceiling of 7 percent in the Bank Act. The explanation is that the banks defined the ceiling as a "discount" rate. What this means is that, if you borrow $100, the lender takes the $7 interest off the loan up front, so the borrower in fact gets $93. The rate of interest is therefore more like 7.5 percent, and if the loan were for three months only, which was often the case, the rate would be higher.

Elsewhere in the testimony, the bankers argued that interest rates on farm loans in Montana, the Dakotas, and Minnesota were in the range of 8 percent to 12 percent, so the belief that local or regional banks would provide cheaper credit to farmers was unrealistic.

Nevertheless, western spokesmen remained adamant that credit policy should be taken out of the hands of the banks and placed in the hands of a central bank which would be independent of government policy. But the westerners were looking for more than a central bank which would assume responsibility for stabilizing the value of the dollar, internally and externally. The western vision was of a central bank which would be an instrument of social policy, providing a flow of steady and cheap credit to agriculture.

BENNETT GETS HIS WAY

After the national tour, the Royal Commission convened a final hearing in Ottawa on September 14, 1933. Lord MacMillan provided the banks with a set of specific questions on which to make their final response. The bankers turned out in full force, with the general managers of the big six all present (Beaudry Leman, one of the six, himself a member of the commission). Morris Wilson, speaking for the Royal Bank, stopped short of opposing a central bank; he concentrated on the difficulties of operating a central bank with so few qualified people in the country and in the absence of a money market which would make possible the direct influence of a central bank on interest rates and credit conditions. Jackson Dodds of the Bank of Montreal, still adamantly opposed to a central bank, produced testimony to show that the Federal Reserve System hadn't contributed very much to solving the monetary problems of the United States during the Depression.

But there was one thing on which all the banks were agreed, and this was that they would suffer a severe loss of earnings if a central bank were created. The chartered bank note issues would disappear, to be replaced by paper currency issued by the central bank. In June 1933, there was an aggregate chartered bank note issue of $137 million, of which the largest issuers were the Bank of Montreal with $35 million, the Royal with $31 million, and the Commerce with $25 million. The banks calculated that they were earning a gross rate of return of 4.5 percent on the assets financed by the note circulation, and that, after expenses and taxes, their net yield was 1.6 percent or about $2 million a year. This was about one-third of the aggregate dividends paid by the banks, so the disappearance of the note circulation was seen as a body blow.

But this battle and indeed the whole war were lost. The Royal Commission Report was accepted by the government, and Lord MacMillan headed for home before the weather got cold. When the Bank of Canada came into being in 1935, the banks were required to withdraw their notes by 1945.

Sir Thomas White and Beaudry Leman dissented from the majority report. They both said that the time was not right for a central bank, and that such an institution would fall under political influence and fail to be independent of the government of the day. Leman even raised doubts as to the constitutional power of the federal government to create a central bank, suggesting that the British North America

Act of 1867 had created a decentralized federation of provinces. (In fact, the BNA Act was very clear and specific in assigning exclusive power over money and banking to the federal government.)

Bennett gave notice of his intention to create a central bank in the throne speech of January 25, 1934, and the act was finally passed in early July. The gestation period was nine months, giving the new governor time to hire a staff and find a place to put them. The bank opened for business on March 11, 1935.

There were two major issues still unresolved: the relationship between the government and the central bank, and the ownership of the Bank of Canada. In a democracy, the elected legislature must prevail on any question that comes within its constitutional mandate. Nevertheless, a central bank has to stand apart from politics, and be seen to be independent of political intervention. A central bank which is the tool of the government of the day would have little credibility in the eyes of the financial system, and even less credibility in the eyes of foreign central banks and international financial markets. This is why, to protect the central bank from short-term political considerations, the governor's appointment is for seven years. If push comes to shove, the government can always get rid of the governor by forcing him into a position in which he has no alternative but to resign. But the resignation of the governor is a very serious matter, since it sends a signal to the world that the government of the day is prepared to override the best financial advice available to it.

There is in fact a basic ambiguity in the relationship between a sovereign government and an independent central bank. This ambiguity was identified in the House of Commons debate in 1934 by William Irvine of the Cooperative Commonwealth Federation (CCF), who is quoted by Fullerton:

> Supposing the central bank was endeavouring to regulate the control of credit in Canada, and supposing the policy it adopted in order to do so was contrary to the policy of the government of the day, and they clashed, which authority would make the decision?

E.N. Rhodes, the Minister of Finance, replied, "Unquestionably the authority of the Governor and the Board of Directors of the bank would prevail." But later he backtracked, the ambiguity remained, and indeed has always remained to this day. Later on we shall see how this issue resurfaced.

The relationship between the government and the central bank is a difficult problem which is not peculiar to Canada. In the United States, the chairman and members of the board of governors of the Federal Reserve System are considered to be at arm's length from the U.S. President and Congress. Even so, the selection of the chairman of the board, and of the staggered appointments to the board, are very much a reflection of the philosophy of the President.

In the United Kingdom, the Bank of England has fallen much more under the thumb of the government in the last two or three decades than would have been acceptable in the past. This is now much more than a theoretical question as the European Community comes together. The view of former prime minister Margaret Thatcher was that the central bank of a united Germany, the Deutsche Bundesbank, would impose a hard-line German approach to monetary stability on the EEC. In her view, a European central banking institution would be too powerful in preventing governments from acting for their own short-term political considerations.

The second issue was ownership. Bennett had made up his mind that the central bank should be privately owned. This seems to have been based on nothing more than his anglophile view of the world; the British thought it was the right thing to do. Even the Federal Reserve System was, in a convoluted way, privately owned. Brownlee, the premier of Alberta, had dissented from this proposal in the MacMillan Report, and he had considerable support in the House of Commons from Mackenzie King and of course from the CCF.

In its first year, the Bank of Canada had a wide public ownership, with no one being allowed to vote more than fifty shares out of 100,000. But there was a general election in October 1935, and Mackenzie King included in his platform a plank to introduce government ownership of the Bank of Canada. When he came to power in 1936, he amended the Bank of Canada Act to give the government 51 percent voting control and he also added enough government-appointed directors to ensure control of the board. In 1938, the Bank of Canada was fully nationalized and all members of the board became appointees by Order-in-Council.

To ensure that there was no conflict of interest, the Bank of Canada Act eliminated from consideration almost anyone who had any practical knowledge about the financial system. Former bankers were excluded (unlike the situation in almost every other industrialized country in the world); bank directors were also excluded, as well as politicians and civil servants at all three levels of government. As a result of the sweeping elimination of almost everyone who was qualified, it has always been difficult to make effective appointments to the board of the Bank of Canada, although there have been some notable exceptions in recent times. (According to this peculiar standard, no farmer should serve on the Wheat Board, no trade unionist on labour panels, no broadcaster on the CRTC, and no one acquainted with the arts and culture on the Canada Council.)

The appointment of the first governor was also a political question. Bennett probably would have preferred an Englishman, whereas, according to Fullerton, Clifford Clark wanted a qualified American. But the political reality was that Canada was in the process of becoming a truly sovereign country, and could not accept a foreigner as governor of the Bank of Canada. Fortunately, the right Canadian for the job was found, in the person of Graham Towers. He was comfortable in his knowledge of the financial structure of international trade, and had some acquaintance with monetary economics; besides, he also held a senior operating job in the Royal, and therefore would be respected by the chartered banks.

Bennett arranged to appoint an officer from the Bank of England, J.A.C. Osborne, as the first deputy governor, to provide Towers with some central banking knowledge. After a search, a francophone assistant deputy governor was found in the person of L.P. St. Amour. (It has always been difficult to attract and hold senior francophone officers in the Bank of Canada. Those who were qualified had much better prospects in the Montreal business or academic community. Besides, there was always the problem of uprooting their families to live in what was essentially an anglophone environment. At one time, Jacques Parizeau was an officer of the Bank of Canada, with brilliant prospects, but his career took him elsewhere.) To round out the first management team, Towers hired Donald Gordon, a gruff and tough young officer in the Bank of Nova Scotia who later on left the bank to be president of the Canadian National Railway.

Towers had only four years to get the bank on its feet before the Second World War broke out. For the first two years of his job, the bankers avoided him, apparently believing that the central bank had nothing to do with their affairs. The Depression was far from over, and money was not tight. In fact there was a great shortage of lending opportunities, and the banks became loaded with government bonds. Apart from the ownership question, the central bank did not become embroiled in political issues. When the war came along, domestic politics were set aside, and for five years the central bank was able to concentrate on developing its technical expertise and recruiting a highly qualified staff.

CHAPTER 7

ABERHART: A THORN IN THE FLESH OF BANKERS

While economic and political forces were converging in the 1930s to create the right climate for a central bank, a quite different political problem emerged for the banks on the Prairies. There, the frustration and anger of the farmers over their economic situation took a much more virulent form than just the demand for a central bank. In Saskatchewan, pressure for radical change led to the formation of the Cooperative Commonwealth Federation at Regina in 1933, an alliance of farm and labour groups. In Alberta, agrarian dissent emerged in the shape of the Social Credit movement, which is the subject of this chapter.

It is no coincidence that both the CCF and the Social Credit parties evolved from elements in the United Farmers of Alberta, a party which governed Alberta from 1921 to 1935. Despite their diverging policies, one thing which they shared was dislike of the existing financial system, and determination to bring it under control.

The CCF gave a political structure to socialist thought in Canada, and has had a profound and lasting influence on all aspects of public policy. The Social Credit movement, on the other hand, had a single-issue approach to public policy. The single issue was that credit had to be brought under control of the state and taken out of the hands of the greedy and wicked financial institutions. When the financial system had been put to rights, the working farmer and labourer would be freed from the shackles of debt and interest, and would be able to operate in an individualistic and even conservative social framework. What gave the Social Credit Party its impetus and its claim to political power in the 1930s was the personality of its founder and leader, William Aberhart.

Before examining the emergence of Aberhart, let us take a quick backward glance at the United Farmers of Alberta. On July 26, 1915, a telegram was sent to the Minister of the Interior in Ottawa from the United Farmers at Empress, Alberta: "Some farmers unable to buy binder twine to harvest crops. Banks will not advance money." The farmers wanted the government to authorize the banks to take security over standing grain in the field in return for binder twine loans.

This set off a flurry of inquiries in the banks. Who were the United Farmers? Was there really a problem in providing credit? The only bank in Empress, Alberta, was a branch of the Union Bank whose manager replied, "There was absolutely no cause for this, because every farmer who in my belief is entitled to credit has been granted quite sufficient to carry him through the harvest."

The huge gap between the perception of the farmers and that of the local bankers seems never to have closed. Despite the buoyant economic conditions which continued through the First World War and through most of the 1920s, the farm community on the Prairies did not believe it was well served by the financial system. As we have seen, the banks could not take security over land and buildings, and were restricted to operating loans. From the early years of the twentieth century until the crash in 1929, much of the mortgage money in the West was supplied by British and European mortgage companies. Also active were the mortgage lenders from eastern Canada, primarily the insurance companies and mortgage loan companies.

The United Farmers of Alberta came to power in the province in 1921. The farmers had organized "locals," much in the manner of a trade union structure, and this powerful grassroots organization had thrown out the traditional Liberal and Conservative parties. The leader of the party and the premier of the province was J.E. Brownlee, whom we have already met as a member of the MacMillan Royal Commission on Banking and Currency. Brownlee was at the very moderate end of the UFA, constantly struggling to keep his more radical elements in line. The UFA was also represented in the federal House of Commons.

In January 1931, Henry Wise Wood retired from the presidency of the United Farmers of Alberta at its Calgary convention. In his farewell address he said, "So long as Mammon reigns, Mars will do the arbitrating, and the masses will suffer ... True social industrialism will provide for the wants of all through the efforts of all." He was succeeded as president by Robert Gardiner, MP. The Calgary superintendent of the Bank of Montreal wrote to his head office as follows:

Mr. Gardiner in his platform addresses asserts that the present worldwide economic depression is almost entirely due to the capitalist system and he has stated that the deflation of 1920 was arranged at a meeting of international bankers in New York at which Canadian banks were represented.

The UFA and Progressive members in the House of Commons decided to put direct pressure for financial reform on the Prime Minister. On April 9, 1931, R.B. Bennett convened a meeting of several bank general managers with representatives of the three Prairie provinces, including Brownlee from Alberta. The CBA subsequently circulated to the banks a memorandum of this meeting, which included the following:

> Mr. Bennett dealt at length with Section 91 of the Bank Act, which, he said, limited the rate of interest that a bank might collect to 7%, notwithstanding which it was well known and quite freely commented upon at the present time, that a higher rate was frequently charged, particularly in the case of western farmers. He felt that the banks were placing themselves in an invidious position by disregarding the requirements of the Bank Act in this respect, and frankly said he did not know how he could defend our position.

The banks took a rather legalistic position, stating that the Privy Council had interpreted the statute to mean that a rate in excess of 7 percent could not be collected through the courts. Jackson Dodds of the Bank of Montreal took a hard-line position; he noted that the average farm loan was about $500 (in fact it was more like $700 or $800) and that a difference of 1 percent was only $5 a year. The Royal had urged the CBA to collect figures on the rate of interest on farm loans, and Graham Towers prepared a format for the other banks to use, in order to get a consistent consolidation. The statistics showed that the banks were charging 7 percent or less for 75 percent of their loans, but the other 25 percent were above 7 percent.

Just a week after meeting the bankers, Bennett met a delegation of western members of Parliament. He invited Henry Ross, secretary of the Canadian Bankers' Association, to come to the meeting. Among those present was Robert Gardiner, the president of the United Farmers. Bennett told the westerners that he had already informed representatives of the banks that he was not going to fight their battles in Parliament. In reporting to the banks on this meeting, Ross recommended that they adopt Morris Wilson's approach (in the Royal) to the problem, that is, that more than 99 percent of decisions on loan applications be made on the spot. The banks were starting to worry about the impact of growing western agitation on the upcoming Bank Act Revision of 1933. As it turned out, Bennett postponed the revision until 1934, to allow his Royal Commission on Banking and Currency to submit its report.

Beaudry Leman, the new president of the CBA, organized the collection of statistics on loans and deposits in the West in order to meet the perennial charge that western deposits were being used to finance corporate loans in the East at the expense of the western farmer. (In the case of the Home Bank, as we have seen, this accusation was true, but it was not the case for the banking system as a whole.) The CBA's consolidated statistics at January 31, 1931 showed the following totals for the Prairie provinces:

Total deposits		$308.5 million
Total loans	319.6 million	
Provincial and municipal bonds		
of Prairie provinces	38.0 million	
Premises	30.0 million	
Cash	12.0 million	
Total assets	$399.6 million	

Adding bond holdings, premises and cash to loans, total assets were $400 million. This gave an excess of assets over liabilities in the Prairie provinces of $91 millions. This appears to have been the first time that the banks collected statistics to meet the accusation that deposits were drained from the West and Atlantic Canada to the benefit of central Canada, but it was certainly not the last.

SANDWELL'S EXPEDITION

The banks were at last becoming concerned about the widespread extent of the criticism in the West. In June 1932, they held a meeting to discuss the publication of a pamphlet defending their position. Henry Ross suggested that the CBA should engage the services of Bernard K. Sandwell, "formerly an assistant professor of economics at McGill," who later became editor of *Saturday Night* magazine.

Sandwell agreed to make an investigative trip to the West, all expenses paid plus twenty-five dollars a day. His mandate was described in an introductory letter to western bankers: "Mr. Sandwell will desire to know what are the common grievances of persons in the West who are critical of the banks; what foundation, if any, there is for these grievances; what remedies it may be within the powers of the bankers to provide."

Sandwell proceeded on his trip, sending back handwritten letters to Henry Ross on his findings as he went along. He met with the leading bankers in the western cities, and also with numerous politicians and farm leaders.

The senior officer of the Royal Bank in Regina sent the following message:

> You are doubtless fully informed regarding the agitation being carried on in this province for the nationalization of banks and other credit organizations. Alderman M.J. Coldwell, a school teacher of Regina, who has for years been active in Labour circles yesterday was unanimously chosen leader of the Labour and Farmers Party at a convention held in Saskatoon. [Coldwell was later to become a national figure as leader of the CCF.]

When Sandwell reached Edmonton, he was invited to speak to the Canadian Club. In reporting to his head office on Sandwell's visit, the manager of the Bank of Montreal was able to put western dissent in context by noting another recent happening:

> For the past ten days the Ministers of the United Church of Alberta have been holding what they call a "school of religion" in Edmonton. Mr. Woodsworth, MP, Winnipeg, has spoken to this Congress three times a day, and has made rather a clever attack on our banking system, dangerous because it is clever; he's a really good speaker. [This of course was J.S. Woodsworth, the long-time leader of the CCF.]

Sandwell's letters and memos to the CBA echoed a concern which Prime Minister Bennett had already raised with the banks:

> Many of the managers in the West were young men just assuming the responsibilities of a career, and any of a timid or conservative nature became ultra conservative in the granting of credit, seeing that there was little prospect of improved prices for the 1931 crop.

When Sandwell got back to Montreal in September, he wrote a five-page report to Henry Ross. He proposed an extensive publicity campaign, including a series of pamphlets on banking, a set of radio addresses, and a series of eight or ten display advertisements in the daily newspapers. At the bottom of the list, he put addresses by bankers to various service clubs. This was the only recommendation that was accepted.

The banks could not agree among themselves on the value of an ad campaign or radio talks. Even the pamphlet idea was not pursued, mainly because the sub-committee of three included Jackson Dodds of the Bank of Montreal and J.A. McLeod of the Bank of Nova Scotia, both extremely conservative men. Sandwell himself must have been discouraged at the failure to follow through on his constructive suggestions. Just at the moment when the CBA was rejecting his pamphlet, he was hired by *Saturday Night* magazine. (Sandwell quite reasonably split the travel expenses for his Toronto interviews between the CBA and *Saturday Night*.) Several years later—in 1936— he wrote a series of articles on banking in *Saturday Night* that were published in pamphlet form.

ABERHART ASCENDS

Just a month before B.K. Sandwell spoke to the Canadian Club of Edmonton in 1932, a chance meeting occurred in that city of two teachers who were engaged in marking high school matriculation exams. One was William Aberhart, and the other was Charles Scarborough. This meeting had far-reaching effects on Canadian political life.

Aberhart, then fifty-three years old, had been born and educated in Huron County, Ontario. John Irving, a chronicler of the Social Credit movement, tells us that, as a young man, Aberhart used to go into the woods to pound his fist on a stump, in order to strengthen his capacity to pound a pulpit. He was a teacher and fundamentalist Bible preacher, and in his twenties had become principal of a high school in Brantford, Ontario. He moved to Calgary in 1910, and resumed his teaching career. Irving writes, "The turning point in his career occurred in 1915 when, by a close vote and with some misgivings, the Calgary School Board appointed him principal of the newly organized Crescent Heights High School."

He was still principal of this school at the time he met Scarborough. But he was also devoting an increasing amount of his time to fundamentalist preaching, and in 1918 he had founded the Calgary Prophetic Bible Conference. He became well-known as a public speaker and charismatic personality, and when he inaugurated radio talks, his reputation spread throughout southern Alberta. The meeting in Edmonton with Scarborough in July 1932 changed the course of his life and that of many Canadians.

Scarborough, an engineer, had been influenced by the writings of Major Clifford H. Douglas, an English engineer. Douglas had published a book, *Social Credit*, in London in 1924. In the annals of crank literature in economics, few books have had an equal impact.

Douglas offered to the world the "A plus B theorem" which states that the cost of all goods is A plus B, A being the sum of wages, salaries, and dividends, and B being all other expenses such as the cost of raw materials, taxes, and bank interest. The sum of A and B is the aggregate cost and price of total output, but the incomes available to buy it are only equal to A. There is a gap of (A + B) minus A. This accounts for "poverty in the midst of plenty" and the problem is to provide the masses with credit to make up the difference. But financial credit has fallen into the hands of bankers, and the state must gain control of the credit system to solve the problem. There should be a "national dividend" and a "just price" for everything. The state should supply people with credit—social credit, based on the potential wealth of the country's resources. Douglas's book was also heavy on moral reform, the cultural heritage of Christianity, anti-communism, and the perception of a Judaic conspiracy to control the financial system.

Aberhart was persuaded with difficulty by Scarborough to read *Social Credit*. But when he finally took it up, Aberhart at once concluded that it provided an explanation for the dreadful economic hardship which he saw all around him. Douglas explained that "the financial system is a centralizing system; it can only have one logical end, and that is a world dictatorship. There seems to be little doubt that the temporary headquarters of this potential world dictatorship have been moved from country to country several times during the past five or six centuries." The Calgary Prophetic Bible Conference took up the study of *Social Credit* with a vengeance. Study groups were created all over the city and the province, and Aberhart incorporated his new economic doctrine into his Bible hour on the radio, which reached a growing and appreciative audience.

At this point Social Credit was still not a political party but an ideological movement. Its emergence as a political force between 1932 and 1935 was due not only to the very fertile ground which Aberhart cultivated, but also to his great personal appeal as a speaker and thinker. In May 1933, Aberhart published a pamphlet titled *The Douglas System of Economics*, which became known as the "Yellow Pamphlet." This explained how a state system of credit would bring purchasing power to the consumer. What made it particularly attractive was Aberhart's proposal that every citizen should get a monthly twenty-five-dollar credit from the provincial government. "This will be distributed through Credit Houses at which, monthly, a credit passbook will be presented by each citizen and an entry of $25 will be made . . . The process will be largely a matter of bookkeeping."

The *Calgary Herald* reported that "the basic idea is that all citizens of a country own its natural resources and are entitled to a share in their distribution, instead of permitting a few financiers to exploit them . . . Mr. Aberhart thought it no use whatever to appeal to Ottawa to introduce some such system. The financial control of government is too well known to need discussion; nor can a political party be counted on, for they are out of date." Aberhart "prophesied the end of all political parties shortly."

But Aberhart had his problems, even within the Social Credit movement. Some felt that he was overreaching himself by his advocacy of impractical financial measures. The secretary of the Douglas Credit League of Canada, C.V. Kerslake, told Premier Brownlee that Social Credit could not be introduced at the provincial level. Brownlee's government, the United Farmers of Alberta, did its best to keep Social Credit at arm's length, but the more it resisted, the greater was the appeal of Social Credit to the rank and file members.

A group of urban members of the movement brought the original guru himself, Major C.H. Douglas, to Calgary to declare that Aberhart's version of Social Credit was unworkable. But in a dramatic turn of events, Aberhart overturned Douglas, who had no personal appeal, and who was unable to explain exactly what he would do to implement Social Credit.

The provincial government, as a defensive action, invited the Agricultural Committee of the legislature to examine Social Credit, with a view to determining whether it could be applied to provincial concerns. Douglas was brought once again from England to Edmonton to give testimony, but once again he had little impact. According to Irving, "Feeling that he [Douglas] had a woolly mind, they [the members of the Agricultural Committee] believed that no more time or money should be wasted on him."

Two witnesses from the University of Alberta challenged Aberhart's theories. One was the Dean of Law at the University of Alberta,

H.R. Weir, who tried to warn his listeners that Aberhart's proposals were not feasible because matters of money and credit were federal under the constitution. Professor George A. Elliott, a very good economist, tried to deal with the "A plus B theorem." But no one was listening. Aberhart produced radio skits lampooning Professor Orthodox Anonymous (Elliott).

Meanwhile, some members of the United Farmers of Alberta were moving towards the CCF, especially Robert Gardiner and William Irvine. They got no encouragement from Brownlee. But in 1934 Brownlee resigned as premier after losing a personal lawsuit brought by the parents of a young secretary in his office. He was succeeded by Robert G. Reid. Thousands of shocked supporters of the UFA migrated to the Social Credit movement. When the UFA's annual convention rejected the Social Credit goals, the Social Credit "crusade beyond politics" went political. On August 2, 1935, the Social Credit Party elected fifty-six members, the Liberals five, the Conservatives two, and the United Farmers not a single seat. Aberhart was premier. A government had been elected which was dedicated to getting rid of the eastern financial establishment altogether.

In the short space of three years, the Social Credit movement had gone from an idea in Aberhart's head to a government in power. Now it was a question of implementing the program. *Saturday Night* magazine pointed out, in November, that the promise of twenty-five dollars a month for 400,000 adult citizens would take $10 million per month or $120 million a year, compared to a provincial budget of $15 million.

One of the great ironies of the impractical Social Credit doctrine was that it was trying to address the very real problem of inadequate demand when widespread unemployment existed. At the very time when Social Credit was coming to power, John Maynard Keynes was preparing to publish his seminal book *The General Theory of Employment, Interest and Money*. Keynes was, by all odds, the greatest economist of the twentieth century. Although by no means alone in the field, he was the first to develop a cohesive theory of macroeconomic behaviour. In contrast to microeconomics, which deals with the economic behaviour of the single household or single company, or the pricing of a single commodity, macroeconomics deals with the aggregate income and output of all units in an economy. It was not until the *General Theory* was published that national income statistics began to be compiled in all countries, and that policy makers had some useful guidance for fiscal policies. Few people realize that the flood of macroeconomic data which report aggregate economic activity today had its origins in the system of thought developed by J.M. Keynes.

There was indeed a problem of inadequate demand and Major Douglas had identified it in a vague sort of way. But the solution was not likely to be found by a fundamentalist Bible preacher, and Aberhart's actual legislative program soon got into serious difficulties. The central problem was that he was trying to replace the banking and currency system with a provincial bookkeeping system of "prosperity certificates" or "scrip." As Dean Reid had pointed out at the 1934 hearings in the Alberta legislative committee, this was unconstitutional, because the British North America Act clearly assigned power over money and banking to the federal government.

Nevertheless Aberhart pressed ahead, and started issuing "Prosperity Certificates." These were pieces of paper something like bank notes, but on the back of each note there were 104 little squares, for each week over two years. It was necessary to buy a one-cent stamp and put it in a square each week, in order to keep the certificate valid. Some of these certificates circulated for several weeks with stamps on them as a form of paper money. Despite the mass support for Social Credit, most people were not too keen on accepting "funny money" in place of real dollars. So the certificate system soon fizzled out.

In April 1936, the *Calgary Herald* reported that the Social Credit government intended to eliminate interest on borrowed funds. Press reports suggested that people were transferring their bank deposits out of Alberta and selling their Alberta government bonds. In fact, the Alberta legislature passed a Reduction and Settlement of Debts Act in late 1936 which had the following provisions: (1) All debts which had been contracted before July 1, 1932, would be reduced by interest payments which had been made since then, which meant that interest payments for the preceding four years by a debtor would reduce the principal owing. (2) After the above, any balance still owing would be repayable over ten years at zero interest. (3) Any debts contracted after July 1, 1932, would have a maximum rate of interest of 5 percent.

This set off a series of court actions and the use of the federal power of disallowance, which meant that, on the recommendation of the Minister of Justice, the federal Governor in Council could disallow a provincial bill. Between 1935 and 1938, eleven Social Credit bills were disallowed or declared invalid by the courts. The Dominion Government referred all its disallowance rulings to the Supreme Court of Canada and was sustained.

STEPHEN LEACOCK'S EXPEDITION

The banks were alarmed by Aberhart's attack on contractual debt and by the whole notion of zero interest on money. They decided that a public relations effort was necessary, even though they had made something of a shambles of Sandwell's recommendations in 1932. Through an unidentified intermediary, they succeeded in engaging Stephen Leacock to undertake a speaking tour in the West in November and December of 1936. He accepted an honorarium of $10,000 plus expenses, which came to about $3,000. The deal was arranged through the advertising agency Cockfield Brown & Co., which submitted a report to the CBA on January 30, 1937. The report begins:

> It is a matter of satisfaction to note that with the tour completed and well behind us, there has not been, so far as we know, one single item of suspicion on the part of anyone that Dr. Leacock was doing a missionary job. It should also be noted that Dr. Leacock himself is completely unaware of the names of his sponsors, and it is a good thing that he should not know in the future.

Fifty-five years later it seems almost inconceivable that the Canadian Bankers' Association and Leacock could have been parties to such a deal. Certainly in my ten years as president of the Canadian Bankers' Association, the idea of financing a propaganda campaign under the table would have been unacceptable to the banks. The world has changed. The banks carry their battles into the public forum for all to see and the CBA does not need to hire undeclared witnesses for its case.

Leacock began his tour in Port Arthur and Fort William on November 27 and 28. As he proceeded west, his speeches became more focused on the Social Credit question. The 1937 report on his tour notes, "When he got to Alberta he really swung into action. His principal speech at Edmonton, at which the acting Prime Minister of the Province sat on his right, was full of biting satire only slightly clothed in humour." The following extracts are typical:

> Take next your Alberta paper money, your Prosperity Scrip that so frightened all the economists of America. Here it is—a prosperity certificate—$1—with a little insert picture of what I take to be God creating Alberta . . . Guard these certificates well. They have been a pleasant interlude in a dull world.

In Vancouver on December 28, Leacock addressed the Foreign Trade Bureau of the Board of Trade. Aberhart happened to be in town, and Leacock invited him to sit at the head table. According to the *Vancouver Province*, Aberhart "laughed heartily at his own expense."

SOCIAL CREDIT LEGISLATION

But Aberhart was not deterred by Leacock's views, nor by the judicial and federal government attack on his legislation. On February 7, 1937, he told the Edmonton Bible Conference, "We must recognize that the real cause of unemployment is the deflation of purchasing power by the money monopolists. The banks actually hold the economic life or death of the people in their hands under the present money monopoly system."

Most newspapers were hostile to Aberhart's program, especially the *Calgary Herald*. Aberhart attacked the *Herald* again and again in his Sunday afternoon radio talks, and tried to get people to cancel their subscriptions. The newspaper courageously held its ground throughout this period. But Aberhart had one supporter of Social Credit, which was the *Ottawa Citizen*. Its publisher was a dedicated convert to Major Douglas's theories.

In late 1936 the Toronto *Mail and Empire* reported that Aberhart proposed to license newspapers. The scheme was dropped, but in 1938 Aberhart returned to the theme with an Accurate News and Information Act, which, according to Rand Dyck (in his book *Provincial Politics*), "would have required them to print corrections at the direction of the government and to supply the source of any information published." Dyck goes on to say, "This clearly violated the principle of freedom of the press, and when even the Attorney General refused to vouch for the validity of the laws before the Lieutenant Governor, Aberhart dismissed him and assumed the position himself."

Litigation sometimes got nasty. A member of the Alberta legislature was described as a "bankers' toady." This brought a criminal action for libel, and two Social Crediters went to jail.

The elimination of interest on borrowed funds started even before the government was elected in August 1935. A flight of deposits had started from the Alberta Government Savings Branch which was a provincial savings office which preceded the Treasury Branches founded in 1938. Its 6,000 depositors found their rights of withdrawal frozen in August 1935, to stop an outflow from Alberta. The freeze on their deposits was still in effect when the Toronto *Mail and Empire* commented on this episode in October: "But if a Province's credit is not good at home, where can it be expected to be good?"

One of the first moves of the new government was to reduce interest on provincial and municipal debt by half. This of course caused a significant backlash, because there were thousands of bond holders who were persons of relatively modest means. Among the casualties of the move, according to the *Financial Post*, were the Toronto Police and Firemen's pension funds, which had $80,000 tied up in Alberta bonds. (The United Church pension fund held bonds as well.) The insurance companies stood to take the biggest losses, but they in turn represented thousands of holders of insurance policies.

(One of the curious characteristics of politicians is that they always think of interest rates in terms of borrowers and never of lenders, even though lenders greatly outnumber borrowers. Probably the reason for the politicians' myopic view is that the borrowers are usually in highly organized and vocal groups and the lenders are not. On one occasion when I had a debate with Ed Broadbent on the CBC's "Journal," he was fulminating about the need to reduce interest rates. I pointed out that millions of people holding term deposits and savings bonds were listening to him and would keep it in mind in the next election. I never heard from him on that subject again.)

Nevertheless, Aberhart was determined to implement his ideological aversion to interest. In 1938 he introduced a package of three bills: the first, the Securities Act, applied a 2 percent tax on mortgages to the lender; the second bill was the Home Owners' Security Act, which required the creditor to pay $2,000 to the debtor (that is, the mortgage lender had to pay the homeowner who owed him money); the third bill, which has had reverberations in modern times, prevented the foreclosure of the home quarter section of a farm. Since most homes were probably not worth more than $2,000, the legal requirement that the creditor pay the debtor that much meant, in effect, the confiscation of the property. Before the Securities Act and the Home Owners' Security Act came into effect in June, however, all three bills were disallowed by the federal cabinet. Aberhart commented, "Ever since the Dominion was brought into being the country has been at the mercy of the financial ogres and money leeches."

But the disallowed acts were only two of a package of nine pieces of legislation. One, the Bank Employees Civil Rights Act, did exactly the opposite of what its title suggests: it required bank employees to be licensed by the Alberta government, and denied the employee any right of appeal to the courts. This bill was attacked in the courts and overthrown.

A more successful initiative was the effort to renegotiate existing farm mortgage contracts to a lower level of interest rates. The Dominion Mortgage and Investments Association, which represented the insurance companies and mortgage loan companies, negotiated interest rate reductions on about 90 percent of farm mortgages, according to the *Montreal Gazette*, in late 1938. Rates were reduced from 7 or 8 percent to 6 percent, as had already occurred in Saskatchewan. The attempt of the government to reduce or repudiate interest on its own obligations was more than the non-bank lenders could stomach. The president of the Dominion Mortgage and Investments Association, J.H. Lithgow, who was general manager of Manufacturers Life, described the Alberta legislation as "of a most vicious and confiscatory character."

But Aberhart did not give up easily. In February 1939 he introduced the Limitation of Actions Act. This would have required all creditors to deal with debtors by June 1, 1940, or the debt would be automatically wiped out. Once again the legislation was disallowed. Then the war intervened and put a stop to the disastrous foray of the Social Credit movement into economic theory and practice.

Aberhart died in 1943, and was succeeded by Ernest Manning, who had been the very first graduate of the Calgary Prophetic Bible Institute. Manning laid Social Credit theory to rest, and to quote Dyck, "he proceeded to undo the damage that the theory had already caused." This involved reimbursing the bondholders for the debts upon which the province had defaulted—$34 million—and for the interest payments which had been reduced or not paid—$25 million.

Manning soon succeeded in restoring the credit of the province, and in 1947 the first oil well blew in at Leduc. Alberta's economy was no longer completely dependent on wheat and cattle. Under Manning, the Social Credit Party became a bastion of conservative free enterprise, and a fortress against the socialist hordes just to the east.

CHAPTER 8

TWO DECADES OF EASY MONEY

Clifford Clark, the deputy minister of finance, said in 1934 that the formation of the Bank of Canada was perhaps the most important legislation passed by Parliament since Confederation. But in its first twenty years, the Bank of Canada was not a visible factor in economic policy to the average Canadian. Throughout that period, the central bank pursued a relatively easy money policy; the rate of interest on government bonds remained at more or less 3 percent, while those who borrowed from banks paid about 4.5 to 5.5 percent. Economic policy was heavily influenced by the belief that chronic unemployment was the main long-term problem. The Bank of Canada shared this view, and rather than try to influence aggregate demand through monetary policy, it tended to intervene for specific purposes, such as curbing the growth in consumer credit or in long-term corporate borrowing from the banks.

However, the founding of the Bank of Canada did introduce a major new element in the relationship between banking and politics. Now there was a third player, independent of the government of the day. For a long time, the role of this new organization was somewhat bewildering to the chartered bankers, who probably sensed that there had been some sort of shift in power away from themselves. And indeed there had been, because the Bank of Canada was charged with advising the government on matters where senior bankers had previously been the principal source of advice.

ANOTHER THORN IN THE FLESH: GERRY MCGEER

Legislation to create the Bank of Canada and to amend the Bank Act in 1934 was something of an epilogue to the MacMillan Report. The commission's report in 1933 had explored the issues thoroughly, and had made specific recommendations for transferring all the gold reserves and the note-issuing power to the central bank.

When the Committee on Banking and Commerce was presented with the draft legislation in the spring of 1934, it conducted a lengthy examination of bankers and other witnesses, but these discussions often wandered off into irrelevant side roads. Considering the economic conditions at the time, one might have expected that the politicians would want to find out how the creation of a central bank would help the government deal with the Depression. Chubby Power, who became one of Mackenzie King's principal lieutenants, did ask the banks what their response to the Depression was, but they had no idea what a monetary policy was, let alone what it should be.

At one point, the committee of fifty members assigned a subcommittee to go to Montreal to interview Sir Herbert Holt, the president of the Royal Bank, whose health was uncertain. Chubby Power wanted to question Sir Herbert on interlocking directorates:

Power: What is the connection, if any, between the Royal Bank of Canada and the Montreal Trust Company?

Holt: None whatever . . . I am the President of both institutions, but their managements are entirely separate and their interests do not conflict in any way.

He went on to acknowledge that the Royal Bank had eleven of the twenty-five directors on the Montreal Trust. Looking back on this dialogue, from the vantage point of 1991, conveys some idea of how far the perception of conflict of interest has changed.

Another witness was Gerry McGeer, a Vancouver Liberal from the British Columbia legislature, who was destined to become the bankers' thorn in the flesh to replace Aberhart. McGeer campaigned against Aberhart in the 1935 Alberta election campaign, flying his own plane around the province. (On one occasion, he was prevented from landing in a farmer's field when the owner declared that nobody opposed to Social Credit could land on his property.)

The proceedings of 1934 provide one of the first examples of McGeer's tirades against the banking establishment, although he had given a preview to the MacMillan Commission. He was opposed to the creation of the Bank of Canada and wanted the banking system to be completely nationalized.

In the legislation proposing the Bank of Canada, we have not only gone backward from the days of 1844, Mr. Chairman, but we are travelling behind the misguided rulers of Rome that were operating 2,000 years ago . . . This war is not between humanity and usury, but it is a war between the right of self government and money dictatorship . . . If we don't waken up to our position and kick these bankers out of control of the money, they are going to kick us out of Parliament.

After three hours the exhausted committee adjourned for lunch. But Gerry McGeer was not through; in the afternoon, he gave the committee another two hours of his monetary know-how. Altogether, McGeer's testimony took up 60 pages out of 700 pages of evidence on the Bank Act revision of 1934. Looking back at this sorry episode, a contemporary witness is bound to feel that the Blenkarn committee is an improvement, or at least not a deterioration.

THE BANK OF CANADA TAKES OVER

Despite the unproductive political posturing in the House committee, the Bank of Canada Act and the Bank Act revision of 1934 were passed through all stages of the Parliamentary process in June and the bills were given royal assent on September 1.

There were two very important matters in the legislative package. One was a corollary to the passing of the Bank of Canada Act, and the other was to give great trouble in the years ahead. The first was the introduction of a cash reserve requirement for the chartered banks, and the second was the retention of the 7 percent ceiling on lending rates.

The Bank of Canada is a government bank, even though for a few years it had some nominal degree of private ownership, as is still the case with the Federal Reserve Banks in the United States. Its mandate is set forth in the preamble to its original act of Parliament in 1934: "To regulate credit and currency in the best interests of the economic life of the nation, to control and protect the external value of the national monetary unit, and to mitigate by its influence fluctuations in the general level of production, trade, prices and employment, so far as may be possible within the scope of monetary action, and generally to promote the economic and financial welfare of the Dominion."

The Bank of Canada gradually displaced the chartered banks as issuers of paper money, and by 1945 became the exclusive source of currency. The balance sheet of the central bank shows as a liability all of the Bank of Canada notes that have been issued, and the offsetting assets consist mainly of government bonds, although they may include gold and foreign currencies. In the earliest years, there was a mandatory gold reserve; when this disappeared, the Bank of Canada was theoretically able to expand the money supply infinitely. This could be done by buying up newly issued bonds from the government and paying the government in the form of deposits to the government's credit. Not only monetary cranks, but sometimes serious economists have worried about this ability of the central bank to inflate itself. In fact, the business of managing the assets of the central bank requires a large element of judgement, constrained by powerful domestic and international forces.

Paper money is only about 10 percent of the means of payment in the hands of the public. The other 90 percent consists of deposits in the chartered banks. (In recent years, the addition of some trust companies, the credit unions, and caisses populaires to the payments system has added a complicating element which would have to be included in a thorough analysis of the contemporary payments system.)

The critical element which gives the central bank its control over the aggregate size of the chartered banks is the requirement that the chartered banks must keep a certain level of deposits—their cash reserves—at the central bank. Contemporary thinking is that these reserves need be no more than sufficient to enable each bank to execute its daily settlements with all other banks. (Indeed, that is already the basis of the required cash reserves maintained at the Bank of Canada by the credit unions and trust companies which are direct clearers in the Canadian Payments Association. See Chapter 14.) In the legislation of 1934, the chartered banks were required to keep 5 percent of their deposit liabilities on deposit with the Bank of Canada. During the first ten or fifteen years of the Bank of Canada's life, this was not difficult to do, as the banks voluntarily kept a conventional cash reserve of 10 percent.

Not only did the banks maintain twice the legal requirement of cash reserves, but they also had enormous secondary reserves of government bonds, acquired during the Second World War. As a result of this very loose application of monetary control in the early years, the managers of the banks were hardly aware of the nature of the central bank's powers, and were more than a little surprised when the Bank of Canada started to exercise them in the 1950s. Nowadays the central bank can influence the cash reserves of the chartered banks on a daily basis, and to quite a high degree of precision. It is mainly through this close control of the cash reserves that the Bank of Canada is able to influence the trend in short-term interest rates.

A legal requirement of a 5 percent cash reserve—or any other percentage for that matter—is a little bit like having a regulation for taxi cabs which requires that one taxi always be idle at the taxi stand. The Bank of Canada's power resides in its ability to change the number of dollars which make up the 5 percent. It can do this in various ways, but most commonly it does so through what are called "open market operations." When it buys securities, it writes a cheque on its own account. This cheque is deposited in a bank by the seller, and that bank in turn puts the proceeds on deposit with the Bank of Canada as a credit. This inflates the number of dollars in the 5 percent cash reserves of the banks, and therefore their ability to extend credit up to twenty times the additional dollars in their reserves. The reverse process is equally possible.

The actions of the Bank of Canada in its "open market operations" are also a signal to the world about its views, because the purchase and sale of securities is done at a market price. If the Bank of Canada chooses to do so, it can influence the price of short-term securities, especially treasury bills. It can also reduce the number of dollars in the 5 percent cash reserve to the extent that it forces the chartered banks to borrow from the central bank. Such borrowings are on very stringent terms, and usually for only one day. The rate of interest at which the banks borrow from the central bank is the "bank rate" and nowadays the bank rate automatically determines the treasury bill rate. This is because the Bank of Canada has developed a system whereby the treasury bill rate is constantly adjusted to 0.25 percent below the bank rate.

THE 7 PERCENT CEILING SURVIVES

The other big issue in the 1934 revision was the retention of the 7 percent interest rate ceiling on loans made by the chartered banks. The MacMillan Commission took the position by a vote of four to one (with Premier Brownlee of Alberta in the minority) that the ceiling should be removed altogether. However, the commission also recommended that, if the government chose not to remove the ceiling, then it should enforce greater penalties for breaches of the law, and should require disclosure so that the facts would be known. The government, mindful of the rising tide of discontent in the West, chose the latter option; the Bank Act of 1934 strengthened the penalties for exceeding the ceiling, and left the ceiling intact. In the four Bank Act revisions with which I had some connection, there was never anything more important than the effort to get rid of the ceiling. But interest rate questions and monetary policy in general were low priorities in the late 1930s, and did not figure in the massive study of federal-provincial relations which was about to occur.

THE ROWELL-SIROIS REPORT IGNORES BANKING

The devastating economic conditions of the 1930s had raised many questions about the adequacy of the government's response to economic problems through appropriate fiscal policies; but they were questions about federal-provincial fiscal arrangements, not about financial regulation. In August 1937, Mackenzie King appointed a Royal Commission on Dominion-Provincial Relations to examine these questions. The commission was originally headed by Newton Rowell, the Chief Justice of Ontario, and Thibaudeau Rinfret, a Supreme Court Justice. Both judges resigned soon afterwards for health reasons, and the commission was chaired by Joseph Sirois, a law professor from Laval. The other members were John Dafoe, the journalist from Winnipeg, and two professors, R.A. Mackay from Dalhousie and H.F. Angus from the University of British Columbia. The secretary of the commission was Alex Skelton, who became the driving force on one of the best Royal Commission reports ever produced in Canada.

Skelton was director of research at the Bank of Canada, whose later career was cut short by a tragic drowning in Africa. In a dull city with a dull Prime Minister, Skelton was larger than life. The son of O.D. Skelton, a Queen's professor who had been one of Canada's leading thinkers on banking issues, he was said to be the only person who could smoke in front of Mackenzie King. (On one occasion when the Prime Minister suddenly called for him to explain some numbers in the Royal Commission report, Skelton grabbed a mouthful of lozenges to cover his alcoholic breath, a not infrequent necessity. With Skelton leaning over his shoulder to explain the figures, Mackenzie King said: "Alex, I don't wish to criticize your personal habits, but I wish you would not chew those confounded lozenges in my presence.")

Skelton gathered together a distinguished group of academics such as the historian D.G. Creighton and no fewer than three future principals of Queen's University: W.A. Mackintosh, J.A. Corry, and John Deutsch. Along with a number of other illustrious economists, lawyers, and businessmen, they produced a series of studies on the Canadian economy that explored the fiscal strains of a regional economy. While the mandate of the Royal Commission was to look at fiscal powers and responsibilities, it is a striking fact that the distribution of regulatory authority over financial institutions between the federal and provincial governments did not receive a single mention. This conspicuous absence was certainly not due to lack of knowledge on the part of the research staff.

In the light of the ongoing federal-provincial battles over the distribution of financial regulatory authority in the last fifteen years, it may seem hard to grasp that the Rowell-Sirois Report completely ignored this area. The reason is simple enough: there *was* no controversy over the distribution of powers fifty years ago. Money and banking were federal matters; the trust companies were fiduciary institutions, not deposit intermediaries; the credit unions were local cooperatives coming under provincial authority, and the Alberta Treasury Branches were just beginning to take shape; securities legislation was not on anyone's agenda.

Even before the members of the Royal Commission were named, the banks wondered whether they should appoint an economist who could help them grapple with fiscal questions which were outside their field of competence. Arthur Rogers, who had succeeded Henry Ross as the secretary-treasurer of the CBA, canvassed the banks for their opinions. The Royal Bank replied: "We think it would be better for the banks as such to hold themselves in readiness to give their opinions on matters regarding which the Commission may ask advice; otherwise to concern themselves only with the problems which are peculiar to the banks." The general manager of Barclays Bank said that making a submission would be a "waste of time" until governments got their debts under control.

The ruminations of the banks continued for several months. In October 1937, Arthur Rogers wrote to the banks that: "As the banks were unpopular in some quarters any proposal they might put forward would be viewed with suspicion." In the end, the CBA decided to form a committee to "survey the debt situation and examine the errors of management in public finance." There was no discussion of the regulatory regime.

The recommendations of the Rowell-Sirois Commission went into great detail as to the allocation of responsibility between the federal and provincial governments but they were set aside because of the war. In August 1945, the federal government returned to the table with a set of fiscal proposals that addressed health policy, social assistance, and fiscal arrangements. But interest in the distribution of financial regulatory powers was just as low in 1945 as it had been before the war.

FINANCING THE WAR AT 3 PERCENT

The outbreak of war in September 1939 brought about a suspension of public interest in financial questions. As far as the banks were concerned, politics were set aside for the duration. Thousands of bankers flocked into the armed services, and a small number of skilled foreign exchange specialists moved to Ottawa to help manage the Foreign Exchange Control Board. The civil service was almost at the height of its professional skill, and the government was able to attract many senior businessmen to help administer the economic controls which were necessary in wartime.

The economy had not recovered from the Depression. In June 1939, there were still 529,000 unemployed, out of a civilian labour force of 4,649,000. By June 1944, at the height of the war, there were 779,000 men and women in the armed forces. Civilian employment had increased from 4,120,000 to 4,485,000, and unemployment was reduced to minimal figures. In five years, the number of income earners went up 15 percent, and the economy went from considerable slack to full stretch. At the same time, output had to be shifted from civilian production to military output and defence production for the Allies. Food, gasoline, and other commodities were rationed, and at the financial level there was tight control on foreign exchange.

It was fortunate that the Bank of Canada had been created a few years earlier, or else the financial administration of the war would have been much less effective. One of the first acts of the government was to create the Foreign Exchange Control Board, coming under the administration of the Bank of Canada. Another major administrative unit was the Wartime Prices and Trade Board, which imposed price controls across the economy.

The chartered banks became in effect the financial arm of a command economy. With the sharp rise in employment and income and the suppression of consumption (for example, no cars were produced in the war), it was essential to drain off the public's excess spending power into savings. This was done in a series of nine

"Victory Loans," each of which was pushed very hard as a patriotic contribution to the war effort and as a good investment. The coupon rate of interest was 3 percent on all the issues, and the bonds matured in fifteen to twenty years, the last issue having a maturity date of 1966. Large numbers of bankers joined the personnel of the investment dealer firms in selling the Victory Bonds to the public.

The financing of the war was a model of fiscal responsibility. Compared to the excessive budget deficits of the peacetime 1970s and 1980s, the wartime deficits in 1939-45 were modest indeed, even allowing for inflation. The government went to great lengths to make sure that it did not leave the Canadian people with a legacy of unbearable debt after the war; its policy was to finance the war to the extent of 50 percent or more from tax revenues. During the 1943-45 period, total federal government expenditures were around the $5 billion mark, of which about $4 billion was defence expenditure. Tax revenues were more than half of this total; the rest was borrowed from the public and from the banks. Altogether, the national debt, consisting of federal government bonds and treasury bills, went up from about $3.4 billion at the end of 1938 to about $12.9 billion at the end of 1945. About three-quarters of this was obtained from the Victory Loan campaigns.

The significance of the successful effort to pay for the war by tax revenues and from the fast-growing savings of the public was that inflation was largely suppressed. Not altogether suppressed, however. The government had to resort to selling securities to the banks to some extent. Even so, the banks bought less than $2 billion of the $10 billion increase in the national debt. The Bank of Canada expanded its holdings of government bonds by about $1.6 billion, but more than half of this was necessary to finance the huge growth in the circulation of bank notes in the hands of the public.

Long before the end of the war was in sight, the government started thinking about the postwar period. A Special Parliamentary Committee on Reconstruction and Re-establishment was created in 1942, and the private sector was invited to make submissions. In late 1943, the banks decided to set up a Postwar Planning Committee. (Most of its members were at the level of assistant general manager, which at that time was a rank held by a few senior officers just below the general manager, who was normally the chief operating officer of the bank.) Several members later went on to higher rank, but the outstanding name on the committee was James Muir, chairman of the committee and later chief executive of the Royal Bank. In contrast to his dynamic and powerful personality as a bank executive, Muir advocated a passive position with regard to postwar planning. In 1944 he wrote: "It seems to me that instead of the banks submitting any definite proposals themselves it would be better if the government would consult the banks . . . with the object of obtaining their views regarding the feasibility of proposals made by other organizations."

This letter reflects the approach to public policy of bankers from the First World War until the 1960s. Bankers were accustomed to waiting for loan applicants to come through the door, and would respond to a proposal initiated by someone else. The concept of marketing their services was almost entirely foreign to the culture of banking. For at least two generations, bankers thought of themselves like doctors, available for consultation, but not seeking out business. The gradual emergence from that culture towards the culture of aggressive competition which exists today was long and painful.

As far as public policy making is concerned, the bankers in effect abdicated leadership. We have already seen that the banks were reactive and even negative in the making of public policy concerning inspection and regulation, and in the formation of the central bank. A long period of relative passivity in the making of public policy may have been a factor which contributed to the perception in Ottawa that the views of bankers could safely be ignored.

LOWERING THE INTEREST CEILING

Although the Rowell-Sirois Report avoided banking and financial legislation, there was a devastating sequel to the 1934 Bank Act revision, and this was the 1944 revision,when the interest rate ceiling on all loans by banks was reduced from 7 to 6 percent.

To understand how this could have happened, it is essential to realize that from Confederation to 1944, interest rates on bank loans and government bonds were generally nowhere near as high as the 7 percent ceiling. For example, the yield on Government of Canada sterling bonds due in 1903 was 4.7 percent in 1871, and 3.9 percent in 1881. By 1900, the yield on 3 percent "sterling perpetuals" was 3.0 percent, rising to 3.6 percent just before the First World War. After the war, Government of Canada long-term bonds got close to 6 percent, but then fell to nearly 3 percent by 1939. Province of Ontario bonds, which normally yield a little more than Government of Canada bonds, had a peak yield of about 6 percent in 1920, and averaged less than 4 percent in the 1930s.

Mortgages on real estate were higher than this, with a peak of about 8 percent in 1920 and an average of 6.3 percent in the 1930s. Consumer credit loans were much higher—in the double-digit figures. But chartered banks were prohibited from making consumer credit loans or from taking residential mortgages, so these rates were irrelevant to the ceiling on bank lending rates.

The Government of Canada started issuing treasury bills in 1931, before the Bank of Canada was founded. In 1934 these yielded 2.5 percent. But by 1939 the rate had fallen to 0.71 percent, and in 1945 it fell to 0.37 percent. By that time, Government of Canada bonds yielded about 1.4 percent. While these numbers seem almost unbelievable today, it must be remembered that the Depression of the 1930s had created an environment in which no one wanted to borrow money, no matter how little the cost. The banks could not find commercial borrowers before the war, and then during the war the huge increase in bank deposits could only be employed in government bonds.

As a result, the CBA did not make much of a fuss about the 7 percent ceiling in 1934, nor indeed about the decrease in the ceiling to 6 percent in 1944. The correspondence in the archives of the Canadian Bankers' Association is illuminating. The secretary of the CBA, Arthur Rogers, asked the banks what they thought about section 91, which was the section of the Bank Act containing the interest rate ceiling. He wondered if the banks would be interested in a proposal to have a 5 percent discount rate ceiling, which in effect would mean an interest rate of almost 10 percent. The discount rate would be applicable only to consumer credit loans, which were becoming more important because of the growing importance of automobiles and consumer durables in the buying plans of millions of households.

Rogers was probably being pushed by the Bank of Commerce, which thought that it was wrong that banks should be restricted to an interest rate of 6 percent on personal loans, when companies operating under the Small Loans Act, and sales finance companies, could charge 12 percent or more. One solution would be to make it clear in the Bank Act that a bank could charge a *discount* rate of, say 5 percent. The significance of the word "discount" is that the rate of interest is applied to the original amount borrowed, even if the borrower pays the loan off in equal monthly instalments. (If you borrow $100 for twelve months at 5 percent, and pay off the loan in equal monthly instalments, then the average rate of interest would not be 5 percent but roughly 10 percent, because your interest cost is $5 on an average loan of $50.)

The Bank of Nova Scotia replied: "We do not quite get the significance of the part [of the discount rate proposal] reading 'is repayable in substantially equal periodic payments over a period not exceeding 18 months.' " The Bank of Toronto got the point: "If the maximum rate expressed in section 91 of the Bank Act is to be reduced to 6 percent we see no reason, particularly since the rate to be permitted is so much less than those finance companies are allowed to accept, why there should be any prohibition against the imposition of proper charges." The Bank of Commerce thought that the rate on consumer loans should be expressed as a monthly rate, which was the way the small loan companies expressed it. The Royal Bank said, "The matter is really immaterial to us and we have no views one way or another as to the inclusion of this feature in the Bank Act." The Banque Canadienne Nationale was opposed outright to the idea of having a 5 percent discount rate on consumer loans: "We consider that such a privilege, if granted to the banks, would lay them open to strong criticism on the part of the general public who had not appreciated the reasons for charging 10 percent interest on such loans." The Imperial Bank objected to the proposal to reduce the interest rate ceiling on ordinary loans to 6 percent but "at the same time we appreciate the matter is not a vital one and may have to be conceded."

At one point earlier in 1944, it appears that Clifford Clark, the deputy minister of finance, was even considering a 5 percent ceiling in place of the 7 percent. Small wonder that the banks decided that discretion was the better part of valour, and argued that the 7 percent ceiling should be left unchanged rather than pressing for a new-fangled discount rate of 5 percent on personal consumer loans, which would be in effect 10 percent. Without a strong push for making small loans to consumers that would be exempt from the ceiling, the proposal died. In the twenty-odd years before that happened, the consumer was at the mercy of the finance companies, which charged 16 to 24 percent on car loans and appliance loans.

The fact that the decennial revision of the Bank Act, scheduled for 1944, was carried out at all is testimony to the power of the Department of Finance and its deputy minister, Clifford Clark. In 1942, when the government and the banks were starting to think about the 1944 revision, the bankers somewhat reluctantly agreed that it would be better to get the revision over with rather than leave it to the vagaries of postwar politics. Arthur Rogers wrote: "The Deputy Minister (Clark) held views similar to the president of the CBA, namely that the revision should be proceeded with in 1944 even if the war were still being waged, as the revision would be completed more expeditiously [1944] because members of Parliament would be impatient with monetary theorists in wartime." This was clearly aimed at Gerry McGeer, but perhaps also at the Social Credit and CCF parties.

But the authorities in Ottawa had an agenda of their own. One was farm financing, and another was term lending for small and medium-sized businesses. Bank lending to agriculture was badly constrained by the century-old prohibition against the taking of mortgage security on real property. The experience of the 1920s and 1930s, confirmed by testimony before the MacMillan Commission, demonstrated that the farmers were badly served by a financial system which could not provide them with term loans for buildings and equipment and such important new developments as rural electrification.

The government's response to this problem was the Farm Improvements Loan Act of 1944. This act copied a piece of legislation which was already on the books, the Home Improvements Loan Act. The idea was for the banks and the government to combine in an effort to provide term credit to farmers. The banks, which had the widespread branch facilities and local knowledge of the farm community, would extend loans at a flat rate of 5 percent. The government would guarantee up to 10 percent of each bank's total pool of farm improvement loans and the total limit on the project was fixed at $250 million. This piece of legislation proved to be very successful in overcoming a significant problem, especially in western Canada.

A similar piece of legislation was the founding of the Industrial Development Bank (IDB), which was accomplished with a special act of Parliament alongside the Bank Act revision of 1944. According to S.R. Noble, a former Royal Bank officer who became the first president of the IDB: "The founders of the bank believe that there has always existed a gap in the credit structure . . . neither the banks nor the security markets have been able to supply adequately the medium and long term capital needs of small and medium-size business."

So the IDB was created as a wholly owned subsidiary of the Bank of Canada with the purpose of filling this perceived gap. The average size of loan turned out to be $40,000 to $50,000, with a range from $3,000 to $200,000. The rate of interest was to be a flat 5 percent, regardless of the term of the loan or its size. While the banks have always felt positive towards the Farm Improvements Loan Act, they have been less than enthusiastic about the Industrial Development Bank, whose name was later changed to the Federal Business Development Bank (FBDB). The IDB could make loans against the security of real property, unlike the chartered banks. (The criticism of the banks that they had left a vacuum to be filled by the IDB was quite misguided, because the banks were prevented by law from that kind of lending.) While the IDB was intended to supplement ordinary commercial lending by the banks, there has always been a running controversy as to whether the FBDB has or has not overextended its mandate into direct commercial competition with the banks, using relatively cheap government money as its source of funds.

FINANCING POSTWAR RECONSTRUCTION AT 3 PERCENT

In Ottawa there was a great deal of apprehension about a postwar recession. There is no doubt that economic thought was heavily influenced by the experience of the 1930s and by the recession after the First World War. Equally important was the pervasive concern that the transition from a wartime economy to a peacetime world would be characterized by widespread unemployment and under-utilized resources. There were about 800,000 men and women in the armed forces and another 1,200,000 in defence production who would have to be absorbed into a civilian economy which had been weak before the war.

John Maynard Keynes had articulated the macroeconomic problem of total demand falling short of total supply in his landmark *General Theory of Employment, Interest and Money*, published in 1936. Keynes's analysis dominated economic thought from then until long after his death in 1946. At Harvard, Alvin Hansen also taught the new generation of economists that there would be a problem of secular stagnation (that is, persistent unemployment) after the war.

One of Keynes's students at Cambridge University was Robert Bryce, about to begin a long career as one of Canada's most distinguished public servants. He, perhaps more than any of his seniors in the upper ranks of the public service, such as W.C. Clark, W.A. Mackintosh, and Graham Towers, was qualified to articulate Keynesian doctrine. Together, this small and talented group saw a need for an extended period of easy money after the war. At the same time, they were much occupied with the need for postwar international monetary arrangements which would prevent the "beggarmy-neighbour" policies of the 1930s. At the time of the Bank Act revision of 1944, the Canadian government was a significant participant in the Bretton Woods discussions which led to the creation of the International Monetary Fund and the International Bank for Reconstruction and Development. While the Bretton Woods discussions were dominated by Lord Keynes and Harry White of the U.S. Treasury, Louis Rasminsky, later to be the third governor of the Bank of Canada, was an influential contributor.

When the war in Europe came to an end in May 1945, followed by the terminal act of the nuclear bomb on Hiroshima in August, there was already a consensus in Ottawa that an easy money policy should be pursued. This meant that bank loans and other forms of credit were to be readily available without causing upward pressure on interest rates. A contemporary observer may find it hard to come to grips with the notion that a 3 percent rate on government bonds was considered high. The Bank of Canada actually encouraged bond yields to fall to 2.75 percent in the immediate postwar years. With bond yields falling, savers were in effect encouraged to look for alternative investments, thus causing the whole spectrum of interest rates to fall. H.H. Binhammer, an economist at Royal Military College, wrote: "The Bank of Canada announced its intention to continue an easy money policy after the war early in 1944 when it reduced the bank rate [from 2.5 percent to 1.5 percent] and supplied the banks with more reserves than they had ever had before." The bank's policy was part of the overall government policy presented in the White Paper on Employment and Income in April 1945. In the White Paper the government committed itself to "the maintenance of a high and stable level of employment and income." Binhammer added, "Following the new Keynesian dogma, fiscal policy was to be the main technique for its accomplishment."

Towers later explained to a House of Commons Committee on Finance, Trade and Economic Affairs why he had not pursued "a rigorous monetary policy" after the war. He said that the government had a moral responsibility to the millions of people who had bought Victory Bonds during the war, and who would be dismayed by a fall in their prices. Moreover, he said, it would have caused a considerable degree of uncertainty among business people and would have discouraged businesses from seeking bank loans to rebuild their inventories of civilian goods.

While monetary policy was very easy, there was little inflation because the federal government managed to throw up budget surpluses for several years after the war. The truth is that it was far easier to be governor of the central bank in Graham Towers's day than it has been in the regimes of Gerald Bouey and John Crow. In the days when the government ran a surplus or a relatively small deficit, the Bank of Canada did not need to promote a high level of interest rates to offset the drain of national savings into government bonds. Especially in the last decade, the balance between the demand for and the supply of savings has been enormously distorted by huge government deficits. The Bank of Canada, like all central banks, has tried to tell the government to curb its appetite, but without success. This conflict between the government and the central bank persists because monetary policy has to be used to offset irresponsible fiscal policy.

Nevertheless, the conviction of Graham Towers that he had to keep bond prices high and stable tended to tie the hands of the central bank in controlling the postwar monetary expansion. Instead of using interest rates as a constraint on market forces, the central bank resorted to various kinds of "moral suasion." Moral suasion, in this instance, was a form of ear-stroking by the authorities, according to which the banks would "agree" to refrain from buying too many government bonds, or "agree" not to extend too much credit to business people which would be used indirectly for capital investment, or "agree" not to add to their holdings of provincial, municipal, and corporate bonds.

"As it was," E.P. Neufeld wrote in *Bank of Canada Operations*, "bank policy tended to accentuate the boom in real investment, and, to the extent that this increased the pressure on scarce domestic supplies and magnified the demand for imported supplies, it contributed both to domestic inflation and to the balance of payments crisis." On the whole, Neufeld thought, the Bank of Canada overdid its easy money policy after the war. But this is not a book about the conduct of monetary policy, and our interest in the central bank's actions is only related to its impact on banking and politics later on.

My first exposure to official life in Ottawa was in the summer of 1947. The Department of Finance and the Bank of Canada each decided to employ a few summer students; after a written competition and some interviews, I was hired by Finance, along with Denis Hudon, a student from Laval. At that time, the Department of Finance occupied the wing of the East Block which fronts on Wellington Street. The Prime Minister's office and the Department of External Affairs occupied the main north-south part of the building.

On some mornings, I would encounter the Prime Minister, Louis St. Laurent, walking up the driveway to the south entrance. My impression is that he had come on the streetcar. In the East Block, my immediate superior was Mitchell Sharp (who later went on to many senior positions in the bureaucracy and in cabinet). Bob Bryce was the assistant deputy minister to Clark, and the one who assigned me a project. He asked me to project the burden of the national debt under various possible conditions for the next twenty years. This required making some assumptions about the Gross National Product, the fiscal position of the government, and the rate of interest.

The results have no doubt been long since lost in the dusty files of the department, but it would be hard to imagine a more misguided projection. Basically, I assumed that a 3 percent rate of interest could be projected far ahead, and that the real questions were the size of the Gross National Product and the budgetary surplus or deficit. At the time the forecast must have seemed worthwhile, because when I returned to McGill in the autumn I wrote a master's thesis on the economic consequences of retiring a national debt completely. In 1991, with the national debt rising by $30 billion per annum, this may seem the most extreme fools' paradise. But in fact the British had completely retired their national debt in the late nineteenth century, and the Americans had done so in the 1920s.

THE LONG RETREAT FROM 3 PERCENT

Five years after the war, the rate of interest on long-term government bonds was still below 3 percent. As we have noted, both Neufeld and Binhammer have concluded that the retreat from easy money was too long in coming. But at the time, Towers had plenty of intellectual support for his position. Fullerton suggests that in the Ottawa hierarchy, it was only C.D. Howe, the influential Minister of Trade and Industry, who foresaw the postwar boom and growing prosperity.

Finally, seven or eight years after the war, the accumulation of economic forces brought about a significant change in the political climate for banking. One of the first things to happen was that the United States started to remove its price controls as soon as the war was over. Consumer prices in the U.S. shot up 25 percent between 1945 and 1947, and American inflation began to spill into Canada. In July 1946, Canada brought the exchange rate back to parity with the U.S. dollar; that is, the official exchange rate was fixed at $1 Canadian to $1 U.S., whereas the Canadian dollar had been worth only 91 cents

U.S. from September 1939. This was only the first of many occasions in the postwar period when Canadian financial policy was driven by international economic forces beyond Canada's control.

In the brave new world of international cooperation which emerged from the Bretton Woods agreements of 1944, member countries (including Canada) which subscribed to the agreements were not supposed to reduce their exchange rate deliberately in order to improve their international competitive position. With a fixed exchange rate, Canada's reserves of gold and U.S. dollars could be depleted by an unfavourable balance of trade or by international capital flows. The exhaustion of the British and European economies in comparison to the booming postwar economy of North America led to a 30 percent devaluation of the British pound against the U.S. dollar in September 1949. When one major trading currency changes value in relation to the key currency (the U.S. dollar), then the other currencies must be adjusted. (If you move one orange in a bowl full of oranges, then all the oranges change position in relation to the others.) Thus, the day after the British devaluation of 1949, the Canadian dollar was devalued by 10 percent against the U.S. dollar but revalued about 20 percent upwards against the British pound.

Less than a year later, the Korean war broke out in June 1950. There was a strong American demand for Canadian exports, and the Canadian dollar was perceived as undervalued by investors. In order to stem the inflow of funds, Canada "floated" the dollar against other currencies in October 1950. This means that the value of the dollar was allowed to find its own level, in response to market forces, rather than being fixed at a specific value defined by the authorities. Thus emerged an historic recognition of the fact that it was extremely difficult to fix the Canadian exchange rate with any confidence that the rate selected would continue to reflect international economic conditions indefinitely.

It was many years before a general system of floating exchange rates would be introduced in Britain and Europe. When this did happen, it had profound effects on the role of the Canadian banks in the world's financial system. But in 1950, the main influence of the floating Canadian dollar was to give the Bank of Canada another degree of freedom in the conduct of monetary policy. However, the addiction to direct controls was still strongly ingrained in Canadian financial policy.

The first response to the strong inflationary pressures of the Korean war was to have another "agreement" with the banks; in

February 1951, the Bank of Canada told the chartered banks to stop increasing their loans to business. This could have been accomplished by reducing the cash reserves of the chartered banks. Even though it was more than five years since the war had ended, the banks still had about one half of their Canadian assets in cash and government bonds. With lower cash reserves, the banks would have had to sell government bonds in order to continue expanding their business loans, which would have caused a fall in the price of bonds.

At long last, in 1951 and 1952, this started to happen. By 1953, the yield on Government of Canada bonds had crept up to 3.7 percent, which may seem low now, but was a considerable change at the time from less than 3 percent. Economic forces were beginning to gather which would eventually bring about a revolutionary change in the asset structure of the Canadian banks. The postwar flood of immigration, booming prosperity, and a vast growth in the needs of the middle class for houses and cars fundamentally changed the political perception of what Canada wanted from its banks. And the demand for bank credit was gradually forcing interest rates upwards, until the 6 percent ceiling on interest rates became a significant, even deadly, constraint.

CHAPTER 9

A HOP, A SKIP, AND A JUMP

In the years 1954-67, the Canadian banking system took a major hop, skip, and jump toward competition and efficiency.

The hop was permission to make loans on houses (1954).

The skip was permission to make loans on cars (1954 and 1967).

The jump was removal of the 6 percent ceiling on bank lending rates (1967).

Taken together, these three leaps forward were almost Olympian in length. They were the result of fundamental economic and social changes taking place in the country, and in turn produced a whole new political climate for the banking system; there was a profound change in the relationship between the chartered banks and the general public. Up to 1954 the banks were the major depository for the public's savings, but not the source of funds for most personal and family borrowing. Bank lending was essentially commercial in nature, with a relatively minor portion of bank assets in personal loans. Then, in a series of moves which removed the barriers to lending against the security of houses and cars, Parliament brought the banks into touch with the rapidly expanding middle class in the suburbs and small towns of Canada.

A HOP . . .

As we have seen, the pessimistic view in Ottawa of the economic transition from war to peace proved to be mistaken. The reconstruction of the economies of Europe and Britain required economic and financial assistance from North America, and Canada shared in that effort. The demand for Canadian primary resources was great, and the Canadian economy took off into strong peacetime growth.

One measure of the spirit of confidence and buoyancy was the birth rate, which from 1945 to 1954 was the highest in the western world. In that period, the natural population increase (births minus deaths) was 18.3 per thousand, compared to 14.2 in the United States and 5.4 in the United Kingdom. Following the repatriation of the armed forces from Europe, which released passenger ships from military duties, immigration jumped to 125,000 in 1948; after slipping back to 95,000 and 72,000 in 1949 and 1950 respectively, it more than doubled to 195,000 in 1951, and averaged about 160,000 in the three years 1952 to 1954.

One of the first economic consequences of the high birth rate and the rising level of immigration was the need for housing. The number of families, which had been growing by an average of 76,000 a year in the decade up to 1951, went up to about 85,000 a year over the next five years. But the number of households is a better measure of housing demand than the number of families, because there was a growing number of "non-family households," such as groups of young working women living together. (In 1956 there were 3,712,000 families and 3,924,000 households.) While many of the immigrant families crowded together in the urban centres, living within their means and building a financial base which was to take them into single-family home ownership before long, there was a pressing need for affordable housing for young married couples. The construction of houses more or less kept up with net family formation up to about 1952, but did nothing to reduce the backlog of demand which had been left from the Depression years and the war, nor did it meet the needs of the growing number of non-family households.

But there was a fundamental problem in the financing of housing which could not be solved by market forces, because it was imposed by legal constraints. The chartered banks were prevented from making residential mortgage loans, even though they held a large proportion of the public's savings. In 1950, for example, the assets of the chartered banks were $8 billion, compared to about $4 billion in the life insurance companies, $800 million in the trust and loan companies combined, and $300 million in the caisses populaires and credit unions. In the years 1951 to 1953, the life insurance companies provided 75 percent of the residential mortgage loans from financial institutions (excluding credit unions); the trust and loan companies provided the rest. In those days, a significant part of the funds for conventional housing finance came from individuals, usually through their lawyers, who acted as agents.

The life insurance companies, lacking a branch system to service mortgages, made residential mortgage loans only in cities with 70,000 or more in population. The trust and loan companies had about 270 branches, only 6 percent of the number of bank branches. In a recent study by J.V. Poapst and E.H. Neave, the lack of available funds in the postwar period for housing in smaller communities is discussed. The study cites a survey which was conducted by the Dominion Mortgage and Investments Association, which was composed of the life insurance, trust and mortgage loan companies:

> The survey covered 41 members, including the major institutional lenders. Respondents were asked to indicate from a list of 162 centres of 5,000 population and over the ones where they did not make one loan in 1952, "irrespective of the size or whether conventional, NHA, residential, commercial, industrial, new or renewal." No lender reported making a loan in thirteen of the communities [Collingwood and Owen Sound in Ontario were examples] . . . In mid 1952 Central Mortgage and Housing Corporation found that in some 75 communities of 5,000 to 50,000 population, National Housing Act joint loans were not available. [CMHC was the Crown corporation which had been created in 1945 as the vehicle for federal housing policy.]

Thus the government had come to the realization that it was the source of supply for residential mortgages in large parts of Canada outside the big cities. In 1953, for example, CMHC financed about 6,000 housing units directly out of its own funds, and shared with financial institutions in "joint loans" on 31,000 other units. Quite apart from its social programs, this was costing CMHC more than $50 million a year, and the government was concerned that it was getting drawn deeper and deeper into housing finance. In those prudent days, the government felt that it should balance the budget, which at that time was about $5 billion in both revenues and expenditures.

In the same year, the government decided to embark on a radical change in housing finance by allowing the banks to make residential mortgage loans. The driving force was quite clearly the senior hierarchy of public servants, especially David Mansur, the president of Central Mortgage and Housing Corp. As far as the banks were concerned, the proposal to bring them into residential mortgage finance came out of the blue. On September 30, 1953, Douglas Abbott, the Minister of Finance, sent a letter to the chief executives of the banks with his proposal to amend the National Housing Act

(NHA). This was one of the infrequent occasions when the decennial revision of the Bank Act was overridden by other legislation. Although the Bank Act was due for revision in 1954, the National Housing Act was drafted to override the Bank Act in March 1954, before the latter was on the Parliamentary agenda.

The government, sensing that there would be considerable opposition to its proposals, was careful to explain to the banks what its motivations were. While Douglas Abbott was writing to the chief executives of the banks, Clayton Elderkin, the Inspector General of banks, wrote to Arthur Rogers at the CBA. He said that the government had contacted Jack Bryden, the president of North American Life Assurance Company and also the president of the Dominion Mortgage and Investments Association. Elderkin said that on the whole, life insurance, trust, and loan companies were not opposed to admitting banks to the mortgage business. The life companies had gradually reduced their holdings of government bonds acquired during the war, and were no longer in a position to fund residential mortgages except through growth in assets. The trust and loan companies were not represented in many communities, and were probably sceptical that the banks would provide significant competition anyway.

But there was much more to the new housing legislation than authorizing the banks to make mortgage loans. The government had decided to get away from the joint-loan program and replace it by an insured loan program which has remained the essence of National Housing Act mortgage loans to this day. Government insurance of funds advanced by financial institutions would be on each individual loan rather than on the whole pool of loans from an institution. By making the insurance applicable to each individual loan, and transferable, both the house and the mortgage became more marketable. This made it possible for the fifty or sixty approved lending institutions to sell their mortgages to other investors, and it also made it possible for individual home owners to sell their property with the government guarantee still applying to the mortgage.

The biggest problem for the banks was the twenty-five-year term to maturity of NHA mortgages. The banks were concerned that the public would perceive them as having put their deposits at risk in illiquid and unsound long-term assets. They sought a meeting with the minister, and in late October 1953 the executive council of the CBA turned out in full force to meet the Minister of Finance, Doug Abbott, and the new deputy minister, Ken Taylor, who had succeeded

Clifford Clark some months earlier. Jim Coyne, the deputy governor of the Bank of Canada, was also present at the meeting. The CBA delegation was led by Ted Atkinson, the general manager of the Royal Bank.

A lengthy memorandum on the meeting prepared by Arthur Rogers gives some flavour of the apprehension the banks felt about getting into the residential mortgage market. L.G. Gillett of the Bank of Toronto said, "The banks generally had been shocked and were still shocked at the proposal to abandon the long-standing plans for maintaining liquidity in our banking system." This was echoed by C.S. Frost of the Bank of Nova Scotia, who "suggested that it was not good sound banking to tie up funds on 25 year obligations."

Coyne thought that the demand for bank funds would be not more than $150 to $200 million a year, and that the central bank would make sure there was enough liquidity so the banks would not feel uncomfortable with that size of program. (In fact, the liquid-asset ratio of the banks, which consisted mostly of cash and government securities, was about 45 percent at the time. After the act was implemented the liquidity ratio climbed up to 48 percent. These ratios are astronomically high by contemporary standards.) The banks did not seem to be satisfied with this assurance, and asked for a clause that would enable them to borrow from the Bank of Canada against the collateral of NHA mortgages. Abbott said he might include some form of borrowing power, "even if it was just window dressing, so long as it does not get the government back into the mortgage business."

In the following weeks, there was a heavy correspondence between the Canadian Bankers' Association and Central Mortgage and Housing as well as several meetings. The government gave way to the banks' fear of being perceived as illiquid by providing a clause which allowed a bank to borrow from the Bank of Canada against the security of NHA mortgages. (This clause has never been acted upon, nor indeed was it ever intended to be used.) Apart from this cosmetic change, the government's proposals were, for the most part, enacted as originally planned. CMHC retained the power to determine the ceiling price of homes eligible under the Act, and could change this price from time to time. CMHC could also determine the maximum percentage of the property value which could be mortgaged. Even more important, the rate of interest on NHA loans was fixed by government decree rather than by market forces. It was this feature of the National Housing Act of 1954 that eventually put political pressure on the government to remove the 6 percent ceiling from bank loans, although this was not a factor at the beginning, when the rate was fixed at 5.5 percent.

In January 1954, Bill 102 to amend the National Housing Act came up for second reading in Parliament. According to Earl McLaughlin, who later became chief executive officer of the Royal Bank, the debate lasted four days and featured fifty-three speakers. In the end, it was referred to the Standing Committee on Banking and Commerce by a vote of 186 to 2. This committee still numbered fifty members, as it had in 1934 and 1944. Its chairman was David Croll, whose long parliamentary career has continued in the Senate until recent times. The committee included many who subsequently became national figures, such as Donald Fleming, Paul Hellyer, Roland Michener, and the fiery and likable CCF member from Nanaimo, Colin Cameron.

The Canadian Bankers' Association's presentation was made by T.H. Atkinson, the president. Atkinson took a conciliatory but ambiguous approach: "We have felt . . . that we were not forced into this against our judgement, although we would not have sought it." He added that the banks "have been referred to occasionally as 'quasi public utilities'." This perception of the role of the banks in the economic system is not one which would be encouraged by a contemporary president of the CBA; it demonstrates, however, that some bankers shared the view that the profit motivation was somewhat modified by social goals. A contemporary would say that the banks are definitely not "public utilities," but should behave like other market-oriented corporations. The social goals should be defined in law, but in such a way as to encourage their achievement through market incentives.

The discussions in the banking committee hearings under Croll were more analytical than those in the 1980s, and the members were less likely to do political grandstanding for the media. Even so, there was plenty of editorial thundering in the newspapers. The *Canadian Statesman* of Bowmanville, in its issue of December 10, 1953, asked, "What evil genius has persuaded the government to force the banks into the mortgage business? Has the government forgotten that the first duty of the banks is to their depositors?" This view was echoed in the West, where the Moose Jaw *Times-Herald* said, "The proposal strikes at the very heart of the Canadian banking system. It will not strengthen it; rather it will weaken it."

The concern that banking safety would be undermined was shared by some mortgage-lending institutions, though possibly the potential competition was a factor in their thinking. The *Financial Times* quoted Morley Aylsworth, president and general manager of the Huron and Erie Mortgage Corporation (the precursor of Canada Trust) as saying, "The soundness of encouraging Canadians both old and new with limited funds at their disposal, to use their meagre resources as a down payment on a purchase of a home is, I feel, open to question."

But the strongest criticism of the bill came from Colin Cameron, whose comments were widely reported. Cameron said that the bill was "a cruel hoax by the government on the Canadian people." He claimed that the insurance companies were vacating the field and that the banks "had torpedoed the federal government's housing proposals," by complaining loud and long that they would have to throw people into the streets in order to get "vacant possession" on a defaulted mortgage loan. K.M. Sedgwick of the Royal Bank said that Cameron's allegation was "just plain silly" and B.M. Currie, general manager of the Bank of Toronto, said that it was "a foolish statement."

The Toronto *Globe and Mail* apparently took its editorial position from the views of the economist Gilbert Jackson, whom we encountered back in the 1920s advocating a return to the gold standard. In a speech to an insurance industry group at the Albany Club in Toronto on February 5, 1954, Jackson said, "Before we change the time-honoured principles of Canadian banking, we should try to find out why the prices of building materials are so high." On February 22, a *Globe* editorial said, "The basic reason for the housing problem (and for the banks' reluctance to get involved in it) is that construction costs are dangerously high, and the basic reason for that is that ... wages are out of line with productivity." (The price index for residential building costs had in fact greatly outdistanced the consumer price index.)

Perhaps the last word was said by R.R. Knight, a CCFer from Saskatchewan, who said that the government scheme would "put a larger number of people in a larger amount of debt over a longer period of time." This was certainly true, but the thousands of families (including the author's) who got themselves into debt when houses cost $12,000 to $15,000 were the ones who had the last laugh. If Knight's comment had been made in the late 1980s, its quality of doom for overextended home buyers might have been more relevant.

The new Housing Act was passed on March 8, 1954, and proclaimed on March 22. By the end of the year, from a standing start the banks had committed $160 million to residential mortgage loans. Over the following three or four years, the banks supplied more than a quarter of all NHA mortgage loans for owner-occupied dwellings. According to Poapst, they supplied $900 million in the years 1955 to 1958, compared to $1,500 million from the life insurance companies and $800 million from the trust and loan companies. For two years, there was very little need for the funding of housing by CMHC, so Doug Abbott had achieved one of his purposes.

Private-sector funding of the housing market could have continued indefinitely, but it did not. The CMHC re-entered the picture in 1956 because it controlled the NHA rate of interest. Unfortunately, as the bureaucratic process usually lags behind market realities, CMHC failed to adjust its NHA rate to the changing level of market rates in the economy. When the National Housing Act of 1954 came into force, the rate of interest on NHA mortgages was almost 2 percent above Government of Canada bond rates (which at that time were 3 percent). But in 1956 and 1957, bond yields started to rise, and the NHA rate lagged behind, first at 5 percent and later at 6 percent. The supply of funds from the financial institutions began to dry up, and Central Mortgage and Housing had to fill the vacuum. Instead of stabilizing the housing market, which one might have expected would be a goal of public policy, CMHC managed to accentuate the fluctuations. This, of course, made it more difficult for the construction industry to plan ahead, and unnecessarily forced building costs and wages upward from time to time.

In late 1959, the NHA rate was boosted from 6 percent to 6.75 percent, after bond yields had exceeded the NHA rate for a short time. Since there was an interest ceiling of 6 percent on the banks, when the NHA rate went above 6 percent, the banks dropped out of the market. Thus the goal of public policy for housing, expressed in the National Housing Act of 1954, was defeated by an arbitrary set of rules about interest rates. This absurd situation was allowed to continue until the Bank Act revision of 1967. In that eight-year period, the absence of the banks from the market for housing finance was helping to build the economic and political pressures which would lead to removing the ceiling in 1967. The hop had happened in 1954, but the skip and the jump were yet to come.

... A SKIP ...

For the banking system, the hop was the power to make residential mortgage loans, and the skip was the power to make personal loans for the purchase of automobiles and other consumer durables against the security of chattel mortgages. The skip was actually a two-step affair spanning the Bank Act revisions of 1954 and 1967. In the 1954 revision, the critical section of the Bank Act (section 75) which defined the business and powers of banks was amended to permit the taking of chattel mortgages and other durable goods. In the event of default, the lender could repossess the car from the borrower and sell it to recover the unpaid debt. This power already existed for other lending institutions, as we shall see, but not for banks.

The second step in the "skip" was the legal confirmation of consumer lending made necessary by the "jump"—the removal of the 6 percent ceiling on bank lending rates in 1967. In reality, the 6 percent ceiling had already been breached for two decades, but the clear legal power for consumer lending was somewhat in doubt until 1967.

After the Second World War, the demand for automobiles was even more urgent than the demand for housing. As soon as manufacturing capacity could be converted back to peacetime use, domestic sales of cars jumped from zero in 1945 to 150,000 in 1948 and then to more than 300,000 a year in the early 1950s. The average price of a new car in the early 1950s was about $2,500. This required financing of about $750 million a year, either in down payments or in consumer credit. Institutions available to provide automobile financing were dominated by the sales finance companies, which were completely unregulated financial institutions (apart from ordinary company law). The sales finance companies consisted of the "captive" companies, such as General Motors Acceptance, owned by the big three automotive manufacturers; the Canadian subsidiaries of large U.S. consumer credit corporations, such as Canadian Acceptance and Commercial Credit; and a few Canadian-owned sales finance companies, such as Industrial Acceptance which eventually became the Continental Bank.

Besides the sales finance companies, there were consumer loan companies such as Household Finance. These companies were regulated under the Small Loan Companies Act, and their lending rates were subject to ceilings which were changed from time to time. In the late 1950s, they could charge 2 percent a month on amounts up to $300, 1 percent a month on amounts from $300 to $1,000, half a percent a month up to $1,500, and beyond $1,500 they were unregulated. Later, the (Porter) Royal Commission on Banking and Finance in 1964 reported that they charged 1.5 percent a month or 18 percent a year for loans exceeding $1,500. The consumer loan companies did some automotive financing, but most of their lending was for personal loans below $1,000.

The typical consumer would arrange financing at an automotive dealership, where the rate of interest usually ranged between 13.5 percent and 16 percent a year, mostly at the upper end. For used cars, rates were higher. Given the 6 percent ceiling on bank lending rates, the sales finance and consumer loan companies could borrow from a bank at 6 percent and lend at 13.5 to 24 percent. The financing arms of the automotive manufacturers were probably a great deal more profitable than the manufacturing business. Some automobile dealers, who were strong enough to bargain with the manufacturers, made personal fortunes by taking a cut of up to 20 percent of the consumer credit interest spread. Thus the 6 percent ceiling on bank interest rates created a situation which was a bonanza for some and an unnecessary burden on the consumer. The banks became very restless with this situation, and political pressure started to build towards a change.

The first breakthrough was a small but critical amendment to the Bank Act in 1954 which gave banks the power to take a chattel mortgage. The amendment was the accomplishment of one bank, and more particularly of one man in that bank, Neil John McKinnon, the general manager of the Canadian Bank of Commerce, and later its chief executive. McKinnon presented "A Brief on Personal Loans" to the banking committee in 1954. He noted that the Bank of Commerce had been operating its personal loan scheme since June 1936, and had made no secret of it. Indeed, evidence had been presented to the banking committee in 1938; the Commerce had, as we have noted earlier, attempted without success to interest the Canadian Bankers' Association, in 1944, in lobbying for a "discount" rate of interest. McKinnon explained to the committee that a borrower under the bank's personal loan plan was required to pay equal monthly instalments into a savings account, which earned the going rate of interest, at that time 2 percent. In effect, this raised the effective rate of interest from 6 percent to 10.46 percent. McKinnon said that the bank had obtained a legal opinion that its interpretation of the Bank Act was valid, and that no one had ever challenged its "discount" method of charging interest.

His brief led to a lengthy discussion at the banking committee hearings, and McKinnon was invited to come back with a proposed amendment to the act. He returned with a draft amendment authorizing chattel mortgages, and also allowing the bank to charge up to 12 percent interest, which he thought was not unreasonable, compared to the 23 percent rate he reckoned the small loan companies were receiving. But it is clear from his testimony that McKinnon was looking at personal loans in the context of the Small Loans Act; in fact he proposed a limit of $3,500 on such loans if provided by a bank, compared to the regulated limit of $1,500 under the Small Loans Act. "We certainly have no intention of going into the automobile finance business, because that is a highly specialized field and demands higher rates than we are suggesting now."

After lengthy questioning by the committee members, McKinnon got support where it counted. Speaking of the Commerce's effective rate of interest of 10.46 percent, the chairman, David Croll, said, "After eighteen years it has become an established practice. For all intents and purposes I think we ought to consider their present method of doing business is within the law." This was supported by Clayton Elderkin, the Inspector General, who said, "The bank does not charge more than Section 91 permits, because Section 91 says that they may charge a rate of discount of 6 percent." Colin Cameron asked him if, in his view, the legal opinion was unassailable. Elderkin replied, "It was accepted when I came on this staff."

The sales finance companies did not go in front of the banking committee to challenge McKinnon. As the Porter Commission observed later on, they did not disclose their rates of interest to the public, and were probably not anxious to have a public debate on the subject.

The banking committee gave McKinnon his amendment on chattel mortgages, but did not comment on the 6 percent interest ceiling. However, by allowing McKinnon's testimony on his discount rate of interest to stand, the committee and the government had in fact given tacit authority to this breach of the 6 percent ceiling.

In the literature on banking, the importance of McKinnon's achievement has been overlooked. Most of the banking texts refer to the chattel mortgage power, but without noting that it was a fundamental change, because it revolutionized the financing of consumer goods in Canada.

When McKinnon gave his testimony to the banking committee in 1954, the Bank of Commerce personal loan plan had about $27 million outstanding. This was less than 10 percent of the personal loans for consumer credit purposes which the chartered banks together had outstanding, but the rest of the industry's loans were made under the 6 percent ceiling rate. They also represented about 1 percent of all consumer credit outstanding at the time, and also about 1 percent of the total Canadian loans of the Commerce.

In the next few years, automobile sales climbed to almost 400,000 a year, and the sales finance companies boomed. But the significance of Neil John McKinnon's encounter with the banking committee was not lost on the newly appointed general manager of the Bank of Nova Scotia, F. William Nicks. (Bill Nicks was a strange combination of conventional banker and maverick. He wore blue felt shoes with his double-breasted suits, and often ate lunch in the ladies' dining room of the National Club. He avoided the normal network of social contacts on Bay Street, and his large stone house, known to the Rosedale neighbours as "Fort Nicks," was closed to all visitors, including bank staff.) Nicks concluded that McKinnon was wrong in thinking that automobile financing was not feasible at 10.5 percent. In any event, he was more than anxious to get one-up on his competitor across the street, whom he detested. But it was not until the eve of his appointment as president and chief executive officer, towards the end of 1958, that Nicks was strong enough in the bank to launch his automotive finance scheme called Scotia Plan Loans.

With the enthusiastic help of the bank's comptroller, Harry Randall, he assembled a small task force and launched his revolutionary project. What made it different from the original Commerce plan was that he introduced the culture of the sales finance companies to banking, and aimed directly at the conditional sales contract business which was their mainstay. (A conditional sales contract is one which requires the borrower to pay principal and interest or else lose possession of the vehicle.) He hired a sales finance professional named Bill Dixon, who in turn hired almost a hundred sales finance company officers in a single year.

When Bill Nicks launched Scotia Plan in October 1958, I had been supervisor of investments in the bank for about two years, and was responsible for the bank's total investment portfolio including the money market operations. When Harry Randall instructed me to raise $100 million in fiscal 1959, I scoffed; it seemed to me inconceivable that we could need more than $10 million or $20 million in the first year. As it turned out, we needed more than $100 million, and the annual report for 1959 shows that I had to liquidate $93 million of the bank's portfolio of government securities. At the time, that was about one-third of the bank's total holdings. I gulped, not realizing that the days of a comfortable cushion of liquidity in the banking system were on their way out.

Scotia Plan loans provided devastating competition for the sales finance companies. With a rate of interest at about 10.5 percent, compared to about 16 percent from the sales finance companies, the public was not slow to catch on. Within a short time, the bank had to place Scotia Plan loan officers in most branches; they worked alongside, but largely independent of, the conventional lending officers in the bank, and were looked upon with suspicion for several years.

Other banks rolled their eyes in disbelief at the antics of the Bank of Nova Scotia. As for the sales finance companies, they were not amused. The presidents of Traders' Finance and Industrial Acceptance made a joint call on Bill Nicks, and told him that if he did not withdraw from the business, they would remove their accounts from the bank. He did not and they did. The figures in the Porter Commission report show what happened. By 1967, the share of consumer credit provided by the sales finance companies had declined from 23 percent to 13 percent, the share of the banks had gone from 16 percent to 36 percent.

By the time the 6 percent interest rate ceiling was removed in 1967, the banks already had almost $3 billion in consumer credit outstanding, of which probably two-thirds was for automobiles. The growth rate continued strongly, especially when some of the banks that had held off until the removal of the 6 percent ceiling joined the competition. By 1990, the banks accounted for 64 percent of consumer credit outstanding and the sales finance companies' share had declined to only 8 percent. There could not have been a more clear-cut case to show that removal of artificial barriers to competition was good for the economy.

For every cut of 1 percent in the consumer credit rate of interest, Canadian consumers as a whole were saving perhaps $30 million or more in the early 1960s, and the reduction in interest rates was probably closer to 5 percent or 6 percent. In addition, the delivery system was greatly improved. The banks had the widespread branch network to serve large numbers of people close to their place of work or their homes, and they developed the highly computerized systems that are taken for granted today. Coupled with their ability to finance residential mortgages, the banks had at last become full-service financial institutions for the average Canadian family.

... A TURBULENT INTERVAL BEFORE THE JUMP

The jump was the removal of the 6 percent ceiling on interest rates in the Bank Act revision of 1967. In the thirteen years between the "skip" and the "jump," there was a certain amount of turbulence. In the first half of this period, monetary policy was interventionist; the banks were frequently asked to conform to goals defined more by the Bank of Canada than by the government of the day. To an increasing extent, this was a consequence of the 6 percent ceiling, which prevented the banks from allowing market forces to determine the best allocation of their resources and which led to pressures for the rationing of credit to one sector or another.

A few months after the completion of the Bank Act revision of 1954, Graham Towers reached his twentieth anniversary as first governor of the Bank of Canada. In January 1955, James Coyne took over the reins of the bank as its second governor. Coyne had been recruited by Towers himself in 1938, when the Bank of Canada's economists met him in connection with the Turgeon Royal Commission on the grain trade. Coyne was a lawyer in an institution staffed mostly by economists, but this did not prevent him from having strong views on economic questions. (Subsequently, economic policy in Canada has tended to suffer when lawyers have been appointed to key economic portfolios.) Jim Coyne was handsome, brilliant, and aloof, someone totally outside the experience of the bankers. Donald Fleming, the Minister of Finance, later described him as "a rather dour person," while Peter Newman called him "an elegant patrician with rather strong ideas." Coyne brought a nationalistic and interventionist perspective to his job, together with a tendency to prefer dramatic solutions. His turbulent reign as governor of the bank ended with his dismissal by John Diefenbaker in July 1961.

Almost from the moment Jim Coyne took over as governor of the Bank of Canada, interest rates began a roller-coaster ride which eventually took the prime rate up to the legal ceiling of 6 percent by 1962. The interest rate on treasury bills climbed from about 1 percent in early 1955 to almost 4 percent in mid-1957, then plunged to 1 percent in mid-1958, followed by a very sharp climb to 5.5 percent in mid-1959. Coyne believed that there was a structural bias in the economy towards inflation which had to be stopped. Although he was responsible for monetary policy, he did not really believe that higher long-term interest rates had much effect on corporate capital investment. This may have had something to do with his bias against foreign investment in Canada, both in the form of lending and of direct equity investment. He felt that the provinces and municipalities were borrowing too much abroad, and that Canadians were inclined to live beyond their means.

The chartered banks were thrown almost immediately into a bewildering series of "agreements" with the Bank of Canada. One of Coyne's first demands was that the banks should call a halt to their headlong competition for corporate accounts, which had led them, he believed, to make excessive long-term loans and purchases of corporate securities.

Coyne also wanted to control the rapid growth of consumer credit. Since the sales finance companies were mostly the subsidiaries of large American parents, and came under provincial law, he could not control their expansion directly. So he asked the banks to provide him with statistics on their lines of credit to the sales finance companies and consumer loan companies. At first, the banks resisted, arguing that they could not disclose the affairs of their customers. After much discussion, it was agreed that the figures would be provided to the Inspector General of banks, W.E. Scott. Once he had obtained the aggregate figures, Coyne clamped down on the banks, asking them not to increase their lines of credit to these borrowers. This forced the banks to turn increasingly to the short-term money market, which was a major factor in the development of the wholesale market for commercial "paper" in Canada. (These are usually thirty- to ninety-day obligations of well-known corporate borrowers sold in large denominations through investment dealers.)

Coyne's next move, in late 1955, was to require the banks to keep a "secondary reserve" amounting to 7 percent of their deposit liabilities in the form of treasury bills and of call loans to money-market dealers. This secondary reserve was on top of the primary reserve requirement, which, since the Bank Act revision of 1954, had amounted to 8 percent of Canadian dollar deposit liabilities plus cash on hand. By forcing the banks to build up their holdings of treasury bills to about 7 percent of deposits, Coyne in effect created a captive market for Government of Canada borrowing at an interest rate of about 2.5 percent at that time. It also put a damper on corporate lending, because the growth in deposits had to be used to buy treasury bills. There was a lengthy and irritable exchange of correspondence between Coyne and the CBA, since Coyne had publicly announced his requirement of a "minimum level of secondary reserves," whereas the banks insisted that they had only promised to "endeavour to reach the target level." Endeavour or not, the banks did reach the target, and it became embedded in their financial structure in the Bank Act amendments of 1967.

In March 1957, Jim Coyne made a new proposal which created an uproar in the banks, the media, and Parliament. In his annual report for 1956, which he embellished upon in a press conference on March 11, 1957, Coyne announced that he was asking the banks to segregate their savings deposits from the rest of their deposit business, and to invest all savings deposits in housing mortgages and longer-term securities of provinces and municipalities. He said that in other countries, the savings were segregated in specialized institutions like Building Societies in Great Britain, and Savings and Loans companies in the United States. If the balance sheets of the banks were segregated in this way, there would be a steadier flow of money for housing and other long-term purposes.

Clearly, Coyne was going beyond the mandate of the Bank of Canada, which is to ensure monetary stability, both internally and externally. He was venturing even further into social policy than he had with his new set of rules on consumer credit and on secondary reserves. There was a huge outcry in the press. Fraser Robertson, the veteran financial writer on the *Globe and Mail*, said, "The Bank of Canada has called on Canada's nine chartered banks to accept a radical program of socialization of their assets." He quoted one banker as saying, "This plan makes the chartered banks the office boys for Ottawa." The next day, Robertson's byline column opened:

> One! Two! Three! Four! Hup! Fall into line there, comrades
> . . . You will learn the fatality of bourgeois attempts to
> sabotage the Bank of Canada.

This rather hysterical view of Coyne's proposals appeared alongside a more judicious analysis by E.P. Neufeld, at that time a young economist at the University of Toronto. Neufeld wrote, "To require the banks to hold specific types of assets against their two kinds of deposits implies a preconceived notion as to what constitutes a desirable distribution of money capital. The more detailed the asset holding requirements are, the greater is the degree of arbitrary allocation of capital."

In Montreal, where Coyne was scheduled to meet the Canadian Bankers' Association on March 14, James Muir, now the chairman and president of the Royal Bank, said, "There was a good deal of shooting before the target was even in sight." He tried to dampen the alarmist stories in the press by saying that the talks were only exploratory. After the meeting, Bill Nicks, now the president of the CBA, announced that the banks had agreed to allocate $150 million to housing in 1957. The Bank of Canada issued a statement confirming that the specific agreement "does not imply either concurrence or disagreement by any bank with the longer run proposals outlined in the annual report." The $150 million agreement was worthy of a two-inch banner headline on the front page of the *Globe and Mail*.

The general perception was that the governor of the Bank of Canada had overstepped his mandate and was dictating social policy. Gordon Ball, the president of the Bank of Montreal, publicly urged the Minister of Finance, Walter Harris, to say that there would be "no fundamental changes in the Canadian banking structure without the fullest possible investigation." The issue was pursued in the House of Commons the very next day, and the Minister of Finance made a statement that the government was not planning any legislation that would segregate savings deposits for housing and long-term investments without a full discussion in the banking committee.

Another initiative of the Coyne era was the "floating bank rate." The "bank rate" is the rate of interest charged by the Bank of Canada to the chartered banks when the latter have to borrow from the central bank in order to meet their legal cash reserve requirement. Although it has a real bite, because it is meant to penalize the borrowing bank, its use has been more as a signal than as an effective rate of interest. This is because banks are supposed to stay within the legal cash reserve requirement without having to borrow from the central bank. However, when the Bank of Canada wants to fly a flag to tell the fleet to change direction, it increases or decreases the bank rate. But on November 1, 1956, the central bank announced that henceforth the bank rate would be set weekly at 0.25 percent above the rate of interest determined on the regular weekly auction of treasury bills. At the time, this was interpreted by many economists as an attempt by the central bank to avoid public responsibility for tight money. Since the general public, then as now, had very little notion of the tools of monetary policy, the blame could be more easily fixed on the chartered banks. However, after thirty years of weekly announcements of the treasury bill rate, and consequently of the bank rate, the public has come to understand in a vague sort of way that, at least in the short run, interest rates are heavily influenced by the actions of the Bank of Canada.

COYNE'S GREAT CONVERSION LOAN

One day in July 1958, Bill Nicks called me into his office and said, "Go home and get your pyjamas and toothbrush. You are going to

Ottawa on the 3:00 Trans-Canada flight. Mr. Coyne is sending over the ticket from the Bank of Canada agency, and you are to say nothing to anyone about this."

When I got to the airport, I found myself with a small group of bond dealers and bankers who were considered to be experts in the recently developed money market and in the management of large bond portfolios. These included Ted Avison of the Commerce, Bill Robson of A.E. Ames, Harold Cameron, a bond dealer, and David Howes of Harris & Partners. When we reached Ottawa, we were all herded into a fourth-floor room at the Bank of Canada, where we met our Montreal colleagues. The RCMP guarded the doors, and a Commissioner of Oaths administered the rites of secrecy. Thereupon the doors opened and the Minister of Finance, Donald Fleming, and Jim Coyne marched in. The governor announced that the purpose of the meeting was to get the endorsement of those assembled for a massive conversion of the national debt from the existing Victory Loan bonds into new longer-term bond issues.

The scheme was presented as a great patriotic enterprise, which required the endorsement of the financial institutions and the expertise of the bond dealers to carry out. The purpose of the "Great Conversion" was to reduce the amount of government debt which had to be "rolled over" at short intervals, and thereby to increase the flexibility of the Bank of Canada. With his forceful personality, Coyne had been able to convince Diefenbaker and Fleming to go along with his grandiose scheme. In the meantime, the twenty-odd money market experts were held incommunicado in Ottawa to help the Bank of Canada carry out the plan.

After the meeting with Fleming and Coyne, we were herded into another room where there were two telephones, one for the Montreal visitors and one for Toronto. We were each allowed one call, under the watchful eye of a Mountie. Frank Case, my opposite in the Royal Bank, placed the first call to James Muir, his chief executive officer. The phone call went something like this: "I have to stay in Ottawa sir . . . no sir, I can't tell you the purpose . . . well, er, sir . . . we're under oath . . . no sir, I am not allowed . . . well, it will be a few days . . . I . . . know sir, I . . . there's nothing . . . I . . . " Frank hung up the phone, looking pale. "Well, what did he say?" we asked.

"He said, 'You're fired!' "

I gulped and picked up the phone to Toronto, expecting a similar response from Bill Nicks. It was similar, but he stopped short of firing me. Muir never fired Frank Case either, but neither did the Royal

Bank participate in the conversion loan. Donald Fleming, who had become Minister of Finance in the Diefenbaker government elected in June 1957, has given a detailed account of the conversion loan in his memoirs, published in 1985. Although Fleming kept detailed notes of his daily life in Ottawa, he was capable of great self-delusion, as Peter Newman and Peter Stursberg later wrote in their political histories of the Diefenbaker era. Fleming asserted that "the financial institutions reacted positively and enthusiastically to the plan." Not quite. The Royal Bank refused to go along with converting its short-term bonds into the new conversion bonds, and Muir persuaded Gordon Ball of the Bank of Montreal to stick with him. Fleming wrote that he received a telephone call from James Muir, in which Muir asserted that no employee of the Royal Bank could withhold information from its chief executive, and he would insist on Case telling him what was going on. Fleming replied to Muir that Frank Case was under oath until the conversion loan was announced in Ottawa the following Monday, and he threatened to prosecute Muir if he tried to force Case to break the oath of secrecy.

While it was true that some institutions and most bond dealers were enthusiastic about the conversion loan, there were some dissenters. One was Harold Cameron. Cameron, a self-educated native of Winnipeg and perhaps the most brilliant mind in the bond market at that time, refused to have his clients drawn into the conversion loan. Another dissenter was myself. After returning to Toronto, I persuaded Bill Nicks to minimize the bank's forced extension of the maturity dates of the bond portfolio, by negotiating trades with the Bank of Canada into other short-term bond maturities. I also wrote a critical attack on the conversion loan, which was later published as an appendix to Douglas Fullerton's book *The Bond Market in Canada.* Peter Newman referred to this book as "the best description of the Conversion Loan," but was unaware that the eyewitness account given in an appendix under the name of C.S. Mallory was written by me. (Given my job, I did not feel free to heap scorn on the conversion loan in my own name.)

Diefenbaker went on television to support the conversion loan, and asserted that the 4.5 percent rate on the 1983 maturity would set a level of interest rates to stand for many years to come. As it turned out, the famous 4.5 percent issue of 1983 never saw par value again. Only a year after the conversion loan was over, it was trading at about $83, which was getting close to a yield of 6 percent.

While the conversion loan was going on in July and August of

1958, the bond market was, in effect, frozen by the Bank of Canada. After the conversion loan was over, when most of the holders of government debt had been muscled into holding longer maturities than they would have voluntarily chosen, Jim Coyne started tightening up the money supply. The rate of interest on treasury bills went from about 1 percent in August 1958 to about 5.5 percent a year later.

The sharp tightening of credit conditions began to produce tension between Coyne and the Diefenbaker government. But this was not the first time that the central bank's policies had led to strain; the Conservatives had complained about tight money during the 1957 election campaign, and according to Fleming, Liberal leader Lester Pearson had exploited the situation for partisan advantage. In his annual report for 1957, published in early 1958, Coyne denied the existence of a policy of tight money. Fleming wrote, "the incident served to embitter my colleagues further against Coyne. Diefenbaker was convinced that Coyne was doing his utmost to sabotage us."

In late 1958 and into 1959 there were renewed concerns about tighter money. The political climate was not improved when Coyne embarked on a "series of precedent-shattering speeches," as Peter Newman wrote in 1963. In Calgary, Coyne asserted that Canada was living beyond its means. As Newman put it, "A study of this statement leaves the impression that he wanted to transform this country into an insular economy, ruled by a government with near dictatorial powers to retain business ownership in Canadian hands."

Fleming noted that Coyne's relations with the chartered banks were strained: "Complaints were frequent and unceasing that he was remote and uncooperative." But it was not only the politicians and bankers who were unhappy with Coyne; the academic community was increasingly restive with what they considered to be inappropriate monetary policy. On December 8, 1960, a letter written by professors Harry Eastman and Stefan Stykolt of the University of Toronto appeared in the *Globe and Mail*. The letter was supported by seventeen economists and was directed to the Minister of Finance, Donald Fleming. It said, "Recent public statements by the Governor of the Bank of Canada have seriously shaken our faith in the wisdom and competence of the Bank's management ... We address you then Minister, to ask that steps should be taken to alter the management of the Bank of Canada ... We plead that you should appreciate the gravity of this situation and that you should act without delay."

(On December 13, 1960, there was a long letter from Governor James Coyne in the *Globe and Mail*. But it was not a response to the open letter by the economists. It was a defence of the Checker cab which Coyne had bought for the Bank of Canada, and a plea for the production of a sensible Canadian-built car. By a strange coincidence, I happened to be making a call on Jim Coyne that very morning. It was extremely cold in Ottawa, and the Governor courteously offered me a ride back to the Chateau Laurier in the bank's car. I accepted, with curiosity, having seen the letter in that morning's paper. When the driver came around to the front door on Wellington Street, I got in, and to pass the time of day, asked the driver what sort of car this was.

"A Checker cab, sir."

"And how does the Governor like it?"

"Not too well. It's hard on his back.")

Later on, twenty-seven other university economists added their signatures to the open letter, and Professor H. Scott Gordon of Carleton University published a pamphlet entitled *The Economists Versus The Bank of Canada.*

Looking back at this episode from the perspective of the excesses of the 1980s, it is ironic that the professional economists of the day were so upset. The authors of the letter were my close personal friends, and many of the signatories were my contemporaries and peers. While I probably shared their views at the time, the profligate fiscal policies which Coyne opposed were minuscule compared to the excesses of the Trudeau and Mulroney eras. In 1960, real growth in the Canadian economy had stalled once more, as it had in 1957-58. There was very little inflation, but, as Gordon wrote in his pamphlet, "The Bank's present view is that we have one continuous, pervading, ever-present problem in Canada—the problem of inflation." He went on to say, "Not only have these movements in bank rate been extremely large, but they do not seem to make much sense from the economic standpoint. The changes in direction in the extent of the movements do not bear any relation to what has been going on in the economy . . . His [Coyne's] public speeches over the past year have been strongly worded, even stringent in tone; they have contained cries of alarm and urgent appeals to action and change . . . The Governor's picture of some of the most fundamental economic processes is, to say the least, peculiar . . . Mr. Coyne is proposing, in effect, that we close the Canadian economy off from the rest of the world."

In the early months of 1961, Donald Fleming asked Jim Coyne to stop making public speeches on matters of government policy. Coyne was unrepentant, even pounding the table at a meeting with the minister on one occasion. The Prime Minister and other cabinet ministers from the West began urging Fleming to get rid of the governor, even though his normal seven-year term of office was due to end in December 1961.

When Fleming sounded out the board of directors of the Bank of Canada, he discovered to his shock and horror (he said later) that on February 15, 1960, the board of directors of the Bank of Canada had voted a pension of $25,000 a year for life to Coyne, beginning with his coming retirement at the age of fifty-one. Later, there was a confused argument as to whether Fleming had been notified; unfortunately, Ken Taylor, the deputy minister of finance, had been absent from the meeting when the pension decision had been taken. His substitute, Wynne Plumptre, had not thought that the matter needed to be reported to the minister. Moreover, the board of directors had obtained a legal opinion that it did not have to seek the authority of the Privy Council to fix the pension policy of the bank, nor had it followed the normal practice of tabling the changes in the Canada Gazette. All of this enraged John Diefenbaker and his cabinet. The pension was half the governor's salary of $50,000, which exceeded that of the Prime Minister, which was then $37,000. (Diefenbaker later told Parliament that his predecessor, Louis St. Laurent, had retired on a pension of $3,000 a year.)

Relations between the governor and the government deteriorated, and a public furor ensued. Coyne refused to resign, even when asked to do so at a meeting of the board of the bank on June 12-13, 1961. The government then introduced a motion in the House of Commons declaring that the position of the governor was vacant. Despite pressure from the Liberal opposition to refer the bill to the House banking committee, Fleming was determined not to give Coyne a platform from which he could flog the government over economic policy. But the Senate, with its large Liberal majority, demonstrated that its meddlesome behaviour in 1990 was not without precedent. The Senate banking committee, chaired by A.K. Hugessen, invited Coyne to appear and in July 1961, the Canadian public was treated to the spectacle of a public attack on the government of the day by the governor of the Bank of Canada. Coyne issued a press release calling Diefenbaker an "evil genius" and accused him of "unbridled malice and vindictiveness." The Senate banking committee, under Hugessen, recommended rejection of the government's bill to the full Senate. But Coyne walked away from the Senate hearings to a public resignation and farewell on the steps of the Bank of Canada.

While the chartered banks were largely bystanders in what Peter

Newman called "the carnage of the Coyne affair," the effects of this sorry episode in Canadian financial history were far-reaching. The most immediate consequence was the promotion of Louis Rasminsky to the position of governor of the Bank of Canada. The second consequence was a review of the relationship between the government and the Bank of Canada. And the third consequence was the appointment of the Royal Commission on Banking and Finance.

In his memoirs, Donald Fleming wrote, "After I became Minister of Finance, I was given conflicting reports on why Coyne was appointed (as governor in late 1954) instead of Rasminsky. Ken Taylor, deputy minister of finance, told me St. Laurent had concluded that Quebec would not accept a Jew as Governor. From another source I was told that St. Laurent thought the chartered banks would not accept a Jew as Governor." Fleming says that Douglas Abbott, who had been Minister of Finance at the time, denied both stories, and said that "Coyne was in fact chosen by the Board of Directors and the government accepted their recommendation." Certainly there was anti-semitism in both banking and politics at the time, but whether it was a factor in the appointment, I was too junior to know. If so, it dates back to an earlier time, because Jim Coyne was appointed deputy governor of the Bank of Canada in 1949, succeeding Donald Gordon. Louis Rasminsky was executive assistant to the governors from 1946 until he became deputy governor when Coyne became governor on January 1, 1955. Thus Coyne had been superior in rank to Rasminsky for five years. After the fact, there was much regret that Rasminsky had not been governor all along, but in fact the succession had been established when Graham Towers was governor and Clifford Clark deputy minister of finance.

The Coyne affair naturally led to a review of the relationship between the government and the Bank of Canada. As we have seen, there was always a degree of ambiguity in the relationship from the very beginning of the central bank in 1935. There is a natural tendency for politicians to evade responsibility for tight money and high interest rates, which are never popular with the electorate. When times were easy, it was not hard for Ministers of Finance to accept responsibility.

Peter Newman has summarized a few examples. J.L. Ilsley, the wartime Minister of Finance, said, "The monetary policy which the bank carries out from time to time must be the government's policy." Douglas Abbott said, "The government, if it were not satisfied with the action taken by the Governor of the Bank of Canada, would have to change the management." But when monetary policy showed some signs of tightening up, Walter Harris as minister retreated from this position. Newman says that Fleming "scornfully accused the government of denying its responsibility for what the Bank of Canada was doing." But then Fleming himself said, "I trust that I am not to be held responsible for what is said by the Governor of the Bank of Canada." In our own day, to his credit, the Minister of Finance has accepted ultimate responsibility by supporting the governor of the Bank of Canada in a time of unpopular policies.

THE PORTER COMMISSION

The third consequence of the Coyne affair was the appointment of the Porter Commission on Banking and Finance. After the publication of the economists' letter in December 1960, Fleming made an informal proposal to cabinet to create a Royal Commission on Financial Legislation. He discussed the matter with Diefenbaker and made a formal proposal on February 2, 1961. The cabinet was reluctant to agree, mainly because there were already other royal commissions under way, but Fleming finally got permission to announce a Royal Commission on Banking and Finance in his budget speech of June 20, 1961. The Order-in-Council naming the commissioners was passed on October 18. The Royal Commission took its name from its chairman, Dana Porter, the Chief Justice of Ontario. There were six commissioners other than Porter, of whom several were among the best qualified in the country. They included W.A. Mackintosh, the vice-chancellor of Queen's, whom we have met earlier; Douglas Gibson, the general manager of the Bank of Nova Scotia and one of the most highly regarded economists in the country; Paul Leman, from Alcan Aluminium, whose father Beaudry Leman had been on the MacMillan Commission; and Tom Brown, a leading investment dealer in Vancouver and a very knowledgeable student of the financial system.

The commissioners gathered together a staff which was perhaps unequalled in quality in our long history of royal commissions. The secretary was Tony Hampson, who later became Chairman of Canada Development Corporation. The joint secretary was Gilles Mercure, later the president of the National Bank of Canada. The research director was Bill Hood, later deputy minister of finance and, in his last appointment, adviser to Simon Reisman on the free trade agreement. There was Bob Johnstone, later a deputy minister, then a consul general in New York and currently executive director of the Ontario Centre for International Business. The platoon of economists was almost a roll-call of the best in the country. They included Harry Johnson, the most distinguished Canadian academic economist of his generation; Grant Reuber, later the deputy minister of finance in the Joe Clark government of 1979, and subsequently president of the Bank of Montreal; Bill Kennett, later the Inspector General of Banks; Jack Young and John Helliwell and Ron Shearer from the University of British Columbia; and Jacques Parizeau, whose career took a different turn afterwards.

Small wonder, then, that after two and a half years, the Porter Commission produced a massive and distinguished report on banking and finance. By the time it appeared, the Diefenbaker government had been overthrown, and sixteen years of Liberal rule had begun. However, the immediate circumstances which gave rise to the Porter Commission were only a small part of the final report, except for the recommendations concerning the relationship between the Bank of Canada and the government. There had been no major review since the MacMillan Commission in 1933, and there were large parts of the financial system which had never been looked at before. Contemporary participants in the long-drawn-out process of financial reform should note with chagrin the difference between the published background work for current legislation and the quality of the Porter report. For one thing, the process has become much more politicized than it was in 1962-63; much of today's research is done behind closed doors in the civil service, and under the direction of political masters.

... AND A JUMP

In general, the Porter report recommended the removal of restrictions on the free flow of funds and advocated greater competition. The report proposed that all deposit-taking institutions be required to maintain cash reserves at the Bank of Canada, except for credit unions and caisses populaires, which would participate in this process only through their "centrals." It recommended a prohibition of interest-rate agreements between the banks and proposed to strengthen the office of the Inspector General of Banks. There were scores of other recommendations, but perhaps the most important one was the recommendation to remove the 6 percent ceiling on interest rates.

The government was thus provided with a comprehensive blueprint for the financial system, including the securities industry as well as the trust and loan companies and cooperatives. But the job had taken longer than intended, and the report of the Royal Commission was not released until April 24, 1964. Meanwhile, there had been two general elections, and at the second of these, on April 8, 1963, the Liberals under Lester Pearson achieved a plurality of 129 seats. There were ninety-five Conservatives, seventeen NDP and twenty-four Social Credit members, of whom most were Créditistes from northern Quebec.

As far as the implementation of the Porter report was concerned, the election of the Liberal government was a disaster, because it brought Walter L. Gordon to the Ministry of Finance. Walter Gordon had become a powerful figure in the Liberal party, and had chaired an earlier Royal Commission on Canada's economic prospects. Although he was the epitome of an establishment figure, he was in many ways hostile to establishment institutions, including the banks. He had become, and remained until the end of his life, one of the leading proponents of nationalism. According to Bruce Hutchison, "Mike Pearson had assured me that the Toronto magnate was the ablest economic brain in the country." This woefully misguided assessment of Walter Gordon was to cost the country dearly.

Gordon proved his economic ineptitude within a few weeks of taking office. In his first budget, he proposed tax measures to restrict foreign investment in Canada, without having thought through their market consequences. Financial markets took a plunge, and the budget had to be withdrawn. But it was more than two years before Pearson was finally persuaded to get rid of Walter Gordon as Minister of Finance.

Walter Gordon ignored the Porter report's principal recommendations to remove the 6 percent ceiling on interest rates and to extend federal control over the deposit-taking activities of non-bank institutions. His interest was primarily in the degree of foreign ownership of Canadian financial institutions.

Meanwhile, the Bank Act revision of 1964 had been delayed because of the tardy completion of the Porter Commission report. It was not until May 1965 that Walter Gordon introduced his version of amendments to the Bank Act. The disappointment of the banking industry was expressed by the president of the Canadian Bankers' Association, Sam Paton, general manager of the Toronto-Dominion Bank. In his presidential address to the CBA's annual meeting, Paton said, "most of the major recommendations of the Royal Commission are ignored." He deplored the fact that the government had failed to listen to the Porter Commission's proposal that "banking" be defined once and for all. The problem was (as it had been from the beginning) that "banking" had never been defined in law. The British North America Act said that the federal government had sole authority over banking, without saying what banking was. The Bank Act said that no one could use the name "bank" unless it was one of the institutions defined as a bank in a list at the back of the Act. In fact, trust and loan companies, credit unions and caisses populaires, and the Alberta Treasury Branches were all doing banking business. But they were not called banks, and therefore were not subject to the Bank Act. The solution for this problem proposed by the Porter Commission was that banking be defined as the taking of chequable deposits with an original term to maturity of not more than 100 days. This definition was designed to bring within the orbit of banking all sorts of short-term deposits, both personal and corporate, which were, in effect, elements in the country's means of payment.

Before Walter Gordon's Bank Act amendments could be dealt with by Parliament, he was forced to resign. He was replaced by Mitchell Sharp. There was another general election on November 8, 1965, but the results left the composition of Parliament almost unchanged. The Bank Act had to be extended twice more to keep the bank charters in existence, and in July 1966, Sharp introduced his version of the Bank Act amendments.

Sharp, who is still active in public service, had organized the Liberal party's Kingston Conference in 1961. I had known him since my brief stint working for him in the Department of Finance in 1947. He had invited me and Michael Mackenzie, now the Superintendent of Financial Institutions, to help him organize the Kingston Conference. Had Pearson understood that it was Sharp and not Walter Gordon who brought economic competence to the Liberal party, the direction of economic policy would have been somewhat different in the years 1963 to 1965. This was particularly true for the Porter report.

Sharp took the Porter Commission report more seriously than Gordon had; he proposed removing the 6 percent ceiling but, mindful of the fact that the Liberal government was in a minority position in the House, he introduced a condition in order to soften the opposition of the NDP and the Social Credit parties. The condition was that interest rates on government bonds would have to average less than 5 percent for a period of three consecutive months beginning after December 31, 1966. Even so, the *Toronto Star* charged that Mitchell Sharp "reverses the principles of liberalism. He is preparing to abandon protection for those people who most need to borrow money cheaply, in favour of higher profits for the money-lending community." The *Toronto Star*, which has always opposed bank profits while trying to maximize its own, was much closer to Walter Gordon than to Mitchell Sharp.

In October 1966, Mitchell Sharp's revised version of the Bank Act amendments finally got through second reading in Parliament. It was now about two and a half years since the Porter Commission report had been published, and the banks were increasingly unhappy with the impact of the 6 percent interest-rate ceiling on their business. In June 1966, Sam Paton, in his second CBA presidential address, said that "competing near-banks are offering interest rates on term deposits which are higher than the chartered banks can charge on commercial loans."

Meanwhile, the Canadian public was getting its first taste of financial company failures due to lack of regulation of the non-bank institutions. In 1965, Atlantic Acceptance failed and there was a royal commission established in Ontario to investigate its affairs. In 1966 a small company called Prudential Finance also failed and there were charges of theft and forgery. Buck-passing between the federal government and the government of Ontario in response to accusations of inadequate regulation got under way and has continued to provide almost unremitting entertainment to this day.

The House of Commons banking committee, by then called the Standing Committee on Finance, Trade and Economic Affairs, was chaired by Herb Gray. (Until recently he was the Liberal leader in the House of Commons. An odd footnote to history is that the only other active politician who was also on the finance committee at the time is Jean Chrétien. All twenty-three of the other members have retired from politics.) The committee met morning, afternoon, and evening from October 25, 1966, to February 23, 1967. In that time, the testimony piled up to more than 2,000 pages. Not all of it was fundamental to improved legislation. Some came from a bloc of nine garrulous Créditiste members from Quebec, headed by Réal Caouette. While this spin-off from the Social Credit philosophy had very little in common with the Alberta roots of the party, it had an unflagging zeal for pure Social Credit doctrine.

The CBA delegation was headed by Sam Paton of the Toronto-Dominion, with John Coleman, chief general manager of the Royal Bank, and Leo Lavoie, vice-president of the Provincial Bank. There was a support group of six or eight senior bankers, among whom I was the resident monetary theorist. Whenever the Créditiste members' turn came up in the twenty-minute rotation, Sam Paton motioned me in from the sidelines to give testimony. The minutes of the proceedings are pock-marked with interminable discussions between Gilles Grégoire and René Latulippe, the Créditiste experts, and myself; there were almost forty pages of testimony on the nature of money and of credit creation. These moments of comic relief provided a respite for the three CBA executive council members, whose principal concerns were the definition of banking and the removal of the 6 percent ceiling.

On the central issues before the committee there was not a lengthy discussion. Mitchell Sharp told the committee that the lawyers in the Department of Justice had been unable to produce a definition of banking which was practical. This left the door open to the many financial disasters which followed in the next twenty years.

As for the 6 percent ceiling, Sam Paton took one last crack at the "trigger" formula which would determine whether or not the ceiling came off. Under the formula, if Government of Canada short-term bonds averaged less than 5 percent for any three-month period beginning January 1, 1967, the ceiling would disappear on January 1, 1968. As it turned out, the critical interest rate averaged 5.16 percent in January and 4.96 percent in February of 1967. Thus the average for March would have to be no more than 4.87 percent for the trigger to fire. Throughout March I held my breath, knowing that the economy was starting to pick up and that short-term interest rates would soon have to rise. Comparatively few people understood that there was a desperate race to the wire, but the Bank of Canada and the Department of Finance knew it very well. Whether there was any digging of fingernails into wet palms I do not know, but in March 1967 the average rate of interest on bonds was 4.57 percent. The trigger went off, and the banking system was saved from a straitjacket which would have created a disaster. It had been 150 years since an interest ceiling had been introduced to the Canadian money-lending business. Sometimes it takes a while.

CHAPTER 10

THE GENDER SHIFT AND SOCIAL CHANGE

THE CLERICAL GHETTO

The banks have been mirrors of social change as Parliament amended their powers to reflect social and political conditions — like the household financing of houses and cars. But the banks have also been a mirror of change in the composition and role of their workforce. The most obvious example is the status of women; this, perhaps more than anything else, reflects the evolving nature of Canadian society and of the banks as a component of that society. The status of women is a high-priority issue, not only for women but for the community in general, and of course for the management of banks. For the past two decades, there has been increasing pressure for the more rapid advancement of women in the workforce, a pressure which is certain to continue. Contemporary observers, who often think that progress is still inadequate, might get some perspective from a glimpse at the past.

One of the first records of a woman being employed by a bank (the bank is not identified) was in 1887. Fourteen years later, there were only five women in that bank. In that year, 1901, the manager of an Ontario branch asked his head office if he should put a screen — "a good high one, too" — around his first female employee, to shut her off from the observation of the public.

In the early years of this century, the most junior bank employees were invariably assumed to be male. In 1905, a banker offered this stricture: "The bank clerk's future rests with himself. He may have to spend years of his life doing routine work, and he will begin his work on a small salary." Another writer said: "A young man, entering on life as a banker, puts in an apprenticeship as truly as the cabinet-maker."

These remarks were made at a time when the banks were flinging their branch networks across the country behind the building of the railways. The need was for young, adventurous, unmarried men who were willing to endure conditions in pioneer communities. It would have been inconceivable for young women to have been hired for such an enterprise. In fact, there was a good deal of grumbling that the rapid expansion of the banks was stretching their male resources to the limit. A banker named A.J.K. D'arcy wrote an essay titled "A Quarrel with the Youthfulness of Bankers": "The public in this country today have to be content to entrust their financial dealings to mere children ... a boy who should still be in school enters the service of a bank ... at a ridiculously early age, [he] is appointed to a position of ledger keeper ... following this advancement he finds himself handling large sums of money in a teller's box."

Another writer, J.P. Buschlen, in his autobiographical *A Canadian Bank Clerk*, wrote in 1913: "Banking isn't the same business it used to be at all. Salaries haven't kept up with the times. A bunch of junior men are now employed to fill posts that experienced clerks used to occupy. The bank makes a policy of recruiting—even going to Europe, where clerks think $5 is equal to a pound sterling—to keep down expenses." In a survey of the leading Toronto banks in 1912, he found that only 13 percent of the employees were over thirty years of age, and only 13 percent were married.

The standards of behaviour required of bank employees were detailed and oppressive. In an unpublished thesis by David Coombs, the author comments on the Rules and Regulations of the Bank of Nova Scotia, issued in 1902. (The other banks had similar rules.) He notes that inspectors visited branch offices and filled out lengthy reports on all officers. They carefully noted punctuality, neatness, penmanship, politeness, diligence, reliability and respectability. There was a ban on smoking in office hours, and employees under the age of twenty-one were prohibited from smoking at all. Rule 19 stated: "Officers in receipt of salaries less than $1,000 [everyone under the rank of manager and many managers too] must not marry under pain of dismissal, unless special permission is first obtained." (This rule remained on the books until the 1940s.) Rule 21 managed to cancel an employee's civil rights: "It is imperative that every officer shall abstain from active political partisanship; and no officer will be permitted to engage in or be a party to an electoral contest of any nature." By abstracting their employees from the political process, the banks established an environment of disenfranchisement and a tradition of non-involvement which had long-lasting implications for the evolution of banking legislation. But the chickens did not come home to roost until many years later.

The gender shift actually started before the First World War, but accelerated under wartime conditions. The Bank of Nova Scotia had twenty-eight female employees in 1911 (out of 626), and 283 in 1916 (out of 1,060). A sociological study by G.S. Lowe notes that the women were mostly stenographers and typists, but there were women in other clerical positions and even a few women tellers.

THE WARTIME SHIFT

When the First World War broke out in 1914, there was a huge drain of young bank employees into the armed forces. The resulting shortage of male staff forced the banks to extend both the number and content of jobs held by women, as noted by Barbara Hansen in her un-published paper "An Historical Study of Women in Canadian Bank-ing, from 1900-1975." She quotes a general circular from the general manager's office of the Bank of Nova Scotia to the branches: "We might just as well realize at once that the services of young women will have to be utilized for ledger-keepers, and at the smaller branches for tellers." In Quebec, not only was the status of a woman as a bank employee very limited, but even her legal status as a depositor was constrained. In the Journal of the CBA in 1917, a lawyer noted "The wife, acting alone, may make deposits up to $2,000 in certain savings banks, and up to $500 in other banks." This helped to ensure keeping her barefoot in the kitchen.

Even before the First World War came to an end, the women were wondering what would happen to their jobs after the war. An article in the CBA's journal of 1917 quoted a female banker: "One woman, who has the supervision of clerks all over the Dominion for an old estab-lished Canadian bank, predicts that with the return of peace scores of girls will joyfully lay down their pens and return to their homes." Another observer thought otherwise: "What is going to happen when the war has ended? . . . There is only a probability of even a small percentage of the women at present employed in the business world being withdrawn when the war is over." Another woman wrote, "Thousands of our men will never return . . . innumerable women—

still quite young—will face widowhood, many with families to support."

In fact, women did not withdraw from employment after the war, although they remained in the clerical ghetto. (The clerical ghetto was not peculiar to the banks. Lowe's study shows that in Manufacturers' Life in Toronto, all the female employees were clerks in 1911, and all except one—a registered nurse—were clerks in 1931.) In an article attempting to explain the impossibility of advancing women beyond clerical jobs, one banker wrote: "It is the prospect of matrimony which interferes with the woman's desire for promotion . . . The first thing we know . . . is that a girl who has shown a keen interest for several years in her work, and has given us reason to contemplate her advancement, becomes dreamy and preoccupied. Then we know that the end is near, and prepare to present her with silver or cut glass." He went on to say that "in most of the Canadian banks, however, the girl employee is given a salary equal to that of the young man doing the same work." This must be among the earliest references (1919) to pay equity in banking, but the author was not very enthusiastic about it. He noted that "the doctrine of equal pay for equal work fails to take into account just what the payment is for." What he meant by this is that the male banker had career possibilities, and that his salary took into account his future prospects as well as his current contribution. For that reason, he thought, a male should be paid more than a female for the same work. The circularity of this argument seems to have escaped him.

MALE MEDIOCRITY AFTER THE WAR

In the inter-war period, the percentage of female employees remained at about 20 to 25 percent of the total staff. Many of the younger men who had returned from the armed services had had enough of regimentation, and did not go back to the banks if they could help it. This fostered a natural environment for male mediocrity, supported by a layer of unpromotable (and therefore uncompetitive) female clerks in the lowest-paying jobs. But when the Depression came in the 1930s, bright young men in the small towns and cities of Canada flocked into the banks, because there was no other place to get a job. During the Second World War, this new generation of young men again departed for the armed forces, and again, many of those who survived never went back to the banks. And so the senior management of the banks after the Second World War consisted of those who had managed to make it through the system during two wars and a depression.

One of the great social consequences of the Second World War, insofar as banking was concerned, was the renewed acceleration in the number of women employed by banks. The change was a further gender shift, but still not a change in the management structure, which remained a male preserve, not only during the war, but for a considerable time afterwards. The gender shift provided the foundation for the rise of women in banking, a rise which is gathering speed but which still faces obstacles.

By the end of the Second World War, the attitude of the male bankers to the women employees was still one of patronizing condescension. Speaking of the wartime years, one manager wrote in an article entitled "Gentlemen — the Ladies" (which was supposed to be laudatory): "It was the young woman, thus recruited, who saved the situation. A mere bobby-soxer, she traded her stool at the soda fountain for one in the bank . . . many an office was staffed almost entirely by young women ranging from 16 to 21." The author went on to say that the young women had acquitted themselves very well, even though they had not received the years of training of the junior male clerks whom they replaced.

Long after the war, attitudes had not changed very much, and women were still confined largely to clerical positions. In 1953, one banker wrote: "With reference to mechanization, the operation of machines has tended to become the prerogative of the female staff due to temperament and a greater affinity for routine occupations." Whether or not greater manual dexterity is in fact a proven biological attribute of women, it has certainly been used in the past to justify a two-tier structure of employment.

In 1951, the Toronto Business and Professional Women's Club ran a series of lectures by women on their jobs in various kinds of business activity. The president of the club, Nazla Dane, who worked for the general counsel of the Life Insurance Officer's Association, wrote to the Canadian Bankers' Association to ask for a woman nominee to talk about banking. The response of the banks is indicative of the times. The Bank of Commerce said they had only one person, Miss Martin, but she was not really qualified in practical banking. The Bank of Nova Scotia had the same problem; although Dr. Lucy Morgan was manager of the economics department, she was not considered to have any practical experience. The Imperial Bank said that it had one person but would not push the matter. The candidates from the Bank of Montreal were thought to be qualified by their connections: one was a niece of the Right Honourable Arthur Meighen, and another was a receptionist in the main branch, but well regarded as the sister of a middle-ranking officer.

But the attitude of men towards the role of women in the banks was not much different from the attitude of society as a whole. In fact, the gender shift in banking was more pronounced than in the labour force generally. At the beginning of the twentieth century, female participation in the labour force was about 13 percent, and at that time it was close to zero in banking. By mid-century, the percentage of women in the labour force had risen to about 23 percent, of whom about one-third were in office work. In banking, the participation rate of women was over 50 percent.

CLIMBING OUT OF THE GHETTO

The rise of women above the clerical level began only in the 1950s and 1960s. The first stage in the climb out of the clerical ghetto was to the teller's position. This started before the First World War, but change came slowly; a female author, writing in 1957, noted: "Women now hold tellers' positions even in the first and second cages in the large city offices." In response to a questionnaire, one bank reported: "We have, for some time, been appointing women and a good number now hold the rank of accountant or assistant accountant." In the same year, the Bank of Montreal claimed credit for the first appointment of a woman "assistant to the manager." By that time, there was a scattering of women in head office staff positions. Dr. Lucy Morgan was manager of the economics department of the Bank of Nova Scotia in 1953, and my first boss in banking. The Canadian Bankers' Association, which now has a woman president and two (out of six) woman vice-presidents, then employed women as "secretaries, stenographers, bookkeepers and junior clerks." The first woman to be ranked as an "acting manager" was Mademoiselle Marie Jeanne LePage, in La Banque Provinciale in 1953. The Bank of Nova Scotia made the first official appointments of female managers in Ottawa and Toronto in 1961.

While the gender shift continued after the war, contrary to expectations, there was also a significant shift towards married women from single women. In 1948, two-thirds of the women in the labour force were single; by 1958 the percentage was less than 50 percent. In banking, the increasing presence of older, married women had profound implications for the lifestyle of bankers. Now there were new elements which the traditional male employee had not considered. He was always prepared to uproot the family on short notice and move on to the next town and a bigger job, because it was a systematic part of his training for advancement. His loyal wife was expected to pull the children out of school and start sewing a new set of drapes. In his climb into management ranks, the young banker could easily move half a dozen times.

But the role of women in banking and in the workforce generally was changing this traditional lifestyle. Mature women with children who were reaching the level of branch accountant or manager were less able to respond to the demands of mobility, because of their roots in the community. Just as likely, the banker's wife might have a job which she was unwilling to abandon for the sake of her husband's career move. And for single parents, mobility was difficult.

Within the last ten or fifteen years, the mobility problem has not been confined to women alone. With changing attitudes about the relationship between work and other values, many young men are now tending to resist transfers. The decline in mobility has had some beneficial consequences for the banks themselves. Quite apart from reducing the disruption of family life and education, the banks are benefiting from more stability in their relationship with customers. One of the strongest criticisms of the banks, especially from the small business community, has been the turnover of account managers, which removed the accumulation of knowledge and experience and trust between the banker and his customer. The frequent transfer of branch managers has undoubtedly had some counterproductive aspects for the banks. Hence the emergence of women as branch managers has had a business benefit, even though the decline in mobility has probably been mainly a response to pressure from men.

THE DECLINE OF REGIMENTATION

The changing status of women in banking during the past twenty or thirty years has to be seen in the wider context of the changing role of the banks in society. As we have seen, the banks were hindered by excessive regulation, especially the 6 percent ceiling on interest rates. While this had not been a problem until the mid-1950s, it then became a significant constraint on freedom and on profitability. Until the mid-1960s, it was unheard-of for the children of the upper and upper-middle classes to seek employment in the chartered banks. The graduates of private schools like Upper Canada College flocked into the brokerage business, but rarely into the banks. On Bay Street and St. James Street there was a huge gap in the social status and incomes of brokers and bankers. The bankers were overwhelmingly young men with so-so high school educations from the small towns and cities of Canada who were prepared to accept a relatively low-paying bureaucratic environment. But the rising population of postwar university graduates was scornful of this working environment, and never went near it. And so the gap between the educational attainments of the bankers and their corporate customers increased.

The legislative amendments which released the banks from their straitjacket of controls—so that jobs became more interesting and better paid—gradually changed the social structure of the banks. When I joined the Bank of Nova Scotia in 1953 with three university degrees, there was only one officer with a university degree among the top forty, except for the professional economists. From small beginnings in the 1950s and 1960s, the employment of university graduates has revolutionized the management structure of the banks.

The changing status of women has to be seen in this wider context of social change. Nowadays the chartered banks compete with other employers for the women graduates of the business schools and law faculties. University graduates, both male and female, tend to work in head office jobs or in large branches. But the banks are decentralized organizations with thousands of branches, usually managed by employees with high school educations and the traditional banking qualities of integrity and a capacity for hard work. Raising the educational qualifications of this large group of employees—about 150,000 of them—has been a major challenge in the last two decades.

In September 1970, the report of the Royal Commission on the Status of Women, which had been appointed in February 1967, was published. It pointed out that there were already in place the Female Employees Equal Pay Act and the Fair Employment Practices Act, both applicable to the banks. It recommended that the government introduce mandatory maternity leave and equality of opportunity. Its recommendations focused on the need to include women in management-training programs and called for an end to the practice of requiring a long period of employment before a woman was considered to be a career person. These recommendations were based primarily on the study of employment in banking by Marianne Bossen, which had been funded as part of the Royal Commission's research program. She found that there were twenty-nine women bank managers in 1969 (the first two women managers had been appointed in 1961). In 1975, when Marianne Bossen took another sounding, she found that there were 186 female branch managers. In 1991, there are something like 1,000. During the 1980s, the banks changed their internal management structures enormously, so that the traditional functions of a branch manager are no longer easily defined.

THE IMPORTANCE OF CONTINUING EDUCATION

In 1967, when the government appointed the Royal Commission on the Status of Women, the banks created the Institute of Canadian Bankers (ICB) as the educational arm of the industry. The institute conducts the largest program of continuing education sponsored by any private industry in Canada. When it was founded (I was its first chairman), only 7.3 percent of the banking students enrolled in it were female—330 out of 4,535. In the 1989-90 academic year, there were about 11,000 bankers in the program, of whom 72.5 percent were women. The course requirements are aimed at upgrading the education of the majority of employees who started work without any post-secondary education. The percentage of women in the institute's program is now exactly equal to the percentage of women employees in the industry.

But the program is barely 10 percent of what the banks spend on education and training, which in 1990 amounted to $180 million. The cost of on-the-job training and continuing education in the banking industry far exceeds that of any other industry in Canada. This is a major factor in accounting for the rapid shift in the relative number of men and women at the middle-management level.

The range of jobs in banks is so great that the traditional classification structure—ledger keeper, teller, accountant, manager, superintendent, general manager, has disappeared. The banks employ more than 25,000 people in computer systems, in jobs which did not exist in 1965. Many of these people are university-educated, some of them with post-graduate degrees in computer science, engineering or business management. There are about 15,000 professionals in the banks, including economists, lawyers, chartered accountants, business-management specialists of all kinds, foreign-exchange traders, money managers, and many others. The job classification system is necessarily complex and wide ranging, and totally lacking in gender bias.

Since job titles are no longer a measure of the changing status of women in banking, it is more useful to look at the information which is required to be published under the Employment Equity Act. This Act became effective in 1986, and applies to more than 600,000 employees who are subject to federal legislation in banking, transportation and other federally regulated activities. (So far, the federal government has not seen fit to apply this law to its own employees, except for those in Crown corporations. There is a vigorous affirmative-action program within the federal public service, but there is no published data comparable to that available for banks. Nor is the government required to publish annual data, as are federally regulated employers. Among the provinces, only Ontario has comparable employment equity legislation.)

There are about 14 million people in the Canadian labour force, and the Employment Equity Act applies to only about 5 percent of them. Some of the federally regulated industries, such as railway transportation and grain handling, are still largely male-dominated occupations, so that the 100,000 women employed by the big six banks represent about half of all women for whom detailed reporting statistics are required in Canada.

At the end of 1989, about 26,000 women were classified as "middle or other managers, or professionals." Only ninety women were "upper-level managers," constituting about 6 percent of upper management in the banks. But this high-level group numbered only twenty-seven in 1987, so that women are in fact rapidly moving into upper-level management. There are also about 26,000 men in the ranks of middle managers and professionals, demonstrating the profound change in the composition of the banks' labour force. The numbers of men and women in the middle-management and professional group from whom the senior executives are drawn are just about equal in number. For any employee, male or female, to reach a level such as senior vice-president, requires work experience of at least twenty to twenty-five years. The representation of women in the highest ranks is therefore, at least in part, a reflection of the age profile of employees; there are few senior executives under forty-five years of age, and the majority of middle-management women are younger than that. Nevertheless top-level bankers are concerned that a "glass ceiling" which limits the advancement of women to the upper echelons is perceived by women to still exist. They have recently commissioned a study at the University of Western Ontario to examine this question.

Since the federal government is not required to observe the same reporting standards which it imposes on federally regulated companies, it is difficult to compare the changing status of women in the public service with what is going on in the banks. However, a recently published study by a task force on barriers to women in the federal public service, titled *Beneath the Veneer*, gives some clues. In 1988, there were 502 women in the federal public service who were classified as "executive" or "senior management." The minimum pay for this upper management group was $56,200, and women constituted 11.7 percent of all employees in these categories. In the same year, there were 1,127 women in banks whose salaries were $50,000 or more, and they constituted 16.9 percent of all employees.

EMPLOYMENT EQUITY AND PAY EQUITY

The status of women in banking has been changing at least as rapidly as in the surrounding society. Since the federal Employment Equity Act requires the publication of detailed statistics on the employees of federally regulated employers, there is a wealth of material which can be used to flog those employers for their failure to advance women rapidly enough. For the other 95 percent of the labour force who are not subject to this level of disclosure, there is less opportunity to be judgemental about the degree of change, or lack of it. Even if the federal government amended the Employment Equity Act to publish data on its own employees as well as those of the Crown corporations, there would still be statistical reports on the status of women for less than 10 percent of the labour force.

Statistics are one thing—attitudes are another. It would be hard to argue that patronizing condescension is no longer common in banking as elsewhere. Social change is an evolutionary process, which only shifts gradually with the transfer of power from one generation to another. One has to look at the composition of the law schools and the business schools to see the shape of the future.

Employment equity has to do with equal opportunity. Pay equity has to do with equal pay for work of equal value. The big six banks have had pay-equity programs in place for at least twenty-five years. In the 1960s, I was a member of a job evaluation committee for the Bank of Nova Scotia. The committee's mission was to evaluate the content of all jobs in the bank up to the level of assistant general manager. With the help of professional personnel consultants, the committee sat for more than two years. Job evaluation is an art and a science, and there is a significant element of subjective judgement. What this means is that a committee is likely to have a protracted discussion with sharp differences of opinion as to the relative value of a specific function. How does one compare the work of a foreign-exchange trader with that of a branch manager? (How does one fix fairly the point score for a hospital orderly versus a nurse versus a doctor?) Personnel firms which specialize in job evaluation have developed elaborate procedures for measuring the parameters of a job. The four general criteria considered are skill, effort, responsibility, and working conditions. One dimension is the number of people under supervision; another is the extent of education or professional skill required to perform the function; another is the level of individual initiative and authority required. There are many other elements involved in job evaluation, but all of them can be reduced to a point score which forms the basis for salary administration. The possibility of inequities always exists, because judgement is required. But the process is supposed to be gender-neutral, and intended to put everyone on an equal footing. Nearly all large employers in Canada, including the banks, have such a process in place, so that pay equity is the intended norm in large Canadian business enterprises. Whether it is fully realized in practice is less certain.

Pay equity means that a woman is paid on exactly the same wage or salary scale as a man for a job of equal value. What it does not mean is that the average pay of women is equal to the average pay of men. The failure to make this distinction is often a source of great confusion in the media. In 1989, the average pay of all male employees of banks was $45,000, and the average pay of all women was $25,600. The largest number of women was in the $17,500 to $25,000 range whereas the largest number of male employees was in the $40,000 to $70,000 range. Pay equity does not mean that the weightings of men and women will be equally distributed along the salary scale; pay equity means that the salary scale is the same for men and women in the same job category. Over time, the profile of jobs occupied by women will shift upwards as the impact of employment equity programs continues. But pay equity has been in place in the banks for a long time.

WOMEN BANK DIRECTORS

The advancement of women in bank management does not satisfy those who believe that the key measure of the status of women is found at the level of the board of directors. At present, there are fifteen women on the boards of the big six banks, out of about 222 directors of whom about 23 are the internal top management. The percentage of female directors is about 7 percent, almost the same as the percentage of senior management who are women.

Fifty years ago, it would not have occurred to banks to have women on the board of directors any more than it would have occurred to the prime minister to have a woman in the cabinet. At the highest level, the appearance of women is the result of a cumulative social change over a considerable period of time. The highest-ranking women emerge in the same way that the highest-ranking men do (except that they have to jump higher and farther at every obstacle): an extended apprenticeship of education, business experience, hard work, luck, and whatever barriers lie across the course. Most women now reaching the top level in any part of society, including bank directorships, are in their forties and fifties and have had lengthy careers. Parachuting people into such positions is practical and feasible in politics, but in most jobs involving a business or professional hierarchy, parachute appointments are usually counterproductive.

Being on the board of a major bank certainly implies stature in the community, but it does not necessarily mean exercising influence. Some bank directors are influential in the affairs of a bank, and some are not. A committee of thirty-five people, by definition, does not make decisions. This applies not only to banks, but to tennis clubs, municipal councils, learned societies, or any other organization one cares to name. At present there are some very distinguished and capable women on the boards of Canadian banks, and they may or may not be influential. But the pool of resources from which women bank directors is drawn is still not very large, whatever impatient activists may say. Many professional women are not eligible for bank directorships; accountants are often prevented by their own professional rules from taking board seats and medical doctors are not suitable by training or inclination. It is far better to add gradually those women who can hold their own with the best of the male board members than to parachute in underqualified women who make it possible for men to say: "There, I told you so!" Having spent about three years in the process of building a consensus among the big six banks to hire a specific woman to succeed me in the presidency of the Canadian Bankers' Association, I think I know whereof I speak.

CHAPTER 11

THE POLITICS OF FOREIGN BANKS

EARLY FOREIGN BANKS IN CANADA

It seems surprising that the foreign presence in Canadian banking has been negligible until recently, compared with the significant—even dominant—degree of foreign investment in manufacturing and in the natural resource industries. Until 1964, there was no constraint on foreign banks entering Canada. Despite this complete freedom of entry, only one very small foreign bank—the Mercantile Bank of Canada—had been established when legislation on foreign banks in Canada was first passed in 1967. There had been some earlier endeavours, which we will examine briefly, but they had all been merged out of existence.

How can this be explained? Perhaps the history of our financial institutions might have gone differently if events in the United Kingdom and the United States had taken a different course. But after a strong initial thrust, British interest in Canadian banking declined and disappeared, only to be revived for a time in the 1920s. The American interest in Canadian banking was mostly in the form of investment capital in the earliest Canadian banks; there is not much evidence that U.S. banks attempted to buy into Canadian banks until the 1960s.

In 1836, a group of investors in London, England, decided to sponsor two new banks across the Atlantic, one in British North America, and the other in the British West Indies. In Merrill Denison's history of the Bank of Montreal, we read that the founders of the Bank of British North America (BBNA) perceived a business opportunity in Lower Canada because of "the high rate of interest there, the great difference of exchange with England, the rapid progress of immigration, and the increasing facility of communication . . . now averaging only twenty days on the homeward passage." They raised one million pounds for a "joint-stock" enterprise (that is, a limited liability company with widely held shares), a sum which exceeded the capital of all the Canadian banks put together at that time.

The Bank of British North America got off to a slow start in Montreal, where its first branch opening coincided with the rebellion in Lower Canada in 1837. But the bank persisted, and became known for the high quality of its staff, many of whom were imported from Scotland. After Confederation, the Bank of British North America was recognized under federal legislation, but it was not brought under the Bank Act until 1890. The BBNA was a major participant in western expansion, and was the first bank to open in British Columbia, in 1859.

Although the BBNA was a strong and successful bank, it was a casualty of the First World War. When the Canadian Lord Beaverbrook seemed to be making a play for control of the bank with a view to merging it with the Colonial Bank of the West Indies, the Bank of Montreal made a pre-emptive move in 1917 and bought the Bank of British North America from its shareholders. This gave the Bank of Montreal seventy-nine branches, and overnight gave it a major presence in the Prairie provinces (thirty-seven branches), where it had been slow to follow the Royal and the Commerce in their period of rapid western expansion.

The Bank of British Columbia was the only other significant British bank in the nineteenth century. It received a Royal Charter in 1862, when British Columbia was a colony centred on Victoria and the area around Vancouver and the lower Fraser Valley was still wilderness. Like the Bank of British North America, the Bank of British Columbia was a joint-stock venture with its head office in London. The creation of the bank was a response to the gold rush of 1858, and its position remained somewhat precarious even after the building of the Canadian Pacific Railway gave it access to the rest of Canada in 1886. The fortunes of its agencies in San Francisco, Seattle, and Portland were volatile, and after a U.S. recession in 1893, the London management acknowledged that "it is very difficult to control people who are 6,000 miles away from the office." There was some question after 1894 as to whether the Royal Charter would be renewed in 1901, and the owners decided to sell out to the Bank of Commerce in that year.

The third British banking venture in Canada was Barclays Bank of Canada, which was chartered in 1928. It opened its doors a month before the crash in 1929 with a distinguished board which included Sir Robert Borden, who had been the wartime Prime Minister, and Louis Taschereau, a long-time premier of Quebec. The unfortunate timing in opening just before the Depression of the 1930s and the Second World War made it difficult for the bank to become profitable. With no dividends coming in, and with British foreign exchange controls preventing the parent bank from putting more capital into its Canadian subsidiary, the British parent initiated a proposal in 1955 to do a share exchange with the Imperial Bank of Canada. The share exchange gave Barclays 10 percent of the Imperial; it appears that Barclays then proceeded to acquire a further 10 percent of the Imperial in the market. This alarmed the board of the Imperial, which sought refuge in a merger with the Commerce in 1961.

Twenty-five years later, in 1980, Barclays Bank decided to take another run at the Canadian banking scene. Barclays Canada now has more offices than any of the foreign bank subsidiaries excepting the Hongkong Bank of Canada and Bank of America (Canada). It also holds the unique distinction of being the only bank in Canada which has been twice licensed to do business.

Until the 1980s, the American presence in Canadian banking was insignificant. Considering the lack of any legislation preventing the acquisition or creation of a Canadian bank by American interests, this is astonishing. More than anything else, it can probably be attributed to the suppression of a national branch banking system in the United States by Congress in 1836, after years of pressure from President Andrew Jackson. The state-regulated banks in the United States were local and regional in character, and did not think in terms of extending their interests elsewhere. Even before Confederation, "the average size of Canadian banks was already much greater than that of American banks," Bray Hammond noted in his *Banks and Politics in America*. "By about 1857 or a little later, the Bank of Montreal was larger than any American bank and probably the largest and most powerful transactor in the New York money market."

But there were other factors. As we have seen in the first chapter, both the Bank of New Brunswick and the Bank of Montreal sought and obtained American share capital in order to open their doors for business. No shareholder could vote more than ten shares in the case of the former, and twenty in the case of the latter. As already observed, the founders of the Canadian banks wanted American capital but not their votes. The earliest bank charters were intended to keep control in the hands of the local establishment in Saint John and Montreal, and later in Halifax, Kingston, and York. The ruling oligarchies were conservative and British and not at all anxious to introduce republican ideas from south of the border. The Colonial Office and the Treasury in Whitehall would probably have discouraged the granting of a charter to any American interests. In any event, there are no recorded cases of American applications for Canadian bank charters.

In the first half of the twentieth century, there were only a few tentative attempts by American banks to get a foothold in Canada. We have seen that J.P. Morgan and its German connection, the Dresdner Bank, invested in the Sovereign Bank in 1907, and soon had to extricate itself from a situation involving dishonest management. Soon afterwards, the Royal Bank appears to have offered a block of minority stock to an American group of investors, but only with a view to raising some additional capital, not to surrender control.

THE MERCANTILE BANK AFFAIR

It was another half century before an American interest in Canadian banking revived. When it did, it led to a celebrated confrontation which became known as "The Mercantile Bank Affair." What emerged from this affair was a new formulation of the Canadian attitude towards foreign banking in Canada. But there was much more involved than the right of access to the Canadian banking business; the Mercantile Bank Affair was an expression of rising Canadian nationalism.

In 1953, the Government of Canada granted a bank charter for the creation of the Mercantile Bank of Canada, a wholly owned subsidiary of the National Handelsbank of Holland. As John Fayerweather wrote later in his thorough study, *The Mercantile Bank Affair*, "It was understood that the bank would specialize in the financing of foreign trade and would not be a significant factor in domestic banking." Without formulating a coherent policy towards foreign banking, the government had set in motion a train of events which eventually led to the licensing of many foreign bank subsidiaries, subject to some significant constraints.

The Mercantile Bank did not do very well, partly because its Canadian management was not shrewd enough to avoid taking over some marginal customers from the big banks, who were glad to foist off some of their doubtful accounts on the newcomer.

In 1960, the Rotterdamsche Bank took over the National Handelsbank, and not long after decided to divest itself of its Canadian stepchild. The successful bidder for the Mercantile was the First National City Bank of New York (Citibank), whose chairman was James Stillman Rockefeller. Under the driving leadership of its president, Walter Wriston, Citibank had embarked on an aggressive worldwide expansion. It was one of the leading banks in the recycling of OPEC oil dollars into loans to the less-developed countries of South America in the 1970s. Long before this tactic was found to be ill-advised, the aggressive American style of Citibank had forced the Canadian government to come to grips with its policy towards foreign banking.

Citibank's agent in Canada was Bob MacFadden, a jovial banker whose strength was public relations. MacFadden called on Louis Rasminsky, the governor of the Bank of Canada, on June 20, 1963, to inform him that Citibank was about to conclude an agreement to acquire Mercantile from the Dutch interests. According to Fayerweather, "the availability of the bank for sale was being openly discussed in banking circles for several months." In fact, an article had appeared in the *Toronto Star* in March, reporting that the Mercantile was on the block. But the stories had apparently not reached Ottawa, and Rasminsky was surprised at MacFadden's disclosure. He advised MacFadden to make his bank's intentions known to Walter Gordon, who had recently become Minister of Finance.

Many years later, in a taped interview with journalist Peter Stursberg, Rasminsky recalled the event: "The National City Bank has had a great deal of experience in foreign countries. They know the sensitivity of every country in the world, including the United States, toward foreign control of banking institutions. I think it was extraordinary that they should have gone as far as they did with the Dutch owners of the Mercantile Bank without making sure that the Canadian government had no objection to what they were doing." He remembers saying to MacFadden: "I don't think that you should proceed a step further without talking to the Minister of Finance." MacFadden asked him how he felt about the purchase of Mercantile and he replied: "Well I'm all in favour of competition, including competition in the banking industry, but I myself have some misgivings about it, and it wouldn't be fair to say that it would be all right so far as I'm concerned." What bothered the governor of the Bank of

Canada was that Citibank's New York management might ignore the sort of advice given to the chartered banks by the Bank of Canada which is called "moral suasion." He was concerned that Citibank might invoke U.S. anti-trust legislation as an excuse not to follow Canadian government policy.

The June 20 meeting was the beginning of a long game called: "Who said what to whom?" The takeover happened to run up against a Minister of Finance who was already on record as very anxious to reduce the American presence in Canada. Walter Gordon had chaired a Royal Commission on Canada's economic prospects, in which he had strongly recommended measures to limit foreign investment in Canada.

By the time Rockefeller and MacFadden were able to arrange to call on the Minister of Finance, on July 18, 1963, Citibank had already concluded in principle its deal with the Rotterdamsche Bank for the purchase of the Mercantile. Despite Rasminsky's recommendation of June 20, the purchase was presented to the Minister of Finance by Citibank as a *fait accompli*. Walter Gordon's response was that, since the deal had not closed, the takeover should not go ahead until the upcoming revision of the Bank Act could deal with the subject of foreign banking in general. His position was that Citibank was taking advantage of a loophole in the law which had made it possible for a major American bank to acquire a Canadian charter without Parliament having considered the matter.

Perhaps even more important—Walter Gordon thought—was the precedent which would be created; he feared a flood of applications from other United States banks which would not stand idly by watching their large New York competitor get an exclusive foothold in Canada. This assessment was not too far off the mark, as we shall see shortly.

Certainly the Canadian government would never have permitted one of the major banks to be taken over by a non-resident even if the Bank Act contained no prohibitive clause. In fact the same can be said of every industrialized country in the world. Within recent times, the Bank of England prevented the Hongkong and Shanghai Banking Corp. from acquiring the Royal Bank of Scotland, which was not even one of the big five "clearing banks" in the United Kingdom. While there have been some fairly significant acquisitions in the United States by Japanese and other interests (including that of the Harris Bank by the Bank of Montreal), it is unlikely that the United States government would permit the sale of one of its first-tier banks to foreign interests except possibly as a rescue operation. As far as Japan and the European countries are concerned, the idea of a foreign takeover of their major banks would be unthinkable. In general, the same applies to major national enterprises in the fields of transport and communications, in Canada and elsewhere.

Despite Walter Gordon's warning, Citibank went ahead with its purchase of Mercantile in September 1963. This set the stage for a showdown between Citibank and the Canadian government, but the confrontation was delayed for more than three years. In that interval, the Porter Commission report was published, the Chase Manhattan Bank made a move to acquire the Toronto-Dominion Bank, Walter Gordon lost the finance portfolio, and a revision of the Bank Act was finally brought before Parliament.

The Porter Commission tried to introduce the ideas of greater competition, less regulation, and more consistency in the application of federal law to deposit-taking institutions. Applying this principle to foreign banking, the Porter Commission recommended that foreign banks be allowed to establish themselves in Canada. Their words were: "We believe that foreign banks should be able to apply for the right to open agencies which would be free to conduct all facets of their business, other than the acceptance of deposits in Canada: this would be comparable to the position of agencies of foreign banks in New York. Such offices would be confined to the main financial centres and licences would be required."

The staff of the Porter Commission was well aware that the large Canadian banks had important agency offices in New York City which were allowed to do a wholesale banking business, but which could not take U.S. dollar deposits from U.S. residents. At that time, U.S. laws relating to the right of establishment by foreign banks were primarily state laws, and New York State would not grant full banking powers to banks from countries that did not offer reciprocal treatment to the New York banks. The overriding U.S. business interest of the Canadian banks was to have an office in New York City, where they could conduct large-scale operations in the New York money market and in corporate lending. Most of the big six Canadian banks also had offices in other states, such as California and Illinois; some of these were corporate subsidiaries or branches of the Canadian parent. Later on, in 1978, under the federal International Banking Act, the right of establishment of foreign banks in the United States was rationalized under one set of rules.

The question of reciprocity was critical to the treatment of foreign banks in Canada. The Canadian banks had established a presence in the U.S. banking market about a century before the Mercantile Affair, so they could hardly support a complete prohibition against any American banking presence in Canada. (The issue of banking reciprocity is far from completely resolved; as the European Community moves towards 1992, there will be issues of reciprocity on the table, as between the United States and Canada on the one hand and the EEC on the other.)

Although the Porter Commission responded to the reciprocity issue by recommending the licensing of foreign bank agencies in the larger cities, it also said: "We think a high degree of Canadian ownership of financial institutions is in itself healthy and desirable, and that the balance of advantage is against foreign control of Canadian banks." The report noted that there was no prohibition on the acquisition of part or all of Canadian banks' shares by foreign banks, and suggested that "this is an anomaly which should be corrected."

THE CHASE MANHATTAN AFFAIR

Walter Gordon was right about one thing. Soon after the public revelation of the Mercantile takeover, David Rockefeller, chairman of the Chase Manhattan Bank of New York, and Allen T. Lambert, chairman and chief executive officer of the Toronto-Dominion Bank, began discussing the feasibility of Chase buying into the Toronto-Dominion. Lambert was one of the leading figures in Canadian banking, but was concerned about the Toronto-Dominion's international competitive position. Chase Manhattan, like Citibank, was interested in broadening its international representation with a Canadian presence, and also wanted to protect its U.S. corporate business connections in Canada from Citibank. Discussions became quite serious, to the extent that Dick Thomson (then assistant to the president, now the chairman and chief executive officer of the Toronto-Dominion), was assigned by Lambert to explore the subject in depth. Thomson spent some time at the Chase head office in New York, and travelled across Canada with a Chase executive. As the discussions went on, however, it was evident that the Chase Manhattan camel wanted to get much more than its head into the tent: it wanted a controlling interest. Lambert and Thomson became concerned that the Chase intended to transfer control of the TD's Canadian corporate business to New York. From then on, the

Toronto-Dominion became more negative about foreign banks than the others of the big six.

The issue came to a head on September 22, 1964, when Walter Gordon announced in the House of Commons a new approach to the foreign ownership of financial institutions in Canada. The occasion was the introduction of amendments to the Insurance and Loan and Trust Companies acts. Gordon said that the government would limit a single non-resident shareholder to 10 percent of the voting shares in these companies, and the aggregate holdings of all non-resident shareholders would be limited to 25 percent in any one of them. At the same time, he announced that "similar provisions would be included in the Bank Act and made retroactive to that date." In this way the 10 percent–25 percent rule was introduced to Canadian financial legislation. But there was a critical difference between the amendments to the loan and trust and insurance legislation and the amendments to the Bank Act which came along a few months later. Almost as an afterthought, the 10 percent limitation on the percentage of voting stock that could be held by a single shareholder was extended, in the case of the banks, to residents of Canada as well. This critical difference became — and remains to this day — a major bone of contention in Canadian financial legislation.

Another critical element was that Walter Gordon's limitations on foreign ownership did not apply to provincially incorporated trust and loan companies, which the federal government did not control. Thus the stage was set for an acrimonious dialogue between the banks on the one hand and loan and trust companies on the other, and also between the federal and provincial governments.

Walter Gordon's stunning announcement put paid to the negotiations between the Toronto-Dominion and the Chase Manhattan banks. (The first published version of this abortive relationship appeared in Denis Smith's biography of Walter Gordon, *Gentle Patriot*, in 1973.) Later on, both Lester Pearson and Walter Gordon talked about the Chase Manhattan Affair in their memoirs. In the third volume of his memoirs, published in 1975, Pearson wrote the following account of what happened after the Gordon announcement of September 22, 1964:

> I remember receiving David Rockefeller at dinner one night at Sussex Drive. I had known him for many years, as well as other members of the family. David, a second or third cousin

of James, was also a banker, the head of the Chase Manhattan Bank. There were just the two of us at dinner that evening. He believed Canada was following a discriminatory, short-sighted, chauvinistic policy in the banking field. He pointed out that they had no trouble in their banking operations in other foreign countries. But here, with their best friends and closest neighbour, they could get nowhere. He was hoping to get some control and eventually, I suppose, total control of a Canadian bank, and had already taken certain steps in that direction. I replied: "Well, there is no use in your going any further. Don't make an issue out of this. We've already got one bank we're having trouble with." We had legislation pending to limit the percentage of non-Canadian ownership in banks. This would have put an end to all foreign efforts to get control of Canadian banks.

Walter Gordon's version of the same event was published in his *A Political Memoir* in 1977. He wrote:

Shortly afterwards, David Rockefeller of Chase Manhattan Bank came to see me in Ottawa. He was to have dinner with the Prime Minister, but came to my apartment for a drink and a talk ahead of time. I had met David Rockefeller on several occasions and knew of the close friendship between his father, the late John D. Rockefeller Jr., and the late W.L. Mackenzie King . . . Rockefeller reminded me that the Chase and the First National City Bank of New York are rivals; that Citibank had bought control of the Mercantile Bank of Canada; and that, if Citibank were coming into Canada, then it was important to him that the Chase should also be represented here. Rockefeller said that he had decided the best way for the Chase to accomplish this objective would be to acquire effective control of the Toronto-Dominion Bank . . . I pointed out that under the proposed legislation his bank would be entitled to acquire a 10 percent interest in the Toronto-Dominion Bank. He replied that this was not enough for his purposes; that he had concluded that anything less than a 20 percent interest would not give the Chase effective control over the management of the Toronto-Dominion Bank. He asked, therefore, if the Canadian government would not reconsider its decision in order that the Chase Manhattan might proceed with its objective. I explained to Mr.

Rockefeller that this was the very thing the proposed legislation was intended to prevent.

In 1980, Peter Stursberg, in his book *Lester Pearson and the American Dilemma*, commented, "Citibank's arrogant and aggressive attitude might be explained by the fact that it was the spearhead for a concerted attack on this country by the Rockefeller interests." There is, of course, no evidence for this absurd interpretation of the rivalry between Chase and Citibank. While Citibank's approach was perhaps "arrogant and aggressive" by Canadian standards, it was consistent with the American approach to public policy, that if an action is not specifically defined as illegal, then it is legal. In a sense, this cultural difference between the Canadian and American approaches to public policy was to surface again in the negotiations on free trade and in the Amex affair.

The Chase Manhattan Bank business probably stiffened the resolve of the Pearson cabinet to introduce restrictive legislation on foreign banking. In May 1965, Walter Gordon finally introduced his Bank Act revision proposals. But the sections dealing with foreign banking—sections 52 to 57—were already circulating in an unpublished version of the bill as early as November 1964. There was a special additional clause aimed at the Mercantile Bank. This clause provided for limiting the total liabilities of a bank to twenty times its shareholders' capital. Since the minister could himself refuse to authorize a larger share capital, the Mercantile was effectively limited to a size of $200 million, or twenty times its capital of $10 million. Although many politicians continued to obfuscate the issue for years, the restrictive clause was clearly retroactive legislation, aimed at the Mercantile alone. Citibank made a public protest against this discriminatory feature in the draft act, and there followed a long public controversy in which Walter Gordon said that he had warned Citibank of his intentions and Rasminsky reaffirmed that he had told MacFadden to clear his takeover proposal with the minister.

But the issue remained unresolved for two more years, mainly because Walter Gordon resigned as Minister of Finance in November 1965. He urged Pearson to call an election and establish a clear majority for a Liberal government in place of the shaky minority elected in 1963. The election gamble failed, and the Liberals gained only two more seats. Mitchell Sharp became Minister of Finance, and a lengthy power struggle ensued within the Liberal cabinet, with the nationalist and leftist Walter Gordon forces (including Allan

MacEachen, Judy LaMarsh, and Edgar Benson) lined up against the more moderate elements led by Mitchell Sharp and Robert Winters. Although Walter Gordon was out of the cabinet, his influence on the nationalist and leftist wing of the Liberal party continued. There was continued pressure on Mike Pearson from Keith Davey and others to restore him to the cabinet.

In the meantime, Gordon published a book in May 1966 titled *A Choice for Canada*. This poured gasoline on the flames of the controversy with Citibank, and the accusations became more acrimonious. The U.S. government handed the Canadian government notes of protest in April and November of 1966, the second of which was described by Canada's ambassador to Washington, Ed Ritchie, as "very rough." Despite the diplomatic pressure, the Canadian government held to its position, and in July 1966 Mitchell Sharp introduced his version of the Bank Act. The sections dealing with foreign banking were essentially unchanged from Walter Gordon's version. Mitchell Sharp said later, "I did accept Walter's restriction on foreign banks. I agreed with it, and I had no difficulty with this at all. Subsequently, we had real trouble over that because he wanted to go a step further at a later stage." Although the draft Bank Act still contained the clause that would freeze Mercantile's size until Citibank sold down to a 25 percent ownership position, Walter Gordon had hardened his position, and wanted Citibank forced to sell down to a 10 percent position. Mike Pearson had to arbitrate between Sharp and Gordon, and finally came down on Mitchell Sharp's side, after Sharp had manoeuvred to get the support of the finance committee.

FIREWORKS AT THE HOUSE COMMITTEE

In November 1966 the bill to amend the Bank Act finally got to the House of Commons Committee on Finance, Trade and Economic Affairs—three years overdue. The committee was chaired by Herb Gray, whose dislike of banks and bankers I was to encounter during the committee hearings and for many years afterwards. But in 1966-67, his attention was focused more on foreign banks than on Canadian ones. It was two months into the committee hearings, January 24, 1967, before the delegation from the First National City Bank of New York had a chance to defend the Mercantile takeover and protest the special section 75(2)(g) which limited its further growth.

As it happened, I was among the small group of bank observers who were present to witness one of the most dramatic sessions the finance committee has ever held. The Citibank delegation, which included James Stillman Rockefeller, Bob MacFadden, Stew Clifford, the president of the Mercantile, and the Mercantile's lawyers, had brought with them a number of public relations flacks. These people proceeded to hand out the Citibank's information package to everyone present, including the members of Parliament, just as the session got under way. Herb Gray spoke very sharply: "I have already given instructions to the representatives of our witnesses that nothing is to be distributed in a way that would interrupt our meeting." According to Fayerweather, "One official of a Canadian bank who was rather sympathetic to Mercantile observed that Rockefeller was visibly shaken by the Chairman's rebuke and that he never fully recovered his composure during the day."

Hostile questioning of the witnesses went on for six and a half hours, and the minutes show that no fewer than twenty members of Parliament managed to get the floor. (Ordinarily, only seven or eight members would attend a session.) Politicians, like the media, have a nose for confrontation and drama.

A week after the traumatic session of the finance committee with Citibank, Sam Paton was asked to give the position of the Canadian Bankers' Association on the subject of foreign banks. As president of the CBA, Paton had to say that on this issue the banks did not have an agreed position. Of all the issues which the banks had had to thrash out between themselves in order to have a consensus, this was one on which a compromise could not be reached. (Thirteen years later, in the Bank Act revision of 1980, the banks were still unable to agree on a common position on foreign banking.)

The vice-chairman of the committee, Ovide Laflamme, invited the individual banks to present their views. On balance, the position of the banks was somewhat ambiguous. John Coleman, speaking for the Royal, said: "What I think we need here is a study in depth." Gordon Sharwood of the Commerce said that his bank endorsed the view of the Porter Commission that there should be agencies, but that if the Canadian banks were set free to compete effectively, branches would be acceptable. Bill Hackett of the Bank of Montreal said, somewhat obscurely, that there should be limited reciprocal arrangements for foreign agencies of banks. The two francophone banks, the Provincial and the Nationale, represented by Leo Lavoie and René Leclerc respectively, agreed with the Royal that there should be further study and a separate act of Parliament. Sam Paton of the

Toronto-Dominion Bank pointed out that there was a serious problem about reciprocity with the United States, because the U.S. federal government did not choose to control the right of establishment of foreign banks. He was putting his finger on a problem which was to become critical when the free trade agreement was negotiated two decades later.

The most extensive statement on the issue was made by myself, because I was under instruction from the Bank of Nova Scotia's chief executive, Bill Nicks, to press the case for foreign banks. Nicks felt strongly—as did his successor Cedric Ritchie—that a restrictive Canadian policy on reciprocity would put at risk the Bank of Nova Scotia's operations abroad, especially in New York and London. As Fayerweather put it: "MacIntosh . . . was highly critical of a restrictive or nationalistic approach to treatment of foreign banks. He advocated an arrangement consistent with a prevailing Canadian open-economy policy of free movement of capital, goods and people." I went on to argue "that agencies did not provide a sufficient degree of reciprocity for some jurisdictions . . . the problem is not confined to the United States."

Oddly enough, the Canadian government never took much interest in the foreign operations of the Canadian banks, even though they were the equivalent of export industries. Walter Gordon dismissed the New York agencies of the Canadian banks out of hand as "inconsequential." (For an accountant whose firm—Clarkson Gordon—audited several Canadian banks, this demonstrates Gordon's extraordinary obtuseness.) The curious lack of concern with encouraging its own banking institutions abroad is in sharp contrast to the attitude of other governments about their banking enterprises. Washington's support for Citibank in the Mercantile Affair was only one small example of this.

The curtain came down on the foreign banking question when Mitchell Sharp appeared before the committee to sum up the government's position. He said that the question of licensing agencies of foreign banks would have to be studied, although he thought "that it would be desirable to wait a few months until there has been time for reflection." The few months turned out to be thirteen years. Sharp also said that he would not consider the establishment of branches of foreign banks, and, strangely enough, the possibility of incorporated subsidiaries of foreign banks was never discussed at all.

Underlying the concern about branches of foreign banks was the belief in Ottawa that branches would be difficult to control. The

Prime Minister put it this way: "We would not find it possible to agree that foreign banking concerns should be allowed to develop in Canada in a way where their policies could be determined by their head offices in a foreign country." In response to this point of view, I had said to the finance committee: "We do not think that there is, in fact, a serious problem with regard to compelling or persuading foreign banking institutions to observe domestic restraints. It is our view that any international bank would not behave in its own best interest and in fact, would behave in a most short-sighted way if it were to attempt to thwart the wishes of the monetary authorities either in matters of domestic monetary policy or in matters of exchange transactions." But this point of view—which reflects the experience of all foreign banks in developed countries—had little effect on the rising tide of nationalist sentiment.

RISE OF THE FOREIGN BANK AFFILIATES

After the Bank Act amendments of 1967 were finally passed into law by Parliament in March, the government and the regulators believed that they had laid the subject of foreign banking to rest. The Mercantile had been put into a $200 million straitjacket, and the Minister of Finance had postponed the question of licensing foreign banks to some indefinite future date. But in an open society, financial markets have a way of flowing around bureaucratic obstacles and overcoming political vacillation. The case of foreign banking was not closed, it was just beginning to open up. The heart of the matter was that the government had failed to take the advice of the Porter Commission by defining banking. Having been presented with a consistent and logical set of proposals for dealing with the problem, the government lacked the courage and clarity of thought to reaffirm the exclusive jurisdiction over money and banking which was defined in the British North America Act.

Not for the first or last time, the government took refuge behind an interpretation of its powers provided by the legal bureaucrats in the Department of Justice. The beauty of an opinion from the Department of Justice from the government's point of view is that it is not available for examination or challenge; it is a one-liner provided to the government behind the scenes, and there is no machinery for challenging such opinions in the courts. In this case, three years of work by the Porter Commission staff, who had been supported by a platoon of the country's best economists, were overturned by an anonymous

lawyer in Ottawa who was not required to reveal any reasons whatsoever for his opinion. All we know is what Mitchell Sharp said to the
finance committee: "I have been advised by law officers of the Crown
and other lawyers to whom I have spoken that Parliament cannot
define banking. This is a clause in the British North America Act and
therefore Parliament cannot say what the British North America Act
means; that is reserved for the court." This absurd piece of sophistry
has not prevented the government from defining banking in a thousand cases, the most important of which have been discussed in
earlier chapters. By ducking the constitutional issues, the Pearson
government left a legacy of unresolved problems in financial regulation which remains with us today.

The Mercantile Bank of Canada remained frozen at $200 million
in assets after the 1967 revision. Then, in early 1971, the majority
Liberal government under Trudeau worked out a deal to "Cana-
dianize" the Mercantile. The Minister of Finance, Edgar Benson,
authorized a series of six issues of $5 million in the capital stock of the
Mercantile, all of which had to be sold to Canadian residents. Citibank's share of the ownership in Mercantile was reduced to 25
percent by 1975, and the Mercantile entered a period of prosperity
and growth. But there were some underlying problems. First, Citibank was investing 100 percent of the effort and getting 25 percent of
the return. Not surprisingly, the parent bank's enthusiasm for its
Canadian subsidiary waned.

The second problem was that Mercantile was essentially a wholesale bank, without the broad base of retail deposits which have been
fundamental to the stability of the big six banks throughout their
history. (The Mercantile was eventually caught in the downdraft
caused by the failure of the Canadian Commercial Bank and the
Northland in the mid-1980s, and in 1985 it sought a merger with the
National Bank of Canada. André Bérard, the present chairman and
chief executive of the National, worked out the deal to absorb the
Mercantile under then chairman Michel Bélanger. The National's
objective was to take a step towards broadening its base to a national
level. The National had already consolidated its position as a major
force in Quebec, as a result of the merger of the National and
Provincial in 1978, thus creating one strong francophone bank.
Clearly the goal of nationwide status was based on the vision of a
continuing economic union.)

The failure to define banking in 1967 showed the First National
City Bank and many others that there was more than one means to an

end. Since the Bank Act prohibited any institution from calling itself a bank unless it was specifically called a bank in the Bank Act, the name of the game was to avoid using the word. There were various ways to do this: one way was to buy a provincially incorporated trust company, another was to create a subsidiary under the Investment Companies Act, another way was to buy or create a leasing company, and still another was to have a venture capital company. By 1979, Citibank had used most of these routes, thereby making a joke of the federal government's failure to define banking. Helen Sinclair, now president of the Canadian Bankers' Association, and then supervisor of a Task Force on Branch Banking (reporting to me) in the Bank of Nova Scotia, co-wrote an article with Martin Krossel which foreshadowed the wrenching constitutional struggles ahead: "Probably the most pragmatic and ultimately the decisive factor behind the government's standoffish attitude vis-à-vis its foreign banking rules is the present strain of federal-provincial relations, and sensitivity over a new Canadian constitution." In July 1974, the Bank of Canada started to publish consolidated figures for "Canadian financial institutions affiliated with foreign banks" in its *Monthly Review*. By then, there were thirty-five or forty foreign banking institutions with Canadian subsidiaries, and their assets were $1.3 billion. Six years later, when foreign banking legislation was finally passed, their assets were $8.3 billion.

Apart from avoiding the word "bank," perhaps the chief characteristic of the foreign bank subsidiaries was that they raised their funds by selling wholesale deposit instruments (usually $100,000 or more) through investment dealers. In order to make this "paper" acceptable to investors, it usually carried the guarantee of the foreign parent, almost always a well-known name like Citicorp or Barclays. Since these Canadian affiliates were not "banks," they were not required to keep cash reserves at the Bank of Canada, and therefore actually had a cost advantage over the Canadian banks. And so a flood of institutions—less regulated than the banks—poured into the country to compete with the banks. Slowly, painfully, the federal government came to the realization that it had not dealt with the foreign banking problem at all.

ALARUMS AND EXCURSIONS

The years 1973-80 in banking could have been described by Shakespeare as a period of "alarums and excursions." Small armies trampled back and forth across the banking stage; there were wild cries, trumpets, volleys of musket fire, confusion and smoke. Five Ministers of Finance dealt with the banking legislation before the Bank Act revision of 1980 was finally passed. The first of these was John Turner, and he was succeeded in turn by Donald S. Macdonald, Jean Chrétien, John Crosbie, and Allan MacEachen. But it was Pierre Bussières, the first Minister of State (Finance), who actually took the revision through Parliament. Every one of these ministers has remained very much in the public eye down to the time of writing.

The opening shot was fired at the Western Economic Opportunities Conference in 1973, when John Turner met with the four western premiers. Turner went along with the western drive for more regional Canadian banks, but the premiers wanted banks controlled by provincial governments. In 1974, John Turner invited interested parties to prepare briefs in preparation for the upcoming Bank Act revision of 1977. Once more, the banks created a Bank Act Revision Committee. The first chairman of the committee was Jim Morgan, the senior investment officer in the Royal Bank. (For convenience and communication, the banks felt that the chair of the Bank Act Revision Committee should be from the same bank that held the two-year presidency of the CBA, and Rowland Frazee, chief operating officer of the Royal Bank, was the president of the CBA.) As it turned out, the Bank Act revision of 1977 was postponed several times, but the Royal Bank team of Frazee and Morgan continued to lead the CBA delegation for a third year. In 1978 Jim Morgan retired, and Frazee was succeeded in the presidency of the CBA by J.A. Gordon Bell, of the Bank of Nova Scotia. I followed Morgan as chairman of the Bank Act Revision Committee, until becoming full-time president of the CBA in 1980.

Meanwhile, in response to Turner's invitation, the CBA submitted a brief to the Minister of Finance in October of 1975. The brief noted that Canada already had about thirty-five to forty affiliates of foreign banks from Germany, Italy, France, Holland, Belgium, Spain, Portugal, the United Kingdom, Greece, Switzerland as well as the United States, Japan, and Hong Kong. It noted that these offices were considerably larger operations than the traditional "suitcase" bank— an expression which described the sort of travelling-salesman type of banking operation, whereby a foreign banker sets up an office in a hotel room and tries to market large commercial loans to Canadian borrowing corporations. The CBA brief noted that there were about 130 Canadian corporations wholly or partly owned by foreign banks and foreign corporations which were doing some sort of banking business. It said: "There are today no laws or regulations or even guidelines for foreign banking operations in Canada. There are no specific provisions for the conditions under which a branch, agency or office may be established by a foreign bank in Canada . . . Foreign banks, either directly or indirectly, exercise far broader powers in Canada than Canadian chartered banks." It recommended that "the operation of foreign banks and their related companies in Canada be clearly brought under federal jurisdiction."

By the time the CBA brief was submitted to Ottawa, there was a new Minister of Finance, Donald S. Macdonald, and reality was beginning to hit the government over the head. In August 1976 the government published a White Paper titled "Canadian Banking Legislation." This document was intended to convey the broad outlines of government policy, leading towards the Bank Act revision. The government had identified forty-eight corporations affiliated with twenty-five foreign banks. It realized, at last, that some coherent method of licensing foreign banks in Canada was required and acknowledged that "a basic conflict arises between the objectives of maximizing competition and ensuring that the control of the financial system remains predominantly in Canadian hands." It went on to define a foreign bank affiliate using the definition which the Porter Commission had proposed, that is, an institution which makes loans and accepts deposits which are transferable by means of a cheque from one person to another.

In the nine years that had passed since the passage of the Walter Gordon/Mitchell Sharp version of the Bank Act in 1967, the government had come around to the view that foreign banks licensed to operate in Canada should do so only through subsidiaries, and not through agencies or branches. The White Paper said: "This will provide in respect of foreign bank subsidiaries a clear identification of capital, assets and profits to facilitate the establishment and enforcement of regulatory controls. In short, the proposal will lend itself most easily to the application of Canadian banking law."

This was a critical change, and one which has continued to be a source of annoyance to foreign banks and a possible source of future problems of reciprocity with the European Community. Perhaps the most important difference between a subsidiary and a branch is that the subsidiary is limited by Canadian banking law in the size of loan it can make to a single borrower. The limitation of loans in relation to capital was a new feature of Canadian banking, part of the fallout of excessive lending to less-developed countries in the 1970s. When

applied to a foreign bank subsidiary, it limited the lending power of
the subsidiary to a percentage of its Canadian capital, rather than to
some percentage of its much larger parent's capital. The American
banks in particular regarded this as unfair, because the Canadian
banks' branches in the United States were capable of making very
large loans to United States corporations, based on the capital of the
parent bank in Canada.

The Department of Finance and Bill Kennett, the Inspector General of Banks, also thought that it would be easier to regulate a foreign
bank if it were required to have an incorporated subsidiary. The new
Bank Act, significantly, required both domestic banks and foreign
bank subsidiaries to maintain within Canada their data-processing
facilities and record-keeping for business booked in Canada, on the
assumption that records held abroad could not be examined adequately. (There is not much of a case for this stricture; the Canadian
banks in their foreign operations through branches certainly do not
escape the attentions of the host-country regulator in any way.)

In order to achieve its twin goals of encouraging competition while
maintaining Canadian control of the banks, the government came up
with an interesting solution. This was to limit the aggregate loans of
all foreign banks taken together to 15 percent of commercial bank
loans in Canada. And in order to prevent one of the large New York
banks becoming dominant, the White Paper of 1976 proposed that no
foreign bank should be allowed to exceed $500 million in assets (that
is, twenty times an authorized capital of $25 million).

In 1977, Jean Chrétien succeeded Donald Macdonald as Minister
of Finance and in May 1978 the White Paper proposals were finally
turned into draft legislation. The revised Bank Act was the size of a
telephone book, because the government had decided to incorporate
the general features of the Canadian Business Corporations Act into
the Bank Act.

Before that, in 1974, the Combines Investigation Act had also been
amended to make it applicable to banks. This made it illegal for banks
to have any sort of agreement on such matters as service charges.
There was already a provision, introduced in 1967, that prevented
banks from making agreements on interest rates, except with a shared
customer or on prior approval by the Minister of Finance. This had
brought to an end a style of banking which had been in place for more
than a century, and which is still the rule in some countries. In
practice, agreements on interest rates had applied mainly to the rate
on personal savings deposits, rather than to lending rates. The pro-

hibition against agreements is enforced by possible criminal charges, so that bankers are very careful to avoid discussing rates. Of course, it is not uncommon for interest rates to move at the same time in response to changes in monetary policy; when the Bank of Canada's "bank rate" changes by a significant amount, most banks generally move soon afterwards, often on the same day. One does not need to conspire in order to respond to obvious monetary forces, any more than the 14,000 American banks conspire when they change their lending rates on the same day, more or less.

In May 1978 the alarums and excursions began in earnest. The revised Bank Act never got off the ground because the parliamentary session ended and Chrétien had to reintroduce the act in November 1978. The CBA appeared before the parliamentary committees—both House and Senate—in November. By this time there were half a dozen smaller banks in the association alongside the big five: the National and Provincial (which had not yet merged), as well as the Bank of British Columbia, the Mercantile, the Canadian Commercial Bank of Edmonton, and the Northland Bank of Calgary. A seventh small bank—the Continental—was in the process of emerging from its previous incarnation as Industrial Acceptance Corporation, a finance company.

The chairman of the House of Commons Finance Committee was Bob Kaplan, who is still active in the current Parliament, and who provides additional evidence of the political longevity of politicians associated with Bank Act revisions. Under Kaplan, the House finance committee held fifty-four meetings and heard 118 witnesses. The Senate committee, whose chairman was the venerable and crusty Salter Hayden (a former director of the Bank of Nova Scotia), met for eighteen days and heard twenty-seven groups. The committee hearings dragged on into 1979, and once again the banks made individual statements before the committee on the question of foreign banks, because they could not arrive at an agreed position for the industry as a whole. Eventually, in March, the Kaplan committee reported back to the House of Commons with a recommendation that both branches and subsidiaries be allowed. The committee proposed changing the ceiling on the aggregate assets of all foreign banks to 10 percent of total domestic assets from 15 percent of commercial loans, which was a sensible simplification in defining the ceiling.

But once again politics brought banking legislation to a halt. Parliament was dissolved in March 1979, before the finance committee's report could be considered. The election in June 1979 brought to office the Joe Clark government—for six months. John Crosbie became the fourth Minister of Finance to deal with the banking legislation. In October, he introduced a Bank Act amendment bill which was substantially the same as Chrétien's, although there were some changes in the sections dealing with foreign banks. The aggregate ceiling on foreign bank assets was reduced to 8 percent of domestic assets; the limit on branching by foreign bank subsidiaries was removed, except for the requirement of ministerial approval; and the foreign bank subsidiary licences were extended for three years instead of requiring an annual renewal.

But the government fell in December 1979 and an election followed, resulting in the return of a majority Liberal government under Trudeau. The fifth Minister of Finance to deal with the banking bill was Allan MacEachen. Once again the bill went back to the finance committee, but by this time exhaustion was setting in. The struggle to amend the banking legislation had now been going on for six years, and the wear and tear on the players was beginning to tell. The government decided to create a new position called Minister of State (Finance) under the Minister of Finance, with responsibility for financial legislation. The first occupant of this position was Pierre Bussières, and he was the one who finally steered the legislation through the parliamentary process.

Meanwhile, the banks had come to the conclusion that the job of president of the Canadian Bankers' Association was too much to be handled by the chief operating officer of one of the big six banks on a two-year rotating basis. The job was absorbing enormous amounts of time in CBA committee meetings, to say nothing of the preparation of briefs and appearances before committees of the House and Senate. In 1979, the banks commissioned a management report from a consultant, who recommended the appointment of a full-time president, preferably a senior bank executive. And so in April 1980, I moved from the position of chairman of the Bank Act Revision Committee of the CBA to the job of full-time president, reluctantly leaving behind my responsibilities for computer systems, law and economics, investments and mortgages in the Bank of Nova Scotia.

In October 1980, the finance committee of the House pushed through some further amendments of the banking bill recommended by Bussières, and in November the House finally gave third reading and passage to the amendments which should have been completed in June 1977. In this last phase of the 1980 revision, there was a prolonged struggle between the banks and the automotive dealers over the power to do car leasing. The dealers wanted to keep the banks out and they won hands down. On one occasion David Lewis (later chairman of Continental Bank) and I met the Progressive Conservative caucus to put the case for bank entry into car leasing. Out of about forty Tories in the room, not one supported us. The matter was succinctly explained to me by Pierre Bussières after he became the Liberal Minister of State (Finance). "Mr. MacIntosh," said Bussières, "there are eight automobile dealers in my riding, and they all support my organization. And the same is true for every member of Parliament. So go away." Twelve years later, nothing has changed.

THE STAMPEDE FOR LICENCES

A very important feature of the foreign banking legislation was that a banking licence could now be obtained by Order-in-Council rather than by a special private Act of Parliament. This was a major departure from the Canadian tradition, which had always required parliamentary approval for individual banks, except for a brief period when "free banking" was tried in the mid-nineteenth century.

Since the new foreign bank subsidiaries were going to be affiliated with strong parent banks abroad, it did not appear necessary to have a parliamentary investigation of each applicant. By 1980, there were known to be about sixty foreign banks with financial subsidiaries in Canada, so that requiring approval of individual bank charters would have clogged Parliament for years to come. The problem was solved by turning over the investigative job to the Inspector General of Banks, who could recommend the granting of licences to the Minister of Finance and thence to cabinet for approval.

By this time, the combined assets of the foreign banks' various financial subsidiaries in Canada were approaching $10 billion, compared to about $150 billion for the domestic banks. But why should quasi banks like Citicorp Canada bother to obtain a banking licence? They were doing very well as they were, especially because they did not have to maintain cash reserves with the Bank of Canada, and were therefore at an advantage compared with the big six banks. The answer was partly stick and partly carrot. The carrot was the power to use the word "bank" (although this was of dubious value to institutions like Citicorp or Chase Manhattan or Barclays). The stick was a clause in the legislation which prohibited foreign bank financial subsidiaries in Canada from placing the guarantee of the parent bank on their wholesale deposit instruments sold in the Canadian money market. This was a critical consideration, because investors would not have placed their funds with relatively small borrowers whose prospects were uncertain without the guarantee of the parent.

Another factor was that practically all of the applicants for foreign bank subsidiary licences in Canada were international banks of great stature in the world's money markets. They were not about to challenge the authority of the Canadian government in the courts.

The scramble to get into position for a banking licence started in 1976, when the White Paper disclosed the government's intention to put an aggregate asset ceiling on foreign banks in Canada. Since there would have to be a rationing process for foreign bank licences and for each bank's share of the total capital, the obvious thing to do was to expand as rapidly as possible to maximize one's share of the market. In the four years prior to passage of the Bank Act in 1980, the financial subsidiaries of foreign banks took on all kinds of commercial lending business at very narrow profit margins, in order to get the business on the books. For Canadian banks, the competition was extremely severe at a time when academics and civil servants were talking about the need for more competition. A whole decade was to pass before many of the foreign bank subsidiaries were subjected to the vigilant gaze of the parent bank at home, and questions raised about profitability.

The foremost bank in the scramble to get in line for a licence was Citicorp, which had created a small family of financial subsidiaries and backed them up with capable American managers and good recruitment policies in Canada. From the beginning, Citicorp was not only the largest of the foreign bank subsidiaries but one of the most profitable. By 1984 it was already rivalling in size its half-sister the Mercantile.

In its final form, the ceiling on aggregate foreign bank domestic assets was fixed at 8 percent of the total domestic assets of all Canadian banks. In mid-1981, when the government started issuing licences, the total domestic assets of the Canadian banks were $220 billion. The ceiling on the aggregate assets of foreign bank subsidiaries was therefore $18 billion. By law, assets could not be more than twenty times capital, so that the aggregate ceiling on the capital of the foreign bank subsidiaries was about $900 million. So the name of the game was to get as large a portion as possible of the $900 million before it was used up. By the end of 1982, the government had granted "letters patent" for a banking licence to fifty-seven foreign bank subsidiaries and the total ration of capital was almost gone. With almost sixty banks sharing about $1 billion in capital, the average foreign bank subsidiary could have only about $16 million in capital and $320 million in assets.

The decision to issue so many banking licences was based as much on a naive theory of competition as on considerations of reciprocity: the greater the number of players, the greater the competition. In my opinion this is debatable. The strongest competitors for the big six Canadian banks are the two largest foreign bank subsidiaries, Citibank Canada and the Hongkong Bank of Canada. (The latter reached its present size by absorbing first the Bank of British Columbia and then Lloyds Bank, formerly the Continental Bank.) There are ten Japanese foreign bank subsidiaries, so that no one of them can achieve the degree of name recognition that is enjoyed by the two largest foreign bank subsidiaries. (By contrast the Australian government, which started admitting foreign banks later than Canada, took a different path by issuing only about sixteen licences.)

But considerations of reciprocity were certainly a factor in issuing so many licences. Apart from the case of Japan, where there was at first a government negotiation on the number of licences to be issued, the decision to apply for a licence was a matter for an individual bank to decide, not its national government. As a result, we have four foreign bank subsidiaries from France and three from Israel. A case could be made that with some countries, a deal should have been worked out to have a "chosen vehicle" in Canada.

In 1990, the total authorized capital of the foreign bank subsidiaries was about $3.5 billion, and their total assets $54 billion. The original 8 percent ceiling on foreign assets is no longer a consideration; in 1984, the ceiling was lifted to 16 percent, partly because of pressure from the more successful and rapidly growing foreign bank subsidiaries, and partly because there was no room left to licence any more new applicants. Then, in 1989, the free trade agreement with the United States exempted the American banks from the ceiling, and the aggregate ceiling for all non-U.S. banks was reduced to 12 percent. Whether the ceiling is relevant at all is doubtful, because the severity of competition, especially in a soft economy, makes further growth very difficult.

What has been the impact of the foreign bank subsidiaries on financial markets and on the Canadian economy? Certainly commercial borrowers have benefited, because virtually all of the lending business of the foreign bank subsidiaries has been to borrowers in the range of $500,000 and upwards. The heavy competition for customers in the "mid-market" ($5 million to $10 million) has resulted in very narrow profit margins on commercial business. With almost sixty additional banks looking for wholesale deposits, the money market and the related foreign exchange market is very finely tuned.

The American banks brought a level of business and technical skill—and the Europeans a level of culture—which has had a significant impact on the financial communities of Toronto and Montreal. The foreign bank subsidiaries have been good employers of university graduates, and they have also greatly increased the breadth and depth of banking knowledge in the accounting and legal professions. They have generated a greater mobility of employees between banks (before 1960, to quit one bank and join another was considered an act of treachery). After the foreign bank subsidiaries were licensed in 1981-82, perhaps 300 to 500 men and women moved from the domestic banks to the newcomers.

Another benefit of the foreign bank subsidiaries has been a capital inflow of about $2.5 billion, on which there has so far been a rather inadequate rate of return. In 1990, the foreign bank subsidiaries as a group earned only 4.8 percent on their capital, a clear indication of the tough competition with the domestic banks.

In the long series of political battles over banking issues in the 1980s, the foreign bank subsidiaries played almost no part. The reason for this is simple enough: the foreign banks are not in the retail banking business, with the notable exception now of the Hongkong Bank of Canada. Battles over service charges, credit-card interest rates, farm loans, regional issues, even small business lending have not involved the foreign bank subsidiaries. At meetings of the Canadian Bankers' Association, where representatives of the foreign bank community were always welcome, attendance was usually limited to the big six; the western banks—The Bank of British Columbia, the Canadian Commercial Bank and the Northland—sometimes involved themselves in specific questions. In banking, the big political questions are always mass-market issues which reverberate from coast to coast. In the United States the same issues exist, but there are no national names which can be the target for members of Congress, so the politics of banking is much more diffuse.

Despite the marginal profitability of most foreign bank subsidiaries, few have given up. One or two have disappeared because their parents disappeared through merger or failure, and one of the largest—Lloyds Bank of Canada—has been merged into the Hongkong Bank of Canada. Many of the foreign bank subsidiaries are niche players, for example, serving an immigrant community which remits money back to the homeland. Even small and unprofitable banks do not want to give up their Canadian licences, if for no other reason than to maintain Canadian representation in a worldwide network.

As a group, the foreign bank subsidiaries have enriched the banking system and the Canadian financial system in general. They have added impetus to the lifting of educational and professional standards of banking personnel. They have provided a broader perspective on world financial markets, and not least, they have implemented a Canadian government policy of reciprocity which was essential for the domestic banks.

THE AMEX FIASCO

On December 17, 1988, Nick LePan, the assistant deputy minister of finance responsible for banking legislation, phoned me to draw my attention to an item in the *Canada Gazette* that day. The item said that the American Express Company was applying for letters patent to become a Canadian bank. After putting down the phone to absorb this stunning news, I sent off multiple copies of a fax message to the banks. There was no use trying to organize a meeting just before the normal Christmas exodus from Toronto and Montreal, so I proposed a meeting on the first working day in the New Year. I asked the members of the appropriate committee on legislation to come prepared to formulate an industry response. I then adjourned with my family to a beach in Puerto Vallarta. Sitting on the beach contemplating the American Express application, my Yuletide spirits did not improve.

After returning to Toronto, I drafted a letter to Michael Wilson which was co-signed by Warren Moysey, then one of the four presidents of the Canadian Imperial Bank of Commerce, and chairman of the CBA executive council. The letter, copies of which went to Tom Hockin (the Minister of State for Finance) and to Michael Mackenzie, the Superintendent of Financial Institutions, said in part: "If the Government of Canada approves this application, it will be creating a precedent whose ultimate consequences for the Canadian financial system are profound and disturbing."

The problem was that the parent of American Express was not itself a bank. It had always been quite clear that a foreign bank subsidiary had to be the offspring of a parent which was itself a bank in its own jurisdiction. In fact this was spelled out in December 1980 in *A Guide for Foreign Banking* issued by the Office of the Inspector General of

Banks. Under a section called "Basic Criteria for Ownership of Foreign Bank Subsidiaries," the first paragraph begins, "The applicant must be a foreign bank." Referring to the Bank Act, the guideline says: "The applicant should be considered a bank by the regulatory authorities in its own jurisdiction . . . ; the applicant should generally be in the business of lending and borrowing money, with the latter including the acceptance of deposits transferable by order." American Express does not meet any of these basic tests. It is not itself a member of the Federal Reserve System, nor subject to the supervision of the Federal Deposit Insurance Corporation in the United States, and is therefore not a regulated bank. (Oddly enough, American Express was 97 percent owned by the Chase National Bank of New York between 1928 and 1933. It was divested by Chase in the fallout from the stock market crash in 1929, and the passage of the Glass-Steagall Act in 1933. Even the Chairman of American Express, James Robinson, "answers such questions" [about Amex possibly buying a U.S. bank] "by noting simply that Amexco *cannot* own a commercial bank".)

With its knack for finding legal loopholes, American Express has established a number of "banking" subsidiaries, none of which qualifies it as a regulated bank under United States federal law. One of its subsidiaries, called American Express Bank Limited, "does not do business in the United States except as incident to its activities outside the United States," according to a submission of American Express filed with the United States Securities Exchange Commission. There are also two or three "non-bank banks" in the American Express network which offer federal deposit insurance protection.

The U.S. Congress has since put a stop to the creation of these institutions, but several hundred of them took advantage of a loophole in U.S. banking legislation. This loophole concerned the U.S. definition of a "bank"—an institution which takes chequable deposits and makes loans. The "non-bank banks" do one or the other but not both, and perform the other half of the banking function through a sister company which either collects the deposits or makes the loans on behalf of the "non-bank bank."

Other criteria for a foreign bank licence in Canada were that "the home jurisdiction should report favourably on the applicant" and that "the applicant should be well supervised in its own jurisdiction." But neither of these criteria can be met by American Express, because there is no federal regulator of the parent in the United States.

The Department of Finance had to stretch the definition of "financial institution" to include American Express Canada. The definitions of a "financial institution" and a "financial corporation" in the Bank Act are not met, even though the notice in the *Canada Gazette* had spoken of converting American Express from a financial institution to a bank.

The precedent was alarming. The very loose interpretation of the Bank Act and the regulations would open the door for any foreign corporation to create a bank in Canada. Later, a CBA study pointed out that the U.S. and Canadian financial subsidiaries of General Electric, General Motors, Sears Roebuck, and Ford all had stronger claims to be called financial institutions than did American Express. The Amex Bank Canada licence had the potential of throwing the whole banking system open to unregulated foreign interests, creating a situation which would have no parallel in the world.

But there were other factors in the Amex application almost as important as the precedent. Amex wanted access to the Canadian payments system and to the ATM (Automated Teller Machine) network which the banks and other deposit-taking institutions had created. This network, which goes under the umbrella name Interac, is one of the most successful technological systems in the world serving bank customers. It is the product of a highly developed data-processing system, an excellent telephone network, and close cooperation among the financial institutions. The cost of the infrastructure runs into billions of dollars. Nevertheless, membership is open to any financial institution which can meet some basic volume criteria, and pay an entry fee of $7.50 a card. (In fact, this fee was paid by the Ottawa civil service credit union.)

American Express wanted access to the ATM network for its cardholders, numbering perhaps 1.6 million in Canada. The parent company does not have access to the national ATM networks in the United States, such as Cirrus and Plus. Instead of paying the entry fee of $12 million to join Interac, Amex has chosen to join a much smaller network operated by the Bank of Montreal, called Circuit. Amex already belongs to a number of regional networks in the United States, thus giving it a makeshift continental system.

A third factor, less important than the first two, but the one which has received most of the attention from bankers, politicians, and the media, was the fact that a foreign corporation was going to be licensed to do things that a Canadian bank could not do. First of all, it appeared that American Express would be able to provide upscale mail-order marketing of luggage and jewellery and travel services, contrary to the

Bank Act prohibition against mixing commercial and financial businesses. Even more irritating was the fact that American Express
marketed insurance products, which the government had steadfastly
refused to allow the Canadian banks to do. It seemed to the banks that
the government was getting the cart before the horse—that it should
think through its legislation on financial institutions before making
major departures from traditional policies on an ad hoc basis to benefit
a foreign corporation. (In December 1990, financial reform legislation—driven by the Amex precedent—proposed that banks and trust
companies be clearly authorized to market insurance products
through credit cards, but not in any other way.)

   This formidable list of obstacles may have occurred to the government, but there were other priorities. The American Express application was made in July 1986, but did not come to fruition until it
received cabinet approval in principle on November 21, 1988—
election day. The fact that the approval process took two years and
four months probably reflects the difficulty that Department of Finance officials were having in justifying approval of the application.
The department managed to keep the application secret from the
industry, even though its acceptance represented a major departure in
principle. (In fact there had been a leak in the *Globe and Mail*'s Report
on Business as early as February 1988 that American Express had
changed its Ottawa lobbyist in search of a banking licence. Later on,
Stevie Cameron in her book *Ottawa Inside Out* wrote: "Someone
approached Mulroney's close friend, Nabisco president Ross
Johnson, in New York. Johnson was on the board of Amex in the
United States, and he was asked for assistance in transferring the
lobby business." But the leak was not noticed at the time. Long after
the public announcement, I learned that one or two bankers had seen
the American Express lobbyists in Ottawa, but for some reason had
failed to raise a flag.)

   In January 1989, the Amex application became a *cause célèbre*. At
the annual meeting of the Bank of Nova Scotia in Halifax on January
17, its chairman, Cedric Ritchie, fired the first shot. He charged that
the government was giving American Express a preferred position,
because his bank was not allowed into the travel business "nor is it
permitted to market merchandise through credit cards." The following day the issue became front page news when Dick Thomson, the
chairman of the Toronto-Dominion Bank, "accused Prime Minister
Brian Mulroney yesterday of striking a special 'deal' with American
Express Company to grant the U.S. financial services giant a bank

licence in exchange for its support of the Canada-U.S. Free Trade deal." Bruce Phillips, Mulroney's director of communications, said that the accusation was "preposterous. The Prime Minister had no personal involvement with this matter." Unfortunately Dick Thomson was unable to document his accusation, and had to retract it after an angry phone call from Michael Wilson. However, Bruce Phillips and Michael Wilson could not deny that Jim Robinson, the chairman of American Express, was not only a personal friend of Mulroney's but chairman of Ronald Reagan's private-sector committee promoting the U.S.-Canada free trade agreement. (In July 1987, Mulroney had joined Jim Robinson in opening a Picasso exhibition sponsored by Amex at the Royal Ontario Museum in Toronto; the big six banks, among the foremost financial supporters of the arts, are not often endorsed at such a level for their numerous endeavours.)

When the banks met with Michael Wilson on January 25, 1989, at the Department of Finance in Ottawa, the mood was angry and confrontational. Wilson denied that the Amex application would set a precedent for other non-bank financial institutions, or even industrial corporations in the United States who might seek a banking licence. He asserted that American Express was a financial institution, but that General Motors Acceptance Corporation and Ford Motor Credit were not. The bankers snorted at this distinction, pointing out that American Express Canada neither made loans nor took deposits, but performed a mixture of commercial and financial activities.

Before leaving Toronto for the meeting, I had prepared a letter to the Minister of Finance requesting a public hearing on the Amex application. This was provided for in the Bank Act, in order to force an inquiry when there was some reason to challenge an applicant. Under the provision, a request had to be made by February 6, a deadline fixed by the Bank Act in relation to the public notice of application for a licence. But the letter was never handed to Michael Wilson, and sadly I took it back to Toronto. A majority of the CBA executive council members voted to withhold the letter, not wanting to put further pressure on the Minister of Finance, and hoping that Michael Mackenzie would call a public hearing anyway.

Meanwhile, a misguided banker on the Ottawa staff of one of the banks had arranged for three or four limousines to ferry the bank delegation from the Sparks Street office of the CBA to the Department of Finance, and thus provide a nice photo opportunity for the TV camera crews and dozens of reporters milling around in the lobby. This conveyed the worst possible image to a national audience, and I should have vetoed it in favour of regular taxicabs. Another mistake was to have invited the president of Lloyds Bank Canada, who was one of the foreign bank representatives on the executive council, to join the delegation. He was a newcomer to Canada, had little knowledge of the issues, and no stake in its outcome. This did not stop him from speaking out very strongly against submitting my letter requesting a public hearing on the issue.

Michael Wilson later announced publicly that the banks did not understand the issue, because the government was going to require American Express to wind down its car-leasing business and separate its commercial functions from its banking subsidiary. We had been trying for a month to find out what the conditions of the licence were, but the Department of Finance would not release them.

After the meeting, the Minister of Finance and the bankers held competing press conferences. Wilson said: "In these discussions, the government is speaking for the consumer . . . and the banks are speaking on behalf of their shareholders . . . we're looking at this as a way of increasing competition, and the banks are looking at it from the standpoint of competition." This assertion was wrong on several counts. First of all, the big banks had never opposed a single one of the sixty other applicants for banking licences already granted. It could hardly be argued that they were opposing more competition. And as for improved service, the facts were the other way around: American Express was trying to get access to the Canadian Interac ATM network, to which it had contributed nothing. Its clientele was an upscale business and professional class, paying $55 or more a year for a charge card, and 30 percent interest a year for late payments.

At the meeting with Wilson, Warren Moysey, the chairman of the CBA delegation, had urged the government to defer the Amex application until the basic principles of financial reform legislation could be resolved after a "full public debate." But the government had committed itself. Wilson said that the banks would be given the power to market insurance products through their credit card system; in other words, the Canadian banks would be allowed to do something in Canada which an American corporation would be allowed to do ahead of them. To call this a deplorable method of making public policy is flattery.

On February 3, 1989, Wilson confirmed his intention to approve the American Express Bank application, but said that the issuance of letters patent would be delayed for up to one year in order that new

financial legislation could be introduced by the government and fully considered by Parliament. As it turned out subsequently, new financial legislation was postponed, and Amex received its letters patent on June 29, 1989. But the licence to operate under the letters patent was not issued until April 25, 1990.

After Wilson's promise of February 3, 1989, to withhold the Amex licence until financial reform legislation could be considered—a promise not delivered—the trusting banks decided to let the February 6 deadline for requesting a public hearing pass. Meanwhile, financial critics for the Liberal and NDP parties, as well as representatives from the Council of Canadians (a nationalistic group) had requested a public hearing. But on May 5, 1989, Michael Mackenzie announced that he would not hold a public inquiry into the American Express application: "The function of an inquiry would be to ensure that all the relevant facts concerning the application would be available to the Minister. I think that requirement has already been set aside. In coming to my decision, I took into account the Minister of Finance's commitment to delay permission for American Express to begin operations for one year to permit time to make changes in banking legislation that would deal with concerns about competitive advantage and related issues." So the Superintendent of Financial Institutions was euchred too.

The American Express fiasco is a textbook example of how not to make public policy. Instead of establishing general principles for financial reform which could be resolved in a democratic forum, and which would provide a guide for particular acts such as the Amex approval, the glaring exception was allowed to precede general policy. And if there were ever a clear-cut demonstration that the political power of the big six banks is only mythological, this is it.

CHAPTER 12

THE DISASTERS OF THE 1980s

Almost everyone agrees that the decade of the 1980s was one of unprecedented greed and stupidity in financial markets. The contribution of Canada's financial institutions to this spectacle was fully in proportion to their share of the global market, though never as spectacular as the excesses in the United States. Fortunately, by 1991 we have put behind us the worst mistakes of the decade in the private financial sector, while still leaving unresolved the deficit-prone proclivities of government.

In this chapter, we will first examine the impact of the oil shocks in 1973 and 1979 on the banks' loans to the Less Developed Countries (the LDCs) and to the domestic petroleum industry, then look at the trust company failures of the 1980s, and finally the two western bank failures. There is a considerable amount of literature on each of these subjects, and in the short space of one chapter it is not feasible to provide a comprehensive account of these events. My purpose is to assess their impact on the political climate in which the ongoing discussions about financial reform took place.

THE LDC DEBT PROBLEM

It has been said that an illiterate has no ancestors except his living grandparents. By this test, most of the world's top bank executives were illiterate in the 1970s and 1980s, because they ignored the lessons of history and the oldest, most basic, commandments of banking:

1. Know thy customer.
2. Do not borrow short and lend long.
3. Lending money is easy—the hard part is getting it back.

4. Spread your risk; don't put all your eggs in one basket.

At the same time, they put far too much faith in a durable cliché:

Companies may fail, but countries do not.

The LDC debt problem was a direct consequence of the "oil shocks" of 1973 and 1979. The first "oil shock" took the price of oil from $2.50 U.S. a barrel in mid-1973 to $11.50 a year later. Why and how did this fivefold increase come about so suddenly? The answer is that the Middle Eastern oil countries had been sending some of their young men to western universities, where they had picked up some knowledge of world economics. They had discovered that they were practically giving their oil away in a world where the demand was great and the resources finite. The politics of oil is a good illustration of the power of ideas.

Some simple arithmetic conveys a notion of the massive scale of the financial problem created by a $10-a-barrel jump in the price of oil. For a country like Saudi Arabia producing 10 million barrels of oil a day, an extra $10 a barrel meant increased revenues of $100 million a day which is $36.5 billion a year. Not all the Organization of Petroleum Exporting Countries (OPEC) were in the Middle East; the "cartel" included countries like Nigeria and Venezuela, but the dominant country in the financial transformation was Saudi Arabia. The governments of these countries had no capacity to reinvest their windfall in global securities markets—nor any inclination to do so. They put most of their huge savings in short-term bank deposits in United States dollars. The world's commercial banking system suddenly had a huge inflow of savings to put to work. Instead of requiring the OPEC depositors to put the money on deposit for extended terms, the world's banks fell over each other in a competitive rush to get thirty-day term deposits. This money was then recycled to the developing countries in Latin America, mostly on what was supposed to be a short-term basis.

Sovereign countries, however, cannot be forced to pay back money, especially in a foreign currency. While governments may not go bankrupt, they may become incapable of generating enough earnings from their exports to pay the interest and principal on their foreign debts. But in the late 1970s, it was not quite so obvious that the commercial banks had broken the cardinal rules of banking: borrowing short and lending long, and making loans to borrowers who could give no assurance of repayment. The less-developed countries like

Brazil, Argentina, and Mexico took off into a period of very strong growth, and all seemed well. Real growth exceeded 5 percent a year and exports were sufficient to pay the interest on the "petro-dollar" loans.

Then in 1979 came the second oil shock, when the price of oil went from about $13 a barrel in mid-1979 to about $35 by mid-1981. This time the numbers became astronomical. Every single day another $500 million flowed into the OPEC coffers and was recycled into the world's money markets through the banks. By 1980, the annual OPEC surplus exceeded $100 billion, even after allowing for huge increases in their imports. The frenzied recycling of oil money went on for several more years.

But then a number of things started to happen which reversed the euphoria of the 1970s. The high price of oil led to conservation measures in the consuming countries and to growth in supply competition from other sources such as the North Sea. At the same time, the OPEC countries indulged in wasteful spending of their surplus savings. Meanwhile, the huge capital inflow to countries like Argentina and Brazil was followed by the loss of immense amounts of money on their military establishments and on government corruption.

The banking rule "know thy customer" had been broken. An immense amount of capital left Mexico, Brazil, and Argentina in the early 1980s, as the military and government elites moved capital to safe havens in New York, London, and Zurich. In the years 1975 to 1986, accumulated capital outflows from Argentina alone were estimated by Morgan Guaranty Trust Company economists to be $33 billion, compared to the country's gross external debt of $49 billion. In Mexico, capital outflows were $60 billion compared to a gross external debt of $97 billion. In Venezuela, capital outflows of $54 billion exceeded the country's gross debt of $38 billion. In effect the commercial banks of the world were lending the LDCs money through the front door, but most of it was going straight out the back door in the hands of a few citizens of the borrowing countries. No wonder that the game of musical chairs came to an end. As the Morgan Guaranty Trust Company wrote in September 1986:

> Psychologically, nothing has contributed more to the
> pervasive sense of frustration over the LDC debt problem
> than the realization that capital flight persisted, if on a much
> reduced scale, almost throughout the period of "involuntary"
> lending [that is, short-term loans becoming long-term, and

accruing unpaid interest]. Creditors, both private and official, are understandably reluctant to provide fresh funds unless the debtors put a stop to the capital flight.

The commercial banks were not alone in their headlong pursuit of bad loans. The International Monetary Fund and the International Bank for Reconstruction and Development (the World Bank)—the official financial organs representing most of the governments in the world—were also lending huge amounts of money and encouraging the commercial banks to do more. One of the most respected authorities on this subject is Rimmer de Vries, the editor of the highly regarded *World Financial Markets* published by the Morgan Guaranty Trust Company. In a statement to a U.S. Senate Foreign Relations Committee in 1983 he said:

> This lending was encouraged by the governments of the industrial countries. They were concerned that the OPEC current account surplus, which jumped from $7 billion in 1973 to $68 billion in 1974, would continue at very high levels because of perceived limits on OPEC's "absorptive capacity."

Both the Canadian and U.S. governments had lent official support to the recycling of petro dollars soon after the first oil shock in 1973. Speaking to the International Monetary Fund in 1974, Canada's Minister of Finance, John Turner, said: "The mammoth scale of financing necessary to alleviate Third World payments imbalances implies that recycling of oil funds is crucial to the effective financing of the payments deficits." This theme was confirmed many times by successive cabinet ministers—Jean Chrétien, Flora MacDonald, and Allan MacEachen—and by the governor of the Bank of Canada, Gerald Bouey. Their counterparts in the U.S. Treasury and the Federal Reserve were singing the same tune. But by 1983, almost everyone except Walter Wriston at Citibank was beginning to get concerned.

Walter Wriston was the chairman and chief executive officer of the First National City Bank of New York, and the guru of the recycling process until his retirement in 1984. He had been in charge of Citibank's European operations when Citibank acquired the Mercantile Bank of Canada, and became president of the bank in 1967, just when the Mercantile Affair was coming to a head. In 1970 he took over as chairman and chief executive officer from George Moore, who remarked, "Walter frightens me." In June 1982, Wriston was quoted by the Associated Press as saying: "Despite rising debt in the Third World, the chance of an international banking crisis is about as close to zero as anything that human beings can predict." But in a biographical sketch of Wriston in the *American Banker* in September 1983 we read:

> Late on August 19, 1982, Paul Volcker, the Chairman of the Federal Reserve Board, telephoned Walter Wriston, the Chairman of Citicorp, and said laconically, "Walter, I have a lot of Mexicans here with a lot of numbers, and the biggest numbers seem to be yours."
>
> Thus began the international debt crisis, which erupted publicly the following day with the Mexican government's request for a moratorium on almost $20 billion debt owed to about 1,400 banks around the world. But the telephone call also accorded Mr. Wriston the recognition he deserved as a principal architect of the banking system's emergence as a major channel for financial flows from surplus to deficit countries, and as a conduit for capital to developing countries.

This was an accurate assessment of Wriston, whose views carried great weight with commercial banks around the world, possibly excluding the Swiss banks, which never had a major exposure to the LDC debt relative to their size. But Wriston never lost the faith. In March 1983, he was quoted as saying: "A year from now, we will be worrying about something else."

Despite this attitude, there was growing apprehension. Pierre Trudeau expressed the changing tone in 1983: "The massive lending by commercial banks to LDCs, viewed at the time as a surprisingly successful recycling of petro dollars . . . has come back to haunt us as a formidable debt and liquidity problem . . . which threatens the stability of the international system." From then on, the governments of the developed countries tried to distance themselves as much as possible from the problems of the commercial banks. Having encouraged the process, governments now told the banks that they were solely responsible for their own folly. Certainly it is true that the bankers were adults and need not have fallen over themselves in the rush to throw money at the developing countries. In 1979 Canadian bankers had been accepting proposals over the telephone to participate in huge syndications to various government borrowers in Mexico and Brazil and elsewhere, with little financial analysis and virtually no knowledge of the borrowers' overall financial situation.

It was several years before the world's commercial banks began to assemble consolidated information which showed the aggregate commitments of the borrowing entities in the developing countries. Until then, banks had been lending money to LDCs with no real idea what the overall aggregate borrowings of each country were, based on the cliché that governments cannot go broke. The Canadian banks were far from alone in this sorry spectacle, in which the top managements of the world's banks failed to observe the most basic rules which they required of their junior subordinates.

Although there was no legal or regulatory limit in Canada on the percentage of a bank's capital that could be employed in loans to a single borrower, there were limits dictated by common sense. But if the boards of directors of the banks asked any questions, there is no evidence of it in the numbers. The New York banks were restricted by a legal limit of 10 percent of the bank's capital to a single borrower, but this was circumvented by treating the governmental agencies of a country like Mexico as separate borrowers. Thus the National Financial Corporation of Mexico was one borrower and its Petroleum Corporation another, although both were wholly owned government agencies. As for "sovereign risk" (that is, the government as the borrower), the banks inexplicably assumed that huge loans to (often corrupt) governments would be able to generate earnings from their exports of goods and services sufficient to pay the interest and principal on their debts. But the economic analysis employed by the new generation of hot-shot lenders in the international divisions of banks to justify the loans was trivial or non-existent, and based on inadequate data.

Although by 1982 it was obvious that things were starting to go wrong, the international lending machine was like a great ship which could not stop for many miles even after being thrown into reverse gear. The price of oil began to fall because of rising supplies and lower demand; world consumption fell from roughly 52 million barrels a day to 46 million barrels a day between 1979 and 1982. The price of oil (in U.S. dollars) fell from $32 a barrel in 1980 to $28 in 1983 and then plunged to $12 in March 1986. The oil-exporting countries in the Persian Gulf suddenly found themselves borrowing money instead of lending it. For the oil exporters in the western hemisphere—Mexico, Venezuela, and Ecuador—the financial situation became disastrous. Inflation, the flight of capital, and military ventures like that of the Argentine regime in the Falkland Islands, turned the promise of the 1970s into the nightmare of the 1980s. Interest payments were chewing up half the exports of countries like Argentina. The situation was not unlike that of home buyers who have committed half their incomes to paying the interest and principal on the mortgage.

By the time the ship stopped, there was no place to go ashore. The total external debt of fifteen less developed countries (including Mexico, Brazil, Venezuela, and Argentina) was more than $500 billion in 1986; of this, about $285 billion was owed to commercial banks and of that, about $24 billion was owed to the Canadian banks. (Not all of this huge sum was in trouble; there were loans to countries like South Korea which were perfectly capable of servicing their external debts; there were short-term loans for the financing of trade, and there were loans to non-government borrowers who were capable of paying, provided they could get the foreign exchange from their governments.) All six of the big Canadian banks were involved, with amounts ranging from about $5.5 billion in the case of the Royal and Montreal to about half that in the case of the National. As a percentage of the shareholders' equity the numbers ranged from about 170 percent in the case of the Bank of Montreal down to 92 percent in the case of the Commerce and Toronto-Dominion.

To put these numbers into perspective, a London-based organization called IBCA Banking Analysis Ltd. calculated in 1986 that the Canadian banks had about $17 billion (in U.S. dollars) in commercial bank loans to Latin American countries. Their numbers for the U.S. banks were $76 billion, for Japan $30 billion, the United Kingdom $29 billion, France $21 billion, Germany $18 billion, and Switzerland $6.5 billion.

Although by 1986 the Canadian banks had already built up their reserves against possible future losses on their LDC loans to $1 billion, the largest loan-loss provisions (out of earnings) were set aside in the following four years. By July 1990, the troubled Third World loans of the big six banks had been cut by almost half, to $13.5 billion, but against this figure the banks held reserves of $9 billion. So the "net exposure" of the big six on the LDC debt had been reduced in four years from about $22 billion to about $4 billion. As a percentage of the shareholders' funds, the remaining troubled Third World loans range from zero in the case of the Toronto-Dominion Bank to about 45 percent in the case of the Bank of Montreal, and average about 20 percent for the big six. In contrast, the five largest banks in the United Kingdom still have about 40 percent of their shareholders' equity in "net exposure" to troubled Third World loans; the three largest United States banks still have about 65 percent. Citicorp, under the leadership of Walter Wriston, was the world leader in the LDC stakes, with about $15 billion (U.S.), equal to about 90 percent of the LDC exposure of the Canadian banking system as a whole. It still has almost twice the exposure to the LDCs as all the Canadian banks combined.

The process of undoing the damage caused by the Canadian banks' participation in the global rush to recycle OPEC oil revenues has been extremely painful for the banks' shareholders and a political liability for the banks. The setting aside of huge reserves to cover possible losses on loans which may or may not be repaid was essential to restore the level of confidence in the safety of banks which they had always been accorded by the public. Fortunately for the banking industry, there was constant and unremitting pressure from Michael Mackenzie, the Superintendent of Financial Institutions after 1986, to increase reserves against loan losses to the maximum extent which the Ministers of Finance and Revenue would allow.

Mackenzie at that time had just retired from the accounting firm of Clarkson Gordon, where he had had a lifetime of experience as a chartered accountant, and more specifically as a bank auditor. His first job was to restore credibility to the function of the Inspector General's office after the failure of the western Canadian banks. The authority of his position was considerably enhanced when the government created the Office of the Superintendent of Financial Institutions (OSFI) with new legislation which went into effect July 1, 1987. Mackenzie promptly began using his clout with the Minister of Finance to require the banks to raise their reserves for possible losses on LDC loans.

There were dozens of agonizing meetings at which the complicated tax and accounting problems were worked out between the banks, the superintendent's office, and government officials. At first the target was 20 percent, then 30 percent, and by 1990 it was 45 percent. At each stage the loss provisions were deductible from income for tax purposes. Some critics argue that the loss reserves should not have been tax-deductible, despite the fact that all corporations pay taxes on their profits and deduct their losses from income. If the tax system were tilted so that the taxpayer shared only in corporate profits but not in losses, the corporate system would wither away.

At the time, most of the banks regarded Mackenzie's pressure on them as excessive and severe. In retrospect, it is now recognized that Mackenzie's stern approach to reducing the risks on the safety of the system was a major factor in restoring domestic and international confidence in the Canadian banking system.

Mackenzie was helped in his drive for adequate reserves by the willingness of most bank executives to bite the bullet. Some banks went much further than they were required to do, mostly by selling off their remaining LDC loans for what they would fetch in the world marketplace. Throughout the troubles of the 1980s, there was always a market of sorts for bank loans to Third World countries. In October 1989, for example, the resale value of loans to Brazil was around 28 percent of their face value; loans to Argentina fetched only about 18 percent, and loans to Mexico about 40 percent. In the case of Mexico, which is the largest LDC borrower from the Canadian banks, there was a special international debt restructuring scheme in July 1989. This also helped some of the Canadian banks to reduce their exposure to Mexico.

Still another factor in the huge downsizing of the LDC debt liability, and perhaps the most important element of all, was the decision of the group of ten industrialized countries to establish a new set of international standards for the capital adequacy of international banks. This process began with a recommendation from Paul Volcker, then chairman of the board of governors of the Federal Reserve System in the United States, to his fellow regulators in 1987. In February of that year, the Federal Reserve and the Bank of England had signed an accord requiring their big banks to observe minimum standards of shareholders' capital to support their assets.

The financial regulators often met at Basle, the headquarters for the Bank for International Settlements, which is a sort of central bank for the European central banks. At the 1987 meeting, Volcker proposed that the U.S.–U.K. accord should be extended to all members of the "Group of Ten." (The "G-10" actually numbered eleven, because it included Switzerland, which is not officially part of the G-10 group. The official members are the United States, the United Kingdom, Belgium, Canada, France, Germany, Italy, Japan, the Netherlands, and Luxembourg.) The chairman of the working committee appointed by the regulators was Peter Cooke, the spokesman for the Bank of England. The Canadian member on the "Cooke Committee" was Michael Mackenzie, who was normally joined at the meetings by a senior officer from the Bank of Canada.

After the Basle agreement was published on December 10, 1987, there was a great deal of jockeying for position among the major powers who wanted specific exemptions. The final terms, accepted by all, became a form of international law. As such, the "Basle Concordat" is a major landmark in international economic history, because it crystallizes a common rule of law across international borders. It is more than a symbol of the international global village — it is the reality of it.

The Basle Concordat established target dates and goals for all banks doing cross-border lending to international financial markets, with an interim target to be reached by 1990 and a final target for the end of 1992. By then each bank is supposed to have a minimum 4 percent of its "risk-weighted assets" in primary capital, which is defined as the shareholders' common equity plus retained earnings. (The percentage varies from zero for the least risky assets — government securities — to 4 percent or more for commercial loans.) But there is also a "second tier" of 4 percent, consisting of various types of "quasi capital" such as preferred stock and long-term debentures. The United States persuaded the other countries to accept up to 1.25 percent of second-tier capital in the form of general reserves against the LDC loans of the big American banks. The British banks got a concession which allowed them to include the revaluation surplus on their real properties, to the extent permitted by the Bank of England. And the Japanese were allowed to include in their capital up to 45 percent of the appreciation on their very large holdings of common stocks. Each concession was made to get an agreement which all the G-10 members would sign. But Mackenzie would not allow any of them to be applied to the Canadian banks. In August 1988, I accused Mackenzie in public of being "too conservative, refusing to give Canadian banks the sorts of concessions U.S., British and Japanese regulators have given their banks."

But in retrospect, Mackenzie was right. By pursuing a rigorous policy, he helped force the Canadian banks to take drastic action to strengthen their balance sheets. Three years later, the benefits of this approach are being felt in both the domestic and international markets. Many of the large American banks have failed to recognize their LDC liabilities to the same extent, and are now less competitive than the Canadian banks in North America. As for the Japanese banks, the concession which allowed them to include almost half of their stock market gains in their capital has turned out to be a boomerang. With a 35 percent decline in the Tokyo stock market in 1989-90, and having started from an extremely low level of capital in the first place — 1 percent or 2 percent of risk-weighted assets — the Japanese have had to pull in their horns. For the first time in almost a decade, the excessively thin margins between borrowing and lending rates in the global banking markets are getting some relief from the artificial conditions caused by the Japanese banks. (A bank can operate on thin margins if the ratio of its capital to its assets is highly levered.) And so the Basle Concordat has already gone some distance towards levelling the international playing field. In a world where huge amounts of investment funds can cross oceans in a matter of seconds, it did not make sense that the major institutions in North America and Europe could be undermined by the effects of the highly speculative Tokyo stock market on the Japanese banks.

The political fallout of the LDC debt problem took various forms. The owners of the trust companies were handed a stick with which to beat the banks; after the fact, they could claim greater wisdom, having been kept immune from the problem by their lack of commercial lending power. (In 1991, their greater wisdom is not so obvious in the real estate market.) The politicians were handed a stick with which to beat the banks about domestic issues such as service charges. And the bankers themselves, weakened by the public perception of their fallibility, were no longer prepared to wrestle with the government on policy questions such as the American Express application. After 1985, I began to feel that, if push came to shove, the pushing and shoving would be done by the Prime Minister and his friends in the trust companies and conglomerates. This had major implications for the direction of financial reform legislation.

THE OIL SHOCK AT HOME

The need to set aside huge amounts for possible future losses on LDC loans was by far the biggest banking disaster of the 1980s. But there was a secondary banking disaster arising from the oil shocks of 1973 to 1979: this was the fallout from an erratic and misguided national oil policy.

As early as 1973 the government decided to pursue a policy of eventual self-sufficiency in oil. The idea was that Canada could shelter itself from the behaviour of the OPEC oil cartel by eliminating oil imports. In the interval, Canada would protect consumers by not following the world price of oil. Even though Canada's reserves of oil from conventional sources were barely sufficient to meet national demand for fifteen years, there were the huge reserves in the oil sands and in frontier oil. No matter that the cost of extracting such oil could be five or even ten times higher than the cost of importing oil, the theory was that Canada could be self-sufficient. (More recently we have watched with fascinated horror the attempt of Newfoundland to be self-sufficient in the production of cucumbers.)

The National Energy Policy was first articulated in 1973, and confirmed in 1976 and again in 1980. In order to shelter the Canadian consumer from the reality of world prices, it was necessary to have a blended price of oil, weighted by the high price of imports and the much lower price of Albertan oil imposed on the western producers. The basic result of the policy was to encourage more consumption and less production than would otherwise have been the case. Not only was the economic policy misguided, but as a political policy it was an unqualified disaster. It created a very deep-seated feeling of betrayal in the West and confirmed what westerners had always thought about selfish eastern interests. In the heavily populated central provinces, it led consumers into a quite false feeling of comfort and self-satisfaction that Canada could pull itself up by its own bootstraps.

Most of the underlying assumptions of the National Energy Policy were erroneous. Oil had been underpriced for fifty years because of the weakness of the producing countries. The oil cartel may have initiated the price rise, but the underlying reality was that the price had not reflected the relationship between demand and supply. Within a few years of the second oil shock, oil production from non-OPEC countries exceeded oil production from OPEC countries, so that a monopolistic price imposed by OPEC was not feasible. Had other producers, like Britain and Norway in the North Sea, wished to undercut the OPEC price, they were perfectly capable of doing so. But their price was the same as the OPEC price, more or less, because that was the price the world was prepared to pay.

After much wrangling and bickering between the federal government and Alberta, an agreement was reached in September 1981 that attempted to reconcile the interests of consumers, producers, and the federal and provincial governments. This energy-pricing agreement set out a bureaucrats' plan for the price of oil over the next decade. As Leonard Waverman said a few years later, it was "an attempt to substitute administered rigidities for an effective market system." Another economist, Wendy Dobson, who later became president of the C.D. Howe Institute, said: "The signal of increasing scarcity is to be found in the price schedule, not in the current price." What she meant was that the price of oil to be received by the Alberta producers would be held to a slow rate of growth for some years. Even so, the schedule predicted the price of "old oil" (existing reserves) rising from $18.75 in 1981 to about $56 five years later. At that time, the U.S. Department of Energy was forecasting the price of oil at $60 U.S. in 1985 and $96 in 1990.

The National Energy Policy had major consequences for the chartered banks, because of their loans to the oil and gas industry. There was official sanction for the universally held belief that the price of oil would double, or even triple, in the next ten or fifteen years. Given that forecast, it was not difficult for oil and gas producers to raise huge sums of money from the banks against the security of their petroleum reserves in the ground. Far from being realized, however, the forecasts proved to be dreadfully wrong. Instead of a controlled Canadian dollar price of $66 a barrel in 1990 under the National Energy Policy, the price was more like $22 Canadian. And instead of a world price of $96 (in U.S.) by 1990, the price was fluctuating below $20 a barrel. Of course this was all forgotten afterwards by governments, who attempted to distance themselves from the financial fallout, just as they had distanced themselves from the LDC debt problem which had arisen from the recycling of OPEC oil revenues.

The competitive rush to make large loans to the petroleum industry in Alberta was the domestic counterpart of the loans to the less developed countries. But there were some major differences: first, the aggregate loans of the big six to the Canadian oil and gas industry never exceeded more than one-quarter of the LDC loans except for a brief period in 1986; secondly, there was not the foreign exchange risk implicit in loans to sovereign countries which had to find enough U.S. dollars to repay principal and interest; and thirdly, most of the loans to the petroleum industry were secured by marketable assets.

In the spring of 1981, four of the big six Canadian banks lent about $2 billion to Dome Petroleum to help finance the company's takeover of Hudson's Bay Oil and Gas (HBOG). Not long afterwards, a further $2 billion loan to Dome was provided by a syndicate headed by Citibank, in which dozens of banks around the world participated. The second loan was negotiated secretly without the knowledge of the lenders on the first loan, and Dome managed to provide security to the Citibank group which the Canadian banks thought was pledged to them. Since Dome was the darling of the nationalists and the flagship of the National Energy Policy, there was a tendency to overlook the fact that the price paid for HBOG probably made the bank loans unsound from the moment the deals were signed. The Dome financing was the largest of all the energy loans, although two government-owned entities—Petrocan and Canadian Development Corporation—between them had larger loans from the Canadian banks.

The Dome financing was hardly in place before interest rates skyrocketed, and the Canadian prime rate soared to 22.75 percent in 1982. Most of Dome's bank borrowings had been done at a "floating rate," that is, a rate of interest which was adjusted from time to time in relation to the U.S. dollar prime rate of the Canadian banks, or to what is known as *Libor*—the London Interbank Borrowing Rate. One financial analyst estimated that for every 1 percent increase in interest rates, the cost to Dome was $50 million. Dome was forced to ask its creditors for relief; this was the opening shot in a five-year battle which ended only with the sale of Dome's assets to Amoco Petroleum in 1987. The directors of Dome (and the bankers) imported a Scotsman named Howard MacDonald to assume control of Dome in place of Jack Gallagher.

Although interest rates declined sharply from the record levels of 1982, Dome's problems were compounded by the decline in the price of oil from $32 a barrel to $12 a barrel. By 1986, Dome was a celebrated basket case. In March 1986, one investment dealer estimated that the big banks had the following amounts on loan to Dome: CIBC $899 million, Bank of Montreal $847 million, Toronto-Dominion $747 million, Royal $183 million, and National $78 million. The Bank of Nova Scotia was not involved in the original financing. The United States banks had loans of $1,054 million, while the European banks had $771 million and the Japanese $202 million. Altogether, Dome's debts were in the order of $6.6 billion.

There were important differences in the ranking of the creditors on the totem pole. The Bank of Montreal considered itself the best secured, and was incensed when Dome proposed that it accept some losses on its loans. Some unsecured creditors were to receive 45¢ on the dollar, and even the shareholders were to be given something. The battle was so bitter between the various creditors that at one point, the Bank of Montreal appeared before a Senate committee to blast the Dome management for having worked out a deal with Amoco on which the bank lenders had never been consulted.

In the end, Amoco paid about $5.5 billion for Dome, and the Canadian banks recovered about 95¢ on the dollar. But for several years, the shaky condition of Dome was used by critics of the banks to demonstrate that the banks were unduly committed to large corporate borrowers. Some analysts in the stock brokerage business, with the lucidity of hindsight for which they are sometimes noted, were very critical of the impact of the Dome loans on bank profits. They tended to forget that they had been pushing the stock when the loans were made. After the Amoco purchase of Dome, no more was heard in the media of the banks' excessive financing of the oil and gas industry. And in the meantime, the National Energy Policy had given way to a less nationalistic point of view, and one which gave more recognition to the legitimate grievances of Alberta.

THE TRUST COMPANY FAILURES

In the late 1980s, the general public became aware of the vast scale of losses on the insured deposits of savings and loans institutions in the United States—about the same as the cost of the war in Vietnam. The size of the numbers is almost beyond comprehension; there are some estimates that it will eventually cost $500 billion or more to clean up the problem, including the cost to taxpayers of interest on loans for the next thirty or forty years. Leaving aside compound interest, estimates of the immediate cost are in the order of $150 to $200 billion. No one knows what the assets of the savings and loan associations will fetch in the market, but by any measure the losses are truly astronomical. Nor is the American problem confined to savings and loan associations; scores of banks are in difficulty, some of them quite large ones.

By comparison, the total of all sums paid out by the Canada Deposit Insurance Corporation (CDIC) since its inception (together with money paid out by the government to uninsured depositors) has been less than $6 billion (nearly all of it in the 1980s). And of this amount, something approaching $3 billion has been recovered from the sale of assets. Most of the remainder is being raised through the higher deposit insurance premiums paid by banks and trust companies. The money paid out by the government to uninsured depositors, however, may never be recovered. These numbers may not look so colossal beside the spectacular excesses in the United States, but they are still very large. Compared to the Home Bank failure in 1923, which cost the taxpayers about $3.5 million, the net losses from the failure of trust companies and banks in the 1980s were roughly 1,000 times greater. Clearly there was something missing in the prudential process, despite all the regulatory standards implemented in banking after 1923. The main thing missing was that the lessons learned in the early decades of the century had been largely ignored in the process of permitting trust companies to become banks without them having to abide by the constraints of the Bank Act. And deposit insurance had opened the door to imprudent practices in small banks as well.

What made the failures of the 1980s particularly troublesome was that several of the most important failures were in western Canada. This undermined the aspiration of westerners to have financial institutions owned and controlled in the West, and thereby contributed to the centrifugal forces in the Canadian confederation. One of the most recent failures to fall into the Canada Deposit Insurance Corporation safety net was Principal Savings and Trust Company of Edmonton in 1987. This was an insured member of the Cormie group of financial institutions, most of which are still involved in ongoing litigation in Alberta.

Gradually the failures of the early 1980s are being paid for. Although there have been significant improvements in the regulatory process, deposit insurance still provides a temptation to financial buccaneers, so one could not say that the problems have all been put in the past. The severity of the problems in the United States is forcing the politicians there to back away, slowly and reluctantly, from the weak and fragmented banking structure which resulted from the crucial decision in 1836 to reject national branch banking.

There are some common themes in the failures of deposit-taking institutions in Canada and the United States, but also some differences. The biggest difference is that, in Canada, there has never been the outright corruption of politicians that has marked the American experience. There is no evidence to date that Canadian politicians or civil servants have been bought off and personally enriched by owners of financial institutions. This is not the same as saying that politicians in Canada have not been influenced by the owners of financial institutions.

The history of the trust company failures in the 1980s began with the granting of licences to applicants who were clearly unsuited by reason of character and qualifications to run deposit-taking institutions. Unlike other corporations, banks and trust companies are dealing in other people's money. For that reason, rules against self-dealing and conflict of interest are far more important than would be the case with, say, a lumber company or a grocery chain.

To open a bank, one had to obtain a specific charter from Parliament, which provided a good opportunity for a public review of the applicant's qualifications. This was changed in 1980 for banks, including the foreign bank subsidiaries, but in that case the applicants were themselves regulated foreign banks.

In the case of federal trust companies, individual charters were abandoned in 1970 in favour of a system of incorporation; at the provincial level, the licensing process was always very casual, and there was no review whatever of the transfer of a licence to a new owner.

An early example in the 1980s was Astra Trust which was granted a federal licence, partly on the strength of a recommendation from an Ontario cabinet minister, even though his own department had refused an Ontario licence. Its founder, Carlo Montemurro, was described in a book by Patricia Best and Ann Shortell on the trust industry as "proven to be a liar and a thief." This book, *A Matter of Trust*, gives a detailed account of several of the most notorious trust company failures in the early 1980s. Among them were Pocklington's Fidelity Trust, Rosenberg's Greymac Trust and Crown Trust, Markle's Seaway Trust, Axton's Dominion Trust, and several other contributors to the Canada Deposit Insurance Corporation's huge deficit.

My purpose is not to repeat the story of the dozen trust company collapses of the 1980s, but to examine the politics which allowed that to happen. Until the 1950s, the deposit-taking function of the trust companies was marginal, and the trust companies had never been viewed as banks. The first trust company in Canada, the Toronto General Trust, was founded in 1872. The first general Ontario legislation on trust companies in 1907 said, "A trust company shall not borrow money by taking deposits." But in 1921 this was changed to allow them to take a deposit "in trust" and to pay interest on it. The same applied in Quebec. There were also federal charters for trust companies that wanted to cross provincial boundaries. As Neufeld has documented, the earliest federal charters had a clause which read: "Nothing in this act shall be construed to authorize the corporation . . . to engage in the business of banking and insurance."

There were several reasons for the banks' absence from the trust business—unlike banks in most countries. The first and best reason was that trust company functions were a matter of property and civil rights, a provincial matter. The federally chartered banks simply did not have the power to perform fiduciary functions, as long as the federal government retained exclusive authority over them. These include taking care of the property of deceased persons. A trust can also be a "living trust" for individuals or institutions, such as managing the assets of a pension fund or the endowments of a charitable trust. It is interesting that the early texts on banking, by Adam Shortt and by R.M. Breckenridge, as well as the histories of the individual banks, do not even mention the fiduciary function. Best and Shortell, however, seem to suffer from a common journalistic myopia towards banks. According to them, "the traditional financial institutions, the banks, were uneasy about taking over the handling of these estates and trustee duties, a kind of business their corporate laws and minds didn't encompass." Whatever their bankerish minds could or couldn't encompass, the plain fact is that the federal government would have had to share administrative authority with the provinces if it had allowed the banks to exercise fiduciary powers.

Apart from the constitutional aspects of the law of property, there was "the prevailing view that to execute a trust required a conscience," as Neufeld has written, and it was difficult to see how a corporate entity could have a conscience. Neufeld goes on to say that "the concept of the corporate trustee is essentially a North American one," and was not imported from England. Since banks could not exercise fiduciary powers under the British North America Act, and since lawyers had a tendency to die eventually, the notion of a corporate trustee who outlived mortal caretakers of property was a sensible solution.

From 1872 onwards the trust companies performed the fiduciary function quite successfully. They may have been stodgy and conservative, but the management of property on behalf of those who are dead or who are unable to act for themselves is by definition a function requiring conservatism. In the introduction to their book, Best and Shortell say: "The old guard's influence is on the wane and the entrepreneurs' star is in the ascendent . . . This book chronicles the shift in mores that has seen an Establishment business dedicated to passing on the wealth of the grandfather to the grandson itself pass into the hands of men whose heritage is a blank page, whose connections are built with skill rather than based on family." This is a puzzling interpretation of the rise of the new wave of trust company owners, since most of them helped to bring the trust company business into disrepute until their wreckage was cleaned up.

There is little doubt that the 6 percent ceiling on bank lending rates was the key factor in fast growth of the trust companies and mortgage loan companies, starting about 1955. The Porter Commission report noted that the assets of the trust companies went from 6.8 percent of bank assets in 1955 to 12.6 percent in 1962. The mortgage loan companies, which were similar to trust companies, did almost as well. The irony of this rapid growth is that it came just after the Bank Act revision of 1954, which gave the banks power to make residential mortgage loans for the first time. But as we have seen in Chapter 9, the 6 percent interest rate ceiling soon became a barrier for the banks, and they dropped out of the mortgage market for some years. The trust companies suddenly discovered that they were able to compete for deposits, and they had no trouble finding profitable assets. There was a pronounced shift towards "intermediation" (taking deposits and making loans), as opposed to the traditional business of "estates, trusts, and agencies." There was a small stampede to incorporate new trust companies: from 1959 to 1964, the number of provincially supervised companies went from thirty-three to forty-seven. The number of trust company branches exploded from 137 in 1956 to 470 in 1967.

The 6 percent ceiling was not the only factor which knocked the banks out of the mortgage market; the trust companies did not have to keep cash reserves at the Bank of Canada, and provincial supervision was relatively loose. The imbalance might have been corrected, and the constitutional power of the federal government restored, if the Minister of Finance had not been Walter Gordon. In 1964 the Porter report said: "In our view the federal banking legislation must cover all private financial institutions issuing banking liabilities." Porter went on to define "banking liabilities" very precisely; the definition would have included the demand deposits and the guaranteed investment certificates of the trust and loan companies, if they matured within 100 days.

But Walter Gordon was a strong nationalist. As we have seen, he ignored Porter's recommendations and concentrated on the foreign ownership question. To be fair, successive Ministers of Finance could have gone back to the Porter report, but they failed to do so.

In Chapter 11 I noted that September 22, 1964, was a historic date in Canadian financial legislation. That evening, Walter Gordon introduced a motion which limited the foreign ownership of federally incorporated trust and loan companies and insurance companies. He said that the new constraints would come into force effective "midnight tonight." The amending bill was tabled the next day, introducing the regulation that a foreign shareholder could not hold more than 10 percent of the shares in a trust company, and the aggregate non-resident holdings in a company could not exceed 25 percent.

Although Walter Gordon declared that the same restriction would

apply to the shares of chartered banks, the relevant change in the
Bank Act did not occur until 1967, more than two years after the
change in the trust and loan and insurance legislation. Best and
Shortell assert that "Bank executives have always had favoured status
with politicians; they forced the federal government to institute a 10
percent ownership limit on their shares in the early 60s, in the name
of nationalism, when the Toronto Dominion Bank was threatened
with a take-over by a U.S. bank." In point of fact, the banking industry
knew nothing of Walter Gordon's intentions and made no comment
whatever on Bill C-123 when it was referred to the Standing Committee on Banking and Commerce in late October 1964. The banks never
appeared before the committee, nor did the insurance companies.
Many of the major insurance companies, such as Mutual Life, Canada
Life, Confederation Life, Manufacturers Life, North American Life,
and Sun Life, were already mutual companies. In several cases this
had come about through emergency legislation in 1957 which had
allowed shareholder-owned insurance companies to turn themselves
into mutual companies. This measure had been taken to forestall
foreign acquisitions of Canadian insurance companies.

As for the trust companies, they too made no comment on the
foreign ownership provisions. When the executive director of the
Trust Companies' Association, E.F.K. Nelson, appeared before
the committee on November 12, 1964, the discussion focused entirely
on sections of the bill which increased the permissible ratio on
residential mortgage loans from 66.66 percent to 75 percent of the
property value. The Banking Committee hearings were quite brief,
and on the last day Walter Gordon reviewed his reasons for introducing the restrictions on foreign ownership. There was no complaint
from the opposition. In fact, the Progressive Conservative and NDP
parties had already commended Walter Gordon for his 10 percent–25
percent rule during the first reading of the bill on September 23.
Oddly enough, the foreign ownership legislation had only been
tacked on to the end of a bill which was intended to enlarge the
business and powers of the trust and loan and insurance companies.

In May 1965, the 10 percent ownership rule was applied almost as
an afterthought to residents as well as non-residents when the draft
Bank Act amendments were first published. This critical change was
never added to the trust company legislation. It was not until late 1966
and early 1967 that the banks brought the subject up for public debate,
and even then they could not agree among themselves about foreign
ownership. The Porter Commission had recommended restrictions

ownership. The Porter Commission had recommended restrictions on foreign ownership and strongly favoured broadly held Canadian financial institutions. Douglas Gibson's testimony to the Standing Committee on Finance, Trade and Economic Affairs reiterated the recommendation of the commission's report (he was chief operating officer of the Bank of Nova Scotia as well as a Porter commissioner). But as recently as December 1990, a member of the House of Commons Finance Committee, John Rodriguez, asserted (to Dick Thomson, the chairman of the Toronto-Dominion Bank): "You opposed the widely held proposal in 1967, and then you changed your tune." Neither accusation is true. The banks did not oppose widely held ownership in 1967, so there was no need to change their tune later on.

Without much discussion or any opposition, the foreign ownership restrictions on trust, loan and insurance companies were given Royal Assent in March 1965. Oddly enough, the trust and loan and insurance companies took little interest in the legislation. It is often said that the decennial revision of the Bank Act has given the banks an unfair advantage through the modernization of their legislation, whereas nothing has been done for the trust, loan and insurance companies. The truth is that there have been several very important amendments to the federal legislation dealing with these companies, and there is no evidence that they felt left out. The principal companies and the associations did not appear before the finance committee in 1954 and 1967, and only briefly in 1964. One group of trust companies did appear in 1967—a group of twelve small trust companies led by Sinclair Stevens, who represented the largest of them, the York Trust and Savings Corp. Stevens was quite persuasive, in the eyes of the committee, in arguing that the banks made it hard for a small trust company to survive. In fact, the banks had just gone out of their way to keep York Trust afloat. It had become caught in a classic mismatch between short-term deposits and long-term NHA mortgage loans, when interest rates increased and squeezed its margins.

Sinclair Stevens was right about at least one thing in his testimony, and that was the close relationship between some of the largest trust companies and the banks. But this was not exactly a great revelation. In 1929 Benjamin Beckhart had described the origins of the trust companies as affiliates of the banks. Denison's history of the Bank of Montreal records the creation of the Royal Trust in 1892 as an affiliate of the bank. The general manager of the bank and nine of the sixteen directors sat on the board of the Royal Trust. Its job was to perform the fiduciary functions which the bank could not handle; the trust company could also help the bank by providing residential mortgage loans to its customers, something else the bank could not do. The Royal Bank had a similar association with the Montreal Trust. In Toronto, the National Trust was part of an interlocking but not an exclusive association involving the Bank of Commerce, Canada Life, and Imperial Life. The other large trust company in Toronto was the Canada Permanent which resulted from a merger with the Toronto General Trust in 1961, and a second merger with the Eastern and Chartered Trust in 1965.

The two big trust companies in Montreal—the Royal and the Montreal—held almost 60 percent of the total assets in the estates, trust, and agency business in Canada in 1969. The reason for such a concentration of assets in the two Montreal companies was that Montreal was the home of the oldest anglophone families with inherited wealth. The two big Toronto trust companies—the National and the Permanent—held about 16 percent of all the estates, trust, and agency assets. Toronto was a latecomer in the building of personal wealth, and London, Ontario, the home of Canada Trust, was even more of an upstart. The dozens of small trust companies shared only a quarter of the total estates, trust, and agency assets, and were much more dependent on intermediation business.

When the Porter Commission looked at the interlocking relationships between the large banks and large trust companies, it concluded that competition would be increased by forcing the banks to sell down to 10 percent where their shareholdings of trust companies exceeded that proportion, and also to eliminate interlocking corporate directorships. This part of the commission report was accepted in the 1967 Bank Act revision. But the banks and trust companies were already drifting apart, because the trust companies had lately expanded their deposit-taking in competition with banks, and by then the banks had little or no influence on their policies.

But the drift of the trust companies into the banking business was constrained by their lack of legal powers to make unsecured commercial loans. In the 1970s and 1980s, the trust companies made increasingly effective political representations to the effect that the lack of diversification on the asset side of their balance sheets placed them at a unfair disadvantage vis-à-vis the banks. More and more, the politicians and the public forgot that trust companies had been created to supplement the functions of banks, not to compete with them directly. The trust companies complained that the banks had been allowed into the mortgage business, forgetting that in 1954 they

had gone on record as accepting the sharing of the residential mortgage field.

Although it was not obvious at the time—or for many years afterwards—the Bank Act revision of 1967 had a decisive effect on the
ownership of trust companies. First of all, it required the four major
companies—the Royal Trust, the Montreal Trust, the Canada Permanent and the National Trust—to relinquish their bank relationships. Secondly, the 10 percent ownership limit which had been
introduced for banks applied only to the non-resident shareholders of
trust and loan companies and insurance companies. Thirdly, the
federal government had once again failed to define banking. Taken
together, these three factors made the large trust companies into
takeover targets. With the banks out of the picture, a series of takeover
battles took place which led to the concentration of ownership of all
the large trust companies and most of the small ones. The consolidation process took about twenty years, starting around 1965, but most
of the big mergers happened in a very short interval from 1979 to
1983.

One of the first mergers was that of British Mortgage in Stratford,
Ontario, which had failed in 1965 after misguided dealings with a
company called Atlantic Acceptance. The government of Ontario
engineered a merger of British Mortgage into Victoria & Grey Trust
Company whose headquarters were in Lindsay, Ontario. Subsequently, Hal Jackman took effective control of Victoria & Grey, and in
1979 also acquired Metropolitan Trust. Later, Jackman was able to
combine Victoria & Grey with the National Trust, retaining the name
of the latter.

In Montreal, Paul Desmarais bought control of the Montreal Trust
from the Canadian Pacific in 1967, but sold his controlling interest in
1989 to Bell Canada Enterprises. The Royal Trust remained broadly
owned until August 1980, when Robert Campeau made his celebrated bid for the company. The management of Royal Trust sought a
"white knight" and a group was formed to outbid Campeau. Among
the bidders were Sun Life, the Oxford Group, the Toronto-Dominion
Bank, several other banks, and most importantly, Olympia & York,
the vehicle of the Reichmann brothers. After the Campeau bid was
defeated, the Reichmanns sold their 17 percent interest to Brascan in
1981. Brascan, a holding company for a major part of the (Edper)
Bronfman interests, then acquired effective control of Royal Trust.

As we have seen, the Bank Act of 1967 required the Toronto-
Dominion and the Bank of Nova Scotia to reduce their interests in the

Canada Permanent to less than 10 percent. The Permanent remained broadly held until the Belzberg family of Vancouver, who owned a small trust company called First City Trust, made a move to gain control in April 1981. (They had already made an unsuccessful approach to Metropolitan Trust before it was merged with Victoria & Grey.) Once again there was a violent confrontation in the stock market between rival groups, and eventually Genstar, a holding company based in San Francisco, succeeded in winning control.

Thus by 1981, the four old major trust companies in Canada, with about 75 percent of all the fiduciary business, had been acquired by controlling shareholders.

Meanwhile, however, another major trust company had emerged. This was the Canada Trust, based in London, Ontario. For many years its management had been generally regarded as being of exceptional quality, and it was also well-known for its outspoken support for the 10 percent ownership limit on deposit-taking institutions. In 1984, its chairman, Merv Lahn, noted "the sad fact that all major Canadian trust and loan companies, apart from Canada Trustco, are now controlled directly, or indirectly, by dominant shareholders." Canada Trust had already fought off an attempt by the Manufacturers Life Insurance Company to acquire effective control in 1982. Like the Canada Permanent and the Royal Trust, the Canada Trust introduced a corporate by-law which prevented any single shareholder from voting more than 10 percent of the voting shares. This apparently decisive protection against a takeover proved to be illusory; if a buyer acquired enough shares, he could overturn the by-law.

In the face of increasing evidence of abusive self-dealing by the owners of some small trust companies, Merv Lahn appealed to the Government of Canada to implement the 10 percent ownership limit on trust companies. His appeals fell on deaf ears. His efforts to hold out for a 10 percent ownership limit are well documented in a recent history of the Canada Trust by Philip Smith called *The Trust-Builders*. In one speech, Lahn said: "The single most important contributing factor [to abusive self-dealing] was the ability, within current law and regulation, for one individual to control a trust or loan company . . . Widely held ownership prevents a crook or a few crooks from looting deposit-taking institutions." His remarks were directed at the scandalous abuse of about a dozen smaller trust companies, and not at the new controlling owners of the major trust companies. The problem was that public policy in Ottawa was driven by the views of a very small number of trust company owners who could not themselves be accused of abusive self-dealing. This group persuaded the Liberal government in the early 1980s, and later the Progressive Conservative government, that closely held financial institutions would be better managed than widely held ones, because there would be a concerned hands-on owner watching over management. Despite the fact that the widely held Canada Trust was clear testimony to the contrary, this view became the prevailing one not only in Ottawa but in the provincial capitals.

The influence of Paul Desmarais of Montreal Trust, Trevor Eyton of Brascan, Hal Jackman of National Trust, and Claude Castonguay of Laurentian Life far exceeded that of the chief executive officers of the banks on the ownership issue. On many occasions I was asked to be the spokesman for the banking industry at financial conferences. At several of these, I had knock-down, drag-out battles in public with Hal Jackman, a friend with whom I agreed on many issues—except on the question of ownership. The top bankers often avoided these affairs, as they were preoccupied in the early 1980s by the credit problems of the recession of 1981-82, and by LDC debt problems. But the image conveyed to the media and to the financial markets was that the owners like Eyton and Jackman were prepared to stand up and speak for themselves, while the bankers were satisfied to rely on a hired gun.

Although Merv Lahn was the outstanding exception to this management style, his views did not prevail. After a strenuous battle in 1984, Genstar made a bid for 100 percent of Canada Trust, putting it out of reach of the Manufacturers Life which was restricted by law to 30 percent. Shortly afterwards, the Montreal holding company Imasco swallowed Genstar itself, and thus the Canada Trust too became closely held. The government, which had been, in effect, a silent partner of the trust company takeovers, suddenly decided that for very large trust companies, it would be a good idea to have 35 percent of the shares held by the public. This afterthought of Tom Hockin, the Minister of State (Finance) in 1986, has remained public policy with the publication of the financial reform legislation which is currently under consideration by Parliament.

While the major companies were being swallowed by large but honest owners, a quite different game was going on with many of the smaller companies. Laws against stealing are not enacted for the 99 percent of the population who do not steal, but for the 1 percent who do. In the last ten or fifteen years, politicians have not been able to understand that limits on the ownership of deposit-taking institutions are not aimed at the honest majority, but at the dishonest minority. The government's solution to the problem of self-dealing was two-fold: more regulation, and when regulation failed, greater use of deposit insurance to bail out the depositors. But as Merv Lahn put it: "Owners will always be several steps ahead of the regulators."

In the late 1970s and early 1980s, the owners were several jumps ahead of the regulators. For example, the *Globe and Mail* reported on October 7, 1989: "Robert Braun, the General Manager of Seaway Trust Company testified yesterday that in the months after William Player secretly became part owner of the firm, about 85 percent of Seaway's mortgage loans went to Player." Mr. Braun said he and the lawyer [Joseph Cornacchia] had talked of "all the fun and all the money you could make if you had control of a trust company." In 1987, William Player was sentenced to fifteen years in prison for his role in defrauding Seaway Trust and two other trust companies. The painfully slow progress of the justice system in Canada has left many other cases unresolved.

Art Mingay, the chairman of Canada Trust and Merv Lahn's colleague, once remarked, "If you look at the people in Canada who have been interested [in acquiring a trust company] they have all been in the real estate business." A common feature of the savings and loan scandal in the United States, the Home Bank scandal in 1923, and the trust and loan company scandals in Canada was the manipulation of real estate transactions for the benefit of the owner of the financial institution. Perhaps the most common method—though not the only one—was to make excessive mortgage loans on commercial properties. Any homeowner can understand that if he buys a house for $100,000, and is able to put a mortgage of $200,000 on it, he can walk away with $100,000 cash for himself. He then uses his engineered profit of $100,000 to buy another house, and repeats the process. In other cases, the real equity ownership in the property, and not just the mortgage, was churned over at artificial prices.

All of this was allowed to go on because of weak licensing and enforcement of the regulations at both federal and provincial levels, political cover-ups in Ottawa and the provincial capitals, and incompetent opposition critics who did not understand what was going on. The politicians' first instinct was to suppress public inquiries and transfer blame to a different level of government. Their second instinct was to pay off angry depositors, primarily with funds from the Canada Deposit Insurance Corporation, but failing that, with tax-payers' money. (The parallel to Sir Thomas White's response to Sir

Henry Pellatt's dealings with the Home Bank, seventy years ago, is almost ludicrous.)

Not only have governments succeeded in avoiding responsibility for huge losses, but they seem to be successful in prolonging the conditions which produced the losses in the first place. Since there will always be a minority of clever and unscrupulous people to manipulate gullible politicians and the public, laws are usually written to penalize such behaviour. But in the case of deposit insurance, the law actually serves to encourage it.

THE USES AND ABUSES OF DEPOSIT INSURANCE

Deposit insurance was first introduced in Canada in 1967, concurrent with the Bank Act revision that year. The first law was passed in Ontario as a response to the mismanagement of British Mortgage in 1965. When the federal government responded with its own legislation only a week after the Ontario bill, the provincial government decided to allow the trust and loan companies under its jurisdiction to apply for membership in the federal plan. The province of Quebec opted out of federal deposit insurance, setting up its own scheme, the Quebec Deposit Insurance Board. (Subsequently, Quebec took care of its financial institution failures itself, unlike Ontario.)

The theory behind deposit insurance was that members of the public could not be expected to assess the financial soundness of institutions in which they place their savings on deposit. Of course this was not meant to apply to the big six banks or the largest trust companies, which were always considered to be sound. The idea was to create a level playing field by making it possible for small institutions to compete for deposits with the big banks. At first, the limit on deposit insurance was $20,000, but this was changed in 1983 to $60,000. In fact $60,000 is not the real limit, because there are different types of accounts eligible for deposit insurance for a single individual, and in a family there can be a number of joint accounts. Altogether, it would be possible to have about $500,000 insured in a single institution, but with dozens of institutions to choose from, even a multimillionaire can be fully insured.

Opposing insurance is like opposing motherhood. The problem was that deposit insurance left the door wide open to imprudent and fraudulent activity. A single individual could own a trust company and use its deposits for funding his own real estate activities. Small

institutions could outbid the banks for deposits, employing the money
in much riskier assets; if the company prospered by taking big risks,
the trust company owner won; if the company became overextended,
deposit insurance would bail out the depositors and there would be no
political outcry. The trust company owner might lose his equity in the
trust company, but no matter, he had already extracted huge profits in
land assembly or through overstated mortgage values.

Between 1982 and 1985, twelve trust and loan companies were
caught in the security blanket of the Canada Deposit Insurance
Corporation. By 1989, the CDIC had paid out the following amounts
for the ten largest:

1982	District Trust	$231 million
1983	Crown Trust	$930 million
1983	Fidelity Trust	$791 million
1983	Greymac Mortgage	$174 million
1983	Greymac Trust	$240 million
1983	Seaway Mortgage	$120 million
1983	Seaway Trust	$300 million
1985	Continental Trust	$113 million
1985	Pioneer Trust	$201 million
1985	Western Capital Trust	$77 million
	Total	$3,177 million

In eight years, CDIC recovered more than two-thirds of this amount
through the disposition of assets, leaving estimated losses at $827
million for these ten companies. (In 1987, two Edmonton-based trust
companies—Northwest Trust and Principal Savings and Trust Company—were added to the list of failures, contributing together about
$400 million to the pay-outs. But the Ontario regulators had learned a
lesson; the Principal Group had not been allowed to conduct business
in Ontario, despite efforts to obtain a licence. Other provinces—
British Columbia and New Brunswick for example—had allowed
their citizens to deposit with the Cormie companies.)

Instead of putting the failed trust companies into liquidation immediately, the Canada Deposit Insurance Corporation adopted a
policy of putting the failed companies in the hands of some other trust
company or foreign bank subsidiary as agent, beginning with the
District Trust in 1982. This infuriated the big six banks because it
meant that the uninsured depositors (those with deposits exceeding
$60,000) would be paid back as well as the insured. This was contrary

to the intent of the deposit insurance legislation, which was designed to protect the unsophisticated small customer. Since the premiums to fund the CDIC were paid almost entirely by the large banks and trust companies, this meant that the major institutions were forced to pay for the mismanagement and fraud of the failed companies. The banks paid 75 percent of the premiums but had no say whatsoever in the policies.

In *A Matter of Trust* by Shortell and Best, we read: "The CDIC is controlled by the groups it insures." Surely nothing in the whole chronicle of the 1980s could be further from the truth. In fact the banks had no voice in the policies of the CDIC—then or now. Until 1988, its board consisted of a part-time chairman with a trust company background and four senior officials in Ottawa: the governor of the Bank of Canada, the deputy minister of finance, the Superintendent of Insurance, and the Inspector General of Banks. There were no representatives from the banks, and this is still the case. In contrast, the boards of the deposit insurance corporations in British Columbia and Ontario, which administer deposit insurance for the credit unions, have two representatives from the credit unions out of nine board members. In the United States, the Federal Deposit Insurance Corporation Board consists of three presidential appointees, all of whom are independent of the Treasury and of the Federal Reserve Board.

In 1986, the government decided to add private-sector members to the board of CDIC. On behalf of the banks, I lobbied long and hard for at least one retired banker who knew something about commercial lending. In July 1986, I sent Tom Hockin, the Minister of State (Finance), a list of thirteen suggestions. The list included academics, retired bankers, and senior business executives. The minister did not bother to acknowledge my letter. The government appointed Ronald McKinlay, a former senior partner of a major accounting firm, as chairman, and four other private-sector directors. There is still no representative from the institutions which pay the premiums on the CDIC board.

Prior to the enlargement of the CDIC's board, its composition was particularly Ottawa-oriented. The board was both judge and jury; the regulators could decide when and how to deal with failing institutions; the governor of the Bank of Canada was in a position to make large loans to a member institution on the assurance from his fellow director, the Inspector General, that the institution was viable. The Bank of Canada had the first claim in the event of default. Later, this inherent conflict of interest was confirmed with a vengeance. In 1985 the Bank of Canada advanced $1.3 billion to the Canadian Commercial Bank, insisting in public that it was sound, on the strength of an opinion from the Inspector General's office which was later shown to be based on insufficient research. In the liquidation process, the Bank of Canada had the first claim on assets, thereby relegating the CDIC's claims to a subordinate position, and increasing the ultimate reliance on the banks and trust companies which pay the premiums. The other three public-sector members of the board—the deputy minister of finance, the Inspector General of Banks, and the Superintendent of Insurance—were all answerable to the Minister of Finance, who might have policy objectives other than the administration of the insurance funds. One was to maintain western-based institutions even when they were perceived to be in serious difficulty.

The failure to separate the insurance function from the regulatory function, as is done in the United States, together with the exclusion of the banks and trust companies from the board, means the structure of the CDIC is flawed.

In November 1984, the CBA published a brief that criticized the deposit insurance legislation and the methods employed by the CDIC to handle the insolvencies. Shortly thereafter there was a regular quarterly meeting of the CBA's executive council with the governor of the Bank of Canada in Ottawa. The Inspector General of Banks at the time—Bill Kennett—was also present, as he normally was at the quarterly meetings. The meeting was perhaps the only occasion in my experience when the relationship between the governor of the Bank of Canada and the banks was strained. Bouey gave the bankers a harsh lecture, with Kennett nodding agreement, on the CBA's public criticism of the CDIC. He pointed out that the most destabilizing credit problems had been those of the large banks. While this was true, the government and the Bank of Canada had shared in the petro-dollar recycling process, both philosophically and practically through Canada's role in the World Bank and International Monetary Fund.

The meeting broke up without changing the CDIC's policy of "winding down" failed institutions, which implied paying out 100 percent of the deposits, including uninsured deposits. Shortly afterwards, the government appointed a working committee on the CDIC, chaired by Robert Wyman, the president of a stock brokerage firm in Vancouver. His two colleagues were André Bérard, president of the National Bank, and Leslie Colhoun, a former president of the National Trust Company. The Wyman Report was released in June 1985, only a few months after the working committee was appointed.

The banks welcomed the report, because it recommended the reform of the CDIC through a greater degree of market discipline. Its key recommendation was to introduce co-insurance. This means that every depositor would have to accept the loss on a small percentage of his or her claim, in the same way that an automobile insurance policy usually has a "deductible." The purpose of co-insurance would be to assign some accountability to everyone, by discouraging the practice of chasing the last quarter percent of interest on deposits without any regard to the risk. Although some of the Wyman Committee's recommendations were accepted, the introduction of market discipline to the deposit insurance process was never adopted. Now—in 1991— the United States is starting to address the same issues, in the wake of the huge losses on the savings and loan associations and banks. In the recommendations of the U.S. Treasury, published in February 1991, there are some striking resemblances to the proposals of the Wyman Committee in 1985, though not on co-insurance.

THE WESTERN BANK FAILURES

The last major banking disaster of the 1980s was the failure of the Canadian Commercial Bank (CCB) in Edmonton and the Northland Bank in Calgary, both in 1985. Although the direct losses absorbed by the CDIC were less than those of the trust companies—$388 million for the CCB and its mortgage subsidiary and $318 million for the Northland—the political fallout was much worse. In the first place these were banks, and the failure of banks had the potential of being more troublesome on the international scene than the failure of some small trust companies. Some bankers and government officials shared the view that the credit rating of Canadian institutions might be downgraded, thereby raising their costs for wholesale deposits in the international markets. More likely was the prospect that the smaller institutions, which depended mainly on wholesale deposits, would be squeezed in the domestic market.

The failure of the Alberta-based banks was an enormous setback to the aspirations of the West and further proof of the deeply held belief that the western economy was in thrall to eastern financial interests. In fact, the failure of the Alberta banks did lead to the destabilization of the domestic wholesale deposit market. It was a major contributing factor to the subsequent disappearance of the Bank of British Columbia, the Mercantile, and the Continental. All of the western-based banks were wiped out in the mid-1980s and at least six of the trust company failures were in the West, including two of the largest ones, Pocklington's Fidelity Trust and Dr. Allard's Northwest Trust Company, both in Edmonton.

The Canadian Commercial Bank was developed by three entrepreneurial financial executives who had already pioneered residential mortgage insurance in Canada. One of them was W.H. McDonald, who had run the mortgage department in the Bank of Nova Scotia in the 1950s. Michael Boyd and Terry Stott were merchant bankers from Greenshields in Montreal. Their idea was to open a new bank in western Canada with a national franchise. Unlike the broadly held banks and trust companies, it was sponsored by a short list of institutional investors, mainly pension funds. The founders had already developed business relationships with this group, primarily through the packaging of residential mortgages. Prominent among the institutional sponsors were the Air Canada and CNR pension funds, the teachers' pension funds in Alberta and Manitoba, the Caisse de dépôt et placement in Quebec, and the Great West Life Insurance Company.

In the early years of the CCB—from 1975 to 1980—the bank seemed to be doing very well. But its portfolio was highly concentrated in loans to the oil and gas industry and in real estate loans in Alberta that were dependent on oil and gas. In 1981-82, the sharp rise in interest rates made the CCB vulnerable, since it was a regional bank which depended mainly on wholesale deposits for its funding. But the problems generated by conditions in the Albertan economy and by the National Energy Policy—which applied also to the large banks—were compounded in the case of the CCB by imprudent lending policies. The bank had ventured into the California real estate market, and its real estate loan portfolio was revealed to be in very shaky condition.

In 1982, Howard Eaton, the president of CCB, decided to live in Santa Barbara, California, and commute to Edmonton. It is said that one of the directors resigned abruptly on hearing this news. The board of directors was disturbed, as was Bill Kennett, the Inspector General of Banks. Then it turned out that Eaton was closely associated with Lenny Rosenberg, the high-flying entrepreneur in Toronto who was involved in several trust company failures. In fact, Rosenberg had acquired 27 percent of the shares of the CCB, which exceeded the 10 percent limit in the Bank Act. Eventually the board got rid of Eaton and promoted the president, Gerald McLaughlan, to chief executive officer in 1983. Later testimony revealed that because of the condition of the loan portfolio, the CCB was probably beyond saving. For two years, the management, the board of directors, the shareholders' auditors, and the Inspector General of Banks kept their heads in the sand, unwilling to recognize the increasing evidence of insolvency.

The story of the unravelling of the CCB between March and September of 1985 is set out in painful detail in the Report of the Commission of Inquiry which was appointed in September that year. There was just one Commissioner, the Honourable Willard Z. (Bud) Estey, then a Justice of the Supreme Court of Canada. The Estey Report rivals the MacMillan Commission Report in 1934 for its speed of production and clarity and exceeds it in thoroughness.

Executives of the big six banks were invited to a meeting in Ottawa on March 22, at which a bail-out of the CCB was arranged. (Later on, Kennett admitted, "We had clearly misunderstood and mis-stated the condition of the CCB when we went into the bail-out.") After a weekend of bargaining, a deal was struck to buy $255 million of the CCB's assets; the big six banks put up $60 million, as did each of the governments of Canada and Alberta, and the other $75 million came from the CDIC. But the public announcement of the deal accelerated the flight of deposits, and by August the Bank of Canada had made loans to the CCB of $1.3 billion. These "liquidity" advances were made on the strength of the central bank's accepting the word of the Inspector General that the bank was still "viable." When Kennett stopped giving this assurance to Bouey, the central bank stopped making loans to the CCB, and the latter was out of business.

The Northland Bank of Calgary opened for business in 1976, about a year after the CCB, and closed its doors in September 1985, coinciding with the demise of the CCB. Although the Northland shared the western aspirations of the CCB, its founding shareholders were largely western credit unions rather than public-sector pension funds. In nine years, it had four chief executive officers, and almost constant turmoil in the top executive ranks. For much of the time it suffered under top management which was inexperienced in banking. Like the CCB, the Northland was geared to the oil and gas industry in Alberta, and by 1985, 45 percent of its loans were based on real estate in Alberta, but also in places like the Cayman Islands.

By 1983, the bank's internal inspector described the loan portfolio as a "time bomb." In order to avoid disclosing the true condition of the bank to the public, the management developed original techniques of "creative accounting." As the later inquiry revealed, "Both banks dealt in the future tense in connection with loan valuations because the present tense, by 1983 at least, represented insolvency." (In other words, the managements estimated the present value of their real estate collateral as it might be at some future date, given optimistic assumptions.) The management got rid of one set of auditors in 1980, and another in 1985. (The firing of a firm's auditors is almost always a sure sign of trouble.) Some directors resigned after making caustic comments about the condition of the bank. But none of this motivated the Office of the Inspector General to act until the collapse of the CCB in 1985. By then it was too late: the Northland's wholesale deposits had also evaporated, and the Bank of Canada had to put its fist in the dike between March and September 1985.

Estey's report examined the circumstances of the founding of the CCB and the Northland as well as the events leading to the collapse. He pointed out that "at the Western Economic Opportunities Conference in July 1973, further pressure for the creation of new banks came from the western provinces: in a joint submission, the governments of the four western provinces stated: 'The branch banking system, characterized by the five major Canadian chartered banks with branches coast to coast, and head offices in central Canada, has not been adequately responsive to western needs.'"

"Western-based banks," the premiers had asserted, "in which there was a degree of public participation, would be more sympathetic to the needs of residents of the West ... in particular, they could provide a substantially greater amount of financial capital than in the past to rural and urban communities." Unfortunately this profound conviction of westerners cannot be shaken by the facts. Estey commented: "The evidence predominantly favours the conclusion that there was no market niche which had been overlooked by the existing banking industry."

By 1985, about 45 percent of the CCB's loans were in the four western provinces, and 36 percent outside Canada altogether. Whether Estey's conclusion that there was in fact no gap in the available supply of bank finance in western Canada was influenced by my testimony, I do not know. On January 22, 1986, I was questioned on this subject by John Sopinka, then Estey's counsel and now a Justice of the Supreme Court of Canada.

Sopinka: There has been some testimony that there is a gap ... or a failure on the part of the larger banks to service the

needs of western Canada. What do you say about that?
MacIntosh: Well, obviously the CBA believes that the
regional banks can be viable. Some of our members are
regional banks, so I could hardly be expected to say otherwise
. . . The problem that we have is the unrealistic expectations
of government . . . that regional banks were going to solve
problems . . . there were quite unrealistic expectations of what
new regional banks in Alberta would be able to accomplish
because they had begun from this obsessive belief that there
was a financial gap in the system.

I then referred to a brief prepared by the Toronto law firm of
Campbell, Godfrey on behalf of the Inspector General which said in
part: "Western Canadian businessmen encountered difficulties in
raising the funds necessary for growth and expansion. As a large part
of the western Canadian economy is resource-based and is inherently
cyclical, businessmen and entrepreneurs found it particularly difficult to raise funds from the existing chartered banks." My response to
this assertion was: "That is a proposition for which there is absolutely
no support in data."

Sopinka: What sort of data base would be expected?
MacIntosh: Numbers. I would expect anybody making an
assertion like that would be able to produce some data that
would support it. [I then went on to explore the data in the
Bank of Canada Monthly Review on inter-regional transfers of
capital by the banks.] Those [statistics] have shown for fifteen
years that there is a large net flow from the east to the west,
specifically from Ontario to all the western provinces . . . The
net transfer to the west of Canada outstanding at the present
time is in the order of $25-$30 billion.
Sopinka: When you ask about documentation, have you talked
to any westerners about that?
MacIntosh: Oh yes, there is massive episodic talk about that.
Over the years, I have talked to many cabinet ministers and
politicians about that. It has been my experience . . . that
[after making] these sorts of sweeping assertions, when you
ask for the chapter and verse so that I can take them back to
our members, they never produce anything except sweeping
generalizations.
Sopinka: We have one real live example. Mel Hurtig said he

could not get financing from the big banks for his
encyclopedia, a great piece of Canadiana.
MacIntosh: That is not a commercial enterprise, as you know,
Mr. Sopinka. That was very heavily subsidized by the
Government of Alberta as a centennial project. It is a very
excellent piece of work, but it is not a commercial
proposition, so do not cite that as a case, please.
Sopinka: I apologize.

Later in the testimony, I noted that the CCB and the Northland, for
the most part, made loans starting at $500,000 and up. This is much
larger than what the banks call "small business" loans, which average
about $50,000 in size. In 1983, the CCB and Northland did not have
one single loan under the Small Business Loans Act on their books;
nor did they have any farm improvement loans.

I concluded that the government was the real culprit in the western
bank failures, because it had encouraged a few small regional banks
and sixty foreign-owned banks to crowd into the marketplace in order
to fill a financial gap which in fact was not there. There were only two
ways to grow: one was to assume unacceptable risks and the other was
to drive profit margins down to the point at which the long-term
viability of the institution was questionable.

In July 1986, an article in *Saturday Night* said: "The CCB collapsed because of dishonesty, incompetence and greed." In a speech a
few months later, I said, with more restraint, that it was "an extended
demonstration of human error." There had been mismanagement by
half-trained bankers, gullible boards of directors and auditors, passive
regulation by the Inspector General of Banks, and a central bank
which allowed considerations of system liquidity to override without
question the Inspector General's perception of solvency.

(In December 1990, Kevin Kavanagh, the president and chief
executive officer of Great West Life, told the House of Commons
finance committee: "My particular company, unhappily, was a 10
percent investor in the Canadian Commercial Bank. I personally
observed that bank with great care as an investment and selected from
our officer group two men [one was Sterling Lyon, ex-premier of
Manitoba] who I thought were very able to be directors and to
represent our interest. Quite frankly, the 10 percent thing [ownership
restriction] did not do us any good . . . In fact, I wondered if there had
not been a larger shareholder, whether the loss of his fortune might
have motivated the ownership in a more productive and positive

way." In other words, 10 percent was not enough to have an effective influence—a really dominant shareholder might have helped Great West to monitor its investment.)

In October 1985, Parliament introduced a bill to pay out the uninsured depositors in full. In effect, the government acknowledged that its assurances had misled large depositors. (The theory was that large depositors should be able to look after themselves; the reality was that the greedy institutions looking for an extra one-eighth percent on their thirty-day deposits, regardless of risk, included not only business corporations but large municipalities like St. Catharines and Kanata in Ontario and Surrey, British Columbia, as well as the Surrey credit union.)

The Estey Report is remarkable for its careful and elegant choice of language. No one was held up to public ridicule, but the weaknesses in the system—and of the players—were revealed for anyone to read. Unlike most public investigations of the banking system, the Estey Inquiry was notable for the presence of two dozen lawyers who heard most of the testimony. The reason for this was that there was the potential for very large financial liability for some of the players, on the grounds of failure to perform their duties. In fact, the liquidator of the two banks, Garth MacGirr of the accounting firm Price Waterhouse, brought suit in August 1987 for $294 million against some officers, directors, and auditors of the CCB. (The plaintiffs were the Government of Canada, the CDIC, and the CCB.) In November 1990, the defendants settled with MacGirr for $82.4 million, which will go to the CDIC, the government, and some other creditors. Under the terms of the settlement, the defendants "deny all liability or fault relating to the allegations."

In the case of the Northland Bank, the liquidator was the accounting firm Deloitte Touche Inc. Here, the two accounting firms which had been the auditors agreed to settle with the liquidator for $43.2 million. Meanwhile, the liquidator has been able to realize enough assets to pay off the Bank of Canada, which had a first claim. As in the case of the Home Bank in 1923, the remaining debris of assets in the two western banks will be realized with difficulty in the years to come.

The result of the collapse of the two Albertan banks was the virtual elimination of regional banks in Canada. The Mercantile Bank of Canada was forced into a merger with the National Bank in late 1985. The Mercantile was not exactly a regional bank, but it was dependent on wholesale deposits and therefore vulnerable to a loss of confidence on the part of a few hundred large depositors. The Continental was somewhat like the Mercantile in that it depended mainly on whole-sale deposits, although its loan portfolio was geographically diverse. It was sold to Lloyds Bank (Canada), which in turn sold out to the Hongkong Bank of Canada.

The Bank of British Columbia had a much broader deposit base, with fifty or sixty branches in British Columbia and Alberta. It depended on the prosperity of the natural resources industries in British Columbia and had already been in difficulty in 1984 because of loan losses. Although the Bank of British Columbia had a good name and grassroots support, the financial analysts and bond-rating services became doubtful about the quality of its loans. An audit of its loan portfolio was conducted by some bankers recruited by the Inspector General. Their report was not encouraging, but Ottawa looked the other way. Recurrent rumours about possible mergers with eastern banks and unfavourable stories in the media helped to accelerate a flight of deposits. Once again, the unravelling of the bank proved to be an unstoppable process; no amount of assurances from the management or from the Inspector General of Banks could halt the erosion of deposits to allow the loan portfolio to recover under better economic conditions.

In November 1986, the government engineered a transfer of the assets and liabilities of the Bank of British Columbia to the Hongkong Bank of Canada. The Canada Deposit Insurance Corporation put up $200 million, two-thirds of which went to the Hong Kong parent bank, and the other one-third to the shareholders of the Bank of B.C. Although several Canadian financial institutions would probably have been pleased to do the same deal, the government had an overriding purpose, which was to preserve an identifiable west coast bank. The takeover was a success, because it enabled the Hongkong Bank of Canada to reach a size sufficient to assure its national stature. The conditions for a viable regional bank were met: adequate capital, good management, and a reduced degree of dependence on the economy of a single region.

With the demise of the two Albertan banks and the Bank of British Columbia as well as the Mercantile and Continental in eastern Canada, the structure of the domestically owned banking system has reverted to something like its shape fifty years ago: six big banks and two smaller domestic banks—the Laurentian and the Canadian Western. The big difference is that now there are about sixty foreign-owned bank subsidiaries of which one—the Hongkong Bank—has some of the characteristics of a broadly based national branch institution. In the 1990s, a similar process is likely to develop in the trust, loan and insurance industries.

It would be quite wrong to suggest that nothing was learned from the experience of the financial disasters in the 1980s. The first step was a great strengthening of the Office of the Inspector General of Banks, and the broadening of its powers to cover all the federally regulated deposit-taking institutions and insurance companies. Another change was the introduction of the new and demanding Basle Concordat standards for the capital adequacy of banks. The third phase—completion of the financial reform package for financial institutions—is still under way as this book is written.

CHAPTER 13

THE TIN EAR SYNDROME: THE BATTLE OVER SERVICE CHARGES

A tin ear carries no sound to the inner ear. This apparently communicable disease was epidemic during the battle over service charges in 1988. Some bankers suffered from the condition, and a case could be made that, with early action, they might have stopped it spreading. But the politicians caught it in a far more virulent form. As the battle went on, the shouting became louder on both sides, but the transmission of ideas was in inverse proportion to the noise. The media, with a few notable exceptions, suffered from the tin ear disease on the right side: no sound penetrated that side of their hearing system — only noises from the political left. This of course contributed to a lopsided discussion of the issues.

The service charge issue contributed to my reputation of being too strident in defending the position of the banks. After many years as spokesman for the banking industry on a great variety of issues, I found the attitudes of politicians and the media more frustrating and infuriating on this issue than on any other. But my frustration was not always with the politicians and media; sometimes it was with members of my own industry.

The event which gave a kick-start to the service charge issue was the publication of a consumer survey arranged by a group called Service d'aide au Consommateur (SAC) in Shawinigan, Quebec. This group was funded in part by the federal Department of Consumer and Corporate Affairs. Its leader and spokeswoman, Madeleine Plamondon, engaged a small research staff to do a comparative study of bank service charges with a view to demonstrating that they were arbitrary and excessive. But the survey was seriously flawed, both conceptually and in terms of conventional sampling techniques. The study acknowledged that "the sampling is not entirely representative from a geographical standpoint." In fact it failed to collect representative information from the caisses populaires, and the survey data on the banks was marred by errors, as the facts had never been checked with the banks themselves.

Among the assumptions made by the SAC was a calculation that the average customer has two "stop payments" a month, a charge which the vast majority of customers never experience in the course of a year. Another service charge in the SAC package was the cost of renewing a mortgage every year, calculated at $85. This was a big factor in the SAC's estimate of the annual cost to consumers of bank service charges, which totalled anywhere from $108 to $248.

The media reported the results of the Shawinigan consumer survey without any effort to analyze or digest it. There were more and more reports that the cost of bank services to the average Canadian household was between $200 and $300. Since the banks in fact had service-charge packages ranging from zero for seniors to around $50 a year, it was obvious that some solid comparative data was needed to set the record straight.

COLLECTING THE FACTS

In the spring of 1987, I set up an internal task force at the Canadian Bankers' Association, under the direction of Joanne De Laurentiis, vice-president of public affairs. By June, the task force thought the issue was sufficiently serious to justify being discussed at the annual meeting that month of the executive council of the Canadian Bankers' Association.

The executive council is the policy-making body of the banking industry, and the president of the CBA is its chief executive and spokesman. Every domestic Canadian bank is entitled to have a seat on the council, in addition to which there are two representatives of the foreign bank subsidiaries in Canada. At one time in the mid-1980s there were as many as thirteen or fourteen present at council meetings; but with the mergers and wind-ups of the last few years, the council size is now down to ten, consisting of the big six, the two foreign bank representatives, and two remaining smaller banks, the Canadian Western Bank and the Laurentian Bank. Whatever the exact composition of the council, it tends to be dominated by the big six, which represent roughly 90 percent of the industry's assets and perhaps 95 percent of the retail business affecting millions of people. The chairmanship of the executive council rotates every two years among the big six, and during my ten years in office, I reported to five different chairmen.

At the June meeting, I told the executive council that Don Blenkarn, the chairman of the House of Commons Committee on Finance, Trade and Economic Affairs, had warned me that he had received a good many complaints from his constituents about increases in bank service charges. These fees had gone up because banks were trying to shift their revenue sources towards fees for specific services and away from dependence on the interest-rate spread between deposit rates and lending rates. There were many examples where the charge for certain services had been sharply increased, such as the charge for an NSF (not sufficient funds) cheque. But the complaints were also about the fact that the banks had provided little explanation or notification of the increases to their customers.

I recommended that the banks examine their disclosure practices, and asked for a supplementary budget to carry out some attitude surveys on service charges, and also to mount a research study. This was agreed to, and over the summer of 1987 the CBA collected information on service charges from all the banks, as well as by the large trust companies and some credit unions. (The Caisses Desjardins in Quebec, however, refused to provide information about their service charges.)

By September, some of the banks were getting wary of collecting and publishing data on service charges. They remembered only too clearly how selective the House of Commons committee had been in collecting data on credit card interest rates a year before. After some discussion, it was decided to discontinue the collection of service charge data until we could see what direction the Blenkarn committee would take. By November 1987, with increasing evidence that the issue was a hot one politically, we reconsidered our options. Several of the banks thought that the pricing of products was a question for individual banks to deal with, and not an industry question. Although this was true, individual banks could not deal with the issue at a political level. In the eyes of the media and the politicians, the question was industry-wide, and therefore it required the association to respond to it.

Meanwhile the need for better information on consumer needs was accelerated by growing criticism. An article in the "Money Guide" of *Canadian Consumer Magazine* was typical of many that appeared in 1987 and 1988. It reported on a study by Decima Research for the Consumers' Association of Canada: "The Decima Study showed that a significant number of respondents believe that consumers need more information on automated teller machines (39 percent) as well as on accounts (41 percent). The experts say that service fees cause part of the confusion. The fees are so complicated—and so little publicized—that it's almost impossible for consumers to keep track of what they've been charged."

In late 1987, the CBA commissioned Environics to do its own survey of public attitudes on financial service charges. This survey found that 57 percent were satisfied with the level of service charges, but 28 percent were dissatisfied. The percentage of dissatisfied customers was higher in the Toronto area. This was not difficult to explain, because for months the *Toronto Star* and the *Toronto Sun* kept up an almost daily attack on the banks over service charges. In Montreal, on the other hand, comparatively little attention was paid to the service charge issue in the francophone media. This was partly because service charges tended to be lower in some of the "common bond" caisses populaires, though in the large credit unions which we surveyed they were actually higher. (A common bond credit union is one whose members come from a particular community, workplace, or church.) But the main factor was that there was no crusading newspaper using its front pages and news columns to magnify the issue. (Later on, when Blenkarn invited the public to send him their complaints, there were far more letters from the Toronto area than from Quebec.)

The Environics study showed that almost half of those who complained about service charges found them vague. The banks were not explaining why there was a fee, why there were changes in fees, or why there were new fees. The cost of cashing cheques was a focus of consumer dissatisfaction. This was not really a problem for the trust companies, whose transactional volumes were a fraction of those of the banks. As for the credit unions, some large ones charged even more than the banks, although there were many which offered their members low-cost service charges because they were not profit-oriented.

In late November 1987, Don Blenkarn phoned me to say that he was sending a research officer representing the finance committee to collect data from the banks. Dr. Terry Thomas of the staff of the

Library of Parliament arrived in Toronto on December 21 to meet a hastily arranged committee of consumer banking officers.

The all-bank committee on service charges which met Terry Thomas promised to get back to him with industry-wide information early in the New Year. The first item on the agenda was to define terms. Since there are more than 200 customer services performed by any given bank branch, the first problem was to identify a list of basic banking services, so that price and product comparisons could be made between banks and non-bank deposit institutions. Before the end of January, the CBA sent a letter to Terry Thomas setting out a precise list of fourteen banking services which the CBA committee thought should be measured. In April these were published and widely distributed, but few papers except the *Financial Post* gave them any attention.

The bank service charge committee agreed on a profile of monthly transactions covering the fourteen services which would be typical for a family of four with two working parents. It assumed, for example, that such a family would write eight cheques a month, make four deposits a month, and make two bill payments for heating fuel and telephone. Terry Thomas agreed that the terms of reference were reasonable, although his report pointed out that no single customer profile could be fully representative of the wide range of users. While Thomas was preparing his report for the Blenkarn committee, the CBA started collecting reports from the individual banks on their charges for the fourteen basic banking services.

It soon became apparent, however, that Terry Thomas was not going to be allowed by the Blenkarn committee to examine trust companies and credit unions, even though they competed with the banks for the same customers. As I was pondering this problem, walking along King Street in Toronto, I encountered Henry Knight, a partner in the consulting firm of Coopers & Lybrand. He had done some other research work for the CBA, and I proposed that he do a special study for us in a hurry. We provided him with our list of fourteen basic banking services and asked him to go out and price these services in the five biggest trust companies and in some large credit unions. We did not know which credit unions to look at, but we suggested that they should be large ones with a significant customer base, and that they be representative of all regions in the country. We stipulated that they should be credit unions which dealt with the general public, as opposed to the great number of credit unions which are "common bond" institutions.

Coopers & Lybrand produced a list of seven credit union names, including the well-known Van City Credit Union and two important caisses populaires near Montreal. The researchers collected their pricing data directly from the institutions involved, and apart from one error in information supplied by Van City in Vancouver (later corrected in our published document), the comparative pricing figures showed that both trust companies and credit unions were charging as much or more than the banks. We also asked Coopers & Lybrand to look into American banking statistics. The Federal Reserve Board had done a study on the costs and revenues of 494 banks, subdivided into small, medium, and large banks. Our consultants also looked at eleven large banks in the United States, which were comparable in size to the big six Canadian banks. The following is an extract from the CBA brief, showing some of the Coopers & Lybrand research:

Average Annual Cost of a Basket of Fourteen Banking Services

	Minimum Monthly Deposit Balance ($ Canadian)		
Annual cost at:	$199	$600	$1,001
6 Banks	$ 84.95	$ 28.54	$ 27.91
5 Trust Companies	97.78	97.78	31.33
7 Credit Unions	73.01	73.01	37.18
11 U.S. Banks	195.93	148.76	142.76

The results were extremely useful for our brief to the finance committee, because they showed beyond doubt that service charges in the U.S. banking system were about twice as high as those in Canada. Moreover, the service charges of small and medium-sized banks were usually as high or higher than those of large banks.

All of this information was incorporated into our brief, which was presented to the finance committee on April 13, 1988, along with the Coopers & Lybrand study. Except for the *Financial Post*, no newspaper published the comparative data. Nor did anyone ever challenge its accuracy, either in the finance committee or elsewhere. The most obvious conclusion from the data was that the level of bank service charges was not the result of attempts to compensate for the huge loss provisions then being made on bank loans to less developed countries (LDCs), as had been commonly charged in Parliament and in the press. Obviously, if small and medium-sized American banks, as well as credit unions and trust companies, had higher service charges than big Canadian banks, but had no LDC debt, there could be no cause-and-effect relationship. This message never got through to the press, although Blenkarn himself understood it. In fact, Dr. Thomas's study had already concluded that there was no relationship between LDC debt and service charges. He had also shown that the rise in service charges was a worldwide phenomenon in the financial system, and not peculiar to Canada.

There were a number of economic forces contributing to this phenomenon. In general, competition for retail deposits had greatly increased, thereby narrowing margins between loan rates and deposit rates. In Canada, both trust companies and credit unions had become strong competitors for the consumer dollar. Computer technology had made possible the calculation of daily interest on deposit accounts, and this had the effect of driving up the cost of deposits to a bank.

The contrast to previous banking experience, during which the savings rate had been 3 percent and the current account rate 0 percent, while the lending rate was 6 percent, could hardly have been greater. Previously, there had been few service charges, because banks made their profit on the interest rate spread. Not only was this no longer feasible, it hadn't even been equitable in the first place. People had learned that it was good business to carry out all their current household transactions—their cheque payments and their utility bill payments and so forth—through the bank at little or no cost, while maintaining their savings deposits in a trust company which was not required to meet the same regulatory standards as a bank with regard to cash reserves and liquidity, and which did not offer high-volume, low-revenue, routine payment services.

Thus the people who generated a high volume of payment transactions were in effect getting their banking facilities free; the costs which they incurred but did not pay for were necessarily covered by someone else. That someone was either the depositor or the borrower; the depositor got a lower rate on his savings and the borrower got a higher rate on his loans. By shifting more of the transactional costs of banking to the users, banks were better able to meet the competition for savings deposits. (Exactly the same considerations apply to the users of credit cards.)

Although the user-pay concept is an equitable one and a sound method of financing costs that can be clearly identified, its use has been undermined by politicians, as in the case of health services. We generally accept the concept of user-pay for public transport, telephones and other utilities, or for crossing toll bridges and camping in public parks. We understand that providing free services to people may result in excessive and frivolous demands for those services. But politicians have coached the Canadian public to believe that certain costs should be paid by someone else, such as higher-income groups or corporations, or foreigners, or whomever. Banking services are often included in the list of services which Canadians expect to be provided as a free public utility. Even spokespersons for the Consumers' Association of Canada have sometimes taken the position that automatic teller machines ought not to incur a transaction charge, apparently on the hypothesis that computer technology only benefits the seller and not the buyer.

DISCLOSURE AND COMMUNICATION

Although it was not difficult to explain the rationale for service charges, and to demonstrate that there was no connection to the LDC debt problem, it was much more difficult to deal with the accusation that the banks were "nickel-and-diming" the customer to death with a variety of charges. The Canadian banks were watching the rapid escalation of service charges in the United States, all of which they could easily monitor in the trade magazines and the newspapers. In the rush to pursue the new world of "user pay," the banks were guilty of doing a poor job in communicating the changed environment to the public, or even to their own employees. Obviously, the head office of a bank cannot hope to explain itself to the general public which provides its customer base, unless it can do so effectively to its own staff.

The problem of communicating to a field staff that may number 35,000 people located in 1,500 branches from coast to coast is considerable. At the logistical level, the banks are extremely efficient in the operation of their coast-to-coast networks. The most striking proof of this is that cheques are cleared from the bank of deposit to the bank of payment within twenty-four hours, wherever the cheques change hands in the country. Cheques deposited in Kapuskasing are flown that evening to North Bay, then to a data centre in Toronto where they are processed. From there they are taken back to the airport, back to North Bay, and back to Kapuskasing by 8:00 a.m. the next morning. This happens throughout the country and is only held up by bad flying weather and such. By contrast, cheque clearing in the United States can take two weeks or more. The efficiency of the

Canadian cheque clearing system is one reason why the banks can give same-day credit for cheques deposited by their customers.

But the cheque clearing system is only one part of the internal communication system of a bank. There is also a daily flow of letters and communications between head office, regional offices, and the branch system. While most of the flow of communications concerns the daily business of the bank's customers, there is a constant flow of instructions concerning the method of handling hundreds of types of transaction. A bank's manuals of procedure are massive ring-binders, which are constantly being updated. On one occasion, when I was in charge of computer systems in my bank, one of the staff calculated that the various manuals, if stacked one on top of the other, would make a pile ten feet high.

The average staff in a Canadian bank branch numbers about eighteen people, of whom many have not had more than two or three years' experience. Even the manager, who might have ten years of experience, cannot keep on top of the constant flood of instructions that comes in each mailbag.

Taking the time to explain why a thing must be done rather than simply setting out the rules which must be followed is a quantum leap in communications. Old-time bankers did not consider that sort of communication was necessary. This attitude is reflected in the anecdote of the branch manager conveying the following warm greeting to a new female employee: "No smoking, no jeans, and no clogs."

The heightened awareness of the need to improve communications within the banks and of course with the general public was a positive outcome of the service charge battle. However, even with a more sensitive attitude to these problems which the current generation of bankers is bringing to the issue, there is still a huge logistical problem. Financial transactions require absolute precision—people are very fussy about the handling of their money. With more than 200 possible types of transaction being conducted in any bank branch, it is essential to have a precise way of recording each transaction. This cannot be left to the casual discretion of a junior employee at the counter, or there would be chaos. While some degree of judgement is required in dealing with individual customer relations, the methodology must be consistent.

Two factors working in opposite directions are affecting the daily workload in a bank branch: the proliferation of services and the use of computers. There is a greatly expanded line of services offered by the banks, such as different kinds of mortgages and different kinds of term deposits. Bank staff are expected by the public to understand and be able to explain the benefits and costs of all the various services. However, this problem is offset to a considerable extent by computerization. In the 1950s and early 1960s, bank managements were rather slow to see the possibilities of computers for their business. Starting in the late 1960s, however, and advancing with increased capital investment and human resources, the Canadian banks now have few equals in computer services for retail banking around the world, and few equals in Canada among corporations which deal with a broad public. The department stores, most trust companies, insurance companies, and the brokerage industry have been far behind the banks in making use of computers. The computer services of the Government of Canada in dealing with the public are about twenty years behind, even for services that are comparatively simple and straightforward, such as Canada Pension Plan records. In some provincial services, such as health insurance, the quality and speed of information systems are sadly far behind, even though the transactional volumes are far less than those in banking.

The rapid introduction of computer technology in banking made possible a level of consumer services which could not have been imagined in the 1960s: daily interest on deposit balances and access to one's bank account from any branch in the country were two examples. The advances in service delivery were matched by an equal advance in consumer expectations but the banks fell short in explaining the changing price structure to their customers.

THE MEDIA ADD CONFUSION

Ensuring more effective disclosure and better communication was only part of our problem in preparing to face the finance committee. Another problem was the widely circulated media story that service charges had escalated by 17 percent a year in recent years. Compared to the consumer price index and wage settlements and other familiar numbers, this looked like gouging. The correct figure was 3.3 percent. The 17 percent number was derived from a misreading of Thomas's published study, which showed that service charge *revenues* had gone up 17 percent a year over several years. However, few reporters took the trouble to analyze the report or to ask for a response on this point. In fact, the 17 percent included corporate revenues such as those derived from contractual payroll programs, but more importantly they included a huge increase in service charge transaction volumes rather than in prices.

The Canadian public, with its growing addiction to ATMs (automated teller machines) and other services, was driving up transaction volumes by about 7 percent a year. Revenues are of course the product of volume times price; after adjusting for volume and the general rate of inflation, the real annual increase in service charges was 3.3 percent. But the 17 percent figure was in general circulation, and it was impossible to have this error retracted by the media.

Another aspect of the service charge issue which caused the banks tremendous difficulty was that of providing a "plain vanilla" or low-cost banking service to low-income groups. The *Winnipeg Free Press* on November 22, 1987, carried the headline, "Service charges cause hardship to seniors, low-income earners." The article, which was by the paper's Ottawa correspondent, reported that "the investigation [Blenkarn's planned study] will include a look at the fees banks charge farmers to search their financial records. Western farmers have complained recently that banks were charging them a flat $500 fee to search through records for interest rate patterns." In this story, the *Winnipeg Free Press* demonstrated an inability to get the facts right in a story about banking. Since the mid-1970s, all the banks had provided free service charge packages to senior citizens. As for the $500 charge for searching records, this was the fee charged by Larry Whaley, a self-proclaimed advocate for farm debtors in western Canada, for conducting a search of bank records to support legal actions against banks for overcharging interest.

The problem of low-income groups had originated, not with senior citizens, but with recipients of welfare cheques, unemployment insurance payments, and so forth. Complaints had been voiced in the House of Commons that it was hard to cash a government cheque at a bank without producing several pieces of identification. This was not a service charge problem, because banks were obliged to cash all government cheques for nothing. The problem was that some people in low-income groups did not maintain a bank account, and therefore had difficulty in proving their identity. There were stories in the press that "money shops" would cash income tax refund cheques on the spot, at a fee of 10 percent or more of the cheque, which might easily be as much as $25.

This particular aspect of servicing low-income groups was a separate policy issue which came in for examination on a different occasion. In Thomas's study, there was a section on "basic banking" for low-income groups. The study looked at mandatory legislation in fifteen states in the United States which called for the provision of "basic banking." However, most of them concerned the provision of banking services for seniors and underage children, which were already well-established throughout Canada. But the obsession of one committee member, Paul McCrossan, with basic banking services was to cause us almost as much grief as any other aspect of the service charge issue.

In the weeks leading up to the finance committee's public sessions on the service-charge issue, the propaganda war in the newspapers accelerated. The greatest theatrical success was that of the *Toronto Sun* on March 9. There was a picture of Garth Turner, the business editor, presenting to committee member Bill Attewell a large carton full of coupons from the *Sun* protesting bank service charges. These had been sent in response to Turner's solicitation, which offered his readers three responses to the question:

Service Charges: Fair or Not?

I don't mind paying for services I use
I don't mind paying any charges the bank brings in
I am being ripped off

According to Turner, the vote was 4 percent for the first option, zero for the second, and 96 percent for the third. (Later, when the House committee hearings were completed, I asked our CBA staff in Ottawa to take a look at the carton full of coupons; it turned out that they were jumbled together in the box, apparently having never been sorted to separate complaints about trust companies and credit unions or even government departments from the rest of the responses.)

The preceding Saturday, the *Toronto Star* had carried a front-page story with a diagram showing five upward-pointing arrows indicating the bank service charge revenues of the big five. The diagram included the revenues from corporate business, but the story was devoted entirely to the retail business. (Even with this glaring error included, the average service charge revenue of the banks increased by 88 percent between 1983 and 1987, compared to 60 percent at Torstar. But Torstar's net profits were up much more than the banks'.)

Rumours began to appear that Thomas's report had been sent back for further work. The *Ottawa Citizen* reported that: "according to one source, the preliminary report was judged to be 'too soft' on the banks." Probably the biggest disappointment to the committee members was that Thomas had destroyed the argument that the growth in service charges was meant to offset the loan loss provisions on Third World debt. At that point, Bill Attewell was still making this assertion to the Toronto papers.

We found Thomas to be a good economist and a fair-minded person. However, the politicians on the committee appeared to believe that the purpose of research was to find weapons to bludgeon the banks. Having failed to get any research support for the doctrine that service charges were too high or that they had been raised to offset losses on foreign loans, the committee leaders tried a new tack. In mid-March, part of the draft report was leaked to the Canadian Press. One article asserted that the banks were "skirting a law that demands they give detailed notice of service charges." Blenkarn had already told the House of Commons that the committee would be spending most of its time examining whether banks were complying with section 201 of the Bank Act, which required a bank to obtain customer consent to charges. Later, when he got the banks and the CBA before the committee, he and McCrossan made much of this issue. The CBA, having been forewarned by the Canadian Press story, brought along Bradley Crawford, of the Toronto law firm McCarthy and McCarthy, its outside legal counsel, as part of the delegation at the finance committee hearings. Crawford is the foremost legal expert on the law of banking, and the author of a revised version of the bible in his field, originally published by Falconbridge in 1905.

As it turned out, the Canadian Press story was wildly exaggerated. In three pages of his report, Thomas had reviewed the law relating to the disclosure of bank service charges. He quoted the act, which says "A bank shall not in Canada, directly or indirectly, charge or receive any sum for the keeping of an account for a customer unless the charges are made by express agreement between the bank and the customer." He pointed out that "many banks and other financial institutions have their new customers sign blanket agreement cards by which the customer appears to waive notification . . . these agreement cards often contain wording that allows the financial institution to require 'reasonable service charges at its discretion.' " He concluded that there was a weakness in the law in defining how information should be conveyed, especially when many customers seldom enter a branch because they use ATMs. There was no suggestion in the report that the banks were "skirting the law."

THE CBA MEETS THE FINANCE COMMITTEE

By the time the CBA appeared before the House of Commons Committee on Finance, Trade and Economic Affairs on April 13, 1988, the banks had been flayed in the press for four or five months.

The finance committee was the pre-eminent product of the parliamentary reform measures introduced by the Conservative government. Blenkarn had taken advantage of the new rules for committees to reduce the size of his committee and to discourage the substitution of casual visiting MPs for absent regular members. At the hearings of the finance committee on the Bank Act revisions of 1934, 1944, and 1954 there had been fifty members on the finance committee; during the revision of 1967 there were about fifteen members, but substitutions occurred frequently. In Blenkarn's regime, there were about eight or ten regular members, with very little substitution. A smaller committee with consistent attendance contributes to the efficient conduct of business (although efficiency may not always be consistent with good sense). Blenkarn has also prided himself on forwarding to the House of Commons reports that have received unanimous support from all three parties. This, of course, has tended to give them significant clout in the House and in the media.

Having dealt with the finance committee and other parliamentary committees from the early 1960s until the service charge sessions of April 1988, I knew that Blenkarn's committee was more focused and carried more weight with the public than its predecessors. I was also aware of Blenkarn's personal courage and his standing in the PC caucus. Having decided, according to some observers, that he would never make it into a Mulroney cabinet because of his outspoken views, Blenkarn had earned the reputation of being a maverick on government policy. He was prepared to contradict the Minister of Finance in public and to challenge the government's position on fundamental issues. His reputation for leading his committee while marching to his own drummer became even more evident after 1988, when he sometimes opposed the government on tax policies.

In terms of energy and intellectual ability, Blenkarn has had few equals as a parliamentary committee chairman. Like most members of the House committee, he had a sincere interest in the welfare of his constituents. But this concern was offset by a thirst for the political advantages to be gained from bashing the banks. His war on service charges was not waged for ideological reasons. Blenkarn strongly supported the market system and free competition and he was not invariably a proponent of government intervention. This distinguished him from John Rodriguez, who usually represented the NDP as a substitute for Michael Cassidy. Rodriguez, a high-decibel member from the Sudbury area, was fond of likening the banks to Colonel Sanders in charge of the chicken coop. During the service charge episode, the Liberal Party was represented by Aideen Nicholson, who was the most open-minded member of the committee. Unfortunately, in the strident exchanges between the chairman and several members of the committee and the CBA delegation, her quiet voice of reason was usually lost in the noise.

In the Canadian parliamentary system, the chairman and majority party members of committees are appointed by the government of the day. When a bill is sent to a House committee for detailed examination after second reading, the intention is that the committee will hear witnesses and make appropriate suggestions to the government for improvements and amendments. In the past, it has not been considered appropriate for a House committee to make radical changes to a bill before sending it back to the House, nor to undertake initiatives on its own. However, because of procedural delays in the House or the government's inability to produce an agreed draft policy, some committees of the House have decided to take up public issues by studying "the subject matter of the bill" even before it reaches second reading. (In the past decade, the Senate has also taken up studying the "subject matter of a bill" partly because it could no longer wait for second reading in the House, and partly to discomfit the government.)

Although Don Blenkarn has made the finance committee a force to be reckoned with in the shaping of financial policies, he has not altered the clumsy and inefficient procedure used by House committees. Each member on the committee is allotted a ten-minute period to question witnesses, pursuing a regular rotation among the two opposition parties and the government party. Each member can take up whatever line of questioning he or she wants, with the result that there is no continuity as to the subject matter under discussion. I can recall instances in 1967 and 1980, when I was a witness before the finance committee, when members would be absent for a short time and then, on resuming their place in the rotation would repeat the questions that had been discussed in their absence. Since the chairman was only a glorified timekeeper—given this ten-minute rotation system—he was powerless to prevent repetitive dialogue or the pursuit of unproductive lines of inquiry by an individual member. But

Blenkarn was different from Bob Kaplan and John Evans—other chairmen whom I had encountered—in that he would intervene unexpectedly with a line of questioning which had nothing to do with the discussion going on. This tactic seemed to be designed to throw the witness into confusion.

The striking difference between attitudes in Toronto and Montreal was reflected in the committee membership. The leading members on the committee—Blenkarn, McCrossan, Nicholson, and Rodriguez—were all from Ontario. There was no one present from Quebec. In fact, MPs from Quebec took little part in the proceedings or in the House of Commons debates. The chief Liberal opposition critic, Raymond Garneau from Montreal, rarely if ever attended; nor did members from the Atlantic provinces, who were insulated from the reach of the *Toronto Star* and the *Toronto Sun*. From the West, Mary Collins, a businesswoman, voiced her concerns about the inability of the banks to cost specific services, but did not appear to share the bank-bashing approach of her Toronto colleagues. The West was also represented by Simon de Jong (NDP, Saskatchewan) and Murray Dorin (PC, Alberta).

The heavy weighting of the finance committee with Ontario members created a special problem for me within the banking industry. At the time, the chairman of the CBA's executive council was André Bérard, then the president of the National Bank and now its chairman. Bérard was not happy about dragging his bank into a problem which was of little significance in Quebec. The financial critic of the Liberal party, Raymond Garneau, easily the most prominent francophone member on financial questions, also kept a low profile. No Quebec politician was prepared to lay a glove on the caisses populaires, which compete with the National Bank, so there was no future for Bérard in attracting any lightning from politicians. While he led the CBA delegation in its April meeting with the finance committee, he preferred to let me carry the battle in public. In this approach he was not alone; most of the senior bankers preferred to let the CBA take the flak rather than create a public relations problem for themselves. I didn't blame them.

When our CBA delegation finally appeared, the tone of the meeting was set by the chairman, Don Blenkarn, who opened with the following welcome:

Mr. MacIntosh, you have said something about needing a half hour. I know your case is a bad case. So, understanding that it is a bad case, we will give you half an hour.

This of course was a declaration to his colleagues and to the opposition members of the committee that it was open season on the bankers.

Leading off our presentation, André Bérard pointed out that we could not deal with the specific service charges of individual banks, because that was a matter for individual banks and not for the association. I then presented a series of charts showing the information which we had developed on the service charges of banks, trust companies, credit unions, and U.S. commercial banks. Our research work was central to our presentation, but Blenkarn never referred to it again in the committee. (Some weeks later he asserted that he had looked at the data but had considered it too biased to be useful because it had been prepared by the CBA.) Although there were a few questions from committee members in the subsequent discussion, there was no attempt to challenge the validity of the data.

A good case could be made that the failure of the finance committee to deal with the factual material which we presented was due to the antiquated procedural methods which have been mentioned earlier. After the CBA's presentation, the chairman invited the official opposition critic Aideen Nicholson to proceed with her questions. Had the procedures allowed the committee to focus on our substantive material, there might have been an effective dialogue on that subject. However, Nicholson decided to examine us on the cost of bank services. Although the Thomas report had already dealt with this subject, pointing out the enormous difficulty in costing products in a multiproduct firm, most committee members were unwilling to accept the idea that calculating the cost of a cheque or of using an ATM machine was a very inexact accounting task. Fortunately, one member of the committee, Murray Dorin, understood the problem. He said, "I am the only accountant on the committee, I think, but I know when you talk about how you cannot figure out what it costs to offer these various services, I am absolutely aware of that. I have run into a number of businesses and you cannot figure out exactly what it costs to do a particular thing when you get a mix of the kind of nature you have."

Out of the blue, Blenkarn suddenly complained that his son's fiancée had not been given credit for a deposit at a bank after 3 p.m. on a Friday. I pointed out that the rules of the Canadian Payments Association, to which all the deposit-taking institutions belong, provided for a cut-off time at the end of the week. The rule is the same for both deposits and withdrawals, and exists so that institutions can settle with each other in a precise fashion. Blenkarn could have asked his research staff to investigate the question, and a written answer could have been prepared. However, the *Toronto Star*'s "news" report on the CBA's appearance focused exclusively on Blenkarn's red herring; the headline was: "Banks run Friday scam MP charges."

As the committee hearing continued, I wondered if the members had read their own staff report, or if they simply could not accept its findings. Terry Thomas had dealt decisively with the Shawinigan consumer group's inclusion of $85 a year for renewing a mortgage: "The assumption that the average consumer renews a mortgage each year is simply wrong. Few consumers renew a mortgage each year. About 60 percent of households are in owner-occupied dwellings, and of these, about 50 percent have no mortgage. In other words only 30 percent of households could renew a mortgage ... some casual information suggests that the average term for a mortgage is over 3 years. Thus about 10 percent of households could renew a mortgage in any year." He concluded that "consumers spend an average of $4.25 for mortgage renewals—some spend $85, but most spend nothing."

This sort of solid, objective analysis seemed to frustrate some of the committee members. John Rodriguez launched an attack on mortgage renewal fees and the following exchange took place:

MacIntosh: I think you should be aware, Mr. Rodriguez, that when the banks started to get into heavy volumes of renewals of mortgages, especially when interest rates got very high a few years ago, some credit unions were charging as much as $500. You say the banks have propped them (renewal fees) up. On the contrary, you are quite wrong sir, the banks have brought the rates down.

Rodriguez: I do not know why you are dragging in the credit unions. Maybe at some point we might want to go see the credit unions and haul them before this Committee and look at their service charges.

But the committee never did. Later on, Blenkarn said that the federal government had no authority over credit unions. This is not true. Just eight years earlier, Parliament had passed legislation to require the admittance of the credit unions to the Canadian Payments Association. Moreover, there is federal legislation which deals with the "centrals" of the co-operative movement, which are in a sense the provincial or regional "head offices" of the individual credit unions.

When the finance committee turned to the question of disclosure, it was more difficult to mount an effective defence. One of the members had walked along Sparks Street in Ottawa, only two blocks from where the committee meetings were being held in the West Block, and had failed to find information on service charges posted in any of the eleven banks and trust companies that he entered. Most of the banks provided this information in brochures which were inserted as "statement stuffers" along with monthly statements or credit card bills. But on the whole, the bank staffs had not been adequately equipped to deal with customer inquiries, partly because the information was changing very rapidly.

Blenkarn said that the banks were bypassing the law by not giving adequate notice to customers of changes in service charges. He asserted that the banks were required to provide customers with an "express agreement" for each and every service charge. (This, of course, would drive the cost of providing a service significantly upwards, to the great disadvantage of consumers.) After an exchange with the CBA's legal counsel on this point, McCrossan said, "You are the lawyer, I am just the actuary . . . we can certainly legislate the future. The past can only be litigated, I guess."

In fact, McCrossan was interested in more than the question of disclosure. He was determined that there should be a law requiring banks to provide "basic banking" services for low-income groups. But most of the banks already had such a package: a low-cost service which provided for a few cheques a month, two or three deposits, two or three uses of an ATM, and a couple of bill payments. And the banks had offered a package of free banking services to senior citizens for more than ten years. But McCrossan wanted a standardized minimum package for no charge at all.

The demand that Parliament legislate the provision of a free service from the private sector was an aberration. Even the most socialist of members had never suggested that the government legislate free postal services, or free rail and bus services, or free bread and milk. As a system for transferring income from upper- to lower-income groups, using the price mechanism is inefficient, inequitable, and arbitrary. How is a bank teller or a clerk supplying bus tickets to know whether a customer has met some means test? In the case of senior citizens or persons on welfare programs, there might be an identity card. But means-tested identity cards are greatly resented by people as a humiliating invasion of their privacy, and are rarely advocated by politicians. What would prevent a well-to-do citizen from asking for a free banking service and resisting any inquiry into his or her affairs? Income transfers can only be administered effectively through the income tax structure, not through commodity prices. But these considerations received scant attention in the press, except for the *Financial Post* and William Johnson's column in the *Montreal Gazette*. On June 7, 1988 he wrote: "The day we require bakers to provide the first loaf of bread free, and clothing stores to provide free underwear, and landlords to offer one free room, it will make sense to pass the committee's recommendations into law." And as Professor John S. McCallum of the Faculty of Management at the University of Manitoba wrote in the *Financial Post*: "In their haste to convict the banks for service charge abuses, it would appear that some are willing to consider the evidence only selectively. That's not particularly fair." But there was no criticism like this in the Toronto daily newspapers.

THE BLENKARN COMMITTEE BECOMES THE GOVERNMENT

Having been neutralized on its position that service charges had been raised to pay for the Third World debt, and that service charges were excessive compared to other institutions, the Blenkarn committee then embarked on one of the most extraordinary episodes of banker-politician confrontation that I can ever recall. This final phase of the service charge war began soon after the April 13 CBA appearance before the House committee in Ottawa. Blenkarn and McCrossan decided to bypass the CBA and go directly to individual banks to force an agreement for a standardized basic package of free banking services. Blenkarn phoned the chief executive officers of the Bank of Montreal, the Canadian Imperial Bank of Commerce, and the Royal Bank, and obtained from the first two an agreement to attend a meeting with a sub-committee of the finance committee, in order to discuss the elements of a free basic banking service.

Fortunately Allan Taylor, chief executive of the Royal Bank, called me up to ask what was going on. This was the first I had heard of Blenkarn's phone calls. Taylor knew that individual banks could not speak for the industry as a whole, and that Blenkarn would attempt to play off one against the other. In fact the press was already carrying stories with headlines such as "The big banks' united front is cracking." (There was some element of truth in this, because two of the banks, the Royal and Montreal, had announced new policies on service charges for their customers; the Royal had decided to introduce a policy of changing its rates only once a year, after considerable notice; the Bank of Montreal had introduced a new low-cost basic account. In both cases, this was partly a response to the fact that these two banks had discovered, when we collected the information through Coopers & Lybrand, that they were at the high end of the spectrum on the fourteen service charges that we had measured. A relatively high percentage of consumer complaints which reached the CBA involved the Bank of Montreal, because of the particular branch strategies it had been following under its CEO, Bill Mulholland.)

After receiving Allan Taylor's call, I phoned the Bank of Nova Scotia and the Toronto-Dominion Bank to ask them whether they would be content to have their positions represented by one or two other banks; I held the phone well away from my ear to get the response. Then I called Blenkarn to say that any meeting with his sub-committee would have to include a representative from each of the big six banks. I offered to gather a group to meet his sub-committee, which consisted of Paul McCrossan, Aideen Nicholson, and Simon de Jong. As it turned out, it was not possible to round up all of the bankers and politicians on short notice. Blenkarn decided to arrange for Paul McCrossan to meet me at the CBA's office in Toronto, the purpose being to explore whether a meeting with all the banks would lead to a voluntary agreement on banking services. This meeting was held on Friday afternoon April 29, 1988, when McCrossan was on his way home for the weekend to his constituency.

Before the meeting, I had a thorough briefing from Joanne De Laurentiis, our vice-president of public affairs, and David Phillips, our vice-president of legal affairs. They told me that if McCrossan could not get a voluntary agreement from the banks, then he would recommend legislation. They added that McCrossan claimed to have received a clearance for an all-bank agreement from Harvie Andre, the Minister of Consumer and Corporate Affairs, whose department was responsible for the Competition Act. Since the act prohibits an agreement among the banks with regard to the offering of a product or service, this was a rather critical point. My staff did not know whether McCrossan had discussed his position with the Department of Finance or with the Minister of State (Finance), Tom Hockin. (As it turned out, he had not.) Another player who was not aware of the Blenkarn committee's attempt to impose a "voluntary" agreement was the Office of the Superintendent of Financial Institutions (OSFI), the organization responsible for regulating the banks on behalf of the Minister of Finance.

At our meeting McCrossan went over his personal list of requirements. Some of them were reasonable, such as improved notification to customers of changed service charges and better explanatory material for customers. These changes were introduced by the banks soon afterwards. But the banks were opposed to any mandatory "plain vanilla" account, free of charges; in fact they were opposed to any common definition of a basic account, since this would prohibit competition rather than increase it.

But the biggest problem was a constitutional one. An agreement between a few members of Parliament and a private-sector group would have no legal standing whatsoever, and would be contrary to the rule of law in a democracy. It would bypass the government of the day and the civil service which administered the law on behalf of the government. It was, in fact, a circumvention of the parliamentary process. But the reporters dealing with the issue did not seem to grasp that there was an issue of due process.

Although the Friday afternoon meeting was cordial, McCrossan did not heed my warning that the banks could not make an agreement with a committee of the House. On Saturday, April 30, I sent an urgent memo to the executive council of the CBA, reporting on my Friday meeting with Paul McCrossan. My memo included the following passage: "We have received a message from Hockin through our chairman, André Bérard, that the government does not wish us to negotiate any deal with the House committee. Obviously the House committee cannot bind the government and cannot even ensure that the government would follow their recommendations in the report, even though McCrossan pretends that with three-party support the government would have no choice but to follow their wishes . . . I do not think it would be useful or even prudent to meet with the House committee or a subcommittee of the House committee for two reasons. First, it would be directly contrary to indications from Hockin. Secondly, the prospects for the conclusion of a unanimous agreement among the banks as to McCrossan's proposal are nil."

On the following Monday, May 2, I canvassed all six bank presidents individually on their feelings and then reported the consensus back to them as follows: "Banks generally agree that any negotiation with the House committee would be a mistake." But the consensus of the presidents was that an informal meeting would have to be held. The banks felt that to refuse a meeting with the sub-committee would be perceived by the press as arrogant and high-handed—the usual perception of the banks no matter which direction we took.

Since Paul McCrossan was leaving shortly for Washington, the earliest date which could be agreed upon was Tuesday, May 10. I confirmed the meeting with Don Blenkarn in a letter to him on May 5, which said:

> The purpose of the meeting is to provide input to you and your colleagues in the preparation of your report on service charges. The bank spokesmen will want to examine with you proposed regulations on disclosure and the need to strike a balance between updated disclosure regulation and the avoidance of costly solutions which would drive service charges up. As I reaffirmed on the phone yesterday, it would not be appropriate to discuss any sort of agreement or arrangement between the banks as to their service products or delivery systems. That would be contrary to the Bank Act, and in any event would be inconsistent with the banks' strongly held view that free market competition is the best assurance of service to the consumer.

Meanwhile, a four-sided turf war was developing in Ottawa, involving the Department of Finance, the Department of Consumer and Corporate Affairs, OSFI, and the House committee. The Department of Consumer and Corporate Affairs felt that it had some responsibility for consumer protection in the field of financial services, and had been trying for some time to work out common concerns with its provincial counterparts responsible for consumer protection. But that ministry also contained the Competition Bureau, which could and would intervene if there were an agreement on service charges contrary to law.

Blenkarn saw Harvie Andre, the Minister of Consumer Affairs, as an ally. On May 3, Blenkarn told me on the phone that Harvie Andre had written a letter to me on April 29, which presumably gave him moral support. Unfortunately, the Department of Consumer and Corporate Affairs was still under the impression that Canada Post could deliver a letter from Ottawa to Toronto in one or two days. In fact, not one but two letters dated April 29 arrived on May 5. The first acknowledged a letter that I had sent to Harvie Andre on March 22, providing information on service charges and fees. The minister hoped that the dialogue would continue. The second letter suggested that the Competition Act wouldn't prevent the development of an industry code of ethics or "the standardization of banking terms." The minister invited the CBA to obtain an "advisory opinion" from the director of investigation and research in the Department of Consumer and Corporate Affairs if we had suggestions along those lines. The letter was copied to Blenkarn, but made no reference to his committee's attempt to force an agreement on basic banking services.

The other two players in the turf war were the Department of Finance and the Office of the Superintendent of Financial Institutions, headed by Michael Mackenzie. The Minister of State (Finance), Tom Hockin, was keeping his head well down. There was no politician alive who would be seen defending the banks, and in any event Blenkarn had the ear of the Conservative caucus. But the departmental officials in Finance, and others in OSFI, were quietly working with the CBA staff to introduce a revised set of disclosure regulations which would correct the problems that some of the banks had already acknowledged. At the same time, however, there was an ongoing tension between Finance and OSFI; Finance considered that it had responsibility for policy questions, and that OSFI's job was to enforce the regulations but not get involved in policy discussions. OSFI, on the other hand, resented the failure of Finance to consult it in its field of expertise.

To complicate the picture, there was a difference of opinion as to whether Canada should follow the British route and create the Office of an Ombudsman to examine and rectify consumer grievances on financial services. Michael Mackenzie thought that an ombudsman would overlap his own jurisdiction. And if any such office were created, it should certainly not be in the Department of Consumer Affairs, because the Department of Finance and OSFI were responsible for regulating the banks.

With these four players tugging in different directions, I felt something like the victim of medieval torture whose arms and legs were tied to four different horses, each pulling outwards.

The meeting of May 10 with Paul McCrossan was held at the small office of the CBA in Ottawa where we had naively assumed we could keep it confidential. But of course the press were waiting in the lobby downstairs, and some of the departing politicians supplied them with their version of the meeting afterwards. Four bank presidents attended: Matthew Barrett from the Bank of Montreal, John Cleghorn from the Royal Bank, Gordon Bell from the Bank of Nova Scotia, and Warren Moysey from the Canadian Imperial Bank of Commerce. The Toronto-Dominion Bank was represented by its senior vice-president and comptroller, Norm Roth. The chairman of the CBA, André Bérard, was absent in Europe, but I was present to represent the CBA. The Blenkarn sub-committee consisted of Blenkarn, Paul Mc-Crossan, Aideen Nicholson, and Simon de Jong. There was also a staff person from each side.

Blenkarn opened the meeting by circulating a draft document entitled "Fair Personal Banking Practices Agreement." Since I had already made it clear in writing that the banks were not prepared to sign an agreement with the committee, the meeting was off to a disastrous start. Paul McCrossan confirmed what we already knew, which was that the committee would propose very tough amendments to the Bank Act if the banks would not agree to the draft document.

But the very first clause started a wrangle. Blenkarn's draft stated, "The parties to this agreement are set out in Schedule A . . . This agreement is endorsed by the Canadian Bankers' Association (CBA), the Canadian Trust Association (CTA), and the Canadian Cooperative Credit Society (CCCS)." This infuriated the bankers, who pointed out that the committee had treated the trust companies with kid gloves and ignored the credit unions. The agreement did not even mention the caisses populaires in Quebec, which were important competitors of the banks. We noted that the committee had completely ignored the data we had presented about competing institutions, and appeared to want to hobble the federally regulated banks in competition with provincially regulated institutions. As for including the credit unions, Blenkarn was talking out of both sides of his mouth; in the committee hearings he had said: "You know perfectly well Mr. MacIntosh, the credit unions are emanations of the provinces . . . What provinces do with their reporting institutions is another matter."

Two of the bankers, whose reputation in the banking industry for abrasive bluntness exceeded my own, asked McCrossan if his proposal to copy the legislation in fifteen American states included anything about the higher U.S. service charges and their record of poorer service and an inferior payments system. One president noted that the Blenkarn committee had gone off to New York to look at international banking centres, but had avoided looking at American bank service charges.

One clause of the agreement required the banks to obtain in writing the agreement of any individual personal customer before changing the service charge. This proposal was attacked by all the banks, who pointed out that it was administratively unfeasible. At least 20 percent of the population changes its address each year, and many do not provide their home addresses to banks at all. With hundreds of millions of transactions a year, it would drive up costs astronomically.

The opposition members on the sub-committee were embarrassed. Aideen Nicholson said that she had never been convinced that there was a problem, but that the banks had handled their public relations very badly. After a while she left the meeting, muttering as she stood up that she had to go to another committee meeting where the egos were not so big. Simon de Jong appeared somewhat uncomfortable, because his own moderate and reasonable approach to the issue was so out of keeping with that of his colleague Rodriguez, who tended to shout.

After about an hour of increasingly hostile bickering, McCrossan stood up and said there was no point in going on—the committee would draft legislation. This reduced the sub-committee representation to two, Blenkarn and de Jong, and shortly afterwards the meeting broke up. Although Blenkarn had said that the meeting would be considered an in-camera session of the finance committee, news stories began to appear almost at once. Jonathan Ferguson in the *Toronto Star* reported: "A deal between MPs and the big banks over the thorny issue of service charges fell apart amid bickering among the presidents of the banks, sources say . . . 'What we were treated to was a one and a half hour lecture on the free market system and that if customers don't like it, they can take their money and go elsewhere,' one source at the meeting said yesterday . . . Then they [the banks] attacked one another for causing the public investigation into service charges by charging customers too aggressively."

The next day, Ferguson's "news" story started off "Don't bend over backwards for the country's big banks; they'll kick you in the teeth. That's the valuable lesson MPs learned this week. And you can just ask Paul McCrossan how much it smarts." The *Star*'s notion of even-handed reporting was headlined "Bankers leave finance committee seething—bankers show arrogance."

Quite a different version of events appeared in the *Financial Post*'s story of May 12, written by Hyman Solomon and Madelaine Drohan. The *Post* story opened "Canadian bankers refused to circumvent normal government channels and endorse House finance committee proposals to revamp bank service charges, bank officials told the Post yesterday . . . Government officials told the Post the Tories were not amused by the plan they said would have made the committee look like the consumer's hero. One of the bankers was quoted as saying, 'We know who makes the decisions in government, and we were not going to be party to moving around them.' "

Meanwhile, the Department of Consumer and Corporate Affairs was trying to head the Blenkarn committee off at the pass. We had already been warned by an official in the competition branch, as noted earlier, that the banks did not have permission to negotiate an agreement with the House finance committee. On May 11, the Competition Bureau followed up an earlier phone call to Bert Waslander, research director for the finance committee, with a hand-delivered letter confirming that an agreement among the banks involving pricing and products would be contrary to the Competition Act.

On May 12, Paul McCrossan phoned me to say that, because of all the leakage in the press, he would have no alternative but to go public. Moreover, he said, he was "going to have to go with very very tough legislation." I asked him why he thought we could have made an agreement when there was a letter to his committee from the director of competition policy which stated that such an arrangement would be illegal. McCrossan was obviously taken aback by my comment, since he had apparently never been shown the letter by Waslander or Blenkarn.

On the following day, this issue finally came out in the open. John Kohut reported in the *Globe and Mail* that: "Proposals by the House of Commons Committee aimed at striking a private agreement with banks on service charges might have conflicted with the Competition Act according to a senior official of the Bureau of Competition Policy ... Section 33 of the Act stipulates banks are not allowed to agree among themselves on a number of issues." Kohut had got his information from David Makin, chief of the financial institutions and markets division of the Competition Bureau Branch.

Since the issue was out in the open, I confirmed to Ginny Galt of the *Globe and Mail* that the banks had told Blenkarn beforehand that we could not and would not sign a deal with his committee. Blenkarn's response was to criticize the bureaucrats: "The Bureau of Competition Policy has been doing everything possible to make sure that anything we do to help consumers is nullified," he said. The *Winnipeg Free Press* had an editorial on May 22 titled "Whose side are they on?" The editorial asserted that "The MPs now find that federal government regulators have joined the battle on the side of the banks. Few will not share Tory MP Don Blenkarn's amazement to find that the committee he chairs is under siege from the Bureau of Competition Policy . . ." In its obsession with bashing the banks, the *Winnipeg Free Press* appeared to be prepared to ignore inconvenient legislation which is intended to protect consumers.

Meanwhile, I had kept Tom Hockin and officials in the Department of Finance, the Department of Consumer and Corporate Affairs, and Mike Mackenzie's office aware of developments. All of the banks were pulling out all the stops to write new brochures and to simplify and explain their various service charges. By the time the finance committee was ready with its report, the government had already drafted its own set of amendments and proposals for voluntary change. But Tom Hockin still kept his head down, not wishing to get caught in the crossfire between Blenkarn and the CBA.

The Blenkarn committee's report on bank service charges was published on June 6, 1988, the 44th anniversary of D-Day. To unveil his report, Blenkarn had called a press conference in the National Press Centre facing the Centre Block of Parliament. I decided that his report had to be answered immediately, while the media were still present. Accordingly, we arranged with the head of the Press Gallery to follow Blenkarn at the same session. The individual banks were more than happy to let me go into the lions' den, because there was nothing to be gained by providing a forum for critics to challenge the price structure and customer services of a single bank, each of which was market-oriented and sensitive to its own name in the marketplace. Although some bankers thought I was too abrasive and undiplomatic with the politicians and the media, they were as angry in private as I was in public. I decided to take with me Joanne De Laurentiis, who was a leavening influence behind the scenes and someone who would present a more conciliatory image.

The finance committee's report turned out to be what we had expected. Some of the proposals, such as those relating to improved information for customers and notification we had already agreed to do, though not in such drastic form as a prohibition against changing service charges more than once a year. The committee proposed to prohibit the charging of a customer for depositing a cheque which had to be returned NSF (Not Sufficient Funds). I had always considered that particular charge to be indefensible, and the CBA had been trying to get all the banks to drop it.

But the proposal to provide a completely free bank account to low-income groups was something we felt very strongly about. In the first place, it was impossible to target low-income families: what would prevent a well-to-do family from maintaining half a dozen "basic banking accounts," and juggling funds from one to the other through an ATM? The extent of government intervention in the market system would have to be enormous. We had already provided the committee with detailed figures showing that each one of the big six banks already had a "basic banking account," costing a customer anywhere from $23.70 a year at the Royal to $44.40 at the Montreal for an account with a $10 minimum balance. Then there were, of course, the millions of senior citizens' accounts which were free of service charges.

But it was not only the substance of the proposals which was so interventionist, but the process which the committee was using. First of all, the committee was aiming its guns only at the federally chartered banks, and giving only lip service to comparable legislation for trust companies and credit unions. Secondly, Blenkarn had tried to castigate the bankers for not negotiating a private deal with their committee, even though this was both illegal and unconstitutional. And thirdly, the finance committee was proposing to introduce its report as a private member's bill. There was nothing in the history or traditions of our parliamentary system to provide for a committee of the House operating in this way. While there had been a recent precedent for a private member's bill being presented in the House and achieving passage — a non-smoking bill — there was certainly no precedent for standing the relationship between the executive and legislative branches of government on its head. Tom Hockin and the government were undoubtedly alarmed about this process, but no one was prepared to challenge the populist Blenkarn in the Conservative caucus. The storm had to blow itself out.

And storm there was. The Press Gallery was almost full; Blenkarn and his sub-committee were sitting in the front row, having stayed on to enjoy the bloodbath; Bert Waslander was sitting with them, but Dr. Terry Thomas was sitting up in the rear seats. My brother Dave, a long-time member of the Press Gallery, and more cantankerous by far than me, was sitting a few seats up, grinning with pleasure. I displayed some large charts showing the comparative service charges of banks, trust companies, and credit unions. These had been available and widely distributed for two months, but no daily newspaper had carried them. We had decided to publish them in the form of large ads, and some of the press photographers used this "photo opportunity" to show the charts. In the course of the proceedings, I knocked over a glass of water while making a gesture; this attracted almost as much press comment as my blast at the committee: "This is a national

sport—a national bloodletting of the banks to satisfy some politicians who are having trouble holding their seats." (As it happens, McCrossan lost his Scarborough seat in the general election which followed.) I said that the report was "schizophrenic, because it acknowledged that there was plenty of price competition for financial services, but nevertheless proposed to introduce anti-competitive restrictions." I called the proposal to introduce a private member's bill a "power play" and "an absurd distortion of parliamentary government in this country."

My remarks did not need much embellishment, and most of the bankers held their peace. One who did not was Susan De Stein of the Toronto-Dominion Bank, who said her bank was "astounded, incredibly angry and frustrated" with the committee report.

The government backpedalled furiously from a confrontation with the Blenkarn committee. Tom Hockin said that he would introduce legislation that would "look pretty similar" to the private bill. According to the *Toronto Star*, "a source in Finance Minister Michael

Wilson's office said his Department was impressed with the quality of the private bill and would be tempted to back it unless Hockin is determined to introduce his own bill."

As for basic banking accounts, Paul McGrath, a senior vice-president of the Toronto-Dominion Bank, said; "All the banks already provide a couple of accounts for next to nothing." Rob Parker, senior vice-president with the Royal Bank, said his bank had about 7 million customers, of whom almost 5 million used low- or no-cost accounts for basic banking services. Helen Sinclair, then a senior vice-president of the Bank of Nova Scotia, said that the MPs had overlooked market reality: "The public wants value for their money, but I am not sure people expect things for free," she said.

John Cleghorn, president of the Royal Bank, said; "Free basic banking service for all customers would constitute an astonishing precedent in a private-sector, highly competitive economy. After financial services institutions are required to give away basic products and services for free, what sector should be next?" One of Cleghorn's senior colleagues, Brian Gregson, wrote to the *Toronto Star* to reply to its editorial of June 8, "It's time to act on bank charges," with the following: "Your editorial contains factual errors and deliberate misinterpretations . . . Since the Star favours free basic services from banks, what about free basic newspapers? You are one of the most profitable papers in one of Canada's most profitable industries—why not publish a free basic newspaper, without advertisements? Or be really popular—one without ads or editorials?"

The *Star*'s editorial also drew a comment from Hugh Brown, who is considered to be one of the best analysts of bank stocks in Canada. He wrote: "In my opinion, Canadian consumers are served by one of the most competitive and efficient retail banking systems in the world . . . Bank shareholders, my clients, comprise millions of Canadians who own shares directly or through their pension funds, mutual funds, or insurance policies. Any detrimental action taken against Canada's banks affects all these shareholders . . . The low valuation of bank shares is partly attributable to an ongoing political fear factor."

The propaganda war had of course spread from the print media to radio and television. I accepted numerous telephone calls for live interviews on radio talk shows, which were sandwiched between reports on traffic conditions over the Lion's Gate bridge in Vancouver or the Halifax-Dartmouth bridge on the east coast. I also debated with Don Blenkarn on *Canada A.M.*, but the most satisfying confrontation occurred on *The Journal*. Barbara Frum asked Blenkarn why he was making such a fuss over service charges when they covered only 20 percent of the costs of these services; there was a long pause, perhaps three or four seconds. I jumped in with "While Don is trying to think of an answer . . ." Timing is everything, and for once I got it right.

In the following fortnight, the finance committee manoeuvred with the government to introduce its proposals as a private member's bill. Since there are normally several dozen bills which private members of Parliament wish to get on the parliamentary agenda, there is a lottery procedure for selecting the few to get priority in the heavy legislative agenda. "By a stroke of luck," the *Financial Post* reported, "it [McCrossan's bill] was selected in a lottery for debate and a vote in the House." The bill was given first reading, and was scheduled for debate in the House on July 12. But Hockin persuaded McCrossan to withdraw it, on condition that the government adopt his proposals in government legislation.

Before this could happen, a public-relations catastrophe happened. Not more than a mile from Parliament Hill, a sixty-two-year-old Ottawa widow, Clara De Gruchy, was charged a $2 service fee by the Bank of Nova Scotia for breaking a $20 bill. This disastrous transaction naturally focused withering criticism on the banking industry, and there was nothing that could be said to improve the situation. (I made inquiries into the circumstance and found out that the branch involved happened to be in a location where there were many coin-operated machines. The manager was attempting to discourage a lot of walk-in non-customer traffic which took up the time of his tellers. Later, Mrs. De Gruchy is said to have made peace with the bank.) But any attempt to explain the situation was of no use—the action of an untrained teller had been an unqualified disaster.

While the public relations situation was hitting rock bottom, the CBA was engaged in day-to-day negotiations with its members, the Department of Finance, and the Office of the Superintendent of Financial Institutions. The government's objective was to get as much as possible of its minimum requirement into a voluntary agreement, and to avoid restrictive legislation in the Bank Act. A major consideration was that the federal government could not legislate for the provincially chartered trust companies and credit unions, and comprehensive financial reform legislation was still some distance off.

By the end of June, Tom Hockin was able to announce a deal that most of the banks had agreed to. They would offer a basic savings account, which provided for six free transactions a month; they would provide thirty days' notice before introducing new fees; they would eliminate fees for closing accounts which had been open for more than a year; they would not charge the depositor of an NSF cheque. There was even an agreement that a bank would not charge a customer for an error caused by the institution, a completely redundant requirement because no business would deliberately charge a customer for its own error.

There were a few loose ends, but Paul McCrossan decided to withhold his private bill to see how the banks would respond to the voluntary agreement. In fact, the Toronto-Dominion Bank never did agree to the imposition of a "basic account," taking the position that "we do not want the government telling us what we can and can't offer via basic services." Another holdout was the Canada Trust, one of the largest trust companies, but not a member of the Trust Companies' Association. The strong-minded chief executive, Mervyn Lahn, finally agreed to go along, after a personal appeal from Hockin. John Evans, head of the Trust Companies' Association of Canada and a one-time chairman of the House of Commons Committee on Finance, Trade and Economic Affairs, said his members were already complying with 95 percent of what the government wanted.

By August, Paul McCrossan had completed his self-appointed task of supervising the financial services industry. He told the CBC: "Well, essentially, they've eliminated all of the fees that we requested they eliminate. Indeed some of them have gone beyond that . . ." Having declared victory, he allowed his private bill to die in Parliament. But the opposition said that the Hockin reform package was "gutless." Rodriguez was so excited that he mixed his metaphors, saying, "This is the biggest bank hold-up since the Great Train Robbery," whatever that means. On August 17, Hockin tabled a report in the House from the regulator, Michael Mackenzie, which confirmed that the banks had complied with the government's request.

So ended the great battle over bank service charges. Although the banks and the CBA had taken a beating over the whole affair, it did contribute to better communication with the public, and with employees. For the consumer, there was a worthwhile simplification of price lists, and a considerable improvement in the available information. The impact on bank costs and revenues was marginal, because the basic economics of financial services in a free competitive market system could not be changed by political rhetoric. The politicians had scored a great triumph, and the Blenkarn committee had established itself as a political force to be reckoned with in national politics.

CHAPTER 14

STOMPING THROUGH THE TULIPS

In this last chapter, we will take a brief tour around the garden of banking and politics, a garden which overlooks the playing field where the drums can be heard. I propose to call this part of the tour "stomping through the tulips," in honour of Danny Kaye's version of the song. At the beginning of the song, he tiptoes through the tulips singing in a very small voice; at the end, he thunders through the flower beds, hollering as he goes. We first encounter international banking centres, which proved to be a feeble plant. This leads to the politics of banks in the securities business, where some strange grafted cross-breeds appear. Then on to free trade, which had a generic relationship to the ownership of securities firms. In the last part of the tour we visit the hybrid terrain of the Canadian Payments Association (CPA). And finally we end the tour with a quick look at corporate governance, where great oaks grow.

THE MONTREAL-TORONTO RIVALRY: INTERNATIONAL BANKING CENTRES

It is probably true to say that the breakdown of the barriers between commercial banking and the securities industry would never have come about had it not been for the absurd federal legislation to create international banking centres in Montreal and Vancouver. What this did was to confirm in plain language that Ottawa intended to use its powers to shift the financial services industry towards Montreal and Vancouver and away from Toronto. This led to great political pressure from the City of Toronto on the government at Queen's Park, which in the mid-1980s woke up to the fact that a huge part of the growth in Toronto was in the services sector, especially in finance.

The Ontario government responded to the Mulroney government's legislation on international banking centres by embarking on a unilateral plan to open up the securities industry to some degree of foreign ownership. This encouraged Quebec to pursue the independent course of financial deregulation which it had already set. It also greatly alarmed the banks, which were severely curtailed in their securities powers by Ottawa. In the end, the barriers against ownership of securities firms by banks broke down entirely; but this came about essentially because of the competition between Montreal and Toronto, and not because of any federal intention to respond to global forces.

The rivalry between Montreal and Toronto is an old one; as we saw in the second chapter, it goes back to the 1820s. In the early 1980s, a number of factors increased the postwar predominance of Toronto as the headquarters for financial services in Canada. When the foreign bank subsidiaries were first licensed in 1981, all but a few chose Toronto for their head office. The resentment about this was so great in Montreal that towards the end of the licensing wave in the early 1980s, the Inspector General of Banks made a Montreal head office location a condition for obtaining a licence.

The influence of Quebec's language legislation is well-known. For the big banks and insurance companies with headquarters in Montreal, the problem of transferring and keeping personnel in Montreal became a serious one. For example, it was extremely difficult to attract and keep the thousands of people required in data processing, since many of them would be required to send their children to French-speaking schools. Most immigrant employees of the banks did not want this for their children. And so the drift to Toronto was accelerated.

When public policy is driven by tax lawyers, chauvinistic businessmen, and municipal politicians, the public welfare is in great danger. This is what happened in the case of international banking centres. In 1981, the Montreal Chamber of Commerce and the Board of Trade commissioned a study by some tax lawyers and accountants which advocated the creation of an International Banking Centre (IBC) in Montreal. These tax experts had noted the creation of international banking facilities in New York City, which were designed to encourage the booking of non-resident international banking transactions in New York rather than abroad (that is, recording the loans and deposits of U.S. banks within the U.S., even though the actual transactions were with non-residents at offshore locations). The legislation had succeeded in transferring hundreds of billions of dollars of offshore banking business to the books of the banks in New York City. But what the Montreal tax experts failed to notice was that the whole exercise had created about two hundred jobs in New York, on repatriated assets exceeding $200 billion. They did not understand that where the banking business was done and where it was booked were not the same thing. The international banking facilities in New York were nothing more than gold letters on the doors of modest rooms in high-rises on Wall Street. Apart from a few clerks, there was almost no employment created at all.

The Montreal Chamber of Commerce overlooked that aspect of the U.S. legislation. They had visions of Montreal becoming the headquarters for scores of financial institutions which had offshore business with foreign corporations and governments. But to attract this imaginary bonanza to Montreal, it was necessary to have federal tax legislation which specified that international banking centres would be lawful only in Montreal. It is not difficult to imagine the technical difficulties of devising tax legislation intended to force financial transactions for offshore customers to be located in one specific city, when money moves freely within Canada and around the globe by computer and wire. To achieve the necessary limitation to one city (later two), it was necessary to employ many lawyers and accountants to invent a complex structure of bureaucratic controls. Although the Department of Finance was in a phase of having tax and labour lawyers as deputy ministers (first Mickey Cohen and then Stanley Hartt), even they had trouble implementing tax legislation to control where business could be done.

But no matter. Political reaction came swiftly, when Ottawa showed an interest in Montreal's scheme. The Vancouver Board of Trade wanted in. Then the politicians in Toronto and Calgary joined the chorus; they also thought that international banking centres were a great idea, provided their cities were included in the legislation. The foolishness and divisiveness of legislation which requires an intricate web of discrimination to offset market forces is apparent. Worse still, it was all to no good purpose, because the possibilities for job creation were almost nil.

In response to heavy political pressure, Marc Lalonde, the Minister of Finance in 1983, commissioned an internal study by his department on international banking centres. This study, by Ron Wilson, examined the factors in the $80-billion business of the big six Canadian banks with non-residents. It came to the conclusion that business corporations, governments, and banks would have no reason to book their mostly U.S.-dollar transactions at a tax-free haven in Montreal. Since there was no intention of giving the Canadian banks a tax advantage — and the banks were not supporting the scheme anyway — there was not much point in creating a complex law to offer a tax-sheltered location to non-residents. Ron Wilson also concluded that "the New York experiment has had no significant effect on employment in the city."

But rational analysis had nothing to do with the political pressure from the Montreal Chamber of Commerce. After the election of the Mulroney government in 1984, a joint proposal from the Montreal Chamber of Commerce and the Vancouver Board of Trade was revived. Michael Wilson commissioned another study, this time by the former governor of the Bank of Canada, Louis Rasminsky, and a former senior deputy governor of the Bank of Canada, William Lawson. After months of study, the two central bankers submitted their report in June 1985. They had consulted a wide range of experts in financial markets in Canada and in New York and their conclusion confirmed what everyone who was qualified already knew: the IBC proposal was not a prudent idea.

But this conclusion was not acceptable to the Mulroney government and the embarrassing report was buried. In February 1986, Michael Wilson announced in his budget speech that legislation to create international banking centres in Montreal and Vancouver would go ahead. This was, of course, consistent with the style of the Mulroney government: make concessions to special interest groups, no matter how costly or ill-considered, and contrary to the best advice available. But in this case it was extraordinary to see a Toronto member, Michael Wilson, defending a budget proposal which was intended to discriminate against his own city. (His dogged determination — even visible anger — in defending an indefensible piece of legislation was repeated a few years later in the Amex case. In both cases, it seemed as though his hard-line posture was in direct proportion to the pressure from the Prime Minister's office and in inverse proportion to his own common sense.)

The Rasminsky-Lawson Report was not published until April 1986, six weeks after the government commitment to go against its advice. Even then it would not have been published, had it not already been leaked to the press. In early March 1986, Al Toulin of the *Toronto Star* quoted from the report: "Decisions about where to book are often influenced by non-banking considerations, notably by government regulations and taxation . . . employment in the banking centres is small . . . and is mainly of a routine nature." Publication of the report released a furious round of political grandstanding in Montreal, Vancouver, and Toronto. In Quebec, the report was labelled as the product of the "Toronto lobby." Many provincial politicians had long since jumped on the IBC bandwagon in Quebec, including Jacques Parizeau, who had once worked for Rasminsky and Lawson in the Bank of Canada; he knew very well that they were not acting as lobbyists for anyone.

In British Columbia, support for a Vancouver international banking centre was multiparty in character: there was Bill Bennett, the Premier; Mike Harcourt, the mayor of Vancouver; and Pat Carney, a Tory cabinet minister. In Toronto, David Peterson and Bob Nixon joined the mayor of Toronto, Art Eggleton, and the Toronto Board of Trade in violent opposition to the discriminatory nature of the IBC legislation. Eggleton tried to draw me, as the president of the Canadian Bankers' Association, into the controversy on his side. But of course I could not do this, because the association represented banks in all parts of the country and it was not our role to take a partisan position between cities. To emphasize the problem, the chairman of the Canadian Bankers' Association was André Bérard, president of the National Bank, headquartered in Montreal. At the annual meeting of the CBA in Vancouver during June of that year, he said that while the banks supported tax legislation to encourage the booking of offshore transactions in Canada, the government should allow "market forces, not Ottawa, to decide where branches emerge." The chairman of the National, Michel Bélanger, described the legislation as "a big fluffy ball."

Almost a year passed from the announcement of the IBC legislation in the budget of February 1986 until the introduction of legislation in January 1987. During that year, there was intense lobbying from all sides. But all the king's horses and all the king's men in Ontario could not stop the bill going forward. I reflected ruefully that on the many occasions when the Canadian Bankers' Association did not get its way, we were criticized as being a flop as a lobby group. But in the political balance of power in Ottawa, even Ontario's nine million citizens fell short.

The anger and frustration in Toronto at federal government policy on IBCs was fundamental in the decisions taken in the summer of 1986 to open up securities markets. Monte Kwinter, Ontario's Minister of Financial Institutions, said in September: "It just doesn't make sense to exclude Toronto." In October he said that Ontario would "fight Ottawa's ludicrous plans." Art Eggleton, the mayor of Toronto, commissioned a study by the management consulting firm Woods Gordon, which reported that Toronto stood to lose at least 350 banking jobs. This calculation was based on data of the same quality as estimates in Quebec that 5,000 jobs would be created. In truth, both estimates completely ignored the available facts. In January, 1987, I told the House of Commons finance committee that the two IBCs in Montreal and Vancouver might create up to twenty-six jobs. This estimate was based on the assumed transfer to Canada of all the offshore eligible assets of the Canadian banks, amounting to $26 billion; the New York experience showed that there were about 200 employees handling $234 billion worth of offshore assets there. Since neither side was paying any attention to the facts, the political bitterness escalated. The prevailing view in Montreal was that Toronto was excessively greedy and selfish; Ontario was not prepared to concede even a minor advantage to Quebec in the development of international financial services. And at Queen's Park, where no love was lost at the Treasury Department and in the Ministry of Financial Institutions for the staff in the Department of Finance in Ottawa, the conviction grew that Ontario had to take strong measures to assure the place of Toronto as the leading financial centre in Canada.

As it turned out, my estimate of twenty-six jobs was an exaggeration. David Dodge, the assistant deputy minister of finance for tax matters, told Blenkarn's committee that perhaps eleven jobs would be created altogether. The finance committee, not averse to the occasional junket, went to New York to look at the international banking facilities for themselves. A spokesman for the Morgan Bank of Canada told them that his bank required only one employee to manage $5 billion. The finance committee at last began to doubt the worth of the legislation; it could have saved $20,000 in travel expenses by paying attention to my testimony in the first place.

On April 30, Blenkarn's finance committee advised the government to withdraw the IBC legislation. Even this was perceived differently in Montreal and Toronto. The *Journal de Montréal*'s headline on April 30 was: "Finance Committee Proposes Two Banking Centres." *Le Devoir*'s headline was: "Ottawa invited to approve the creation of banking centres." But these optimistic reports were slightly premature. On May 1, the Toronto *Globe and Mail* reported: "Finance committee rejects bank centre plan" and the *Toronto Star* said: "The all-party committee rejected Wilson's plan." The government, faced with the revolt of the Blenkarn committee, shelved the income tax amendments until the fall.

During the summer recess, Mulroney changed the composition of the finance committee, which is a clear demonstration that when push comes to shove, the government of the day can force a committee to support its legislation. When the committee reconvened in December, Blenkarn was forced to swallow his feelings, and the IBC legislation was approved by a narrow margin. But not before Norman Warner, the member from Cornwall, had seriously proposed that the Mohawk Akwesasne Reserve become the site for international banking centres. Presumably he meant that the bingo halls could be converted into banking halls.

On December 17, 1987, the legislation was finally passed by the House of Commons. Mulroney was given a standing ovation in Montreal. But there was no stampede to open an international banking centre. Most of the applicants were not commercial banks at all, but private Swiss investment banks and the like. In Vancouver, the Canadian Imperial Bank of Commerce, banker to the province for more than a century, was among the first to open an IBC. Late in 1988, the Royal Bank and the Bank of Montreal followed suit. Professor Michael Goldberg at the University of British Columbia said: "We're going to get a critical mass." But some of the financial journalists saw through the political cosmetics. Hugh Anderson described the IBC legislation as a "gimcrack" in the *Montreal Gazette*, adding that "a gimcrack is a showy object of little use or value." Christopher Waddell wrote in the *Globe and Mail*: "The scheme has become a textbook example of what can go wrong when illusion triumphs over reality."

The significance of the international banking centre controversy was not the predictable failure of the legislation to achieve anything worthwhile for the Canadian financial system: the importance was the political fallout on securities legislation.

THE MONTEBELLO BREAKTHROUGH

In June 1986, Monte Kwinter, Ontario's Minister of Financial Institutions, stunned financial markets by announcing that Ontario would permit banks, trust companies, and foreign financial institutions to acquire up to 30 percent ownership in a broker or investment dealer licensed in Ontario. When asked by the *Financial Times* how much he had consulted with Ottawa, he replied: "About as much as took place when they decided to make Vancouver and Montreal international banking centres." This says it all.

Kwinter's announcement set in motion a train of events which would not stop until most of the big investment firms in Canada had been swallowed up by the major banks. This was certainly not what either Ontario or the other provinces or the federal government had intended; it was the result of escalating divisiveness encouraged by politicians and originated by businessmen who did not do their homework.

The regulation of the securities industry in Canada had, for a long time, been more a question of practice than of constitutional law. In the mid-nineteenth century, the Bank of Montreal had been the sole fiscal agent for the Government of Canada, including the placement of its bond issues in the London market. So it could hardly be said that banks did not have the power to underwrite securities. In fact, this function had never been seriously challenged, and the banks were major players in the distribution of Government of Canada marketable debt, Canada Savings Bonds, and also provincial and municipal government securities. Until 1980, the Bank Act was ambiguous about the power of banks to underwrite corporate securities. There were one or two cases in which banks were minor members of corporate underwriting syndicates—Bell Telephone and General Motors Acceptance, for example. But these were certainly exceptions, and the banks had never considered themselves to be underwriters of corporate bonds and stocks.

As for the distribution of securities to the public, there were various levels of involvement. Banks actively distributed federal government securities, both as agents in the case of Canada Savings Bonds, and as principals in the case of marketable debt; they sold provincial bonds to customers, but only in the sense of taking orders initiated by customers; and they were prevented by the Bank Act from advertising the sale of municipal securities. As for corporate securities, banks could buy them for their own account, but they were essentially no more than incidental order-takers for corporate stocks and bonds through the branch system. Stock transactions had to be placed with a licensed broker. When mutual funds became important in the 1960s and 1970s—especially for Registered Retirement Savings Plans—some of the banks developed equity funds which were managed by independent fund managers. Most bankers were reluctant to get involved in the distribution of stocks and equity mutual funds because they felt that if their recommendations did badly, the customer would take his banking business elsewhere.

The provincial governments, especially in Ontario and Quebec, had gradually asserted increasing authority over the securities markets over many decades. Some of the other provinces also had securities commissions, but their regulatory standards still tend to be those applicable in Ontario in the 1950s.

The Bank Act revision of 1980 defined more precisely the extent of a bank's power to "deal in" securities. The White Paper of 1976 leading up to the Bank Act revision said: "The power of banks to underwrite corporate securities or to act as agent in the private placement of corporate securities will be withdrawn." Banks did not make an issue of this policy, nor did they fight the prohibition against engaging in the management of mutual funds. The CBA's official response to the White Paper noted that "Banks will be prohibited from offering equity and bond plans and RRSPs except where the funds for this purpose are handed over to arm's-length management." Although I was chairman of the Bank Act revision committee of the CBA, and personally opposed to this constraint, I could not generate any interest in taking a stand on this question, and we let it go by default. In the end, the revisions to the Bank Act in 1980 eliminated any possibility of a bank underwriting corporate securities for secondary distribution to others, and put constraints on the distribution of corporate securities and mutual funds.

Meanwhile, from the mid-1970s onwards, the provincial securities commissions increasingly required banks to observe their laws and regulations in dealing with the public. On the whole this was not unreasonable, because the securities commissions had a mandate to protect the public from unqualified sellers of securities, which certainly included the untrained staff of bank branches. The encroachment of the securities commissions on banks was not hindered by the Department of Finance or the Inspector General of Banks, because the federal government had, in effect, opted out of securities regulation. The Department of Consumer and Corporate Affairs commissioned a huge study advocating a National Securities Commission, but this was quietly buried. A dual regulatory regime developed, in which banks found themselves reporting to provincial securities regulators as well as to their own federal regulator, the Inspector General.

Until 1986, there was no thought of allowing banks to own securities dealers. The successive policy documents leading towards the Bank Act revision of 1990 gave no hint that a major change was soon to come, for the simple reason that none was foreseen. But there were several important skirmishes which helped to define the frontier between provincial regulation of securities and federal regulation of banking. One of the most important and memorable of these was the Green-Line battle in the spring of 1983. This began when the Toronto-Dominion Bank decided to offer a discount brokerage service to the public. The bank argued that it could take unsolicited orders for stocks and relay them to brokerage firms through a relatively advanced information system which reduced the cost of each transaction.

The "Green-Line" scheme was challenged by the investment industry, and the matter went to a hearing before the Ontario Securities Commission. What made the occasion memorable for me is that I had to appear on the witness stand for a whole day on behalf of the Canadian Bankers' Association, which supported the Toronto-Dominion's case. The Securities Commission eventually ruled in the Toronto-Dominion's favour.

Although it had nothing to do with ownership, the Green-Line decision confirmed a very important event which had already occurred in April 1983: the deregulation of brokerage commission rates. Up until then, there was a monopolistic structure of brokerage fees, protected by statutory authority delegated to the Investment Dealers' Association and the stock exchanges by the provincial securities commissions. The survival of this cartel arrangement long after price-fixing had been made illegal for most goods and services, including bank interest rates and service charges, is a sociological study beyond the scope of this book. My own theory is that it was extremely easy for brokers to confer trivial favours on politicians by offering them a few shares of stock in underpriced new issues or by supplying good tips. The wonderful world of fixed commissions had for generations guaranteed the incomes of some mediocre people, including the less talented children of the establishment. Those who could not conceivably get into a law school or medical school, or even earn a decent degree in commerce, could still find a comfortable home in the brokerage industry.

All this had come to a dismal end in April 1983. The Green-Line discount brokerage service could not have existed before then, as every trader of stocks in both primary distribution and secondary markets had to observe the fixed commission rates. The breakdown of the fixed commission structure meant the certain end for many small firms, and decreased profit margins for the survivors. Unfortunately for the banks, they did not understand that the world had changed, but the partners of the investment brokers understood very well.

In a speech in December 1983 Peter Dey, chairman of the Ontario Securities Commission, said: "By definition, we believe a financial segment can have only one core function — and it should be protected from competition from other segments. For the securities industry, the core function is underwriting." He added that another function which was essential to and supportive of the core function was a full-service brokerage. In contrast to the unsolicited order-taking aspect of the Green-Line discount brokerage service, a full-service broker could provide analysis and advice to the customer. Dey was articulating a view about drawing the line between commercial banking and investment underwriting which I shared with many others. But some of the leading bankers were expressing more and more interest in full investment powers. In November 1984, for example, Rowland Frazee, the chairman of the Royal Bank, told the Canadian Tax Foundation that banks should be allowed to under-write securities, and that the traditional separation of functions in the Canadian financial market was coming apart, with or without govern-ment policy changes. From that time on, I had to advocate a position about which I had personal reservations. By the mid-1980s the CBA had shifted from the position of simply trying to retain the existing powers of the banks in securities markets, to the British style of opening up the securities business completely.

In the years 1982-85, several studies done in Ontario proposed some degree of outside ownership of securities dealers, but none of these recommended more than a minority ownership of securities dealers by banks. In fact, a 1982 report of the Ontario Securities Commission under its chairman, Henry Knowles, recommended an outright prohibition on the ownership of dealers by banks and trust companies. The Knowles report summarized the views of several highly qualified lawyers and some federal regulators as well, who argued for maintaining the separation of the "core functions" in financial services. By February 1985 the commission had shifted position under the chairmanship of Peter Dey, and recommended that a single institution be allowed to own up to 30 percent of a dealer and that foreign ownership also be permitted up to 30 percent. Later in 1985, an Ontario Task Force on Financial Institutions, chaired by

Professor Stefan Dupré, modified the Dey report by proposing that the ownership of a dealer by a single institution be limited to 20 percent. As for foreign ownership, Dupré recommended that Ontario avoid making unilateral concessions to foreign investors until the negotiation of satisfactory arrangements for international trade in services, which would involve federal-provincial agreements.

While these changes were going on in Ontario, the province of Quebec had become in many ways the leading edge of change in the financial services industry. Since the "Quiet Revolution" in the early 1960s, the educational system had been revolutionized, and there was a whole new generation of business-oriented men and women, who owed no allegiance to traditional institutions and were therefore inclined to be agents of change. A major element in capturing the pinnacles of industrial power was to use the instruments of government for that purpose. One of the first achievements was the creation of Hydro Quebec; within two decades, the new generation proved that it had the engineering and industrial know-how, together with the necessary management and financial skills, to operate one of the largest enterprises in the country very successfully.

In the financial field, Quebec made a major departure from the rest of Canada by taking control of its share of the Canada Pension Plan flow of funds. By combining the universal pension plan with its own provincial employee plans, Quebec was able to turn the Caisse de dépôt et placement into a major financial investor, controlled by Quebec. (Among other things, the Caisse became the largest single shareholder of most if not all the big six banks at one time or another.) Financial legislation was tilted in the direction of favouring the Caisses Desjardins, the large credit union movement in Quebec. For example, in recent years Quebec has authorized the Caisses Desjardins to sell insurance products, something which cannot be done by banks and trust companies.

In December 1965, the Government of Quebec appointed a study committee to report on the financial institutions coming under provincial authority. The mandate of the committee was extended several times, so that its final report was not published until June 1969. The study was going on throughout the momentous period when the federal government was introducing limits on the foreign ownership of banks, removing the 6 percent interest rate ceiling, and opening up consumer credit financing to banks. The chairman of the committee was Jacques Parizeau, then an economist and not yet launched on his political career. Other members of the Parizeau committee were Michel Bélanger, then deputy minister of industry and commerce, subsequently chairman of the National Bank, and now co-chairman of the Bélanger-Campeau Commission on the constitution; and Douglas Fullerton, who had helped René Lévesque put together Hydro Quebec, and whose career included managing the investment portfolio of the Canada Council.

The Parizeau report came to be regarded as a seminal document in the development of the Canadian financial system, mainly because it represented a striking departure from the concept of the four separate pillars of banking, insurance, securities, and fiduciary functions. The Parizeau report proposed that deposit-taking and all the other functions could be contained in a common ownership structure, although it provided for separate licensing of each function.

Already in 1969 there were signs of a different perspective on relations between Quebec and the rest of Canada. For example, the report said: "If our aim is to maintain control of financial institutions in Quebec hands, we do not see why a New York group should be treated differently from Toronto or Winnipeg groups." In the committee's eyes, the rest of Canada was just as "foreign" as New York. There was an open attitude towards foreign investment in Quebec financial institutions, but this was an easy promise for Quebec to make, because the principal instruments of financial power—the Caisse de dépôt and the Caisses Desjardins—were beyond the reach of foreigners.

It was this background of the Parizeau report in Quebec and the federal government's decision to create international banking centres in Montreal and Vancouver that convinced the Peterson government in Ontario to take decisive action to sustain Toronto's competitive position in financial services. And there was a policy ready to hand, because the New York investment dealers were knocking on the door, asking for access to the Canadian securities markets. The culmination of this thinking was Monte Kwinter's statement of June 1986 to allow both domestic and foreign ownership of securities firms up to 30 percent.

On June 14, I told Al Toulin of the *Toronto Star*: "By the time Ottawa gets around to deciding [how to respond to Kwinter], the stadium will be shut down and everyone will have gone home." Two days later, Dick Thomson said:

> The Ontario government is obviously recognizing that there is
> a problem in the fact that Canada and the provinces and the

major corporations are no longer using Canadian dealers. And the reason is that the Canadian dealers have not got the presence abroad that the foreign dealers do and the Canadian dealers don't have enough capital.

By September, there were a few signs that the message was getting through; Tom Hockin, the Minister of State (Finance) told the *Financial Times* of London: "There is a disposition to consider a few changes in the Bank Act." But our experience with Tom Hockin was that he had no great conviction about defending federal institutions from provincial policies. We felt that we had to reach Michael Wilson to emphasize the urgency of the situation.

Sunday, October 19, 1986, was an important milestone in the evolution of the Canadian banking system. On that day, Michael Wilson, the Minister of Finance, landed in a helicopter on the front lawn of the Chateau Montebello. His purpose was to have Sunday lunch with the chief executive officers of the big six banks. Over lunch, Wilson agreed in principle that the banks should be allowed to increase their access to the securities business in Canada, either through acquisition or by creating their own internal facilities. The deputy minister of finance, Stanley Hartt, was also present. It could be inferred that Wilson's concession would also gain the essential agreement of the Prime Minister.

The Montebello meeting was hardly a secret. The private dining room used by the banks could only be reached by walking through the main dining room; the chief executives were well-known to the establishment folks from Montreal and Ottawa who were among the weekend guests; and there were casual references to the meeting in the press afterwards. The chief executives had each brought along three of their most senior officers, and I was present as scribe and information resource. It was most unusual for the senior bankers to spend the weekend together, as opposed to the occasional quarterly business meeting with the governor of the Bank of Canada or the Minister of Finance. In fact there was probably no precedent in Canadian banking experience. But it was not unusual for the chief executives to encounter each other at the annual meetings of the International Monetary Conference, a gathering of top bankers from around the world, or at the Reserve City Bankers' Conference in the United States. At one of those meetings, it had seemed strange to some of the big six chief executives that their only opportunities to discuss very general issues on the future of the financial system seemed to be held under the auspices of the American Bankers' Association. This is what gave rise to the Montebello meeting, which was chaired by Don Fullerton of the Commerce. Beforehand, he asked me to canvass the banks and rough out an agenda. The chief executives had already decided to invite Michael Wilson, and had in fact settled on the time and place to suit the convenience of the Minister of Finance.

On the preceding Friday evening, the group of twenty-five from Toronto and Montreal had assembled for a round-table discussion of priorities. Gradually a consensus emerged on Saturday that the banks should put the case strongly to Wilson for broadening the powers of banks in the securities industry. The reasons for making the case were already well-known. Dick Thomson of the Toronto-Dominion and Allan Taylor of the Royal Bank had made speeches in which they had urged Ottawa to reconsider its opposition to the banks being more fully involved in the investment business. In the world financial markets, commercial bank lending was being turned increasingly into the business of buying and selling the securities of major corporations; "commercial paper" (typically thirty-day marketable obligations of corporations) was displacing bank loans. In 1986, about 85 percent of cross-border transactions in the global money markets were in the form of securities. This "securitization" of world banking was likely to leave the big Canadian banks out in the cold, and the Canadian investment dealers were too small to compete with the major securities firms in New York and London.

This theme was turned into a short brief to the minister by a sub-committee, while the others played golf and tennis. On Sunday morning, it was presented to the chief executive officers for their approval—at least, to five of them; Bill Mulholland, the chief executive of the Bank of Montreal, had come late to the meeting and left early, without telling his colleagues. Even in his absence, the Minister of Finance was persuaded that Canada's place in the world's financial system was in danger of serious erosion. The British were just then revolutionizing their system in a "Big Bang"; in that same month they had in effect eliminated all barriers between banking, investment dealing, and insurance. The Germans and Swiss already had "universal banks," which were equipped to deal in either commercial bank loans or securities, as they chose. The Americans and Japanese still maintained barriers between banking and the securities business, but even there, the walls were starting to break down.

Leaving aside global considerations, Wilson could see that the federal government was allowing Ontario and Quebec to set the agenda for financial change in Canada. Having been a vice-president of Dominion Securities, he could certainly recognize the threat to the major Canadian investment dealers if New York firms like Salomon Brothers and First Boston got a major foothold in Toronto. He agreed that drastic action was necessary to prevent the fragmentation of the Canadian financial system in a rapidly changing world. And so the Montebello meeting was a major milestone for the banks.

Before this departure from the traditional separation of commercial banking from underwriting could be turned into official government policy, the whole issue was blown wide open by the Bank of Nova Scotia. On November 12, 1986, the Quebec Securities Commission granted the bank a licence to create a subsidiary in Quebec called Scotia Securities, a full-service dealer. The Quebec government was furious that Paul Guay, the chairman of the Quebec Securities Commission, had taken this step without consulting the Quebec Minister of Finance. The Department of Finance in Ottawa was also surprised and infuriated, but the genie could not be put back in the bottle. I was also astonished at this move by my former colleagues, but took advantage of the opportunity by saying to a *Globe and Mail* reporter: "If they [Ontario] do nothing, you won't need an international banking centre to have a transfer to Montreal," (meaning, all the banks would shift their securities business to the permissive Montreal location). In early December, Monte Kwinter, for Ontario, and Tom Hockin for the federal government, struck a deal. It was agreed that banks and trust companies would be allowed to go to 100 percent ownership of investment dealers, and Ontario would amend its Securities Act accordingly. Foreign investment dealers would be permitted to go to 50 percent ownership right away, and to 100 percent by June 1988, thus giving domestic financial institutions a lead time of one year over foreigners.

The official announcement of the federal government's approval of the ownership of securities dealers by banks came on December 18, 1986, when Tom Hockin released a strategy paper: *New Directions for the Financial Sector*. There was one terse sentence in a short paragraph on financial subsidiaries: "They [banks, trust, loan, and insurance companies] will be permitted to own securities dealers." The announcement had all the earmarks of a late addition to the text. The following February, I made one of my worst predictions ever to the Canadian Press: "If you pay two and a half or three times book value [for an investment dealer] and then lose all the staff next month, you've got to be stupid . . . I would be surprised to see a bank buy in —at least at those kinds of prices." Four months later I told the *Toronto Star* that the big banks had decided to get into the stock brokerage business by creating new companies rather than by buying existing investment dealers: "They're not going to buy the Wood Gundys because that would surely prove to be too expensive." But five of the big six banks ignored my free public advice.

After the new Ontario securities legislation became effective on June 1, 1987, there was a complicated takeover game. In November, one observer was quoted in the *Financial Post* as saying: "The banks will blow their brains out trying to get into the business and the dealers will be fighting each other to sell to the highest bidder." A senior partner of an investment dealer said: "You can't have a guy in the investment bank earning $1 million and a guy running another part of the bank earning $200,000." This neatly expressed the clash of corporate cultures. The Bank of Montreal bought 75 percent of Nesbitt Thomson at 2.4 times the book value for a price of $291 million. Even the stock market crash of October 1987 did not discourage the bidding. The Bank of Nova Scotia paid $419 million for 100 percent of McLeod Young Weir in November 1987. In December, the Royal Bank bought 75 percent of Dominion Securities for $385 million, and in January 1988 the CIBC bought 65 percent of Wood Gundy for $190 million, after a deal with the First National Bank of Chicago aborted. The National Bank of Canada bought 73 percent of Levesque Beaubien for $100 million. Only the Toronto-Dominion stood aside from the rush to pay premium prices for discount merchandise. A few of the foreign banks joined the rush: the Security Pacific Bank of California bought 49 percent of Burns Fry, and later on some of the medium-size brokerage firms were bought by Deutsche Bank, Sanwa of Tokyo, and Citibank.

The problem was that the pricing of the takeovers was done at a time when the investment dealers had just come through a period of booming business and high profits, but where the underlying fundamentals had changed. With the end of fixed brokerage commission rates and the rise of discount brokers, profit margins in the brokerage business were fundamentally narrowed. And the crash of October 1987 reduced confidence in capital markets generally. The economics of the retail securities industry was shifting the market towards mutual funds. The leveraged buyouts and corporate mergers of the 1980s were coming to an end in an orgy of excesses. But there was always the flood of new government bond issues to finance the deficit, so the bond underwriting departments had something to do.

The downsizing of the brokerage industry began soon after the banks paid high prices for the investment dealers. But it would be misleading to attribute the decreased size of the major investment firms to the cultural change brought about by bank acquisition of dealers. In February 1990, Merrill Lynch sold its retail stock brokerage business to Wood Gundy, now a subsidiary of the Commerce. Several other New York brokerage firms also retreated from the Canadian market. The downsizing and withdrawal was a symptom of market conditions, rather than the consequence of the imprudent rush to buy into the securities industry.

The crumbling of the barrier between commercial banking and securities business forced the regulators to work out completely new arrangements to cover their responsibilities. What would be the relationship between a bank and its controlled investment subsidiary if the bank had to supply capital to the underwriting part of the business, thereby possibly eroding the capital requirements of the bank under the Basle Concordat? What sort of disclosure should there be to investors when the placement of securities issues implied that a bank was getting a loan off its books? Should a bank or trust company have to maintain identifiable separate premises in a branch for its securities business? There were dozens of problems like this, some of which still remain to be worked out. There was a new awareness of the "conflict of interest" problem, although it had always been there; the investment dealers had a clear conflict of interest between the underwriting function and the retail distribution function. The issuer of corporate or government securities was assured that he was getting the highest price possible, while the buyer of the securities was immediately told that the purchase price was very competitive. This inherent inconsistency has not been resolved by financial deregulation, but then, it had not been resolved under the old regime either.

A BIRD IN THE BUSH

Ten months after the agreement between the federal government and the Government of Ontario to open up ownership of the securities industry to Canadian banks and trust companies — and also to foreign securities firms — the Canada-U.S. Free Trade Agreement (FTA) was tabled in the House of Commons. The structure of the financial services industry was well down the list of priorities in the free trade deal, but it was certainly a consideration. The United States had been pushing for some time to add the service industries to the list of items to negotiate under the General Agreement on Tariffs and Trade (GATT). The U.S. government felt that it had been very generous in providing access to United States financial markets for foreign institutions including banks and brokers. It also perceived Europe and Japan and most of the Third World as protectionist in varying degrees. But there had been resistance to adding financial services to the GATT agenda, with opposition coming particularly from Brazil and India. What the Americans wanted was "national treatment." What this means is that foreigners should be given the same degree of access, without discrimination, as domestic institutions in the host country.

From the beginning, I felt that the concept of "national treatment" was a threat to Canada's bargaining position, and started thumping some warning drums. The problem was that "national treatment" in the United States was a very restrictive term compared to the Canadian situation. As we have seen in earlier chapters, the United States had abandoned nationwide branch banking in 1836; the U.S. federal government could not (or more correctly would not) negotiate nationwide branching, because it had conceded its powers to the states. On the other hand, "national treatment" in Canada meant nationwide branch access. This was a significant difference which meant that any bargaining was inherently biased against the Canadian position, unless the U.S. federal government was prepared to reassert its constitutional power.

There was also an important functional bias. And this is where the Ottawa-Queen's Park deal on the ownership of securities dealers came into the picture. Under the agreement, by June 1, 1988, any one of the sixteen U.S. bank subsidiaries in Canada could own a full service investment dealer. But in the United States, commercial banking and investment banking had been separated by the Glass-Steagall Act of 1933. That act had put up a wall between banking and securities dealing, because of abuses which had occurred in the period leading up to the crash in 1929.

Since foreign banks would have to observe the same restrictions as domestic American banks, "national treatment" meant that Canadian banks could not own securities firms in the United States. But the major Canadian investment dealers like Wood Gundy and Dominion Securities already had substantial offices in New York. The logical conclusion was that the Canadian dealers would have to shut down their American offices once they became subsidiaries of Canadian banks. What the American negotiators offered to Canada was a promise that, if the Glass-Steagall Act were amended or the Federal Reserve's regulations were altered in the future, the Canadian banks would obtain equal benefits. This was the bird in the bush. The bird in the hand was the fact that Canada was offering Americans immediate access to the investment business in Canada, as well as nationwide branch banking.

The Canadian trade negotiator, Simon Reisman, was an old friend of mine. We had gone overseas together in the war, and had been frequently in touch since my short sojourn in the Department of Finance in 1947. On one occasion when he was deputy minister of finance, I had burst into his office shouting that he did not know what he was talking about on some issue under discussion, but in less polite language; he yelled back at me to get out of his office at once — also not politely. With me at the time was Louise Cannon, then my assistant on government relations, and now a senior vice-president of the Bank of Nova Scotia. She turned white at the appalling insults being exchanged, assuming (not unreasonably) that the bank's welcome at the Department of Finance had been eliminated forever. But it was just an army barrack exchange, not to be taken seriously. We quickly resumed our normal kind and gentle demeanour.

Reisman had delegated the negotiations concerning the financial services sector to Bill Hood, who came out of retirement to undertake the job. Hood had had a distinguished career, first as a professor at the University of Toronto, and later as an officer at the Bank of Canada and then, finally, as deputy minister of finance. I knew Hood well too, but this proved to be of no advantage in trying to make the case against the concept of "national treatment." After spending some time with him on various occasions, I reported back to the banks that the government was prepared to trade off an unbalanced and unequal deal in banking for the sake of gains elsewhere. In fact most banks were supportive of the Free Trade Agreement in general, even though they considered that the trade-off in banking was handing over a bird in the hand for a bird in the bush.

In order to accord "national treatment" to the Americans in banking, it was necessary to remove the restrictions which limited the aggregate assets of all foreign bank subsidiaries in Canada to 16 percent of total domestic bank assets; and it was also necessary to remove the requirement that an American bank obtain a certificate of approval from the Department of Finance for each branch opening.

As for the 10 percent–25 percent ownership rules which had been introduced by Walter Gordon in September 1964, the 10 percent rule for individual owners remained but the 25 percent rule on aggregate foreign ownership was removed. This gave Americans equal treatment with Canadians in the ownership of banks. Some critics tried to argue that six Americans could band together, each owning 10 percent, and get control of a major Canadian bank. But this is not so, because the pooling of votes in a shareholders' agreement contravenes the Bank Act, in that the 10 percent limit applies to any shareholder and his associates.

Although our lobbying had little effect on Hood and Reisman, it did at least secure the substantial position of the Canadian banks in the United States market which already existed. To be fair, the Americans had a case for saying that the Canadian banks already operated across state boundaries within the United States, which the American banks were prevented from doing by the MacFadden Act of 1927. Most of the big six banks had units in half a dozen states or more. All of them had agencies in New York; there were still one or two wholly-owned subsidiaries in California, and there were branches and representative offices in Oregon, Texas, Illinois, Massachusetts, and elsewhere. The Bank of Montreal had even acquired the Harris Bank of Chicago, quite a large bank.

Under the U.S. International Banking Act of 1978, a foreign bank was required to select a home state, and could not add units in other states. But the forty or fifty different units of the Canadian banks were grandfathered at the time (that is, their licences were accepted as having preceded the new legislation). For that reason, the guarantee in the Free Trade Agreement that their multistate operations would not be rolled back into strict conformity with the interstate prohibitions was of vital importance. But everyone knew that the American unit banking system was breaking down for the economic reasons which have been discussed in earlier chapters. There was an expectation that in due course, interstate banking would spread from regional groupings and emergency takeovers of failing institutions, to a wider interstate branching model, more like the Canadian system. And in fact, this has been happening.

As for the Glass-Steagall Act, the U.S. regulators allowed the major Canadian dealers to continue performing some functions in New York, and quite recently there has been a further move towards full-service investment banking by subsidiaries of some American and Canadian banks.

The assurance that they would not be rolled back from their existing position may not have seemed much of a negotiating success for the banks. Nevertheless, most of the banks took the view that the Free Trade Agreement should be supported. Allan Taylor of the Royal Bank was the most positive, while Cedric Ritchie of the Bank of Nova Scotia opposed it. Although most of the top bankers stayed out of the political debate, I felt there was enough agreement to make the following comment to the House Committee in November 1987:

> For the banking industry, what is good for Canada is good for the banks. The banking industry is supportive of the free trade deal. I say this despite the fact that our industry has some specific reservations . . . In trade, both sides gain by definition . . . Some of the critics of the deal seem to believe that the only right deal is a deal in which Canadians gain, but not the Americans. When critics cite the fact that the Americans make some gains out of the deal, of course they do. Why would they enter into a deal in which they made no gains at all? The purpose of a deal is to trade to your mutual advantage.

In December 1987, I joined a large group of business associations and corporate leaders who provided moral support to Donald Macdonald and Peter Lougheed when they held a large press conference to support the Free Trade Agreement. The CBC gave little or no coverage to the press conference that evening, although it found plenty of time for its daily diet of opposition to the FTA, a pattern later confirmed in a content analysis by the Fraser Institute.

In late 1990, the extension of the GATT to cover agriculture and the service industries foundered on disagreements about agricultural subsidies. Had Canada not concluded the Free Trade Agreement with the United States, it would be a divided and heavily indebted country facing the prospect of going it alone in international trade and services, including banking.

At the insistence of James Baker, the U.S. Secretary of the Treasury at the time, final negotiations in Washington in December 1987 about financial services were taken away from Reisman and his opposite, Peter Murphy, and lodged in the U.S. Treasury and the Canadian Department of Finance. The reason for this was the fear on the American side (and probably on the Canadian side) that a trade deal would tie the hands of either government on fiscal and monetary policy. The recent assertion of Sinclair Stevens that there was a secret commitment by the Bank of Canada to maintain a high exchange rate would have been exactly the opposite to what the authorities wanted, which was flexibility without commitments for the future. Stephen Langdon, financial critic for the NDP, raised the point during my testimony to the House Committee on External Affairs on November 4, 1987:

> Langdon: So we have a trade deal based on a 76¢ dollar. This could fall apart in two or three years if changes brought the dollar to 90¢ or par.
> MacIntosh: It was agreed in the trade negotiations that the exchange rate and monetary policy would be left out of the arrangement. This was the only way they could go. There are so many other variables . . . You cannot possibly relate trade balances alone to the forecast for exchange rates between Canada and the United States.
> Langdon: Precisely.

Reisman's deputy trade negotiator, Gordon Ritchie, assured Canadians that no commitment on the exchange rate was asked or given. As between Ritchie who was there, and Sinclair Stevens who was not, the choice seems clear.

The impact of the Free Trade Agreement on the banks has not been very significant as yet. There has been little pressure for additional banking licences coming from American banks. There have been a few acquisitions of investment dealers and brokers by banks, but there have also been some withdrawals from the Canadian market. Although the U.S. bank subsidiaries in Canada were released from legal limits on their growth (except for the constraint on large loans in relation to capital), conditions have been so competitive that removal of the ceiling on size has not been significant. The parent banks have had capital adequacy problems at home, and the U.S. investment brokers have also been preoccupied by domestic problems. In the long run, some American banks may gain a strong foothold in Canada, but the reverse is perhaps more likely. The big six are better equipped to operate branch networks than the large U.S. banks, and may also have an advantage in capital adequacy.

As for the Free Trade Agreement in general, most banks consider that it has been in the national interest and that the exodus of some manufacturing plants can be explained by the excessive costs which have been built into the Canadian economy.

BANKING SWITCHGEAR

One of the conspicuous omissions in this book is the story of data processing in the banking industry. I have chosen to leave it out because the harnessing of computer technology was largely driven by market forces and the rapid modernization of bank managements, rather than by political factors. In fact, the dead hand of government, whenever it has laid its pale fingers on the financial system, has often produced inaction or excruciatingly slow progress. Millions of Canadians can confirm the fact that the direct electronic transfer of Old Age Security and Canada Pension Plan funds did not even start until 1990, and family allowances remain to be done. This was after twenty-five years of "pilot tests." The relatively simple and standardized monthly distribution of pensions to about four million people could have been in place at least two decades ago, had it been in step with banking technology.

The government's tardiness in replacing cheques with direct electronic funds transfers has been the result of a combination of politics and bureaucracy in Ottawa. Successive governments resisted electronic transfers, because the politicians in all parties wanted to take credit for the millions of cheques going into Canadian households in the form of pensions and family allowance payments. The Public Service Alliance, a union of federal civil servants, helped the politicians to delay changes; they opposed technological innovation in principle, on the grounds that it would reduce the employment of civil servants. In a press release on February 2, 1984, the Alliance said: "Federal government moves to implement Direct Funds Transfers— direct payments of salaries to banks—threaten public service employees with loss of jobs, loss of privacy and pay cheque delays because of computer foul-ups . . . Alliance President Pierre Samson is leading a lobby against further implementation of DFTs which are already being used for National Research Council employees, some Canadian Forces pensions and some public service pensions."

Another major obstruction was the postal unions, which resisted the reduced flow of first-class mail. Overcoming these layers of resistance to automation has been a continuing challenge for the banks and other financial institutions since the mid-1970s. Even then, persuading federal politicians to catch up to the state of the art might not have happened, had it not been for the political influence of the caisses populaires and credit unions. In the 1980s, their participation in the legal structure of the payments system became an important political factor, because they shared with the banks a common interest in payments technology. The politicians and civil servants found themselves facing a united front of financial institutions who wanted more action.

In the years leading up to the Bank Act revision of 1967, the near-banking institutions—the trust and loan companies and the credit unions—pressed for direct participation in the payments system. The operation of the clearing and settlement system had been in the hands of the Canadian Bankers' Association for almost a century. The first clearing house was founded in Halifax in 1888, but the Montreal clearing house which started a year later became the ultimate clearing house for all inter-bank transactions in Canada.

A clearing house is nothing more than a shared meeting place where messengers from different banks can exchange packages of cheques. The customer of bank A deposits a pay cheque made out by his employer who happens to deal with bank B. When bank A receives the cheque, it credits the account of its customer, but it must then recoup the value of the cheque from bank B by presenting the cheque for payment. Once or twice a day, each bank gathers up all the cheques on every other bank, adds up the total, and presents them for payment in a package. Since each bank owes every other bank, the function of the clearing house is simply to settle the differences between each pair of banks. It is a multilateral exchange, and on any given day, depending on the flow of customers' business, only the net differences have to be paid by one bank to another. This is the "settlement" process. It depends on two things: complete trust in the other institutions, and a precise set of rules to make it work.

The rules and regulations of the Montreal clearing house in 1889 began with the decree: "The hour for clearing shall be 10 a.m. precisely." In 1901, this rule had become more elaborate: "At the appointed time, the manager calls out 'Ready!' and rings a bell. Each messenger from the 18 banks then delivers the parcels in his possession, and receives in return other parcels." There were substantial fines for errors or for lateness.

The settlement rules are now vastly complex and technical. They deal with such issues as the precise location of the machine-readable numbers on a cheque and the quality of the paper. There are exact scientific and engineering standards for plastic cards (to access ATMs), since the payments system has moved partly away from paper cheques towards electronic interchange.

But more than anything else, the payments system depends on mutual trust. A recent article said: "On a typical weekday evening, an average of 9 million payments are processed at the cheque processing centres of the 14 direct clearers in 8 regional settlement points, located from Halifax to Vancouver. This represents more than two billion cheques and other payment items per year. About $60 billion is processed daily with a recent peak of just over $100 billion per day." This does not take account of the growing volume of electronic transactions, most of which are still intra-bank, but some of which are direct electronic funds transfers between institutions.

When the Canadian Bankers' Association was formed in 1891, it took responsibility for the Bank Circulation Redemption Fund, which was an insurance pool created by Parliament in 1890 to make sure that the bank notes of individual banks were paid in full if a bank defaulted. In 1900, an act of Parliament gave the CBA power "to establish in any place in Canada a clearing house for banks, and to make rules and regulations for the operation thereof." But the rules required the approval of the Treasury Board, which is the financial administrative arm of government. This ensured that legal power over the payments system resided in the state.

When the Bank of Canada was founded in 1935, every chartered bank was required to maintain an interest-free deposit at the central bank. The clearing houses across the country continued to be operated by the Canadian Bankers' Association, but the settlements between banks were carried out through their deposits at the Bank of Canada. The role of the Bank of Canada in the settlement system is much more than an administrative convenience; it is also the mechanism through which the central bank can deliberately change the aggregate deposits of all the banks taken together. The central bank's ability to change credit conditions rests in part on this fundamental legal connection between the banks and the central bank. (Some of the other key elements of monetary policy are the ability of the central bank to influence securities markets and the foreign exchange market and to manage the federal government's debt.)

As we have seen in earlier chapters, the trust and loan companies and the credit unions did not emerge as significant factors in the payments system until the 1950s. Bradley Crawford, the principal authority on banking law, writes that until 1945, "Payment orders written by their customers upon their demand deposits were popularly believed not to qualify as 'cheques' within the meaning of the Bills of Exchange Act." In other words, a cheque drawn on a trust company or a credit union was not considered to have valid legal status as a means of paying a debt. As these "near-bank" institutions grew in strength in the 1950s and 1960s, they began to pressure Ottawa to remove the monopoly of the Canadian Bankers' Association on the administration of the clearings system. They had three complaints: first, that they didn't have a voice in the operation of the clearing system; secondly, that the banks were putting them at an unfair advantage by charging too much for acting as the clearing agents for their cheques; and thirdly, that they lacked the prestige and advertising value of having their own names exclusively on the cheques, since they had to have the name of their clearing agent as well.

In 1964, the Porter Commission recommended that the trust and loan companies and credit unions be admitted to the clearing system. But they added a proviso that the "near-banks" would have to maintain cash reserves at the Bank of Canada, just like the chartered banks. In lobbying for implementation of the Porter Commission recommendations, the Canadian Co-operative Credit Society—the central national organization of the provincial credit union bodies other than the caisses populaires—opposed the requirement to keep interest-free cash reserves at the Bank of Canada. Except for Sinclair Stevens's group of small trust companies, there were no representations by the trust and loan companies at the committee meetings leading up to the Bank Act revision in 1967. Political attention was mainly concentrated on the Mercantile Affair, so the pressure to change the payments system attracted little interest.

In the five-year struggle to amend the Bank Act, which was completed in 1980, the decision to take the operation of the payments system away from the Canadian Bankers' Association went largely by default. The government's White Paper of August 1976 said, "Near-banks have no voice in the operation of the clearing system." It noted that, with the growing importance of electronic funds transfers, the near-banks were apprehensive that they would have no voice in the planning of the future payments system. The government said that it would transfer the CBA's powers to a new Canadian Payments Association, which would include the caisses populaires, credit unions, and the trust and loan companies. It spelled out some conditions: all federally incorporated deposit-taking institutions would be required to join; provincially incorporated companies were permitted to join, provided they were prepared to accept the deposit insurance standards of the Canada Deposit Insurance Corporation or its provincial equivalent.

In October 1976, the CBA's public brief on the White Paper was very mild. It said that the Canadian Payments Association "will remove a long standing complaint of the credit unions, caisses populaires and trust companies." The brief proposed that the banks have a voice on the board of directors proportional to their size in the clearing system, and that there be an effective system of inspection and control of the near-banks. The tone of resignation in this response made it easy for the government to get the legislation through the finance committee. The credit unions and caisses populaires did not appear as witnesses. When the trust and loan companies showed up, they talked mainly about preventing the banks having enlarged powers in residential mortgages. The CBA was not asked to testify on this section of the Bank Act, and did not volunteer to do so. On October 1, 1980, the finance committee approved the draft Canadian Payments Association Act in little more than an hour.

Although the banks accounted for more than 80 percent of all cheques passing through the payments system, they were given only equal representation with the near-banks on the board of directors. The chairman (who has a deciding vote) was to be an officer of the Bank of Canada; the first appointee was Serge Vachon, who remains chairman in 1991. The board of directors was structured in such a way as to provide representation to four "classes" of financial institution: banks, trust and loan companies, credit unions and caisses populaires, and "other" institutions, which included the Alberta Treasury Branches. The CPA is a strange animal in the Canadian corporate system. It combines the public and private sectors in a single board of directors, with the added wrinkle that the private-sector directors represent four classes of financial institutions.

Its public aspect is that responsibility for the payments system is defined in the act of incorporation, and in the by-laws which have to be approved by Order-in-Council. Its chairman and deputy chairman are officers of the Bank of Canada. The formulation of policy and planning and operations are under the control of the representative board of directors, which in turn exercises its authority through a detailed set of rules and regulations.

After the CPA was created it took two years to transfer management from the CBA in Toronto to the new CPA management in Ottawa. The objective was to make the transition completely transparent to the general public. As one of the directors of the CPA in the years 1981 to 1989, I had a schizophrenic role: on the one hand, I had to preside over the liquidation of a function which our association had managed for a century; on the other hand, I had to share the challenges of the successor organization which had brought new players to the table. The evolution of the personal relationships on the board of directors was an interesting exercise in human dynamics. The bankers were wary of the directors who had arrived by virtue of their political clout and who had limited expertise in the technology of the payments system. The newcomers were suspicious of the bankers' willingness to share authority.

After a decade of meetings, there is now an atmosphere of mutual respect and harmony, reflecting a common experience and a shared challenge. The near-banks soon learned that their long-held belief that the banks overcharged them for clearing services was mistaken. (Only two out of the four trust companies which meet the test of processing 0.5 percent of the clearings volume have elected to become "direct clearers" like the banks.) The bankers found that the representatives from the caisses populaires and some of the other institutions brought mature technological skills to the table. The Canadian public-private model has been closely observed by some of the members of the European community, and has influenced the development of their own payments systems.

As for the general public, the transfer of responsibility for the payments system from the CBA to the CPA was such an obscure event that few people noticed. This is because the clearing and settlement system takes place behind the scenes, and does not directly affect the relationship between a customer and an institution. Indirectly, the general public is greatly affected, because the efficiency and soundness of the payments system is translated into the speed and accuracy of ordinary customer transactions. The payments association is somewhat analogous to the association of telephone companies, which have to make arrangements among themselves for connecting their phone lines across provincial boundaries and for dividing up the revenues of a long-distance telephone call. The telephone user only sees the end product, which is the use of a telephone. Behind the telephone there is an elaborate network of intercompany relations.

But the payments system is a great deal more complex than the interconnection of telephone companies. There are about 120 members of the Canadian Payments Association, of which only fourteen institutions are "direct clearers." All the others use a direct clearer as their agent. And unlike the telephone analogy, there is a high degree of financial risk in the payments system. While millions of cheques are small ones, there are a small number of payments which run into the tens of millions or even hundreds of millions of dollars. In the event of a single institution failing, there is a question as to who holds the bag for payments which happen to be in process of clearing at the instant of failure. The failure of one institution can generate a domino effect on others, as we became painfully aware after the failure of the two western banks in 1985. One of the chief purposes of the ongoing financial reform legislation in recent years has been to foresee and prevent financial failures which could spread through the whole system.

On balance, the Canadian Payments Association has been an effective Canadian response to the political pressure to include near-banks in the banking system, a problem which was created by the failure to define banking in the ten successive revisions of the Bank Act.

THE FUTURE OF THE SYSTEM

A hundred years after the foundation of the Canadian Bankers' Association, it appears that the end is in sight on the long road to the latest Bank Act revision. The complete package of banking, fiduciary, and insurance legislation will come into effect on a common starting date. After a breathing space of a year or two, the lobbying will start up once again for the next revision, which is due five years after the current one. The banks will have a laundry list which includes issues left over from the current package. In particular, there will be ongoing battles over car leasing and the distribution of insurance.

Meanwhile, perhaps one of the least satisfactory features of the current legislation is the misguided treatment of governance in financial institutions. After the current draft legislation has been passed by Parliament, trust companies will have almost identical powers to chartered banks. But there will still remain one important difference between them. By law, the banks will remain broadly held, with any individual shareholder limited to no more than 10 percent of the votes. But the trust companies can be wholly owned by a single shareholder, including an American holder because of the Free Trade Agreement (although the Minister of Finance will have the power to prohibit the takeover of a big institution by a big institution).

There is no conceivable justification for having a dual system of ownership of institutions which do exactly the same thing. The absurdity of two ownership structures in a single system is testimony to the lack of courage and clarity of thought on the part of the government. The lack of courage comes from fear of the provincial governments, which have been happy to promote the competitive strength of trust and loan companies coming under their own jurisdiction. Since 1967 the federal government has had ready at hand a decisive weapon of central control, the Canada Deposit Insurance Corporation. Without federal deposit insurance, no deposit-taking institution could operate successfully across provincial boundaries. Hence the enforcement of CDIC standards on provincial institutions, or on federal institutions which threaten to migrate to the provinces, would be inescapable. But the government has failed to make the CDIC an instrument to enforce common standards. A provincially incorporated institution without federal deposit insurance would probably wither away.

This unsatisfactory resolution of the ownership problem has been highly political. The appointment of Trevor Eyton, chairman of Brascan, and of Claude Castonguay, chairman of the Laurentian Group, as senators, is convincing evidence as to where political power really resides in the financial system. Seventy years ago, their counterparts would have been Sir Herbert Holt of the Royal Bank and Sir Edmund Walker of the Bank of Commerce. The trust company owners, with the support of the provinces, have persuaded Ottawa that what is good for the banking system in the rest of the industrialized world is not good for Canada. The argument is that the broadly held banks are governed by self-perpetuating managements which cannot be removed by their beholden boards of directors. And—the argument goes—a dominant shareholder has an interest in making the management deliver the goods.

What makes this argument particularly ludicrous is that the most broadly held financial institutions are the mutual insurance companies. The votes in these companies, which include seven of the ten largest insurance companies in Canada, are held by millions of policyholders. If the bank managements are beyond the reach of a few thousand shareholders, it would seem that the mutual insurance company managements are even further beyond the reach of the policyholders. The largest stadium in the country would not contain the annual meeting of a life insurance company, if even a small percentage of policyholders showed up. As it happens, the topmost company in Claude Castonguay's Laurentian Group is a mutual insurance company.

The philosophy of the more accountable dominant shareholder has been frequently expounded by the trust company owners. Until the late 1970s trust company presidents shared the views of the bankers that broadly held deposit-taking institutions were a good thing. But after the takeovers of the early 1980s, the trust company managers naturally shared the views of their owners. Thus in July 1988, Michael Cornelissen, the chief executive of Royal Trustco, said: "The 10 percent ownership restriction on banks doesn't necessarily work in the interest of providing greater accountability to shareholders." Accountability to shareholders means timely disclosure. At the very least, it means disclosure sometime or other. But Royal Trustco is part of the extremely convoluted and interwoven Hees-Edper group of companies. On February 8, 1991, the Toronto *Globe and Mail* reported: "Michael Cornelissen, the architect of Royal Trustco's dramatic expansion into foreign markets, offered to resign after the company chalked up huge losses in the final quarter of 1990. The chief executive told a room full of financial analysts last week that his offer was rejected by the board of directors." The concern of the financial journalists in this case was the question of timely disclosure to the shareholders.

As Phillip Mathias wrote recently in the *Financial Post*: "A curious analyst would take weeks to comb out, and piece together, all the preferred-share links reported in the many disclosure documents of the four dozen or so public companies in the Hees-Edper empire." If he and other financial analysts, after exhaustive study, are unable to sort out the true underlying earnings of public companies which are closely controlled at the top by one shareholder, it is far from clear that accountability is improved by the controlling shareholder.

As we saw in Chapter 12, most of the fourteen trust companies which collapsed in the 1980s were closely held. Very recently we have had another striking example of a closely held trust company, Standard Trust, falling afoul of the regulators. After allegedly having failed to disclose the actual state of loan-loss provisions, as suggested by the Superintendent of Financial Institutions, the directors of Standard Trustco have been accused of paying a non-cash dividend upstream to the controlling shareholder, also against the regulators' advice. The Ontario Securities Commission has instituted action against the directors. The case is an interesting commentary on the assertion of some conglomerate owners that they are a source of capital to their subsidiary deposit-taking institution. And once again, timely and accurate disclosure by a dominant shareholder was apparently lacking.

The overwhelming evidence of the last ten or twenty years is that closely held deposit-taking institutions are an unnecessary hazard in the structure of Canada's financial system. Although some of them rank among the best managed deposit-taking institutions, there are too many examples of self-dealing and excessive risk-taking to ignore.

Instead of dealing with the obvious consequences of closely held ownership, the federal government is now proposing to require that one-third of the board of directors of deposit-taking institutions be "unaffiliated." An unaffiliated director is supposed to be independent by virtue of having no significant business dealings with the financial institution of which he or she is a director. This proposal is meant to deal with the allegation that the board of directors of a bank is a committee of large borrowers. Since the first loyalty of a bank director who is an executive of a borrower is to the line of credit of his or her own company, that director is most unlikely to challenge the chief executive officer in matters of bank policy. Unfortunately this allegation is very often true, but it is even more likely in the case of a company with a dominant shareholder. The solution is not to create two classes of directors, one of which is said to be independent and unaffiliated, and therefore presumably more capable of giving good advice to the management of a bank. There is no precedent in Canada or elsewhere for creating two classes of directors. The banks have been opposing this approach to governance for several years, and will probably continue to do so in 1991. The trust companies, on the other hand, have declared themselves comfortable with the proposal. It is not clear how certain trust company directors can remain "unaffiliated" and "independent," when they can be quietly removed by the dominant shareholder if they create a nuisance. In the real world, this is exactly what happens.

The real problem is that the boards of the banks are too large. There is no such thing as an effective committee with thirty-five people on it. Everyone knows that the board of a golf club or a symphony orchestra or a parent-teachers' association cannot be effective with thirty-five people. Power necessarily gravitates to an executive committee or to a small group around the chief executive officer. The banks have always taken the position that their boards are necessarily large to accommodate the wide range of regional and geographical interests across Canada. But there are other ways to achieve regional representation, such as through prestigious advisory committees in different cities and provinces.

The real problem in governance is to have a board of directors which is small enough to be cohesive and accountable. Currently, the Bank Act sets out the minimum size of a bank's board of directors, but it also should set a maximum size of around fifteen. With that size of board, there would be a degree of accountability which is not possible when power is vaguely diffused among thirty-five people, as is the case at present, with the big six Canadian banks having an average of thirty-five directors each. This compares with the four largest U.S. banks, which have an average of twenty directors, the four largest U.K. banks (nineteen), the two largest Australian banks (fourteen), and the two largest German banks (thirteen).

In order to prevent a smaller board of directors being nothing but a cheering squad for the chief executive officer, the financial legislation should require a nominating committee of the board of directors over which the chief executive officer does not exercise veto power. With a smaller board of directors, who are not answerable for their tenure to the chief executive, the governance of the banks would be improved. And since a smaller group of directors would have to take more responsibility and be more accountable, they should have to limit the number of their other directorships in order to devote adequate time to their bank directorship. And of course they should be paid accordingly. If these measures had been in place, the banking system might have avoided some of the embarrassing dynasties which have not improved the public perception of the governance of our great institutions.

Almost two centuries of banking and politics has had one constant theme: the creation of institutions where people can, with confidence, keep their savings, and where they can transact their household affairs conveniently. These core functions remain at the heart of the banking system, even though there are now many layers of elaborate superstructure around the core. Next to the exchange of money and the storage of savings there is the key function of investing the savings productively. For banks, their role in the capital market is to lend money to industry, agriculture, and governments to finance the production of goods and services and to finance community activities.

In the past fifty years, the banking system has been modified out of recognition by political and market imperatives. The simple folksy branch in Orillia, Ontario where Stephen Leacock was rattled by the wickets, is no more. In those days, the system was not very competitive, but neither was it structurally unsound like the American system. Over time it was gradually modified to meet the changing needs of the population, while still meeting the test of public confidence. As we have seen, the bankers were human after all, which they proved by making some dreadful mistakes of judgement. Despite the calamities of the 1980s, the banking system has emerged in a condition which looks very strong when measured against contemporary international standards. The whole financial system is relatively efficient, competitive, and user-friendly. The cooperative efforts of the banks, large trust companies, caisses populaires, and credit unions have given Canada an automated network of easily accessible facilities which is not exceeded anywhere in the world. The challenge for the future is to retain that level of competitiveness and build on it for generations to come.

Sources

The following abbreviations have been used:

BARP – Bank Act Revision Proceedings, Extracts and Synopses of Debates and Proceedings, 1913, 1923, 1924, and 1925, Canadian Bankers' Association, Toronto, 1933

BNSA – Bank of Nova Scotia Archives

CBAA – Canadian Bankers' Association Archives

CBAJ – *Journal of the Canadian Bankers' Association*, now called *The Canadian Banker*

CPBW – Canadian Press Business Wire

FINTREA – House of Commons Standing Committee on Finance, Trade and Economic Affairs; called Standing Committee on Banking and Currency until 1967

FP – *Financial Post*

FT – *Financial Times* of Canada

GM – Toronto *Globe and Mail*

M&S – McClelland and Stewart Publishers, Toronto

MT – Monetary Times of Canada

OUP – Oxford University Press, Toronto

PADF – Public Archives, Department of Finance

RRCBF – Government of Canada, Report of the Royal Commission on Banking and Finance (Porter Commission), 1964

TS – *Toronto Star*

Chapter 1

"Democracy does not love banks": G.P. de T. Glazebrook, *Sir Edmund Walker*, OUP, Toronto, 1933, p. 133; "worst bitchers": P.E. Trudeau, TS, June 1, 1976; "breakdown of market compartmentalization": William D. Coleman and Grace Skogstad, *Policy Communities and Public Policy in Canada*, Copp Clark Pitman, Toronto, 1990, p. 92ff.

Chapter 2

"A good banker" and "not struck with admiration": Bray Hammond, *Banks and Politics in America*, Princeton University Press, 1957, pp. 667 and 669; "a rude instrument": Donald Creighton, *John A. MacDonald, The Young Politician*, Macmillan of Canada, Toronto, 1952, p. 243; Market share data: R.M. Breckenridge, *The History of Banking in Canada*, U.S. Washington, Government Printing Office, Washington, 1911, appendix tables (see also individual bank histories listed in bibliography); "A circumstantial story": Adam Shortt, *History of Canadian Currency and Banking 1600-1880*, Canadian Bankers' Association, Toronto, 1982, p. 649.

Chapter 3

Market share data from CBAJ, 1895-6, p. 648; "without a currency": Francis Rowe, "Early Banking in Newfoundland," *The Newfoundland Quarterly*, Fall 1971; "Your Directors beg": BNSA, Bank of Liverpool, President's address to shareholders, Dec. 1875; "It was soon evident": Joseph Schull and J.D. Gibson, *The Scotiabank Story*, Macmillan of Canada, Toronto, 1982, p. 55; "Among the shareholders": ibid., p. 57; "as a consequence of loans": R.M. Breckenridge, op. cit., p. 169; "a system of absentee landlordism": Victor Ross, *A History of the Canadian Bank of Commerce*, OUP, Toronto, vol. 1, 1920, vol. 2, 1922, p. 129ff.; "black and white beans": Schull and Gibson, op. cit., p. 105; "banks with large capital": BNSA, Annual Report of the Bank of New Brunswick, 1912, and Schull and Gibson, op. cit., p. 106 ff.; "small townbanks suffered": Ronald Rudin, *Banking en français: The French Banks of Quebec*, University of Toronto Press, Toronto, 1985, p. 79; "Rumours are frequent": Ross, op. cit., p. 330ff.; "In Winnipeg, on Main Street": Pierre Berton, *The Last Spike*, M&S, Toronto, 1971, p. 52.

Chapter 4

"If we take the initiative": Schull and Gibson, op.cit., p. 97; "Is it your opinion": National Monetary Commission, "Interviews on the Banking and Currency Systems of Canada," *in* Breckenridge, op. cit., p. 50; "parish work at St. George's Church": Nancy Whynot, "An Investigation into the Rise and Fall of The Sovereign Bank of Canada," unpublished thesis, University of Guelph, 1979, unpaginated; "to the extent of $3,500,000": John Ballaine, *Strangling of the Alaskan Railroad*, Seattle, 1923, quoted in State of Alaska Archives and Records Centre correspondence with author, May 16, 1990; "the advertising practice": PADF 14474 and CBAA 85-518-24; "a few shares in the Sovereign Bank": PADF, Whynot file 13890; "obvious to Jemmett": Whynot press files; "I now beg to state": Whynot letter file, March 1, 1906; "I wish to correct": PADF, Whynot file 616-3; "Major Stewart was granted leave": Whynot letter file, MT, Sept. 19, 1908; "You are familiar with the circumstances": Breckenridge, op. cit., p. 173ff.; "in February 1909": Whynot letter file; "It would be farcical": CBAA 87-515-12; "There are just two points": CBAA 87-518-24; "came a cropper": PADF, Whynot file, April 3, 1918; "I fail to see why," "So far as Mr. Jarvis's arguments," "A rumour is abroad," "providing for some independent inspection," "our friend McLeod," "I do not take seriously," and "good enough to give": BNSA file HAR-1; "Those who are familiar": Toronto *Mail and Empire*, 1931 (see *Maclean's* below); "Have We a Canadian Dreyfus?": E.C. Drury, *Maclean's*, Sept. 15., Oct. 1,Oct. 15, 1933; "crystallized public sentiment": Benjamin Beckhart, *The Banking System of Canada*, Henry Holt, New York, 1929; "at the annual meeting": CBA Executive Council meeting minutes, CBAJ, 1909; "members of the Association": CBA Executive Council meeting minutes, CBAA 87-506-03, 1910; "The audit which is provided," "government inspection would be," "Every Minister of Finance," and "government inspection of banks": BARP, 1913.

Chapter 5

"Love of liberty": Carlie Oreskovich, *Sir Henry Pellatt, The King of Casa Loma*, McGraw-Hill Ryerson, Toronto, 1982, p. 182; "The amount locked up": Zebulon Lash, CBAA-89-518-04; "government could have closed": Report of the Royal Commission, 1924, CBAA 87-518-10; "We consider him a man of means" and "He is always hard up": BNSA, Pellatt file; Home Bank liabilities data: CBAA 87-518-03; "Never at any time": CBAA 87-518-12; "If the Bankers' Association": *Toronto Telegram*, Dec. 12, 1923; "First Statement," "depositors in that institution," and "disclosures of crookedness": CBAA 87-518-03; "No facts were at any time": CBAA 87-518-10; "failure of Home Bank": CBAA 87-518-12; "Despondent because of long illness": Toronto *Mail and Empire*, Nov. 26, 1923; "like Christmas presents," "moral claim in equity," and "exactly the same feelings": CBAA 87-518-11; "The less a director knows": CBAA 87-518-12; "Home Bank fiasco": *Western Record*, July 14, 1925; 1925 market share data: *Canada Gazette*.

Chapter 6

"The government should appoint" and "Pease had a rough ride": Douglas H. Fullerton, *Graham Towers and His Times*, M&S, Toronto, 1986, p. 38; "properly administered central": BARP, 1933; "Many runs upon the banks": RoyalCommission on Banking and Currency (MacMillan Commission), Proceedings and Report, Ottawa, 1933; "a highly permissive, open-ended": George Watts, "The Origins and Background of Central Banking in Canada," *Bank of Canada Review*, May 1972; "it would be financial suicide": Robert Bryce, *Maturing in Hard Times*, McGill-Queen's University Press, Montreal, 1986, p. 33-35; "if Leacock lost": David M. Legate, *Stephen Leacock*, Doubleday, Toronto, 1970, p. 183; "Canada will have no monetary stability": Clifford Curtis, "The Canadian Monetary Situation," *Journal of Political Economy*, June 1932; "instrumental in swinging": Fullerton, op cit., p. 43; "financial and economic upheaval": CBAJ vol. 40, p. 162; "Without wishing to be flippant": J.A. McLeod, presidential address, CBAJ, Nov. 1932, p. 16; "Bennett had no doubt observed": Fullerton, op. cit., p. 41; wheat prices: F.H. Leacy, *Historical Statistics of Canada*, Statistics Canada and Social Science Federation of Canada, Ottawa, second edition, 1983, table M228; "Canadian banks of the future": Royal Commission on Banking and Currency, Winnipeg hearing, p. 1690; "The records show": MacMillan Commission report, Sept. 19, 1933; "emphasis on liquidity": W.T. Easterbrook, *Farm Credit in Canada*, University of Toronto Press, Toronto, 1938, p. 127; "rate paid on time deposits" and "banks . . . reluctantly were compelled to break": Royal Commission on Banking and Currency, MacMillan Commission report, p. 33ff; "Supposing the central bank" and "authority of the Governor": Fullerton, op. cit., p. 49.

Chapter 7

"Some farmers" and "absolutely no cause": CBAA 87-529-01; "so long as Mammon" and "Mr. Gardiner in his platform": CBAA 87-529-07; "Mr. Bennett dealt at length" and consolidated statistics: CBAA 87-529-09; "formerly an assistant professor," "Mr. Sandwell will desire," "you are doubtless," "For the past ten days," and "Many of the managers": CBAA 87-529-13; arrangement with *Saturday Night*: CBAA 87-529-15; "The turning point": John A. Irving, *The Social Credit Movement in Alberta*, University of Toronto Press, Toronto, 1959, p. 7ff.; "a centralizing system": Clifford H. Douglas, *Social Credit*, W.W. Norton, New York, 1933; "distributed through Credit Houses": Irving, op. cit., p. 88; "the basic idea" and "prophesied the end": ibid., p. 58; "a woolly mind": ibid., p. 154; Saturday Night pointed out: *Saturday Night*, Nov. 23, 1935; "It is a matter of satisfaction": CBAA 87-529-26; "When he got to Alberta" and "take next your Alberta": CBAA 87-529-26; "We must recognize": CBAA 87-529-88; "required them to print" and "This clearly violated": Rand Dyck, *Provincial Politics in Canada*, Prentice-Hall, Toronto, 1986, chapter 9; "But if a Province's credit": Toronto *Mail and Empire*, Oct. 24, 1936; "ever since the Dominion": CBAA 87-551-12; "Of a most vicious": MT, Dec. 3, 1938; "to undo the damage": Dyck, op. cit., p. 467.

Chapter 8

"Clifford Clark . . . said in 1934": FP, Sept. 15, 1934; "What is the connection": BARP, 1933; "flying his own plane": Irving, op. cit., p. 286; "In the legislation": BARP, 1933; "Alex, I don't wish": oral history, possibly apocryphal; "We think it would be better," "waste of time," "As the banks were unpopular," and "survey the debt situation": CBAA, 87-523-01; "It seems to me": CBAA 87-516-35; "We do not quite get," "If the maximum rate," "matter is really immaterial," "We consider that such a privilege," and "matter is not a vital one": CBAA 87-507-40; "Deputy

Minister held views": CBAA 87-507-40; "founders of the bank": CBAA 87-543-26; "Bank of Canada announced" and "Following the new Keynesian": H.H. Binhammer, *Money and Banking and the Canadian Financial System*, fourth edition, Methuen, Toronto, 1982, pp. 573ff.; "a rigorous monetary policy": Graham Towers, FINTREA, Proceedings, March 18, 1954, reported in E.P. Neufeld, editor, *Money and Banking in Canada*, Historical Documents and Commentary, Carleton Library, No. 17, M&S, Toronto, 1964; "bank policy tended to accentuate": E.P. Neufeld, *Bank of Canada Operations, 1935-54*, University of Toronto Press, Toronto, 1955, chapter 5.

Chapter 9
Population statistics: Leacy, op. cit., Tables A248-259 and A339-350; Financial statistics: RRCBF, and Economic Council of Canada, *First Annual Review*, Ottawa, 1964, and E.H. Neave and J.V. Poapst, *Studies of Canadian Residential Mortgage and Consumer Credit Markets*, Canadian Bankers' Association, Toronto, 1990, and Binhammer, op. cit., and Neufeld, *Money and Banking*, op. cit.; "survey covered 41 members": Neave and Poapst, op. cit.; correspondence between Elderkin and Rogers, "banks . . . had been shocked," "not good sound banking," and "just window dressing": CBAA 87-537-04; "not forced into this" and "'quasi public utilities'": T.H. Atkinson, testimony to FINTREA, March 1954; "What evil genius": Bowmanville *Canadian Statesman*, Dec. 10, 1953; "The proposal strikes": Moose Jaw *Times-Herald*, Feb. 27, 1954; "soundness of encouraging," "a cruel hoax," "just plain silly," "a foolish statement," and "Before we change": CBAA 87-551-15; "reason for the housing problem" and "put a larger number": Toronto *Globe and Mail*, Feb. 22, 1954; Data on consumer credit: RRCBF, and Neave and Poapst, op. cit.; "We . . . have no intention": N.J. McKinnon, testimony to FINTREA, 1954, pp. 285ff. and 806-822; "After eighteen years": FINTREA, 1954, p. 590; "bank does not charge": ibid., p. 601; "It was accepted": ibid., p. 608; "a rather dour person": Donald M. Fleming, *So Very Near*, M&S, Toronto, 1985, vol. 1, p. 275; "an elegant patrician": Peter C. Newman, *Renegade in Power: The Diefenbaker Years*, M&S, Toronto, 1963, p. 295; bewildering series of "agreements": CBAA 87-525-05; Coyne's request for sales finance company statistics": CBAA 87-540-16 and 87-525-05; irritable exchange of correspondence: CBAA 87-559-07 and 87-540-16; Coyne [asked] the banks to segregate: CBAA 87-559-07; "Bank of Canada has called," "This plan makes," "One! Two! Three!" and "To require the banks": GM, March 12 and 13, 1957; "a good deal of shooting," "does not imply," and two-inch banner headline: CBAA 87-540-16/17; "no fundamental changes": CBAA 87-551-11; not planning any legislation: GM, March 26, 1957; "financial institutions reacted positively": Fleming, op. cit., page 498; "the best description": Newman, op. cit., Chapter 21; "incident served to embitter": Felming, op. cit., p. 455; "series of precedent-shattering": Newman, op. cit., p. 301; "A study of this statement": ibid., p. 304; "Complaints were frequent": Fleming, op. cit., p. 303; "Recent public statements": Eastman-Stykolt letter; "Banks' present view": H. Scott Gordon, *The Economists versus the Bank of Canada*, Ryerson Press, Toronto, 1961; "evil genius": Fleming, op. cit., p. 338; "carnage of the Coyne affair": Newman, op. cit., pp. 295ff.; "After I became Minister of Finance" and "Coyne was in fact chosen": Fleming, op. cit., p. 302; "The monetary policy," "if it were not satisfied," "scornfully accused," and "I trust that I am not": Newman, op. cit., pp. 300ff.; "Pearson has assured me": Bruce Hutchison, *The Far Side of the Street*, Macmillan of Canada, Toronto, 1976, p. 25; "most of the major": CBAJ, summer 1965; definition of banking: RRCBF, p. 378; "reverses the principles": TS, quoted in John T. Saywell, editor, *Canadian Annual Review*, University of Toronto Press, Toronto, 1966, p. 317; "competing near-banks": CBAJ, summer 1966, p. 13.

Chapter 10
"A good high one too": Jessie Murray, "Women in the Banking World," CBAJ, col. 23, 1916, p. 316; "bank clerk's future": G.E. Kingsford, CBAJ, vol. 12, 1905, p. 167; "a young man's future": CBAJ, 1905, p. 253; "A Quarrel with the Youthfulness of Bankers": CBAJ, vol. 18, 1911, p. 208; "Banking isn't the same": J.P. Buschlen, *A Canadian Bank Clerk*, William Briggs, 1913, Toronto Reprint Library, University of Toronto Press, Toronto, 1973; "officers in receipt of salaries" and "It is imperative": David G. Coombs, "The Emergence of a White-Collar Work Force in Toronto, 1895-1911," unpublished thesis, York University, Toronto, 1978; "We might just as well realize": Barbara Hansen, "An Historical Study of Women in Canadian Banking, 1900-1975" *Canadian Women's Studies* vol. 1, Winter 1978/79; "wife, acting alone": W.F. Chipman, CBAJ, vol. 24, 1917, p. 115; "One woman, who has the supervision": Agnes Graham, CBAJ, vol. 24, 1917, p. 316; "What is going to happen" and "Thousands of our men": Jean Graham, "The Woman Employee and the Canadian Bank" CBAJ, vol. 26, 1919; "prospect of matrimony," "in most Canadian banks," and "doctrine of equal pay": CBAJ, vol. 26, 1919, p. 364-5; "A mere bobby-soxer": T.W.H. Thompson, CBAJ, vol. 54, 1947, p. 126; "reference to mechanization": Walter L. Lund, "Women in the Banking World," CBAJ, vol. 60, 1953, p. 122; "Women now hold tellers'" and "We have, for some time": Halen Stephens, "Women in Canadian Banking," CBAJ, vol. 64, 1957, p. 115; "acting manager" and first appointments of women managers: Naomi Mallory, "Now They Are Managers," CBAJ, vol. 68, 1961-62, p. 129; 29 women bank managers: Marianne Bossen, *Manpower Utilization in Canadian Chartered Banks*, Special Study No. 4, Royal Commission on the Status of Women, Ottawa, 1971; 186 women branch mangers: Marianne Bossen, *Employment in Chartered Banks, 1969-75*, Bossen and Associates, Winnipeg, 1975, p. 28; labour force statistics: Leacy, op. cit., Tables D124, D160; Institute of Canadian Bankers statistics: correspondence from ICB, Dec. 13, 1990; employment equity statistics: CBA file EEICDA, July 18, 1990; women bank directors: CBA data, Oct. 30, 1990.

Chapter 11
History of Bank of British North America: Denison, op. cit., vol. 2, pp. 155, 247, 330ff.; "high rate of interest": ibid., vol. 1, p. 67; "very difficult to control people": Ross, op. cit., vol. 1, p. 345; "average size of Canadian banks" and "By about 1857": Hammond, op. cit., pp. 662ff.; "understood that the bank": John Fayerweather, *The Mercantile Bank Affair*, New York University Press, New York, 1974, pp. 50ff; "availability of the bank for sale": ibid., p. 52; "The National City Bank," "I don't think that you should proceed," and "Well I'm all in favour": Louis Rasminsky *in* Peter Stursberg, *Lester Pearson and the American Dilemma*, Doubleday, Toronto, 1980, pp. 236ff.; "We believe that foreign banks," "We think a high degree," and "this is an anomaly": RRCBF, pp. 373ff.; Dick Thomson was assigned by Lambert: interview with A.T. Lambert, Dec. 17, 1990; Lambert and Thomson became concerned: a different view appears in John D. Wilson, *The Chase*, Harvard Business School, Boston, 1986, p. 173 and footnote 2; "Somewhat to his [Rockefeller's] surprise, Lambert himself raised the possibility of Chase's acquiring a 25 percent interest in the bank"; this abortive relationship: Denis Smith, *Gentle Patriot*, Hurtig Publishers, Edmonton, 1973; "I remember receiving": Lester B. Pearson, *Mike*, vol. 3, 1957-68, University of Toronto Press, Toronto, 1975, pp. 130ff.; "Shortly afterwards, David Rockefeller": Walter L. Gordon, *A Political Memoir*, M&S, Toronto, 1977, p. 211ff.; "Citibank's arrogant . . . attitude": Stursberg, op. cit., p. 239; "very rough": Fayerweather, op. cit., appendix E, reprinted from Peter C. Newman, *The Distemper of Our Times*, M&S, Toronto, 1968; "I did accept Walter's": Stursberg, op. cit., p. 241; "I have already given": FINTREA, Proceedings, Jan. 24, 1967; "One

official of a Canadian bank": Fayerweather, op. cit., p. 94ff.; "What I think we need" and testimony of other bankers: FINTREA, Proceedings and Evidence, Jan. 1967, pp. 1594ff.; "MacIntosh was highly critical": Fayerweather, op. cit., pp. 94ff.; "agencies did not provide": ibid., pp. 106ff.; "inconsequential": ibid., p. 62; "desirable to wait": FINTREA, Proceedings, Feb. 2, 1967, pp. 1652ff.; "not find it possible": Fayerweather, op. cit., p. 91; "We do not think that": FINTREA, Proceedings, pp. 1594-5; "advised by law officers": FINTREA, 1967, p. 1629; "the most pragmatic": H.S. Sinclair and M. Krossel, CBAJ, vol. 86, no. 1, p. 9; "There are today no laws" and "operation of foreign banks": CBA, Industry Brief on the 1977 Revision of the Bank Act, Oct. 1975; "a basic conflict arises" and "This will provide": Government of Canada, White Paper on Canadian Banking Institutions, Aug. 1976; "If the Government of Canada approves": Moysey/MacIntosh letter to Michael Wilson, Jan. 4, 1989; "Amexco *cannot* own a commercial bank": Peter Z. Grossman, *American Express*, Crown Publishers, New York, 1987, p. 356; "does not do business": Don Steinberg, "American Express vs. the Canadian Banks," unpublished study, University of Western Ontario, 1990, p. 4; leak in the *Globe and Mail*: GM, *Report on Business Magazine*, Feb. 1988, p. 55; "Someone approached Mulroney's": Stevie Cameron, *Ottawa Inside Out*, Key Porter Books, Toronto, 1989, p. 178; "nor is it permitted to market": GM, Jan. 18, 1989; "accused Prime Minister" and "had no personal involvement": GM, Jan. 19, 1989; "In these discussions": GM, Jan. 26, 1989; "function of an inquiry": GM, May 6, 1989.

Chapter 12
"Psychologically, nothing has": Morgan Guaranty, *World Financial Markets*, Sept. 1986; "lending was encouraged": ibid., Feb. 1983; "mammoth scale of financing": John Turner, speaking at the annual meeting of the International Monetary Fund, Sept. 1974; theme was confirmed many times: CBA, "Recycling the Petro Dollars of the Seventies," Sept. 1987; "Walter frightens me": M.S. Mendelsohn, *American Banker*, Sept. 19, 1983; "Despite rising debt": CPBW, June 12, 1982; "Late on August 19": Mendelsohn, loc. cit.; "A year from now": *American Banker*, March 11, 1983; "The massive lending": Pierre Elliott Trudeau, speaking at the Canadian Institute of International Affairs, Ottawa, May 6, 1982; "too conservative": GM, Aug. 20, 1988; an agreement was reached in September 1981: Memorandum of Agreement Between the Government of Canada and the Government of Alberta, Sept. 1, 1981; "an attempt to substitute": Leonard Waverman, "Canadian Energy Policy After 1985" *in* Edward Carmichael, editor, *Canada's Energy Policy, 1985 and Beyond*, C.D. Howe Institute, Toronto, Oct. 1984, p. 47; "signal of increasing scarcity": Wendy Dobson, *Canada's Energy Policy Debate*, C.D. Howe Institute, Toronto, May 1981; one investment dealer estimated: Burns Fry Ltd. various issues on banking, oil loans, and capital adequacy, Spring 1981, Sept. 25, 1981, Jan. 19, 1982, Oct. 1, 1982, Oct. 2, 1985, March 14 and 18, 1986, Jan. 1988, June 9, 1988, March 15, 1989, Oct. 16, 1989, Nov. 20, 1990; "proven to be a liar": Patricia Best and Ann Shortell, *A Matter of Trust*, Viking Penguin Books, Toronto, 1985, p. 188; "A trust company shall not borrow" and "Nothing in this act": E.P. Neufeld, *The Financial System of Canada*, Macmillan of Canada, Toronto, 1972, p. 289, and RRCBF, chapter 10; "the traditional financial": Best and Shortell, op. cit., p. 8; "the prevailing view" and "concept of the corporate trustee": E.P. Neufeld, *The Financial System*, op cit., p. 291; "old guard's influence": Best and Shortell, op. cit., introduction; "In our view the federal": RRCBF, p. 363; "Bank executives have always": Best and Shortell, op. cit., p. 14; "You opposed the . . . proposal": FINTREA, Minutes and Proceedings, Dec. 4, 1990; "the sad fact": Best and Shortell, op. cit., p. 49; "single most important" and "Owners will always be": Philip Smith, *The Trust-Builders: The Remarkable Rise of Canada Trust*, Macmillan of

Canada, Toronto, 1989, p. 204; "Robert Braun, the General Manager" and "all the fun": GM, Oct. 7, 1989; "If you look at": Best and Shortell, op. cit., p. 117; "CDIC is controlled": ibid., p. 246; "We had clearly misunderstood," "Both banks dealt," "at the Western Economic Opportunities Conference," "Western-based banks," "The evidence . . . favours," and Sopinka-MacIntosh dialogue: Report of the Inquiry into the Collapse of the Canadian Commercial Bank and the Northland Bank, Hon. Willard Z. Estey, commissioner, Aug. 1986; "CCB collapsed because of dishonesty": *Saturday Night*, July 1986, p. 38; "My particular company": FINTREA, Proceedings, Dec. 1970; "deny all liability": Ernst and Young, Price Waterhouse, and Deloitte Touche, joint press release, Dec. 4, 1990.

Chapter 13

"sampling is not": Service d'aide au consommateur, *A Study of Service-Related User Fees at Financial Institutions*, Shawinigan, Que., March 1987; "Decima Study showed": Craig Toomey, "Nickeled and Dimed?" Money Guide, *Canadian Consumer Magazine*, Nov. 1987; Environics survey: Environics, Report to Canadian Bankers' Association, Dec. 1987; Table of service charges: Report prepared by Coopers & Lybrand Consulting Group on Service Charge Comparisons, March 25, 1988 (also appendices and updates, 1988 and 1989); "Service charges cause hardship": *Winnipeg Free Press*, Nov. 22, 1987; "Service Charges: Fair or Not?": *Toronto Sun*, Feb. 28, 1988; front-page story with a diagram: TS, March 5, 1988; "according to one source": *Ottawa Citizen*, Mar. 12, 1988; "skirting a law": Canadian Press, Mar. 1988; "A bank shall not in Canada" and "many banks and other financial institutions": Terence J. Thomas, *Financial Service Charges in Canada*, Research Branch, Library of Parliament, Ottawa, March 8, 1988; "Mr. MacIntosh, you have said" and "I am the only accountant": FINTREA, Minutes and Proceedings, April 1988; "Banks run Friday scam": TS, April 24, 1988; "assumption that the average" and "consumers spend an average": Terence Thomas, op. cit.; "you should be aware" and "You are the lawyer": FINTREA, April 1988; "The day we require bakers": *Montreal Gazette*, June 7, 1988; "In their haste to convict": FP, June 8, 1988; "big banks' united": TS, April 2, 1988; "We have received a message" and "Banks generally agree": CBA correspondence; "purpose of this meeting": MacIntosh-Blenkarn correspondence; "standardization of banking terms": Andre-MacIntosh correspondence; "parties to this agreement": CBA files; "You know perfectly well": FINTREA, April 1988; "A deal between MPs and the big banks": TS, May 12, 1988; "Don't bend over" and "Bankers leave . . . seething": TS, May 14, 1988; "Canadian bankers refused": FP, May 12, 1988; "Proposals by the House of Commons Committee": GM, May 13, 1988; "The Bureau of Competition Policy": GM, May 20, 1988; "Whose side are they on?" and "MPs now find": *Winnipeg Free Press*, May 22, 1988; "a national sport," "schizophrenic, because it acknowledged," and "an absurd distortion": TS, June 7, 1988; "astounded, incredibly angry": GM, June 7, 1988; "a source in Finance Minister": TS, June 7, 1988; "All the banks already provide," "public wants value," and "Free basic banking service": FT, June 13, 1988; "It's time to act": TS, June 8, 1988; "Your editorial contains": TS, June 25, 1988; "In my opinion, Canadian": TS, June 16, 1988; "By a stroke of luck": FP, June 28, 1988; "we do not want the government," "essentially they've eliminated," and "biggest bank hold-up": GM and TS, June 7-8, 1988.

Chapter 14

A study by some tax lawyers and accountants: Montreal Chamber of Commerce and Board of Trade, Committee for Economic Promotion of Montreal, International Banking Centres, Nov. 30, 1981; "New York experiment": Ronald Wilson, "The International Banking Centre Issue," Department of Finance, Ottawa, July 1983;

joint proposal . . . was revived: Montreal and Vancouver Boards of Trade, Joint proposal to Minister of Finance, Feb. 7, 1984; two central bankers submitted their report: Louis Rasminsky and William Lawson, "Report to the Minister of Finance on International Banking Centres," June 1885, published April 1, 1986; already been leaked to the press: TS, July 6, 1985; "Decisions about where": TS, March 8, 1986; "market forces, not Ottawa": CPBW, June 20, 1986; "a big, fluffy ball": *Vancouver Province*, Aug. 26, 1986; "doesn't make sense": GM, Sept. 9, 1986; "fight Ottawa's ludicrous plans": TS, Oct. 17, 1986; Dodge . . . told Blenkarn's committee: GM, Feb., 1987; "Finance Committee Proposes": *Journal de Montreal*, April 30, 1987; "Ottawa invited to approve": *Le Devoir*, April 30, 1987; "Finance committee rejects": GM, May 1, 1987; "all-party committee": TS, May 1, 1987; Norman Warner . . . proposed: TS, Dec. 2, 1987; "a critical mass": TS, Jan. 16, 1987; "a gimcrack is": *Montreal Gazette*, April 9, 1987; "scheme has become": GM, Feb. 11, 1987; Kwinter announcement, Government of Ontario press release, June 11, 1986; "About as much as took place": FT, June 16, 1986; "The power of banks" and "Banks will be prohibited": "White Paper: The Banks' Assessment," No. 4 in a series, CBA, Oct. 1976; a huge study advocating a National Securities Commission: Philip Anisman et al., *Proposal for a Securities Market Law in Canada*, Department of Consumer and Corporate Affairs, Ottawa, 1979; ruled in the Toronto-Dominion's favour: OSC, Oct. 31, 1983; "By definition, we believe": Peter Dey, Ontario Securities Commission, address, Dec. 6, 1983; Henry Knowles recommended an outright prohibition: Henry Knowles, Report to the Minister of Consumer and Commercial Relations, Dec. 31, 1982, vol. 4; Dupré report: Ontario Task Force on Financial Institutions, Toronto, Dec. 1985; "If our aim is to maintain": Report of the Study Committee on Financial Institutions (Parizeau report), Goverment of Quebec, 1969; "By the time Ottawa gets around": TS, June 14, 1986; "Ontario government is obviously recognizing": FT, June 16, 1986; "a disposition to consider": *Financial Times* (London), Sept. 12, 1986; the Quebec Securities Commission granted the bank a licence: *Montreal Gazette*, Nov. 14, 1986; "If they do nothing": GM, Nov. 20, 1986; "They will be permitted": Tom Hockin, *New Directions for the Financial Sector*, Department of Finance, Ottawa, Dec. 18, 1986; "If you pay two": CPBW, Feb. 19, 1987; "not going to buy": TS, June 26, 1987; "The banks will blow": FP, Nov. 9, 1987; "You can't have a guy": FP, Dec. 8, 1986; "what is good for Canada": House of Commons, Minutes of Proceedings and Evidence, Standing Committee on External Affairs and International Trade, Nov. 4, 1987; press conference to support the free trade agreement: GM, Dec. 18, 1987; "we have a trade deal": House of Commons, loc. cit., Nov. 4, 1987; "Federal government moves": News release, The Public Service Alliance of Canada, Feb. 2, 1984; "hour for clearing": John Knight, CBAJ, vol. 10, 1902, pp. 41ff., and CBAJ, vol. 5, 1897, p. 148; "On a typical weekday evening": Avi Poriah, CBAJ, July/Aug. 1991; "to establish in any place" and "Payment orders written": Bradley Crawford and John Falconbridge, *Banking and Bills of Exchange: A Treatise on the Law of Banks, Banking and Bills of Exchange and the Payments System in Canada*, 8th edition, Canada Law Books, Toronto, 1986, pp. 347 and 377; "Near-banks have no voice" and "will remove a . . . complaint": "White Paper: The Banks' Assessment," op cit.; few people noticed: John Roberts, "The Quiet Evolution," CBAJ, Oct. 1982; "10 percent ownership": Peter Newman, *Maclean's*, July 1988; "Michael Cornelissen, the architect": GM, Feb. 8 and 12, 1991; "A curious analyst": FP, Feb. 12, 14, and 15, 1991.

BIBLIOGRAPHY

Baines, Christopher. "A Study in Fraud: The Failure of the Home Bank (1923)." Unpublished thesis, University of Toronto, 1977.

Bank Canadian National 1874-1974. Montreal: Bank Canadian National, 1974.

Bank of Nova Scotia. "Canada's First Chartered Bank." *Monthly Review*, May 1956.

Baskerville, Peter, editor. *The Bank of Upper Canada.* Toronto: Champlain Society, 1987.

Beckhart, Benjamin. *The Banking System of Canada.* New York: Henry Holt, 1929.

Berton, Pierre. *The Last Spike.* Toronto: McClelland and Stewart, 1971.

Best, Patricia, and Ann Shortell. *A Matter of Trust.* Toronto: Viking Penguin Books, 1985.

Binhammer, H.H. "Eleventh-Hour Proposals for Bank Act Revisions." *Journal of the Canadian Bankers' Association*, vol. 84, no. 5 (Sept.-Oct. 1977).

Binhammer, H.H. *Money and Banking and the Canadian Financial System.* 4th edition. Toronto: Methuen, 1982.

Bliss, Michael. *Northern Enterprise.* Toronto: McClelland and Stewart, 1987.

Boreham, Gordon. *Money and Banking*, 2nd ed. Toronto: Holt, Rinehart & Winston, 1979.

Bossen, Marianne. *Employment in Chartered Banks, 1969-75.* Winnipeg: Bossen and Associates, 1975.

Bossen, Marianne. *Manpower Utilization in Canadian Chartered Banks.* Ottawa: Special Study No. 4, Royal Commission on the Status of Women, 1971.

Breckenridge, R.M. *The History of Banking in Canada.* Washington: Government Printing Office, 1911.

Brown, George W., David M. Hayne, and Francess G. Halpenny, editors. *Dictionary of Canadian Biography.* Toronto: University of Toronto Press, various volumes.

Bryce, Robert. *Maturing in Hard Times.* McGill-Queen's University Press, 1986.

Buschlen, J.P. *A Canadian Bank Clerk.* Toronto: William Briggs, 1913. (Toronto Reprint Library, University of Toronto Press, 1973.)

Cameron, Stevie. *Ottawa Inside Out.* Toronto: Key Porter Books, 1989.

Canada Deposit Insurance Corporation. *Annual Reports.* Ottawa, 1982-89.

Carmichael, Edward, editor. *Canada's Energy Policy, 1985 and Beyond.* Toronto: C.D. Howe Institute, 1984.

Coleman, William D., and Grace Skogstad. *Policy Communities and Public Policy in Canada.* Toronto: Copp Clark Pitman, 1990.

Creighton, Donald. *John A. MacDonald, The Young Politician.* Toronto: Macmillan of Canada, 1952.

Curtis, Clifford. "The Canadian Monetary Situation." *Journal of Political Economy*, June 1932.

Denison, Merrill. *A History of the Bank of Montreal.* Toronto: McClelland and Stewart, vol. 1, 1966, vol. 2, 1967.

Dobson, Wendy. *Canada's Energy Policy Debate.* Toronto: C.D. Howe Institute, 1981.

Douglas, Clifford H. *Social Credit.* New York: W.W. Norton, 1933.

Dyck, Rand. *Provincial Politics in Canada.* Toronto: Prentice-Hall, 1986.

Easterbrook, W.T. *Farm Credit in Canada.* University of Toronto Press. 1938.

Easterbrook, W.T. and Hugh G. Aitken. *Canadian Economic History.* Macmillan of Canada, 1956.

Economic Council of Canada. *First Annual Report.* Ottawa, 1964.

Fayerweather, John. *The Mercantile Bank Affair*. New York: New York University Press, 1974.

Federal Task Force on Housing and Urban Development. *Report*. Ottawa, 1969.

Financial Observer Newsletter. Don Mills, Ont.: CCH Canadian Ltd., various issues.

Firth, E. *The Town of York 1815-34*. Champlain Society, 1966.

Fleming, Donald M. *So Very Near*, vol. 1. Toronto: McClelland and Stewart, 1985.

Flint, David. *Sir Henry Pellatt*. Fitzhenry and Whiteside, 1979.

Fullerton, Douglas H. *The Bond Market in Canada*. Toronto: Carswell Co., 1962.

Fullerton, Douglas. *Graham Towers and His Times*. Toronto: McClelland and Stewart, 1986.

Glazebrook, G.P. de T. *Sir Edmund Walker*. Toronto: Oxford University Press, 1933.

Gordon, H. Scott. *The Economists versus the Bank of Canada*. Toronto: Ryerson Press, 1961.

Gordon, Walter L. *A Choice for Canada*. Toronto: McClelland and Stewart, 1966.

Gordon, Walter L. *A Political Memoir*. Toronto: McClelland and Stewart, 1977.

Griffin, Major General Frederick. *Sir Henry Pellatt*. Toronto: Ontario Publishing Co., 1939.

Grossman, Peter Z. *American Express*. New York: Crown Publishers, 1987.

Guthrie, Anna L. "History of the Statutory Ceiling on Bank Lending Rates in Canada." *Journal of the Canadian Bankers' Association*, vol. 74, no. 4 (Spring 1967).

Hammond, Bray. *Banks and Politics in America*. Princeton, N.J.: Princeton University Press, 1957.

Harvey, M. "The Economic Condition of Newfoundland." *Journal of the Canadian Bankers' Association*, vol. 3, 1896, and vol. 4, 1897.

Hébert, Lorenzo. "Les banques au Canada en 1867." *Journal of the Canadian Bankers' Association*, spring 1967.

Hutchison, Bruce. *The Far Side of the Street*. Toronto: Macmillan of Canada, 1976.

Ince, Clifford. *The Royal Bank of Canada, A Chronology 1864-1969*. No date, no publisher.

Innis, H.A. *The Cod Fisheries*. New Haven: Yale University Press, 1940.

Irving, John A. *The Social Credit Movement in Alberta*. Toronto: University of Toronto Press, 1959.

Jamieson, A.B. *Chartered Banking in Canada*. Toronto: Ryerson Press, 1953.

Johnson, J.K. *Canadian Directory of Parliament, 1867-1967*. Ottawa, 1967.

Leacy, Frank, editor. *Historical Statistics of Canada*, 2nd ed. Ottawa: Statistics Canada and Social Science Federation of Canada, 1983.

Legate, David M. *Stephen Leacock*. Toronto: Doubleday, 1970.

MacIntosh, R.M. "The Bank Act Revision of 1954." *Journal of the Canadian Bankers' Association*, vol. 62, 1955. (Reprinted in Neufeld, E.P., *Money and Banking*.)

MacIntosh, R.M. "The Banking Situation Today." *Journal of the Canadian Bankers' Association*, vol. 73, no.1 (spring 1966).

MacIntosh, R.M. "Foreign Banks in Canada." Address to Empire Club of Toronto, Dec. 9, 1982.

Marsh, James H., editor in chief. *Canadian Encyclopedia*. 2nd edition. Edmonton: Hurtig, 1988.

Masters, D.C. "Toronto and Montreal." *Canadian Historical Review*, vol. 22, 1941.

McIvor, R. Craig. *Canadian Monetary, Banking and Fiscal Development*. Macmillan of Canada, 1958.

McLaughlin, W.E. "Mortgage Lending by Canadian Banks." *Journal of the Canadian Bankers' Association*, vol. 62, 1955.

Mishkin, Frederick S. *Asymmetric Information and Financial Crises*. New York: National Bureau of Economic Research, 1991.

Monthly Review (formerly *Statistical Summary of the Bank of Canada*). Ottawa: Bank of Canada, various issues.

Morgan, Henry James. *Canadian Men and Women of the Time: A Handbook of Canadian Biography of Living Characters*. 2nd edition. Toronto: University of Toronto Press, 1912.

Moritz, Albert and Theresa. *Leacock, A Biography*. Toronto: Stoddart, 1985.

Naylor, Tom. *The History of Canadian Business, 1867-1914*, vol. 1. Toronto: James Lorimer, 1975.

Neave, E.H., and J.V. Poapst. *Studies of Canadian Residential Mortgage and Consumer Credit Markets*. Toronto: CBA, 1990.

Neufeld, E.P. *Bank of Canada Operations, 1935-54*. Toronto: University of Toronto Press, 1955.

Neufeld, E.P. *The Financial System of Canada: Its Growth and Development*. Toronto: Macmillan of Canada, 1972.

Neufeld, E.P., editor. *Money and Banking in Canada*. Historical Documents and Commentary, Carleton Library, No. 17. Toronto: McClelland and Stewart, 1964.

Newman, Peter C. *The Distemper of Our Times*. Toronto: McClelland and Stewart, 1968.

Newman, Peter C. *Renegade in Power: The Diefenbaker Years*. Toronto: McClelland and Stewart, 1963.

Oreskovich, Carlie. *Sir Henry Pellatt: The King of Casa Loma*. McGraw-Hill Ryerson, 1982.

Organization of Economic Cooperation and Development. *Statistics on External Indebtedness*. Paris: OECD, 1990.

Pearson, Lester B. *Mike*, vol. 3, 1957-68. Toronto: University of Toronto Press, 1975.

Perry, J. Harvey. "Bank Act Revision 1980." *Journal of the Canadian Bankers' Association*. vol. 87, no. 6 (Dec. 1980).

Perry, J. Harvey. "Bank Act Revision: Report from a Survivor." *Journal of the Canadian Bankers' Association*, vol. 87, no. 4 (Aug. 1980).

Perry, J. Harvey. "The Legal Basis of Banking." *Journal of the Canadian Bankers' Association*, vol. 87, no. 3 (June 1980).

Perry, J. Harvey. "Origins of the Canadian Bankers' Association." *Journal of the Canadian Bankers' Association*, vol. 74, no. 1 (spring 1967).

Plumptre, A.F.W. *Central Banking in the British Dominions*. Toronto: University of Toronto Press, 1940.

Ricker, J.C. and J.T. Saywell. *Nation and Province*. Toronto: Clarke Irwin, 1963.

Rogers, Irene. "The Bank of Prince Edward Island." *Canadian Paper Money Journal*, vol 13, no. 4 (Oct. 1977).

Ross, Victor. *A History of the Canadian Bank of Commerce*. Toronto: Oxford University Press, vol. 1, 1920, vol. 2, 1967.

Rowe, Francis. "Early Banking in Newfoundland." *Newfoundland Quarterly*, fall 1971.

Royal Commission on Banking and Currency. *Report*. Ottawa, 1933. (Also Minutes of Proceedings.)

Royal Commission on Banking and Finance. *Report*. Ottawa, 1964. Also fifteen background studies by staff members and others.

Royal Commission on Life Insurance. *Sessional Paper No. 123*. Ottawa, 1906.

Rudin, Ronald. *Banking en français: The French Banks of Quebec*. Toronto: University of Toronto Press, 1985. (Rudin's work is unique on the history of francophone banks, and has been used extensively as the source on Quebec banks.)

Sarpkaya, S. "Counting Canada's Banks." *Journal of the Canadian Bankers' Association*, vol. 85, Dec. 1978.

Sarpkaya, S. "How Many Banks Have Been Established?" *Journal of the Canadian Bankers' Association*, vol. 85, Oct. 1978.

Schull, Joseph. *100 Years of Banking in Canada, A History of the Toronto-Dominion Bank*. Toronto: Copp Clark, 1958.

Schull, Joseph and J.D. Gibson. *The Scotiabank Story*. Toronto: Macmillan of Canada, 1982.

Shortt, Adam. "History of Canadian Currency and Banking 1600-1880." *Journal of the Canadian Bankers' Association*, 1982. (This volume assembled all of Shortt's articles from the *Journal of the Canadian Bankers' Association*.)

Slater, D.W. "Modern Capitalism and Canadian Economic Policy." *Journal of the Canadian Bankers' Association*, vol. 73, no. 2 (summer 1966).

Slater, D.W. "Decennial Revision of Canada's Banking Acts." *Journal of the Canadian Bankers' Association*, vol. 73, no. 3 (autumn 1966).

Slater, D.W. "Special Drawing Rights — A New International Money Era." *Journal of the Canadian Bankers' Association*, vol. 74, no. 4 (winter 1967).

Smith, Denis. *Gentle Patriot*. Edmonton: Hurtig Publishers, 1973.

Smith, Philip. *The Trust-Builders: The Remarkable Rise of Canada Trust*. Toronto: Macmillan of Canada, 1989.

Stewart, Roderick and Neil McLean. "Forming a Nation." *Toronto Illustrated*, 1893.

Stratton, Carson G. *Report of Senate Standing Committee on Energy and Resources*. June 15, 1987.

Stursberg, Peter. *Diefenbaker: Leadership Regained*. Toronto: University of Toronto Press, 1975.

Stursberg, Peter. *Lester Pearson and the American Dilemma*. Toronto: Doubleday, 1980.

Thompson, Austin S. *Jarvis Street*. Toronto: Personal Library Publishers, 1980.

Thomas, Terence J. *Financial Service Charges in Canada*. Ottawa: Research Branch, Library of Parliament, 1988.

Thomas, Terence J. and Basil Zafirion. *The Proposed Amex Bank of Canada*. Library of Parliament, May 1989.

Toronto Reference Library. *Biographical Scrapbooks*, vol. 68 and microfilm T606.3 (Sir Herbert Holt); microfilm T686.3, vol. 1, Aug. 9, 1923 (J. Mason).

United States Bureau of the Census. *Historical Statistics of the U.S.* Washington: U.S. Bureau of the Census, 1960.

Walker, B.E. "A History of Banking in Canada." *Journal of Commerce*, New York. Reprinted, Toronto, 1899.

Western Economic Opportunities Conference. *Proceedings, Calgary, July 24-26, 1973*. Ottawa, 1973.

Whynot, Nancy. "An Investigation into the Rise and Fall of The Sovereign Bank of Canada." Unpublished thesis, University of Guelph, 1979. (The author assembled a file of newspaper clippings and selections from the Public Archives of Canada which were invaluable.)

Wilson, John D. *The Chase*. Boston: Harvard Business School, 1986.

INDEX